19th Industrial Conference on Advances in Data Mining (ICDM 2019)

New York, New York, USA
17-21 July 2019

Editors:

Petra Perner

ISBN: 978-1-5108-9517-1

Printed from e-media with permission by:

Curran Associates, Inc.
57 Morehouse Lane
Red Hook, NY 12571

CURRAN ASSOCIATES INC.
proceedings
.com

Some format issues inherent in the e-media version may also appear in this print version.

Printed with permission by Curran Associates, Inc. (2020)

For permission requests, please contact ibai-publishing
at the address below.

ibai-publishing
Arno-Nitzsche-Str. 45
04277 Leipzig, Germany

info@ibai-publishing.org

Additional copies of this publication are available from:

Curran Associates, Inc.
57 Morehouse Lane
Red Hook, NY 12571 USA
Phone: 845-758-0400
Fax: 845-758-2633
Email: curran@proceedings.com
Web: www.proceedings.com

Table of Content

Petra Perner (Ed.)

Advances in Data Mining

Applications and Theoretical Aspects

19th Industrial Conference, ICDM 2019
New York, USA, July 17 – July 21, 2019
Proceedings

Petra Perner (Ed.)

Advances in Data Mining

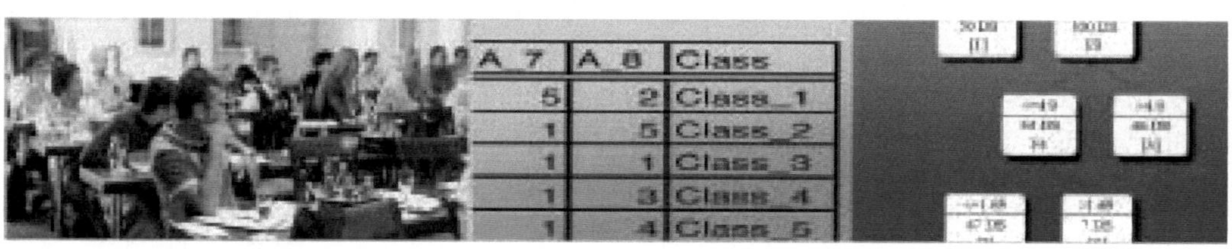

19th Industrial Conference on Data Mining, ICDM 2019
New York, USA, July 17-21, 2019

Proceedings

ibai - publishing

Preface

The nineteenth event of the Industrial Conference on Data Mining ICDM was held in New York (www.data-mining-forum.de) running under the umbrella of the World Congress on “The Frontiers in Intelligent Data and Signal Analysis, DSA 2019” (www.worldcongressdsa.com).

After the peer-review process, we accepted 39 high-quality papers for oral presentation, which are published in the ICDM Proceeding by ibai-publishing (www.ibai-publishing.org. The topics range from theoretical aspects of data mining to applications of data mining, such as in multimedia data, in marketing, in medicine, and in process control, industry, and society. Extended versions of selected papers will appear in the international journal *Transactions on Machine Learning and Data Mining* (www.ibai-publishing.org/journal/mldm).

In all, twenty one papers were selected for poster presentations, which are published in the ICDM Poster Proceeding by ibai-publishing (www.ibai-publishing.org.

A tutorial on Data Mining and a tutorial on Case-Based Reasoning were held after the conference.

The conference was running in an inspiring atmosphere. The presenters of the oral presentations gave excellent talks and the audience acknowledged each talk with excellent questions. The poster presenters presented well prepared posters and gave in front of their posters a summary of their work in five minutes for the audiences. Afterwards the audience could step to the poster that they were interested in. The audience had a lot of questions and they gave valuable comments and new directions for the work in progress. In all was the poster session a very successful session.

We would like to thank all reviewers for their highly professional work and their effort in reviewing the papers.

We also thank the members of the Institute of Applied Computer Sciences, Leipzig, Germany (www.ibai-institut.de), who handled the conference as secretariat. We appreciate the help and understanding of the ibai-publishing publishing house (www.ibai-publishing.org) that handled the papers and published the proceedings.

Last, but not least, we wish to thank all the speakers and participants who contributed to the success of the conference. We hope to see you in 2020 in New York at the next World Congress on “The Frontiers in Intelligent Data and Signal Analysis, DSA 2020” (www.worldcongressdsa.com), which combines under its roof the following three events: International Conferences Machine Learning and Data Mining MLDM (www.mldm.de) , the Industrial Conference on Data Mining ICDM (www.data-mining-forum.de), and the International Conference on Mass Data Analysis of Signals and Images in Artificial Intelligence and Pattern Recognition with Applications in Medicine, Biotechnology, Chemistry and Food Industry, MDA-AI&PR (www.mda-signals.de).

July 2019 Petra Perner

Volume Editor

Petra Perner
Institute of Computer Vision and Applied Computer Sciences, IBaI
PF 30 11 14
04251 Leipzig
E-mail: pperner@ibai-institut.de

19th Industrial Conference on Data Mining ICDM 2019

www.data-mining-forum.de

July 17 – 21, 2019, New York, USA

Chair

Prof. Dr. Petra Perner

Institute of Computer Vision and applied Computer Sciences, IBaI

Program Committee

Ajith Abraham	Machine Intelligence Research Labs (MIR Labs), USA
Mohamed, Bourguessa	Universite du Quebec a Montreal - UQAM, Canada
Bernard Chen	University of Central Arkansas, USA
Jeroen de Bruin	University of Applied Sciences JOANNEUM, Austria
Antonio Dourado	University of Coimbra, Portugal
Stefano Ferilli	University of Bari, Italy
Geert Gins	Glaxo Smith Kline, Belgium
Warwick Graco	Australian Tax Office ATO, Australia
Aleksandra Gruca	Silesian University of Technology, Poland
Pedro Isaias	The University of Queensland, Australia
Piotr Jedrzejowicz	Gdynia Maritime University, Poland
Martti Juhola	University of Tampere, Finland
Janusz Kacprzyk	Polish Academy of Sciences, Poland
Mehmed Kantardzic	University of Louisville, USA
Lui Xiaobing	Google Inc., USA
Eduardo F. Morales	National Institute of Astrophysics, Optics, and Electronics, Mexico
Samuel Noriega	Universitat de Barcelona, Spain
Wieslaw Paja	University of Rzeszow, Poland
Juliane Perner	Novartis Institutes for BioMedical Research (NIBR), Switzerland
Rainer Schmidt	University of Rostock, Germany
Moti Schneider	PCCW Global, Greece
Victor Sheng	University of Central Arkansas, USA
Kaoru Shimada	Fukuoka Dental College, Japan
Gero Szepannek	University of Applied Sciences Stralsund, Germany
Joao Miguel Costa Sousa	Technical University of Lisbon, Portugal
Markus Vattulainen	Tampere University, Finnland
Zhu Bing	Sichuan University, China

Ensemble of Customized DenseNet with SVM for Refining Iris Contact Lens Features

Meenakshi Choudhary, Venkanna U. and Vivek Tiwari

DSPM IIIT Naya Raipur, India
{meenakshi,vivek,venkannau}@iiitnr.edu.in

Abstract. Although, Iris Recognition (IR) has achieved sublime progression, yet is prone to be forged by contact lenses. Since, contact lens conceals the iris texture and inhibits sensor from capturing genuine iris. Moreover, cosmetic lenses are prone to forge the IR system by registering an individual with fake iris signature. Therefore, it is foremost to detect presence of contact lens in human eyes prior to access an IR system. In this paper, a novel Densely Connected Contact Lens Detection Network (DCLNet) is proposed, that is a deep convolutional network with dense connections among layers. DCLNet has been designed through a series of customization over Densenet121 with addition of Support Vector Machine (SVM) classifier on top. It accepts raw iris images without segmentation and normalization. To ascertain the strength of proposed model, comprehensive experiments are simulated on two publicly available databases (IIIT-D Contact Lens and Notre Dame (ND) Contact Lens 2013). Experimental results vindicate that DCLNet enhances Correct Classification Rate (CCR) up to 4% as compared to state of the arts.

Keywords: DCLNet, DenseNet, Contact Lens Detection, Convolutional Neural Network (CNN), Support Vector Machine (SVM).

1 Introduction

Among all biometric traits, human iris is prevailing due to its complex texture with discriminating patterns. During last decade, researchers achieved improved performance in Iris Recognition (IR) with state of the art accuracy up to 99% [1]. Nevertheless, IR encounters various challenges, specifically with unconstrained image acquisition. Further, the surrounding factors such as pupil dilation [2] and sensor interoperability [3-4] significantly affect iris recognition. Furthermore, IR system is prone to be forged through contact lenses that contain two variants: Transparent (Soft) and Textured (Cosmetic or Colored). Transparent lens does not modify iris texture, yet changes the reflection property of iris region to great extent. On the other side, textured lens interpolates iris with high intense color and overlays the actual texture with exterior texture printed over it. With aforesaid features of contact lenses, these may be exploited to forge the IR system [5]. Therefore, contact lens detection is considered as a performance influencing constituent for IR system.

To accomplish contact lens detection, several approaches have been proposed in literature. Previously, Lee *et al.* [6] attempts to generate purkinje image (focused enough for recognition) using collimated Infra-Red Light Emitting Diode (IR-LED). The authors also proposed an IR camera (with wavelength 760nm and 880nm) and reported False Recognition Rate (FRR) as 0.33%. However, this approach requires additional hardware. Afterward, He *et al.* [7] incorporated statistical textural analysis to select distinctive features based on Gray Level Co-occurrence Metrics (GLCM) with Support Vector Machine (SVM), to classify between fake and real iris. However, only lower half region of eye images is examined. Similarly, Wei *et al.* [8] employed Co-occurrence matrix, Iris-Textons and, edge sharpness to identify fake iris. Furthermore, He *et al.* [9] used Local Binary Patterns (LBP) for several iris sub-regions, then trained a model with Adaboost learning for the most discriminative LBP feature identification. Later, by using similar approach, Yadav *et al.* [5] analyzed the influence of contact lens on iris recognition then, proposed a region oriented LBP method to reduce it. All aforementioned techniques depend upon manual feature extraction from iris images (i.e. handcrafted features), and employs hand-coding to generate corresponding iris templates.

In recent years, researchers [10-11] have started utilizing Convolutional Neural Networks (CNN), to automatically extract features from iris images, that are used to classify given image to accurate lens category, using classifiers such as Softmax, SVM [12] etc. Earlier, Silva *et al.* [13] built a CNN with Softmax classifier for deep image representation; however, due to shallow architecture it exhibited degraded performance. Consequently, Raghavendra *et al.* [14] introduced a CNN model with 15 layers namely 'ContlensNet', trained on multiple patches of normalized iris images. Nevertheless, it demands pre-processing of iris images. Conversely, the GHCLNet [15] shows better performance without pre-processing and normalization. However, it uses two parallel ResNet50 [16] models (each with 170 layers), therefore it possess very complex architecture and is computationally expensive to train.

1.1 Research Contribution

In this paper, Densely Connected Contact Lens Detection Network (DCLNet) has been proposed to identify contact lenses in iris images captured from distinct sensors. The prime contribution is two-fold:

- The proposed work attempts to customize DenseNet121, a well-known CNN model pre-trained on ImageNet (animal dataset). The customized model is then fine-tuned on Near Infra-Red (NIR) iris images to learn complex iris patterns.
- The layer specific feature analysis is carried out to inspect the contribution of individual layers of proposed model in contact lens detection, where the iris patterns learnt by random layers are visualized.

The remaining paper is organized as; Section 2 describes the background, architecture and working of proposed model. Section 3 represents the experimental results, performance comparison with state of the arts and layer specific feature analysis. Finally, Section 4 concludes the work.

2 Proposed Model: Densely Connected Contact Lens Detection Network (DCLNet)

The proposed model utilizes DenseNet121 [17] as fundamental building block with quite customization. It enables feature reuse at consequent layers within a dense block, and therefore enhances the feature map generation. It addresses vanishing gradient problem as well, using direct paths to all prior layers, to route residuals throughout backpropagation.

2.1 Model Designing and Fine-Tuning

Figure 1 depicts schematic design of proposed model that employs DenseNet as feature extractor and SVM as classifier. DenseNet121 endues 4 dense blocks with 6, 12, 24 and 16 dense layers respectively. A bottleneck layer is placed between dense layers that performs 1*1 convolution. Therefore, a dense block has following sequence of layers; BN→ReLU→Conv(1×1)→BN→ReLU→Conv(3×3). Here, BN, ReLU and Conv represents Batch Normalization, Rectified Linear Unit and Convolution respectively. At the end of dense block, a transition layer is used, that performs 1×1 convolution and average pooling [17]. The transition layer is defined by; BN→Conv(1×1) →AvgPooling(2×2). These collectively constitute over 400 layers. Since this model is huge and couldn't be trained with available iris images in dataset, DCLNet selects only up to first two dense blocks (with approx. 50 layers) for feature extraction. The output of pooling layer (pool_2) after second dense block represents the iris features learnt by DCLNet. Then, a flatten layer is added to form 401408 dimensional feature vector. For further down-sampling, three fully connected layers are added i.e. $fc1$, $fc2$, $fc3$ with 512, 128, 3 units, with $fc3$ as output layer. Two dropout layers (with probability 0.4) are also used to remove overfitting in fc layers. In our experiment, SVM exhibits better performance than Softmax, therefore, Multiclass SVM (with Radial Basis Function (RBF) kernel) is added as classifier on top. The entire model design ends up with total 56 layers including Batch Normalization, ReLU and Dropouts. Since initial layers are aimed to constitute basic features such as points, edges, blobs etc. they are not involved in training and remaining layers are fine-tuned. In proposed model, initial 27 layers are kept freeze and rest 29 layers are retrained as shown in Fig. 1 on NIR iris images of contact lens datasets. Table 1 describes the learning parameters used by the model.

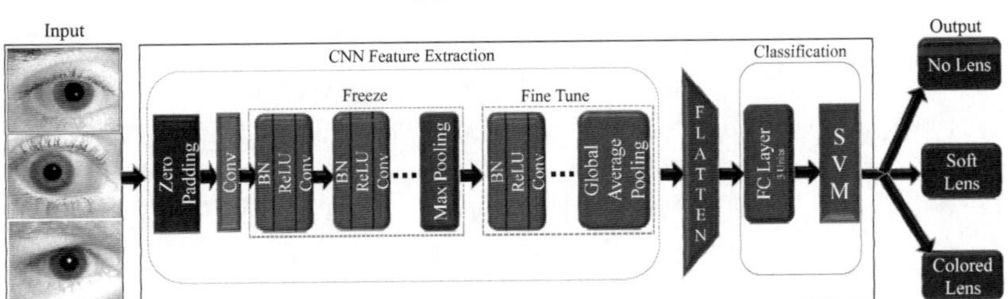

Fig. 1. Proposed Model Design

Table 1. Learning Parameters of DCLNet

No.	Parameters	Value
1	Optimizer	SGD
2	Momentum	0.9
3	Learning Rate	0.0001
4	Batch Size	32
5	Epochs	50

2.2 Image Augmentation

A deep convolution network requires large number of images per subject to learn feature representation. In order to generate more training images, augmentation techniques are used such as shearing, flipping, rotation, rotation after shearing, shearing after rotation at various angles and directions etc. Due to the fact that large image size creates more parameters that leads to overfitting [18-19], the input image is down-sampled to 128×128. Subsequently, further augmentation techniques are incorporated to generate identical but pixel based position variant images.

2.3 Feature Extraction

The model begins with a zero padding layer where, the length of output feature map is given by (1) [17].

$$o = \frac{(w - k + 2p)}{s} + 1 \tag{1}$$

where o = length of output feature map, w = input length, p = size of zero padding, k = filter size, and s = stride. Furthermore, each convolutional block is represented by BN→ReLU→Convolution. BN takes a mini batch of features from previous activation layer and normalizes them by subtracting each element by the Batch Mean and dividing by Standard Deviation as given in (4).

$$\mu_B \leftarrow \frac{1}{N}\sum_{i=1}^{N} x_i \tag{2}$$

$$\sigma_B \leftarrow \frac{1}{N}\sum_{i=1}^{N} (x_i - \mu_B)^2 \tag{3}$$

$$x_i \leftarrow \frac{x_i - \mu_B}{\sqrt{\sigma_B^2 + \epsilon}} \tag{4}$$

where x_i and N denote individual and total number of elements in Batch respectively. μ_B and σ_B denote mean and standard deviation of mini batch (B). The first convolution layer uses a filter of 5×5 and the convolution operation is expressed as:

$$Y_j = \sum_i X_i * w_{i,j} + B_j \tag{5}$$

where X_i and Y_j represents the ith input and the jth output feature map respectively. The $w_{i,j}$ is the kernel convolving over set of pixels $i \in X_i$. B_j denotes the bias and * denotes convolution. The ReLU layer is used to impose non-linearity by using $Y'_j = max(0, Y_j)$. The Max-pool layer attempts to down-sample the convolved feature maps by applying max-pooling across 2×2 pixels with stride of 2 while retaining same depth. It is mathematically represented by following expression [20].

$$z^{i}_{j,k} = \max_{0 \le m,n < s} (Y^{i}_{j.p+m,k.p+n}) \tag{6}$$

Here, $Z^i_{j,k}$ represents a neuron in i^{th} feature map $Y^i_{j,k}$, computed over an $(p \times p)$ region. After last dense block, a global average pooling layer is used. For an iris image, let $f_k(x,y)$ is the activation of kth unit, at spatial location (x,y) in last convolution layer. Then, for unit k, the global average pooling results $F^k \rightarrow \sum_{x,y} f_k(x,y)$. Next, the flatten layer is used to rearrange the output feature map from Global Average Pooling to 401408 dimensional vector to feed them in *fc* layers. The output of fully connected layer l is denoted as

$$z^{(l)}_{j} = \sigma^{(l)} \left(\sum_{i=1}^{M^{(l-1)}} z^{(l-1)}(i).w^{(l)}(i,j) + b^{(l)}(j) \right) \tag{7}$$

where $Z_j^{(l)}$ represents j^{th} output of lth layer. $M^{(l-1)}$ is the term representing the number of neurons in $(l-1)^{th}$ layer, $w^{(l)}(i,j)$ is the weight on connection between i^{th} neuron of layer $l-1$ and j^{th} neuron of layer l, $b^{(l)}(j)$ is bias for neuron j in layer l, $\sigma^{(l)}$ is the activation for layer l.

2.4 Network Implementation Description

The proposed DCLNet has been implemented in python using Keras [21] library with Tensorflow [22] at backend. The system configuration is as: Intel Scalable processors Xeon 4114, 64GB DDR4 RAM, GTX 1080Ti 11GB GPU card.

3 Experiments

This section describes experimental setup and result interpretation based on IIIT Delhi (IIITD) Contact Lens and Notre Dame (ND) Iris datasets by following validation protocols. DCLNet is trained and tested on raw iris images (without segmentation and normalization) and Correct Classification Rate (CCR) has been chosen as a primary measure for performance comparison.

3.1 Description of the dataset and validation protocols

This subsection provides details about the datasets namely: ND Cosmetic Contact Lens 2013 database [23] and IIITD Contact Lens Iris Database [24]. The proposed architecture is trained and validated on these two datasets based on the given evaluation protocols.

ND Database: The ND database is composed of two separate datasets ND-I and ND-II. ND-I contains images captured using IrisGuard AD100 [25] sensor and conceptually partitioned into training and probe sets of 600 and 300 images respectively. Whereas, images of ND-II were captured using LG4000 sensor [26]. It is divided into training and probe set of 3000 and 1200 images.

IIITD Database: It contains total 6570 iris images collected from 101 subjects; with Conget and Vista sensors are used for image acquisition. Since each subject contains left and right iris, collectively they form 202 unique iris instances. The dataset is given with an evaluation protocol as 50 subjects should be used for training and rest 51 for testing the model performance.

3.2 Experimental Outcomes

In this subsection, several experiments are performed on aforementioned datasets with three validation strategies *i.e.* intra-sensor validation, inter-sensor validation and multi-sensor validation.

Intra-sensor validation

Training and validation performed on images captured from same sensor is termed as intra-sensor validation. Table 2 presents the performance comparison of proposed DCLNet with existing methods such as; Deep Image Representation (DIR) [13], ContlensNet [14] and GHCLNet [15]. As, both datasets have two sensors, Table 2 contains total four experiments that calculate CCR for individual lens category, where C-C represents "Colored-lens to Colored-lens", N-N is "No-lens to No-lens" and S-S is "Soft-lens to Soft-lens" classification. Final result is obtained by averaging individual CCRs.

Table 2. Model Performance (in CCR %) for Intra-Sensor Validation

Data Base	Classification	DIR [28]	ContlensNet [29]	GHCLNet [30]	DCLNet
IIITD-Conget	C-C	73.00	100	100	99.10
	N-N	35.50	68.68	89.86	94.19
	S-S	98.21	93.62	91.26	92.33
	Average	69.05	86.73	93.71	95.20
IIITD-Vista	C-C	55.88	100	100	100
	N-N	60.80	74.50	94.6	93.19
	S-S	98.30	87.50	91.88	92.89
	Average	72.08	87.33	95.49	95.36
ND-I	C-C	99.75	100	100	98.50
	N-N	84.50	93.25	91.67	89.49
	S-S	73.75	97.50	87.50	90.86
	Average	86.00	96.91	93.05	92.95
ND-II	C-C	97.00	100	99.75	99.93
	N-N	73.00	88.00	95.24	92.86
	S-S	65.00	97.00	89.74	94.45
	Average	78.33	95.00	94.91	95.74

It is observed that, with IIITD-Conget sensor, the proposed DCLNet exhibits average CCR of 95.20% with minimum hike of 2% than all state of the arts. With Vista Sensor, DCLNet performs better than DIR and ContlensNet [14], and comparable to GHCLNet [15] with 95.36% CCR. For ND-I database DCLNet achieves average CCR% of 92.95, which is less than state of the arts. This is due to less number of images available in ND-I dataset for training. However, with ND-II, model gives 95.74% of CCR, which is best among all state of the art models.

Inter-sensor validation

Inter-sensor validation is performed on pair of sensors. With IIITD dataset, DCLNet model is trained and tested pair-wise among Conget and Vista sensors. Whereas, with ND dataset, the experiment is done on pair of ND-I and ND-II. Consequently, four different cases occur as presented in Table 3 that indicates the performance of proposed model for different sensor pairs.

Table 3. Model Performance (in CCR %) for Inter-Sensor Validation

Exp.	Training Database	Test Database	Classification Type	DIR [28]	ContlensNet [29]	GHCLNet [30]	DCLNet
1	IIITD-Conget	IIITD-Vista	C-C	89.61	100	99.25	99.83
			N-N	06.00	96.19	93.40	89.55
			S-S	45.47	88.23	83.37	81.74
			Average	45.51	94.80	92.01	90.37
2	IIITD-Vista	IIITD-Conget	C-C	38.15	78.91	85.36	99.82
			N-N	48.67	87.75	96.74	81.43
			S-S	42.25	87.75	65.73	79.26
			Average	43.08	84.80	82.61	86.83
3	ND-I	ND-II	C-C	94.00	97.50	100	97.92
			N-N	75.00	68.50	81.25	83.00
			S-S	65.00	98.00	93.27	92.90
			Average	78.00	88.00	91.51	91.27
4	ND-II	ND-I	C-C	97.00	100	98.00	100
			N-N	80.00	81.33	91.90	92.00
			S-S	49.00	90.03	81.84	84.34
			Average	75.33	90.45	90.58	92.11

It is observed that, when DCLNet is trained and tested on Conget and Vista images respectively, it under performs with respect to ContlensNet [14] and GHCLNet [15]. However, when Vista dataset is used for training and Conget for testing, DCLNet achieves best performance with minimum hike of more than 2%. For ND dataset, when training and testing is performed on ND-I and ND-II respectively, DCLNet performs better than DIR [13] and ContlensNet [14] and comparable to GHCLNet [15] with 91.27% accuracy. Similar results are observed, when the model is trained and tested on ND-II and ND-I respectively, i.e. hike of 2%.

Multi-sensor validation

Here, images from heterogeneous sensors are combined to form multi-sensor database. In this view, Conget and Vista sensor images are combined to form IIITD-Combined dataset. Similarly, ND-I and ND-II images are merged to constitute ND-Combined dataset. The average reported CCR is 95.36%. Table 4 represents the DCLNet performance comparison with state of the arts for multi-sensor validation.

Some key observations are, with IIITD-Combined dataset, the performance of DCLNet is reported as 94.93%, which outperforms all state of the arts. With ND-combined dataset, DCLNet performs best among all state of the arts with 96.04% CCR.

Table 4. Model Performance (in CCR %) for Multi-Sensor Validation

Database	Classification Type	DIR [28]	ContlensNet [29]	GHCLNet [30]	DCLNet
IIITD-Combined	C-C	61.07	98.50	99.73	99.87
	N-N	47.55	96.56	91.87	92.82
	S-S	97.99	88.90	92.85	92.10
	Average	69.28	94.65	94.82	94.93
ND-Combined	C-C	99.60	100	100	99.93
	N-N	77.40	95.40	91.67	93.89
	S-S	71.40	82.40	95.04	94.32
	Average	82.80	92.60	95.57	96.04

3.3 Analyzing Discrimination power of DCLNet

The proposed DCLNet is additionally assessed against more robust and consistent measure i.e. Receiver Operating Characteristics (ROC). It represents comparison between True Positive Rate (TPR) and False Positive Rate (FPR) returned by classifier, based on each possible threshold value. Another useful metric "Area Under the Curve (AUC)" is also employed that measures the performance of DCLNet across all possible thresholds.

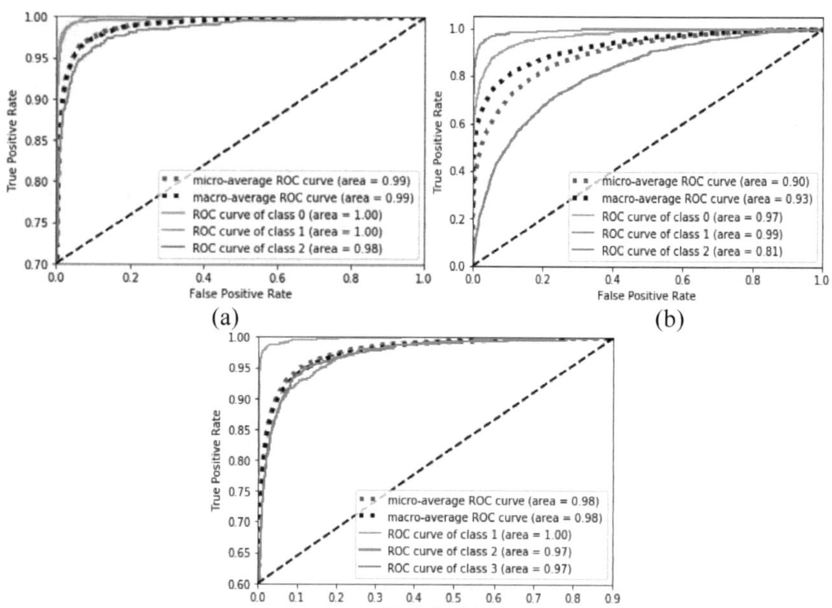

(c)

Fig. 2. ROC plot for DCLNet (a) Intra-sensor validation over IIITD Vista, (b) Inter-sensor validation on ND-II and ND-I, (c) Multi-sensor validation over IIITD Dataset

Here, three finest ROC curves are plotted for Intra, Inter and multi-sensor validation. The ROC plot shown in Fig. 2(a) depicts the generalizability of DCLNet for Intra-sensor validation on IIITD-Vista. It makes correct prediction for Colored, No Lens and

Soft Lens with AUC=1, 1 and 0.98 respectively. It performs best for Vista, due to enriched quality of images with clearer iris texture.

The ROC plot depicted in Fig. 2(b) is constructed for DCLNet while it is trained and tested on ND-II and ND-I sensor respectively, where classes 0, 1, 2 represent No lens, Colored lens and Soft lens respectively. The model's performance is considerably impressive for Colored and No Lens categories with higher AUC of 0.99 and 0.97 respectively. However, slightly less AUC of 0.81 has been observed for soft lens, since it is misinterpreting Soft lens as No lens. This is due to poor quality of iris images in ND dataset that causes difficulty in accurately classifying between No lens and Soft lens. Figure 2(c) depicts the ROC plot for DCLNet, while it was trained and tested on Vista and Conget sensor respectively. Here, classes 1, 2, 3 denote Colored lens, No lens and Soft Lens respectively. The model is accurately predicting Colored lens with AUC=1 and also exhibits good prediction for No lens and Soft lens images with AUC=0.97.

3.4 Results and Discussion

The experimental outcomes infer that the proposed model performs better or at least comparable to existing frameworks. With Intra-sensor validation DCLNet achieved best CCR in majority cases. Further, for Inter-sensor validation, the distinct classification accuracy of DCLNet deficits for some classes, yet average performance is greater or equivalent to state of the arts. In case of multi-sensor validation, DCLNet unveils best accuracy. Moreover, our substantial contribution is that DCLNet endues less complex architecture with optimum layer configuration, fewer training parameters, and revealing analogous performance with state of the arts.

ContlensNet [14] incorporated iris normalization by utilizing OSIRIS V4.1 tool [27] that exhibits limited accuracy due to some factors such as occlusion, illumination, and unconstraint image acquisition. Moreover, it involves added efforts to create patches of 32*32 size from normalized iris images. The proposed DCLNet is less computation intensive, still attaining similar, in fact improved performance deprived of iris segmentation and normalization. GHCLNet [15] shows better performance in most cases, however, computationally expensive. The proposed DCLNet can achieve comparable performance with fewer layers and learning parameters.

3.5 Individual Layer Features Visualization and Analysis

Figure 3 visualizes the features learned by distinct convolutional layers of DCLNet. It is perceived with each lens type, that early layers (9th and 16th) learn broad features such as points, dark pixels, blobs etc. and spawn 128 feature-maps of size (56*56). Afterward, 19th convolutional layer seeks for corners and edges with 32 feature maps of identical size. The 33rd convolutional layer shows major contribution in unravelling iris region from sclera. In this view, it can be deduced that as convolutional layers have enough potential to discover deeper patterns in iris images, therefore iris segmentation and normalization are not necessary. Accordingly, by diving deeper in the network, the layers learn further precise features analogous to three lens categories. At the end, the 47th convolutional layer learns lens discriminating patterns.

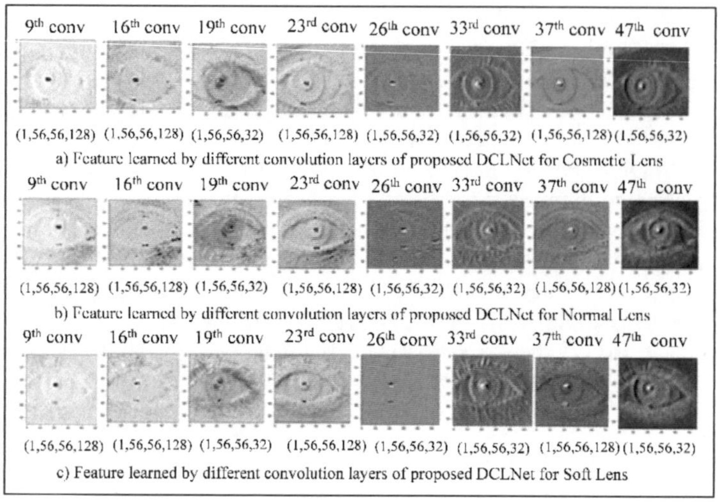

Fig. 3. Layer Specific Visualization of Iris Features

4 Conclusion

Contact lens detection has been a prominent subject in the territory of iris recognition. As the contact lens dissimulates the genuine iris texture and can probably be exploited to counterfeit the Iris Recognition system. Numerous techniques were suggested in literature to resolve such issue. Conventional techniques incorporated hand-crafted iris features and attained satisfiable results. Recently, convolutional networks have been employed to accomplish this task. The proposed DCLNet is a densely connected convolutional network with fewer number of layers and learning parameters. Due to the dense connections amongst layers, it learns more key features. Moreover, it doesn't demand iris segmentation and normalization. For performance assessment, comprehensive tries are conducted on two global databases with three evaluation protocols. The qualitative results signify that proposed model attains comparable outcomes with state of the arts and even superior in some experiments.

References

1. Daugman, J.: How iris recognition works. IEEE Transactions on Circuits and Systems for Video Technology, 14(1), 21-30 (2004).
2. Hollingsw, K., Bowyer, K., Flynn, P.: Pupil dilation degrades iris biometric performance. Computer Vision and Image Understanding, 113(1), 150-157(2009).
3. Arora, S., Vatsa, M., Singh, R., Jain, A.: On Iris camera interoperability. In: 5th International Conference on BTAS, pp. 346–352, IEEE, Arlington, VA, USA (2012).

4. Bowyer, K., Baker, S., Hentz, A., Hollingsworth, K., Peters, T., Flynn, P.: Factors that degrade the match distribution in iris biometrics. Springer Identity in the Information Society, 2(3), 327-343 (2009).
5. Yadav, D., Kohli, N., Doyle, J., Singh, R., Vatsa, M., Bowyer, K.: Unraveling the effect of textured contact lenses on iris recognition. IEEE Transactions on Information Forensics and Security, 9(5), 851-862 (2014).
6. Lee, E., Park, K., Kim, J.: Fake iris detection by using purkinje image. In Proceedings of the International Conference on Advances on Biometrics (ICB '06), of Lecture Notes in Computer Science, vol. 3832, pp. 397–403. Springer, Hong Kong (2006).
7. He, X., An, S., Shi, P.: Statistical texture analysis-based approach for fake iris detection using support vector machines. In Proceedings of the International Conference on Advances on Biometrics (ICB '07), of Lecture Notes in Computer Science, vol. 4642. Springer, Berlin, Heidelberg (2007).
8. Wei, Z., Qiu, X., Sun, Z., Tan, T.: Counterfeit iris detection based on texture analysis. In: 19th International Conference on Pattern Recognition, pp. 1-4. IEEE, Tampa, FL (2008).
9. He, Z., Sun, Z., Tan, T., Wei, Z.: Efficient iris spoof detection via boosted local binary patterns. In: Advances in Biometrics (ICB 2009), of Lecture Notes in Computer Science, vol. 5558, Springer, Berlin, Heidelberg (2009).
10. Qin, H., El-Yacoubi, M.: Deep representation-based feature extraction and recovering for finger-vein verification. IEEE Transactions on Information Forensics and Security, 12(8), 1816–1829 (2017).
11. Proenca, H., Neves, J.: Deep-PRWIS: periocular recognition without the iris and sclera using deep learning frameworks. IEEE Transactions on Information Forensics and Security, 13(4), 888– 896 (2018).
12. Benıtez-Pena, S., Blanquero, R., Carrizosa, E., Ramırez-Cobo, P.: On Support Vector Machines under a multiple-cost scenario. In: Advances in Data Analysis and Classification, pp. 1-20. Springer, Berlin Heidelberg (2018).
13. Silva, P., Luz, E., Baeta, R., Pedrini, H., Falcao, A., Menotti, D.: An approach to iris contact lens detection based on deep image representations. In: 28th SIBGRAPI Conference on Graphics, Patterns and Images, pp. 157-164. IEEE, Salvador (2015).
14. Raghavendra, R., Raja, K., Busch, C.: ContlensNet: Robust iris contact lens detection using deep convolutional neural networks. In: Winter Conference on Applications of Computer Vision (WACV), pp. 1160-1167. IEEE, Santa Rosa, CA (2017).
15. Singh, A., Mistry, V., Yadav, D., Nigam, A.: GHCLNet: A generalized hierarchically tuned contact lens detection network. In: 4th International Conference on Identity, Security, and Behavior Analysis (ISBA), pp. 1-8. IEEE, Singapore (2018).
16. Menotti, D. *et al.*: Deep representations for iris, face, and fingerprint spoofing detection. IEEE Transaction on Information Forensics and Security, 10(4), 864–879 (2015).
17. Huang, G., Liu, Z., Maaten, L., Weinberger, K.: Densely connected convolutional networks. In IEEE Conference on Computer Vision and Pattern Recognition (CVPR), pp. 2261-2269. IEEE, Honolulu, HI (2017).
18. Liu, N., Zhang, M., Li, H., Sun, Z., Tan, T.: Deepiris: Learning pairwise filter bank for heterogeneous iris verification. Pattern Recognition Letter, 82(2), 154–161(2015).
19. Proença, H., Alexandre, L.: Toward covert iris biometric recognition: Experimental results from the NICE contests. IEEE Transactions on Information Forensics and Security, 7(2), 798–808(2012).

20. Scherer, D., Muller, A., Behnke, S.: Evaluation of pooling operations in convolutional architectures for object recognition. In: International Conference on Artificial Neural Networks (ICANN), of Lecture Notes in Computer Science, vol. 6354. Springer, Berlin, Heidelberg (2010).
21. Chollet, F. *et al.*: Keras. https://github.com/fchollet/keras, 2015.
22. Mart, A. *et al.*: Tensorflow: Large-scale machine learning on heterogeneous systems, https:/www.tenssorflow.org.
23. The ND Contact Lens Database 2013, http://www3.nd.edu/ cvrl/CVRL/Data_Sets.html.
24. The IIIT-Delhi Contact Lens Iris Database, https://research.iiitd.edu.in/groups/iab/irisdatabases.html.
25. Irisguard, Washington, DC, USA, ad100 camera, 2013, http://www.Irisguard.com/uploads/AD100ProductSheet.pdf.
26. Lg, Riyadh, Saudi Arabia, LG 4000 camera, 2011, http://www.lgIris.com.
27. D. Petrovska and A. Mayoue, "Description and documentation of the biosecure software library," technical report, BioSecure, Project No IST-2002-507634, 2007. Available: https://biosecure.wp.tem-tsp.eu/evaluation-framework/.

An Efficient Approach for Mining Weighted Frequent Patterns with Dynamic Weights

Umama Dewan[1], Chowdhury Farhan Ahmed[1], Carson K. Leung[2][0000−0002−7541−9127](✉), Redwan Ahmed Rizvee[1], Deyu Deng[2], and Joglas Souza[2]

[1] University of Dhaka, Dhaka, Bangladesh
farhan@du.ac.bd
[2] University of Manitoba, Winnipeg, MB, Canada
kleung@cs.umanitoba.ca

Abstract. Weighted frequent pattern (WFP) mining is considered to be more effective than traditional frequent pattern mining because of its consideration of different semantic significance (weights) of items. However, most existing WFP algorithms assume a static weight for each item, which may not be realistically hold in many real-life applications. In this paper, we consider the concept of a dynamic weight for each item and address the situations where the weights of an item can be changed dynamically. We propose a novel tree structure called compact pattern tree for dynamic weights (CPTDW) to mine frequent patterns from dynamic weighted item containing databases. The CPTDW-tree leads to the concept of dynamic tree restructuring to produce a frequency-descending tree structure at runtime. CPTDW also ensures that no non-candidate item can appear before candidate items in any branch of the tree, and thus speeds up the construction time for prefix tree and its conditional tree during the mining process. Furthermore, as it requires only one database scan, it can be applicable to interactive, incremental, and/or stream data mining. Evaluation results show that our proposed tree structure and the mining algorithm outperforms previous methods for dynamic weighted frequent pattern mining.

Keywords: Data mining · Knowledge discovery · Weighted frequent pattern mining · Dynamic weights.

1 Introduction

Discovery of meaningful and hidden knowledge from a large collection of data is the main goal of data mining [4, 7, 10, 13, 16, 19]. Frequent pattern mining [12,17,18] is an important data mining problem where the patterns that occur frequently in a database are mined. However, in real-life scenarios, the frequency of a pattern cannot be considered as a sufficient indicator to find the meaningful patterns in large transaction databases. It is because, through frequency, only the number of transactions in the database containing the pattern is reflected. In many cases, the items in a transaction can be considered to have different degrees of importance (weight). For example, in retail applications, an expensive product generally contributes a large portion of overall revenue although it may not appear in many transactions. For this reason, *weighted frequent pattern (WFP) mining* [6, 21–23] was introduced to discover more useful knowledge by considering different weights for different items. Some real life examples where weight-based pattern mining can be applied are market data analysis where the price of products is an important factor, web traversal pattern mining where different web pages have different strength of impact.

Even though WFP mining considers diverse application specific weights for different items, still it cannot reflect real world environment where the significance (weight) of items vary with time. Most of the existing WFP algorithms consider static weight for an item. But in real life, the significance of an item can be affected by many factors. Consumer behaviors change with time which affect the significance of products in retail market. For example, the demand of jackets increase in winter, but their demand are quite likely to decrease in summer. Again, at one period of time, the demand of a particular design or material of jacket (e.g., jean jacket) can increase or decrease considering the current trend and other factors. It signifies that considering different weights for a particular item for different times is a requirement for several real-life applications.

Motivated by these real world scenarios, a new strategy for handling dynamic weights in WFP mining was introduced [2]. However, the algorithm uses a less compact tree structure (CanTree [14, 15]) and requires long mining time. The main focus of the current work is to solve these problems all together. Our *key contributions* of this paper include:

- A novel, highly compact tree structure—namely, *Compact Pattern Tree for Dynamic Weights (CPTDW)*—is proposed to mine frequent patterns with dynamic weights that significantly improves the performance with a single database scan.
- A phase-by-phase tree restructuring method—namely, path adjusting method—is proposed for dynamic weighted frequent pattern mining, which improves the degree of prefix sharing in the tree structure.
- A single-scan mining algorithm is developed based on the above tree structure, that can be applied for finding dynamic weighted frequent patterns over a data stream.
- Performance characteristics of a pattern-growth mining approach for dynamic weighted frequent pattern mining were observed through extensive experimental study.

The remainder of this paper is organized as follows. The next section discusses the required preliminary concepts with related works. Section 3 describes our proposed methodology with proper examples. Section 4 presents our evaluation results to show the supremacy of our proposed approach. Finally, conclusions are drawn in Section 5.

2 Preliminary Concepts and Related Works

2.1 Frequent Pattern Mining

The support/frequency of a pattern signifies the number of transactions that contain the pattern in the transaction database. Frequent pattern mining is used to find the complete set of patterns that satisfies a minimum support threshold in the transaction database. The *downward closure property* states that, if a pattern is infrequent, then all of its super patterns must be infrequent and can be pruned.

The Apriori algorithm [1] is the first solution for the frequent pattern mining problem. However, it needs several database scans and suffers from the level-wise-candidate-generation-and-test problem. *Frequent Pattern (FP)-Growth* [9] solves this problem by using an FP-tree based technique which requires only two database scans. There has been several research works which are being used to devise new algorithms or to improve the existing works for finding frequent patterns.

2.2 Weighted Frequent Pattern Mining

The weight of an item is a non-negative real number that is assigned to reflect the importance of that item in the transaction database. For a set of items $I = \{i_1, i_2, ..., i_n\}$, the weight of a pattern, P $\{x_1, x_2, ..., x_n\}$ is given as follows:

$$Weight(p) = \frac{\sum_{q=1}^{length(P)} Weight(x_q)}{length(P)} \tag{1}$$

For example, consider (i) an item "a" has weight 0.7 and frequency 2, and (ii) an item "b" has weight 0.3 and frequency 5. Then, according to Eq. (1), the weight of itemset "ab" will be $\frac{0.7+0.3}{2} = 0.5$. The weighted support of a pattern is the result of multiplying the pattern's support with the weight of that pattern:

$$WSupport(P) = Weight(P) \times Support(P) \tag{2}$$

A *weighted frequent pattern* is the pattern whose weighted support is at least the minimum threshold.

Example 1. If (i) an item "a" has weight 0.7 and frequency 2 and (ii) item "b" has weight 0.3 and frequency 5, then $WSupport(\text{"a"}) = 0.7 \times 2 = 1.4$ and $WSupport(\text{"b"}) = 0.3 \times 5 = 1.5$ according to Eq. (2). If the minimum support threshold is 1.2, then both "a" and "b" are weighted frequent patterns.

In real-life applications, normalized weight values are assigned to each item based on their price. Normalization process is required to adjust the differences among data from various sources so that a common basis of comparison is being created [22, 23]. Based on the normalization process, a specific weight range can be determined so that the final item weights can be within that range.

Some weighted frequent pattern mining algorithms [6, 21] have been developed based on Apriori technique, which makes the use of candidate generation-and-test paradigm. These algorithms require multiple database scans, and result in poor mining performance. Moreover, WFP mining is more challenge because the weighted frequency of a pattern does not satisfy the *downward closure property*.

Example 2. Continue with Example 1. With Eqs. (1) and (2), $Weight(\text{"ab"}) = \frac{0.7+0.3}{2} = 0.5$ and $WSupport(\text{"ab"}) = 0.5 \times 3 = 1.5$, but $WSupport(\text{"a"}) = 1.4$ and $WSupport(\text{"b"}) = 0.9$. For the minimum support threshold of 1.2, pattern "b" is infrequent but item "ab" is frequent, which means *downward closure property* is not satisfied.

WFIM [23] and its extension WIP [22] maintain the property by multiplying each item's frequency by the overall maximum weight.

Example 3. Continue with Example 2. Item "a" has the maximum weight of 0.7. By multiplying it with the support count of item "b", 2.1 is obtained. As a result, "b" will not be pruned at an early stage and pattern "ab" will not be missed. However, at the final stage, the overestimated pattern "b" will be pruned by using its actual weighted support.

2.3 Dynamic Weighted Frequent Pattern Mining

In dynamic weighted frequent pattern mining, weight of each item changes dynamically in each batch based on the importance of that particular item. The dynamic weighted support of a pattern is the result of adding the weighted supports of that pattern in each batch. A dynamic weighted frequent pattern is the pattern whose dynamic weighted support is greater than or equal to the minimum threshold. Dynamic weighted support of a pattern P is:

$$DWSupport(P) = \sum_{j=1}^{N} Weight_j(P) \times Support_j(P) \tag{3}$$

where N is the number of batches. Consider an item "a" has weight 0.7 and frequency 2 in first batch and weight 0.3 and frequency 5 in the second batch. Then, according to Eq. (2), the weighted support of pattern "a" in the first and second batches are $0.7 \times 2 = 1.4$ and $0.3 \times 3 = 0.9$, respectively. So, the total $DWSupport(\text{"a"}) = 1.4 + 0.9 = 2.3$ according to equation (3). If the minimum support threshold is 1.2, then "a" is a dynamic weighted frequent pattern.

Zhang et al. [24] proposed a strategy to find association rules in dynamic databases by weighting. However, they considered one weight for a database containing a group of transactions. By doing so, the recently added groups of transactions are highlighted over the previously added groups. However, this assumption is not realistic because the importance of an item or itemset can vary with time.

Ahmed et al. [2] proposed a *dynamic weighted frequent pattern mining (DWFPM) algorithm* to dynamically handle the changing item weights. It exploits pattern growth mining technique that removes the level-wise candidate generation-and-test methodology of the dynamic weight algorithm [24]. Furthermore, it requires only one database scan which makes it eligible for using in incremental, inter-active and stream data mining. However, the CanTree structure [14, 15] used in this algorithm results in a less compact tree structure and incurs very high mining time due to the canonical order of its tree structure.

3 Our Proposed Approach

3.1 Tree Construction

To capture transactions having items with dynamic weights, we construct a *compact pattern tree for dynamic weights (CPTDW)*. A header table is maintained with the tree structure. The first value of the header table is the item ID. The second value of the header table contains each item's weight value in a batch-by-batch fashion, and the third value of header table contains the I-list of items which contains the current frequency value of each item in a batch-by-batch manner. Our CPTDW builds an FP-tree [9] like compact frequency-descending tree structure with a single-scan of transaction database. At first, transactions of the first batch are inserted into the CPTDW tree one by one according to a predefined item order (e.g., lexicographic order). After inserting a batch of transactions, the CPTDW tree structure is dynamically restructured by the current frequency descending item order and I-list is updated accordingly using the path adjusting method [3, 11]. In summary, CPTDW tree can be constructed in two phases:

1. **Insertion phase:** Transaction(s) of a batch is scanned, according to the current item order of I-list, transactions are inserted into the tree and the frequency count of the respective items is updated in the I-list.
2. **Restructuring phase:** The I-list is rearranged according to the frequency descending order of the items and the tree nodes are restructured according to the newly arranged I-list.

The construction of CPTDW starts with the insertion phase. The first insertion phase begins by inserting the first transaction of the first batch in a lexicographic item order into the tree. The tree will be restructured after the insertion of all the transactions of the first batch. The tree is restructured by using the *path adjusting method* [11]. The paths in a prefix-tree are adjusted through recursive swapping of the adjacent node in the path until the path completely achieves the new sorted order. Thus, bubble sort technique is used to process the swapping between two nodes. One of the basic properties of FP-tree is that the frequency count of a node cannot be greater than the frequency count of its parent node. To maintain this property, the *path adjusting method* inserts a new node of the same name as a sibling of the parent node in the tree when

Algorithm 1 Path adjusting method algorithm.

Input: Let X, Y and Z be three nodes in a path in a prefix tree where X is the parent of Y, Y is the parent of Z and Y and Z nodes are needed to be exchanged for path adjustment. Consider *nodeName.name*, *nodeName.count* and *nodeName.child* refer to the name, the support count (in the referred path) and a child of a node. Therefore, the path adjusting is performed according to the following algorithm:

function EXCHANGE
    Exchange parent and children links of Y and Z
function INSERTION
    Insert Y' to X as a new child node such that $Y'.name = Y.name$
    Set $Y'.count = Y.count - Z.count$
    Assign all children of Y except Z to Y'
    Set $Y.count = Z.count$
function MERGE_NODE(P,Q)
    Set $Q.count = Q.count + P.count$
    for each child node of Q **do**
        for each child node of P **do**
            if $Q.child == P.child$ **then**
                Call MERGE_NODE($Q.child$, $P.child$)
            else if $Q.child$ not equals $P.child$ **then**
                Add $P.child$ and its sub tree to $Q.child$ list
function MERGE
    if C is another child node of X and $C.name = Z.name$ **then**
        Call MERGE_NODE(C,Z)
        Delete C and its sub tree
function PATH_ADJUST
    if Y and Z need to be swapped and $Y.count > Z.count$ **then**
        Call INSERTION( )
    Call EXCHANGE( )
    Call MERGE( )
Repeat to **Call** PATH_ADJUST with next two nodes of Y and Z in another path to be exchanged and **Terminate** when no further node exchange is required.

the parent node needs to be exchanged with any child node which has a smaller count value. Otherwise, if the frequency counts of both the nodes are equal, then a simple exchange operation between the two nodes is sufficient. However, after swapping, if two sibling nodes contain the same item due to the exchange operation, then they should be merged. This insertion and restructuring phases are executed alternatively until all the transactions of all batches are inserted into the tree and restructured in the frequency descending order according to a batch-by-batch fashion. The pseudo-code for path adjusting method is shown in Algorithm 1.

Consider the example database of Table 1. At first, the items of the first batch are inserted according to the lexicographic order as shown in Fig. 2(a). Then, they are sorted in frequency descending order based on path adjusting method [3,11]. Figure 2(b) shows the tree structure after restructuring the transactions of

Table 1: An example of transaction database with dynamic weights

Batch	TID	Transactions	Weights
1st	T1	a, d, e	a: 0.9 b: 0.5 c: 0.3 d: 0.45 e: 0.2
	T2	c, d, e	
	T3	b, a, e	
2nd	T4	b, d	a: 0.7 b: 0.55 c: 0.4 d: 0.2 e: 0.3
	T5	a, c, e	
	T6	b, c, d	
3rd	T7	d, e	a: 0.5 b: 0.7 c: 0.8 d: 0.6 e: 0.5
	T8	b, e	
	T9	c, b, e	

the first batch. Figure 2(c) shows the tree after inserting the transactions of the second batch based on the item order which is achieved after restructuring the transactions of the first batch. Then, the items are sorted in frequency descending order based on their current frequency which includes their frequency count of both the batches. Figure 2(d) shows the tree structure after restructuring. As frequency information for each batch is kept separately in each node of the tree, it can be easily discovered which transactions have occurred in which batch. At the same way, Fig. 2(e) shows the tree structure after inserting the transactions of the third batch. Figure 2(f) is our final CPTDW tree structure which is achieved by inserting and restructuring all the transactions of all batches. Our proposed CPTDW tree structure has the following properties:

- **Property 1:** The items in the tree are sorted according to the frequency descending order.
- **Property 2:** The total frequency count of any node in the tree is greater than or equal to the sum of total frequency counts of its children.
- **Property 3:** The tree structure can be constructed in a single database scan.

3.2 Mining Process

According to the FP-growth mining algorithm [9], while creating a prefix-tree for a particular item, all branches prefixing that particular item are taken with their frequency value. After that, the conditional tree is built from the prefix tree by deleting the nodes containing infrequent items. CPTDW algorithm performs the same type of mining. The mining operation of CPTDW is done in a top-down approach [20]. As discussed in Section 2.2, the main challenge in weighted frequent pattern mining is that, the weighted frequent pattern of an item does not hold the *downward closure property*. So, to maintain this property, global maximum weight GMAXW has to be used. GMAXW is the maximum weight of all the items in the global database. In our case, this is the highest weight among every weight in all of the batches. For example, in Table 1, item "a"

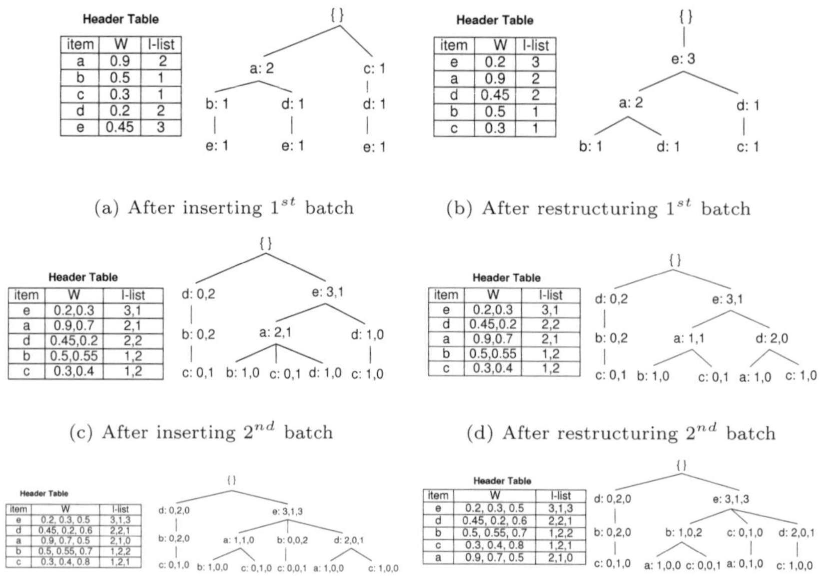

(a) After inserting 1st batch

(b) After restructuring 1st batch

(c) After inserting 2nd batch

(d) After restructuring 2nd batch

(e) After inserting 3rd batch

(f) After restructuring 3rd batch

Fig. 2: CPTDW Tree construction

has the GMAXW of 0.9. The local maximum weight LMAXW is needed while doing the mining operation for a particular item, and it is not always equal to GMAXW.

As our CPTDW tree is sorted according to the frequency descending order, LMAXW could be anywhere for a particular item. We start our pattern growth mining operation from the top-most item of the CPTDW tree structure. So, for this case, LMAXW is the weight of the first item for sure. After that, for the second item, we compare its weight with the previous LMAXW and consider the larger one as the current LMAXW. By moving in this way, LMAXW calculation for each time can be saved.

We consider the database presented in Table 1, the tree constructed for that particular database in Fig. 2(f) and minimum support threshold 1.2. Here, GMAXW is 0.9. After multiplying GMAXW with the total frequency of each item, we get a: $3 \times 0.9 = 2.7$, b: $5 \times 0.9 = 4.5$, c: $4 \times 0.9 = 3.6$, d: $5 \times 0.9 = 4.5$, and e: $7 \times 0.9 = 6.3$. So, all items are single element candidates. We start the mining process with the top-most item of the CPTDW tree, "e". For "e", LMAXW is 0.5, frequency of "e" is $3+1+3 = 7$. By multiplying the frequency of "e" with LMAXW, we get $0.5 \times 7 = 3.5$, which is greater than minimum support threshold 1.2. So, single element pattern "e" is generated.

After that, we consider item "d" as it is the second top most item in Fig. 2(f). So, the prefix tree of "d" is created by taking all the branches prefixing item "d"

Algorithm 2 Mining and Test_Candidate Procedure.

```
procedure PROCEDURE_MINING(T, H, α, LMAXW)
    for each item β of H do
        if (frequency(β) × LMAXW <δ) then
            Delete β from H and T
    Let CT be the Conditional tree of α
    Let HC be the Header table of Conditional tree CT
    for each item β in HC do
        Call TEST_CANDIDATE(αβ, frequency(αβ),δ)
        Create Prefix tree PT_α β with its Header table HP_α β for pattern αβ
        Call Mining(PT_α β, HP_α β, αβ, LMAXW)
procedure TEST_CANDIDATE(X,B,δ)
    Let Dynamic weighted support of X be DW_X
    Let frequency(X_k) denotes frequency of pattern X in kth batch
    Let weight(X_k) denotes weighted average of pattern X in kth batch
    Set DW_X = 0
    for each Batch B_i in B do
        DW_X = DW_X + (frequency(X_{B_i}) × weight(X_{B_i}))
    if DW_X ≥ δ then
        Add X in the Dynamic weighted frequent pattern list
```

as shown in Fig. 4(a). For creating conditional tree, the nodes that cannot be candidate patterns must be deleted from the prefix tree. For item "d", LMAXW is 0.6. After multiplying the frequency of the item in the header table shown in Fig. 4(a), we get e: $3 \times 0.6 = 1.8$. As the value is greater than the minimum support threshold value, that is 1.2, so no node should be deleted from the prefix tree which signifies that, the prefix and conditional tree for item "d" is same. So, the candidate patterns "de" and "d" are generated at this point.

The same procedure is conducted for all the items in the I-list of Fig. 2(f) for finding out all the candidate patterns of our example database. The pseudo-code of the mining procedure is illustrated in Algorithm 2 and the operations are shown in Fig. 4. After generating all the candidate patterns, we calculate the actual DWSupport of each candidate pattern according to Eq. (2) to check whether they are actually frequent or not. This calculation is shown in Table 2.

4 Performance Evaluation

In this section, we present the overall performance of our proposed algorithm CPTDW over several datasets. The performance of our proposed algorithm CPTDW in compared with the existing DWFPM algorithm [2].

Experimental environment and datasets. To evaluate the performance of our proposed tree structure and algorithm for dynamic weighted frequent pattern mining, we have performed several experiments on IBM synthetic dataset (e.g., T10I4D100K) using synthetic weights and real life datasets (e.g., retail, chess, mushroom, pumsb*, connect, pumsb) using synthetic weights and real-life

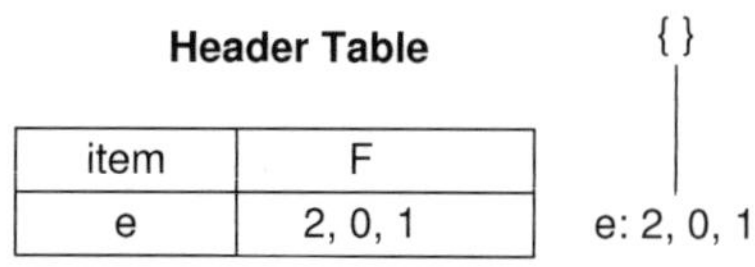

(a) Prefix and Conditional Tree for "d"

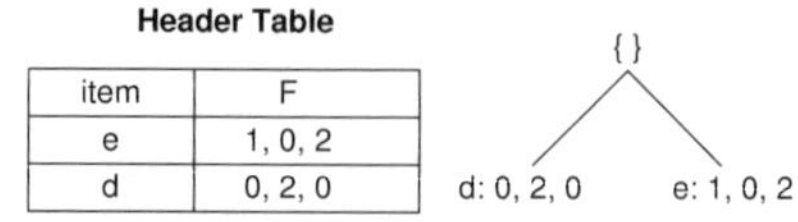

(b) Prefix and Conditional Tree for "b"

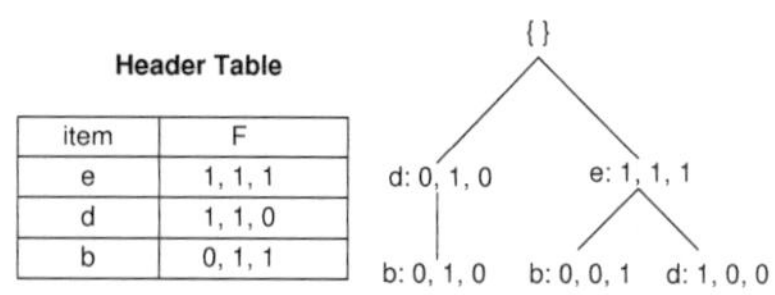

(c) Prefix and Conditional Tree for "c"

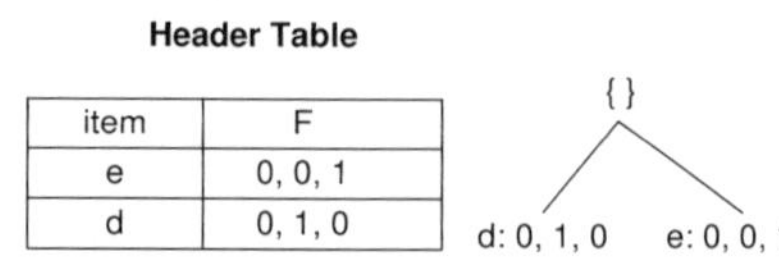

(d) Prefix Tree for "bc"

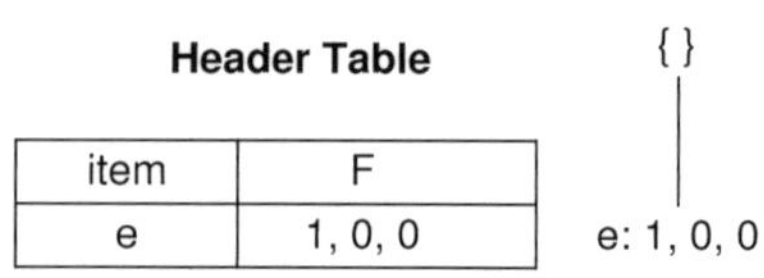

(e) Prefix Tree for "cd"

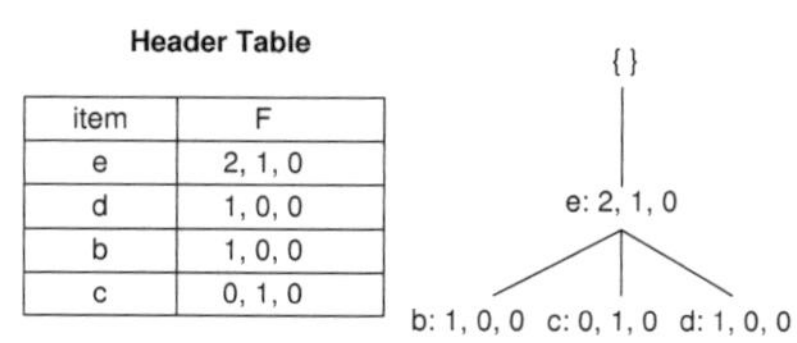

(f) Prefix Tree for "a"

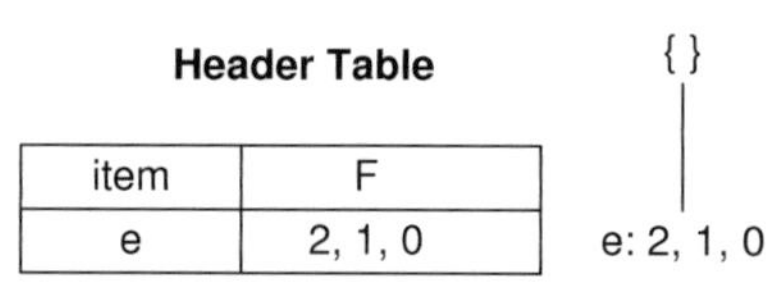

(g) Conditional Tree for "a"

Fig. 4: Mining Operation

dataset (e.g., chain-store) with real weight values. All the datasets are collected from frequent itemset mining dataset respiratory [5]. The performance of the proposed algorithm is compared with the existing algorithm DWFPM [2], with respect to runtime (aka execution time) and memory usage. Our programs are written in Java programming language. Programs were run in a time sharing environment with the Linux 16.04 operating system on a HP Notebook, 64 bits machine, Intel(R) Core(TM) i3-6100U CPU, 2.30GHz processor, 4GB RAM, 100MHz clock, and 500 GB of main memory. We have divided all the datasets in such a way that each batch contains at most 10 transactions. The minimum support threshold values of 2%, 3%, 10% and 15% are used to conduct the experiments.

Table 3 shows some important characteristics of synthetic and real-life datasets. Dense and sparse natures of datasets are very useful properties. A dense dataset contains many items per transaction and small number of distinct items. For the *chess* dataset in Table 3, it has a total of 75 distinct items, an average

Table 2: DWSupport calculation of the candidate patterns of CPTDW algorithm

No	Candidate patterns	DW support calculation	Results
1	e: 3,1,3	$(0.2 \times 3) + (0.3 \times 1) + (0.5 \times 3) = 2.4$	Passed
2	de: 2,0,1	$(\frac{0.45+0.2}{2} \times 2) + (\frac{0.6+0.5}{2} \times 1) = 1.2$	Passed
3	d: 2,2,1	$(0.45 \times 2) + (0.2 \times 2) + (0.6 \times 1) = 1.9$	Passed
4	be: 1,0,2	$(\frac{0.5+0.2}{2} \times 1) + (\frac{0.7+0.5}{2} \times 2) = 0.95$	Pruned
5	bd: 0,2,0	$\frac{0.55+0.2}{2} \times 2 = 0.75$	Pruned
6	b: 1,2,2	$(1 \times 0.5) + (0.55 \times 2) + (0.7 \times 2) = 3$	Passed
7	ce: 1,1,1	$(\frac{0.3+0.2}{2} \times 1) + (\frac{0.4+0.3}{2} \times 1) + (\frac{0.8+0.5}{2} \times 1) = 1.25$	Passed
8	cd: 1,1,0	$(\frac{0.3+0.45}{2} \times 1) + (\frac{0.4+0.2}{2} \times 1) = 0.675$	Pruned
9	bc: 0,1,1	$(\frac{0.55+0.4}{2} \times 1) + (\frac{0.7+0.8}{2} \times 1) = 1.225$	Passed
10	c: 1,2,1	$(0.3 \times 1) + (0.4 \times 2) + (0.8 \times 1)= 1.9$	Passed
11	ae: 2,1,0	$(\frac{0.9+0.2}{2} \times 2) + (\frac{0.7+0.3}{2} \times 1) = 1.6$	Passed
12	a: 2,1,0	$(0.9 \times 2) + (0.7 \times 1) = 2.5$	Passed

Table 3: Dataset characteristics

Datasets	#trans.	Avg. trans. len. (A)	#distinct items (D)	Dense & sparse characteristics ratio $R = \frac{A}{D} \times 100(\%)$
T10I4D100K	100,000	10.1	870	1.16
mushroom	8,124	23	119	19.327
chess	3,196	37	75	49.33
pumsb*	49,046	50.48	2,088	2.42
retail	88,162	10.3	16,470	0.0625
Chain-store	1,112,949	7.2	46,086	0.0156

transaction length of 37, and 49.33% items are present in every transaction. If $R > 10\%$, then the dataset is considered *dense*, which may generate many long frequent patterns and dynamic weighted frequent patterns. If $R \leq 10\%$, then the dataset is *sparse*. The dataset *chess* is too dense and the dataset *mushroom* is moderately dense. Similarly, datasets *T10I4D100k* and *pumbsb** are moderately sparse datasets; datasets *retail* and *Chain-store* are too sparse datasets.

Synthetic dataset with synthetic weight. We used IBM synthetic dataset *T10I4D100k* developed by the IBM Almaden Quest research group. The dataset was obtained from the frequent itemset mining dataset respiratory [5]. The dataset do not provide weight values. According to the real world scenario, the weight values of each item was heuristically chosen to be in the range from 0.1 to 0.9, and randomly generated by using a log-normal distribution. The pattern generation times for this dataset for both the existing DWFPM algorithm and our proposed CPTDW algorithm are shown in Fig. 6(a).

Real life datasets with synthetic weight. We used real-life datasets *chess, mushroom, pumsb** and *Retail* obtained from the frequent itemset mining

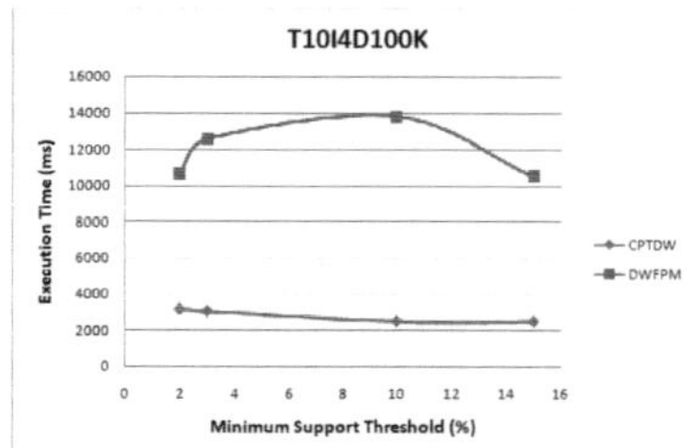

(a) Runtime on *T10I4D100K* dataset

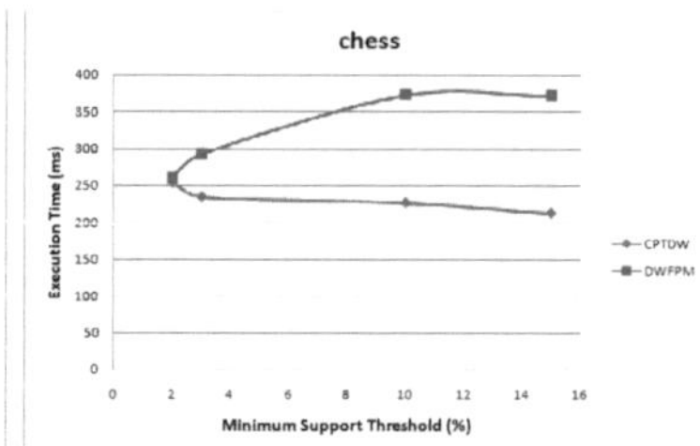

(b) Runtime on *chess* dataset

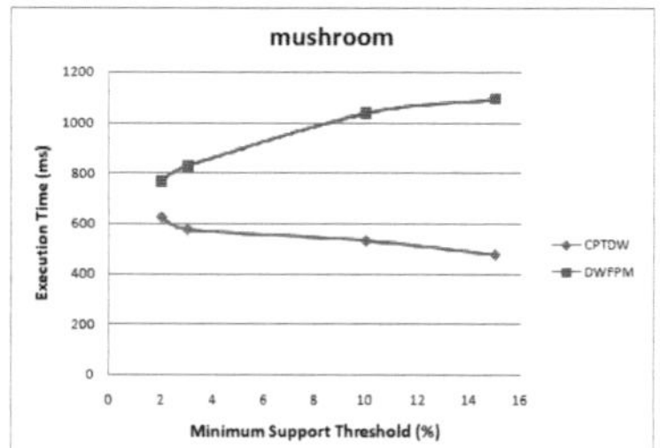

(c) Runtime on *mushroom* dataset

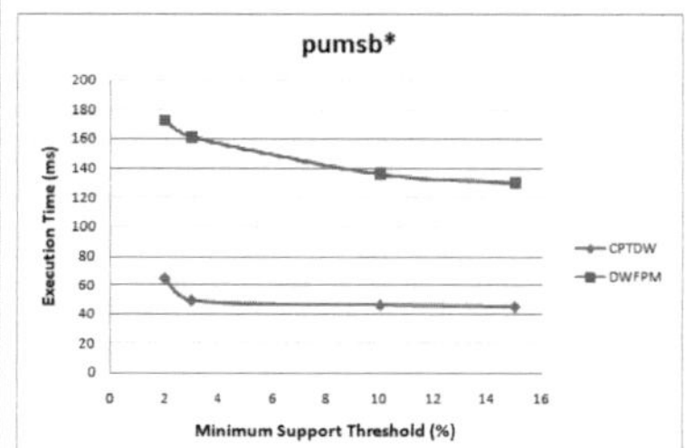

(d) Runtime on *pumsb** dataset

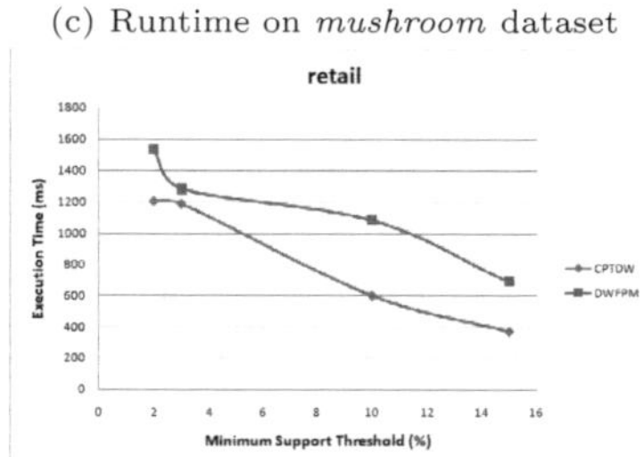

(e) Runtime on *retail* dataset

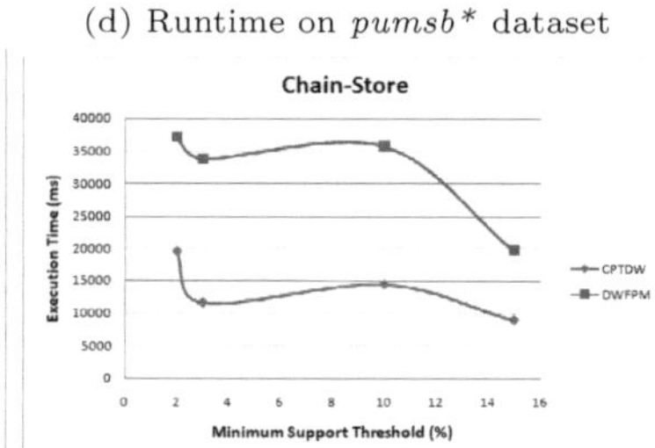

(f) Runtime on *Chain-store* dataset

Fig. 6: Experimental Results

dataset respiratory [5]. These datasets do not provide weight values. So, weights for items were generated randomly by using log-normal distribution. The pattern generation times for these datasets for both the existing DWFPM algorithm and our proposed CPTDW algorithm are shown in Figs. 6(b)–6(e).

Real life dataset with real weight. We used real-life dataset *Chain-store* obtained from SPMF, an open-source data mining library [8] consisting of multiple data mining applications and databases. This dataset was taken from a major chain store in California. We have taken real weight values for items from their utility table. The experiment is conducted on the first half transactions of the total transactions of the dataset. The pattern generation times of the DWFPM and CPTDW algorithms for this dataset are shown in Fig. 6(f).

Scalability of CPTDW. The experimental results on different datasets show that our proposed algorithm can easily handle large number of transaction containing databses (e.g., *T10I4D100k*, *Chain-store*). Hence, these experimental results demonstrate the scalability of our proposed algorithm to handle large

Table 4: Node count of CPTDW and DWFPM algorithms

Dataset	Node Count (CPTDW)	Node Count (DWFPM)
mushroom	12	21
pumsb	21	61
pumsb*	36	70
Chain-store	789	804

Table 5: Runtime Distributions of CPTDW and DWFPM Algorithms

Dataset	Tree construction time of CPTDW (ms)	Overall runtime of CPTDW (ms)	Tree construction time of DWFPM (ms)	Overall runtime of DWFPM (ms)
T10I4D100K	1,033	3,925	283	6,001
chess	19	37	3	40
mushroom	13	38	2	44
pumsb*	21	285	3	424
retail	36	367	10	518

number of transactions and distinct items. Our CPTDW algorithm outperforms the existing DWFPM algorithm by using an efficient tree structure and pattern growth mining technique in terms of runtime and memory usage.

Memory usage. Research on prefix-tree based frequent pattern mining shows that, the memory requirement for the prefix tress is low enough to use the gigabyte range memory available nowadays. Table 4 shows the total number of nodes of the prefix-trees at the time of generating dynamic weighted frequent patterns for different datasets for both the CPTDW and DWFPM algorithms. We have handled our tree structure very efficiently. Our CPTDW tree can represent transaction information in a very compressed form because transactions have many items in common. By using more prefix-sharing, our tree structure can save memory space.

Runtime distribution. Recall from Section 3.1 about our CPTDW tree construction process, CPTDW requires several swapping operations to restructure the tree structure in frequency descending order after the insertion of the transactions of each batch. So, there might arouse an issue that, CPTDW should require more time for the tree construction which is true. However, observed from Table 5, although CPTDW requires more time to construct the tree structure, we get a significant gain in overall runtime due to the frequency descending compact structure of the tree. For the following experiments presented in Table 5, the datasets were divided into 15 unique symbols and the minimum support threshold value of 3% is used.

5 Conclusions

Although there have been several efforts in mining weighted frequent patterns, they are not designed for handling many real-life situations where the importance of an item varies dynamically over time. Our key contribution of this paper is to provide a new tree-based approach to efficiently mine dynamic weighted frequent patterns. By storing batch-by-batch frequency and weight information, our compact pattern tree for dynamic weights (CPTDW) algorithm discovers accurate knowledge about dynamic weighted frequent patterns. CPTDW is applicable to real time data processing because it requires only one database scan. By using an efficient tree structure and mining approach, our CPTDW saves memory space and time consumption. Extensive performance analyses shows our algorithm is efficient when applied to both sparse and dense datasets, and can handle a large number of distinct items and transactions. As ongoing and future work, we are extending the current work for (i) incremental and interactive mining on databases with dynamic weights and for (ii) sliding window based dynamic weighted frequent patterns mining over data streams.

Acknowledgements

This project is partially supported by NSERC (Canada) and University of Manitoba.

References

1. Agrawal, R., Srikant, R.: Fast algorithms for mining association rules in large databases. In: VLDB 1994, pp. 487–499 (1994)
2. Ahmed, C.F., Tanbeer, S.K., Jeong, B., Lee, Y.: Handling dynamic weights in weighted frequent pattern mining. IEICE TIS E91-D(11), 2578–2588 (2008)
3. Ahmed, C.F., Tanbeer, S.K., Jeong, B., Lee, Y., Choi, H.: Single-pass incremental and interactive mining for weighted frequent patterns. ESWA 39(9), 7976–7994 (2012)
4. Barkwell, K.E., Cuzzocrea, A., Leung, C.K., Ocran, A.A., Sanderson, J.M., Stewart, J.A., Wodi, B.H.: Big data visualisation and visual analytics for music data mining. In: IV 2018, pp. 235–240 (2018)
5. Bayardo, R., Goethals, B., Zaki, M.J. (eds.): Proc. IEEE ICDM Workshop on FIMI 2004 (2004)
6. Cai, C.H., Fu, A.W., Cheng, C.H., Kwong, W.W.: Mining association rules with weighted items. In: IDEAS 1998, pp. 68–77 (1998)
7. Fan, C., Hao, H., Leung, C.K., Sun, L.Y., Tran, J.: Social network mining for recommendation of friends based on music interests. In: IEEE/ACM ASONAM 2018, pp. 833–840 (2018)
8. Fournier-Viger, P., Lin, J.C., Gomariz, A., Gueniche, T., Soltani, A., Deng, Z., Lam, H.T.: The SPMF open-source data mining library version 2. In: ECML PKDD 2016, Part III. LNCS (LNAI), vol. 9853, pp. 36–40 (2016)
9. Han, J., Cheng, H., Xin, D., Yan, X.: Frequent pattern mining: current status and future directions. DMKD 15(1), 55–86 (2007)

10. Hoi, C.S.H., Khowaja, D., Leung, C.K.: Constrained frequent pattern mining from big data via crowdsourcing. In: BigDAS 2017. AISC, vol. 770, pp. 69–79 (2017)
11. Koh, J., Shieh, S.: An efficient approach for maintaining association rules based on adjusting FP-tree structures. In: DASFAA 2004. LNCS, vol. 2973, pp. 417–424 (2004)
12. Leung, C.K., Hoi, C.S.H., Pazdor, A.G.M., Wodi, B.H., Cuzzocrea, A.: Privacy-preserving frequent pattern mining from big uncertain data. In: IEEE BigData 2018, pp. 5101–5110 (2018)
13. Leung, C.K., Jiang, F.: Efficient mining of 'following' patterns from very big but sparse social networks. In: IEEE/ACM ASONAM 2017, pp. 1025–1032 (2018)
14. Leung, C.K., Khan, Q.I., Hoque, T.: CanTree: a tree structure for efficient incremental mining of frequent patterns. In: IEEE ICDM 2005, pp. 274–281 (2005)
15. Leung, C.K., Khan, Q.I., Li, Z., Hoque, T.: CanTree: a canonical-order tree for incremental frequent-pattern mining. KAIS 11(3), 287–311 (2007)
16. Liu, J., Chang, Z., Leung, C.K., Wong, R.C.W., Xu, Y., Zhao, R.: Efficient mining of extraordinary patterns by pruning and predicting. ESWA 125, 55–68 (2019)
17. Perner, P.: Mining frequent subgraph pattern over a collection of attributed-graphs and construction of a relation hierarchy for result reporting. In: ICDM 2017. LNCS (LNAI), vol. 10357, pp. 323–344 (2017)
18. Phan, H., Le, B.: A novel parallel algorithm for frequent itemsets mining in large transactional databases. In: ICDM 2018. LNCS (LNAI), vol. 10933, pp. 272–287 (2018)
19. Rahman, M.M., Ahmed, C.F., Leung, C.K.: Mining weighted frequent sequences in uncertain databases. Inf. Sci. 479, pp. 76–100 (2019)
20. Tanbeer, S.K., Ahmed, C.F., Jeong, B., Lee, Y.: Efficient single-pass frequent pattern mining using a prefix-tree. Inf. Sci. 179(5), 559–583 (2009)
21. Wang, W., Yang, J., Yu, P.S.: WAR: weighted association rules for item intensities. KAIS 6(2), 203–229 (2004)
22. Yun, U.: Efficient mining of weighted interesting patterns with a strong weight and/or support affinity. Inf. Sci. 177(17), 3477–3499 (2007)
23. Yun, U., Leggett, J.J.: WFIM: weighted frequent itemset mining with a weight range and a minimum weight. In: SIAM SDM 2005, pp. 636–640 (2005)
24. Zhang, S., Zhang, C., Yan, X.: Post-mining: maintenance of association rules by weighting. Inf. Syst. 28(7), 691–707 (2003)

How to Achieve High Classification Accuracy with Just a Few Labels: A Semi-supervised Approach Using Sampled Packets

Shahbaz Rezaei and Xin Liu

University of California, Davis, CA 95616, USA
{srezaei,xinliu}@ucdavis.edu

Abstract. Network traffic classification, which has numerous applications from security to billing and network provisioning, has become a cornerstone of today's computer networks. Previous studies have developed traffic classification techniques using classical machine learning algorithms and deep learning methods when large quantities of labeled data are available. However, capturing large labeled datasets is a cumbersome and time-consuming process. In this paper, we propose a semi-supervised approach that obviates the need for large labeled datasets. We first pre-train a model on a large unlabeled dataset where the input is the time series features of a few sampled packets. Then the learned weights are transferred to a new model that is re-trained on a small labeled dataset. We show that our semi-supervised approach achieves almost the same accuracy as a fully-supervised method with a large labeled dataset, though we use only 20 samples per class. Duting inferene, based on a dataset generated from the more challenging QUIC protocol, our approach yields 98% accuracy. To show its efficacy, we also test our approach on two public datasets. Moreover, we study three different sampling techniques and demonstrate that sampling packets from an arbitrary portion of a flow is sufficient for classification.

Keywords: Transfer Learning · Semi-supervised Learning · Network Traffic Classification · Packet Sampling · QUIC Protocol Classification

1 Introduction

Network traffic classification is one of the key components of network management and administration systems. It has been used for Quality of Service (QoS) provisioning, pricing, anomaly detection, malware detection, etc. Depending on the usage scenario, traffic may be classified based on protocols (e.g. UDP, TCP or FTP), traffic-types (e.g. voice, video or downloading), application (e.g. Youtube, Facebook or WeChat), user-actions, operating system, etc [12]. Due to the inherent differences of traffic in these applications, a model, approach or dataset that is used for one application cannot be used for another application. As a result, due to the lack of general approach, designing an accurate traffic classifier for an application of interest a has been time-consuming and cumbersome task.

Classical machine learning approaches have been extensively used for more than a decade and showed good accuracy. However, the emergence of new applications and encryption protocols has dramatically increased the complexity of the traffic classification problem. Recently, deep learning algorithms have been developed for traffic classification. Deep learning approaches are capable of automatic feature selection and capturing highly complex patterns, and thus demonstrated high classification accuracy in comparison to other methods.

However, deep learning requires a large amount of labeled data during training. Capturing and labeling a large dataset is a non-trivial and cumbersome process. First, current Internet traffic is mostly encrypted that makes DPI (Deep Packet Inspection) based labeling impossible. Hence, most labeling procedures capture each traffic class in isolation. However, this is only possible at the edge of a network or in an isolated environment. Unlike labeled dataset, unlabeled data is abundant and readily available in the Internet. Therefore, it motivates us to study how to use easily-obtainable unlabeled datasets to dramatically reduce the size of labeled dataset needed for accurate traffic classification.

Furthermore, to make our approach practical, in particular for high speed links or data centers, we propose to use sampled data packets instead of an entire flow. Using sampled packets also reduces memory and computation complexity needed for entire time series features [12]. In summary, in this paper, we make the following contributions:

1. We propose a semi-supervised approach that utilizes large quantities of unlabeled data and just a few labeled samples. Specifically, we first train a model on a large unlabeled dataset and then re-train the model with a few labeled data on the target classification problem.
2. We study three different sampling methods on the encrypted traffic classification problem: Fixed step sampling, random sampling, and incremental sampling. We show that good sampling methods can almost achieve the upper-bound accuracy in certain datasets.
3. We evaluate the proposed approach using captured QUIC traffic and show that our semi-supervised approach using sampled packets can accurately classify QUIC traffic that has fewer unencrypted fields during handshake.
4. We test our approach on different public datasets. Surprisingly, we show that we can train a model using a completely separate unlabeled dataset and then retrain the model with a small number of labels in the target dataset and still achieve good accuracy.

2 Related Work

In pre-deep learning era, traditional machine learning algorithms had been commonly used for traffic classification [16]. However, due to their simplicity, manual feature extraction, and inability to capture complex patterns, their accuracy has declined [12]. Recently, several studies develop deep learning models, such as Convolutional Neural Network (CNN) and Long Short-Term Memory (LSTM), for network traffic classification in a fully-supervised fashion. In [18], authors train six different CNN models based on LeNet-5 model on a public dataset with 12 classes. They convert 249 statistical characteristics into a 2-d 16×16 image and report high accuracy. In [9], authors use CNN, LSTM and various combinations on a private dataset captured at RedIRIS, a Spanish academic and research backbone network. They use time series features of the first 20 packets, including source port, destination port, payload size, window size, etc.

In [10], a framework comprising a CNN and Stacked Auto-Encoder (SAE) is trained on a dataset containing 12 VPN and non-VPN traffic classes. They use raw header and payload bytes as input. In [2], Reproducing Kernel Hilbert Space (RKHS) is used to convert the time series features of a flow to an image. Then, produced images are used as input to a CNN model. The only study that investigate QUIC protocol is [14]. They capture five Google services: Google Hangout Chat, Google Hangout Voice Call, YouTube, File transfer, and Google play music. They use CNN model and report high accuracy. They capture 150GB of data and train the model in a fully-supervised manner.

In [12], a general framework, covering all previous deep learning-based traffic classifiers, is introduced that can deal with any typical network traffic classification task. The paper provide a seven-step training process, including data capturing, data pre-processing, model selection and evaluation, etc. The framework also requires large enough dataset for training. In summary, in comparison, all work discussed above assumes large quantities of labeled data. Furthermore, packet sampling is not considered in their approaches.

3 Problem Statement

As discussed earlier, deep learning models have been adopted for (encrypted) traffic classification. Because deep learning approaches are capable of automatic feature selection and capturing highly complex patterns, they demonstrate high classification accuracy. However, a critical challenge is that deep models require large amounts of labeled data during training. Capturing and labeling a dataset is a non-trivial and cumbersome process.

First, because encryption mechanisms are heavily used in today's Internet, labeling a dataset captured in an operational network is almost impossible unless an accurate classifier is already available. As a result, labeling process is usually done by assuring that only one target class is available during capturing by turning off all other applications on the device used to generate traffic. This is typically done in an isolated environment or at the edge of the network. Traffic distribution in such an environment may differ from an operational network, especially at the core of the network. In addition, to capture large amounts of labeled data, previous studies often runs scripts to automatically perform certain actions that can be captured and labeled without manual labor. However, we will show that network traffic generated by scripts may have a different distribution from that of human-generated traffic, causing poor performance on real traffic.

In contrast, unlabeled data is abundant and readily available in an operational network. Capturing a large unlabeled dataset is an easy task. There are also many large and publicly available datasets. Hence, our objective is to use easily-obtainable unlabeled datasets to significantly reduce the size of labeled dataset needed for training an accurate traffic classifier. We only have a few labeled samples for each class that we are interested in, called target classes. We call this dataset D_l. At the same time, we assume we have a large unlabeled dataset D_u. This unlabeled dataset D_u may contain numerous flows from various traffic classes, even from classes that we are not interested in, i.e. they do not exist in D_l. The goal is to leverage the two datasets to train a traffic classification model for a target task while heavily exploiting D_u dataset for training.

4 Methodology

4.1 Key Components

Our objective is to obtain an accurate traffic classifier with only a small number of labeled samples from each traffic class. To achieve this objective, we propose a semi-supervised learning approach. There are three key components in the proposed scheme. The first is the classification model trained through semi-supervised learning. Specifically, we pre-train a model with D_u and then transfer the model to a new architecture and re-trained the model with D_l. This is called semi-supervised learning. This approach considerably reduces the number of labeled data needed for the second supervised learning part. Moreover, the pre-trained model can be reused for other network traffic classification tasks.

In order to use an unlabeled dataset, D_u, we pre-train a model, F, such that it does not need human labor for labeling[1]. An important step in the pre-training stage is to decide the target of the regression function. We choose a set of statistical features for this purpose, such as average packet length, average inter-arrival time, etc. Moreover, the input of the model is a set of packets sampled from the entire flow. For each packet, we only observe length, direction, and relative time. In other words, F is pre-trained to estimate statistical features of the entire flow by taking a set of sampled packets as an input. The idea is based on the assumption that not all traffic patterns are valid and a model pre-trained on a large unlabeled dataset will lay on a manifold of valid patterns and hopefully can estimate statistical features.

Next, the pre-trained model, F, will be used as a part of another model, G. Then, G will be re-trained with a small labeled dataset. Since a part of the model has already observed many traffic patterns, G needs considerably less human-labeled data. Note that F might not necessarily be an accurate estimator of statistical features. But, it will be re-trained quickly to help the classification task since it has already seen numerous traffic patterns during the pre-training.

The second key component is the features, including input features and the pre-training targets. As it is categorized in [12], there are three input features heavily used for network traffic classification tasks: time series features (such

[1] We use pre-training and re-training to distinguish between the first and second step of our semi-supervised approach.

as packet length and inter-arrival time), statistical features obtained from the entire flow (such as average packet length and average byte sent per second), and header/payload features (such as TCP window size field, TLS handshake data fields and data content). Header/payload data features have been used for classification of encrypted traffic such as TLS 1.2 [10, 13]. These methods rely upon unencrypted data fields or message types exchanged during handshake phase of TLS 1.2. However, state-of-the-art encryption protocols, such as QUIC and TLS 1.3, aim to reduce the number of handshake messages to improve the speed of connection establishment. As a result, fewer unencrypted data fields and packets are exchanged that makes it harder for header/payload based approaches to achieve high classification accuracy. Furthermore, statistical features require the model to observe the entire flow before classification which is not efficient in practice. However, statistical features present useful information of flows, and thus we use statistic features as the target, not input, in the pre-training stage.

The third component of our approach is sampling. As discussed earlier, statistical features and header/payload features have their limitations. Therefore, we aim to use time series features. Specifically, we use time series features of only a part of a flow as an input to predict the statistical features as a regression target. Additionally, instead of using only the first few packets, which is used in most studies based on time series features [2, 3, 9], we sampled a fixed number of packets from a flow for the input. First, in practice, sampling is the only practical solution in some scenarios, such as in high bandwidth links or data centers. Moreover, sampling obviates the need to start capturing from the beginning of a flow or capturing the entire flow. Furthermore, storing the entire flow needs a large amount of memory and a model trained on would be more complex. Additionally, it allows the model to capture patterns from different part of a flow, not just the beginning of a flow. The approaches that used the first few packets can only capture specific patterns taken place at the beginning of a connection. However, these patterns may not necessarily be distinguishable from one class to another. For instance, user-specific behaviors, such as changing the quality of Youtube video, renaming a file in a Google Drive, etc., are mostly performed at the middle of a flow, not within the first few packets. Finally, it allows us to sample a single flow several times which serve as a data augmentation method.

4.2 Semi-supervised Learning

We used Convolutional Neural Network (CNN) as a part of the model architecture because of its shift invariant feature. CCN uses same set of small filters to cover the entire receptive fields. Hence, it allows the model to be shift invariant, that is, a pattern can be captured by CNN even if it is shifted to another region of input. Recall that we used sampled packets as an input to the model and as a data augmentation technique we sampled multiple times from different part of the flow. Hence, same set of patterns may be observed in different part of the input. Thus, the shift invariant model is more suitable.

As shown in Fig. 1, a CNN-based model is first pre-trained with an unlabeled dataset. Then, the learned weights of the convolutional layers are transferred to

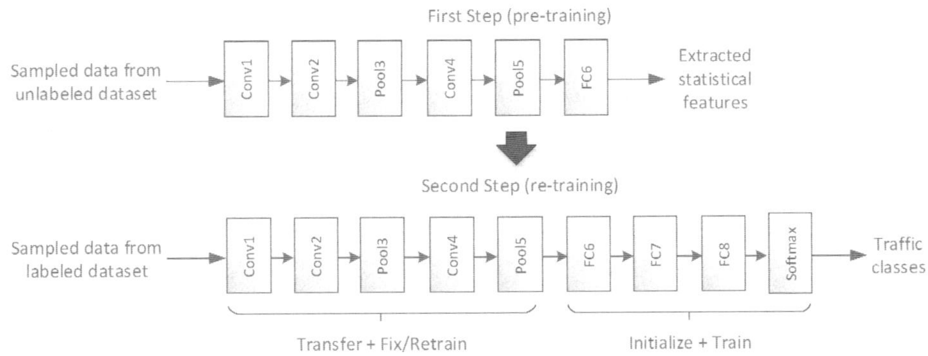

Fig. 1: Semi-supervised steps and model architecture

Table 1: Structure of the CNN model

-	Conv1	Conv2	Pool3	Conv4	Pool5	FC6	FC7	FC8
Number of filters/neurons	32	32	-	64	-	256	128	128
Kernel size	5	5	3	3	3	-	-	-

a new model with more linear layers. Finally, the new model is re-trained on a small labeled dataset. The details of the model structure is presented in Table 1. We use max pooling and Rectified Linear Unit (ReLU) activation function. Batch normalization is also used after convolutional and max pooling layers.

The input of the model is a 1-dimensional vector with 2 channels. The first channel contains inter-arrival time of sampled packets and the second channel contains the packet length and direction combined. To combine the packet length and direction, we multiply the direction (+1 or -1) with packet length. So, if packet length is positive, it shows packet length in forward direction, otherwise it shows the packet length in backward direction. Moreover, we normalized the input data range in [-1,+1] by considering the maximum value of 1434 Bytes and 1 second for length and inter-arrival time.

4.3 Sampling Techniques

In this paper, we used 3 different sampling methods to examine the effect of sampling on performance of the traffic classification task.

- **Fixed step sampling:** In fixed step sampling, a fixed number, l, is chosen and only packets that are l packets away from are sampled.
- **Random sampling:** This technique simply samples each packet with probability $p < 1$. This is a common technique in operational networks with high bandwidth because it requires less memory and computational overhead.
- **Incremental sampling:** Incremental sampling has three parameters, (l, α, β). Similar to fixed step sampling, it samples packets that are l packets away

from, but it increases the value of l by multiplying it by α after sampling each β packets.

During data augmentation, we sampled a flow 100 times from the beginning of the flow when random sampling was used. However, it would have given us the same set of packets if we had started from the beginning of a flow multiple times when using fixed step or incremental sampling. Hence, we started sampling at different part of a flow 100 times, if the flow was long enough.

4.4 Datasets

As explained earlier, our semi-supervised approach needs an unlabeled dataset for the pre-training stage and a labeled dataset for the re-training stage. In this paper, we conducted experiments with three datasets:

QUIC Dataset: This is a dataset captured in our lab at UC Davis and contains 5 Google services: Google Drive, Youtube, Google Docs, Google Search, and Google Music [5]. We used several systems with various configurations, including Windows 7, 8, 10, Ubuntu 16.4, and 17 operating systems. We wrote several scripts using Selenium WebDriver [17] and AutoIt [1] tools to mimic human behavior when capturing data. This approach allowed us to capture a large dataset without significant human effort. Such approach has been used in many other studies [14, 8, 3]. Furthermore, we also captured a few samples of real human interactions to show how much the accuracy of a model trained on scripted samples will degrade when it is tested on real human samples. During preprocessing, we removed all non-QUIC traffic. Note that all flows in our dataset are labeled, but we did not use labels during the pre-training step. We used class labels of all flows to show the accuracy gap between a fully-supervised and semi-supervised approach.

Unlabeled Waikato Dataset: WAND network research group at the university of Waikato published several unlabeled traces from 2009 to 2013. In this paper, we use Waikato VIII [6] captured at the border of the University of Waikato. The entire dataset is unlabeled and it is not clear what traffic classes exist in the dataset. However, the dataset definitely do not contain QUIC traffics because it was captured before the emergence of any practical implementation of QUIC protocol. We use Waikato dataset to pre-train the CNN model. The dataset is extremely large and due to the limited time and computational budget, we only used traces of the first month, around 4% of the entire dataset.

Ariel Dataset: Ariel dataset [4] was captured in a research lab at Ariel university over a period of two months. The original paper [11] used a fully-supervised method to classify three category of class labels: operating system, browser, and application. However, only the operating system and browser labels are available in the public dataset. In this paper, we only use a small portion of the dataset to re-trained a pre-trained model to test our methodology.

For all datasets, We ignore short flows because when short flows are sampled, there will not be enough packets to feed a classifier. In our evaluation, short flows are those with less than 100 packets before sampling.

5 Evaluation

5.1 Implementation Detail

We used python and implemented the CNN architecture using PyTorch. We used a server with Intel Xeon W-2155 and Nvidia Titan Xp GPU using Ubuntu 16.04. The CNN model has already been explained in section 4.2. During the pre-training, we trained the model with Adam optimizer and MSE loss function for 300 epochs. We used 24 statistical features as targets of regression. We used minimum, maximum, average, and standard deviation of packet length and inter-arrival time. For each one, we considered forward, backward and both flow directions that gave us a total of 24 features. During the supervised re-training, we used Adam optimizer with cross-entropy as a loss function[2].

There are two category of performance measures to evaluate a classifier: macro-average and micro-average metrics [15]. Whenever the accuracy of the entire model is shown, we used macro-averaging where the accuracy is averaged over all classes. For pre-class performance evaluation, we used micro-averaging metrics, including accuracy, precision, recall, and F1, similar to [14].

5.2 QUIC Dataset

We first pre-train our model on QUIC dataset consisting of 6439 flows without using class labels. Recall that because we sample each flow up to 100 times, total number of samples during the training is 544744. We use 24 statistical features calculated from flows as regression targets. Then, we transfer the weights to a new model and re-train with class labels. For this step, we capture 30 flows for each class and divide the training and test with different number of flows [3]. We also perform cross-validation. Moreover, we train the same model without transferring the weight to show the performance gap.

To tune the hyper-parameters, we separate 30 files for each target class and conduct greedy search. We train the model with only 20 labeled flows and validate with other 10 flows. This small number of training data may not yield optimal parameters, but it is consistent with the assumption that a limited amount of labeled data is available for the supervised training we conduct. We find that the model shown in Fig. 1 is accurate enough and a deeper model does not yield higher accuracy. We also find that re-training or fixing the convolutional part of the transferred model during re-training does not significantly change the accuracy. Note that we use these same hyper-parameters for other experiments without re-tuning them. Hence, these sets of hyper-parameters seem to be acceptable across different datasets, which makes our proposed approach more practical. The sampling parameters we use for fixed, incremental and random

[2] Codes are available at https://github.com/shrezaei/Semi-supervised-Learning-QUIC-

[3] In the entire paper, we use flow to refer to an unsampled flow and sampled flow for the sampled case. In other words, a dataset with 30 flows per class contains up to 3000 sampled flows per class because each unsampled flow is sampled multiple times.

sampling are 22, $(22, 1.6, 10)$, and $1/22$, respectively. We also sample only 45 packets from the entire flow.

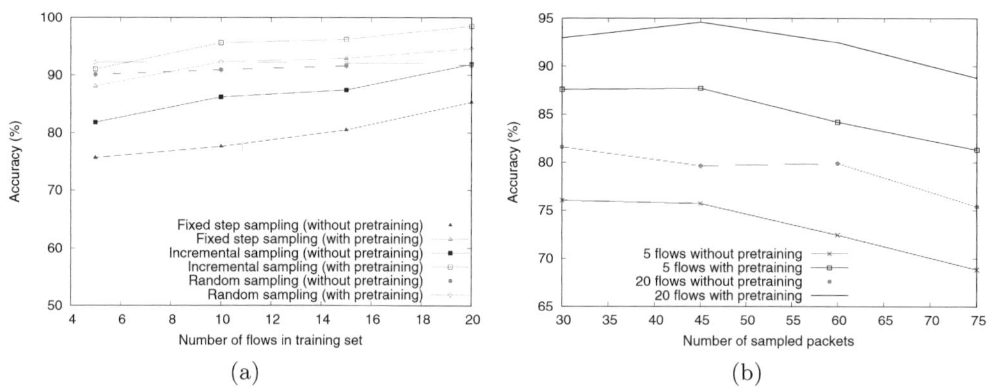

Fig. 2: Accuracy of QUIC dataset vs: (a) Supervised training set size (b) number of samples in fixed step sampling

Fig. 2(a) presents the accuracy of our model with various settings. It shows that increasing the size of the training set improves the accuracy except for random sampling. The reason is that during random sampling, we always started sampling from the beginning of the flow each 100 times we sampled a flow. Hence, the data augmentation method with only 5 files gives the model enough data to capture the patterns corresponding to the beginning of the flow. However, the accuracy of random sampling barely increases as the training size increases. We conjecture that this is because imposing randomness during random sampling makes it more difficult for the model to fit to the true distribution. Fixed step and incremental sampling methods work with sampled flows captured from different parts of a flow. Therefore, if different parts of a flow show different patterns, data augmentation of these two methods reveals more patterns. Hence, increasing the training size boosts the accuracy.

As shown in Fig. 2(a), incremental sampling outperforms other sampling methods. When random or fixed sampling is used, it is not easy to capture both long and short patterns. Incremental sampling allows sampled flows to contain many packets in short range and some packets in long range. That is why incremental sampling outperforms other sampling methods. Furthermore, the figure clearly shows the efficacy of our transfer learning model on fixed step and incremental sampling, as expected. Our method improves the accuracy around 10% when compared with a model without the pre-training step.

Table 2 represents the accuracy of the CNN model when the entire labeled dataset is used in a supervised manner. In that case, we do not conduct the first step pre-training because the entire dataset is used to train the second model. This gives us the upper-bound for the accuracy of a fully-supervised learning

Table 2: Accuracy of QUIC dataset with different sampling methods

Supervised training size	Fixed step	Random	Incremental
20 flows per class	94.60%	91.35%	98.53%
Entire dataset	96.50%	96.92%	98.99%

when sampling is used. The accuracy of incremental sampling is close to the upper-bound when only 20 flows per class are used for re-training. But, fixed sampling and random sampling require larger labeled training set during the re-training. To find how much sampling degrades accuracy, we also train a Random Forest (RF) classifier that takes statistical features as input and predicts the class labels. The accuracy of RF is 99.87% which shows that sampling degrades performance up to around 4% for our dataset. Note that we deliberately avoid using deep models such as CNN for this part because the input is a set of statistical features which is not suitable for a shift-invariant model, such as CNN. In our experiment, fully connected neural network is also unnecessarily complex to be trained with our relatively small dataset. Note that our dataset has only around 6500 flows. When using statistical features as an input, it is not possible to augment the dataset. As a result, total number of data points used during training RF was around 100 times fewer than training a model with sampled data.

In the second experiment, we study the effect of number of sampled packets on the accuracy of the model. We change the number of sampled packets from 30 to 75. We set the parameters of fixed step sampling method so that it always covers around the range of 1000 packets. Interestingly, the accuracy drops when we increase the number of sampled packets, as shown in Fig. 2(b). Increasing the number of sampled packets improves the accuracy of statistical feature prediction. However, it is harder for the model to learn class labels when input dimension is larger because of the small training set.

Fig. 3(a) presents the performance metric of our best model, that is, a model re-trained on a pre-trained model using 20 training flows with incremental sampling. The high performance metric shows that it is possible to train a good classifier with as small as 20 flows for each class if our semi-supervised approach is used. Therefore, it dramatically reduces the data collection and labeling that are the most time-consuming and labor-intensive steps.

To study whether automatically generated data with script represents human interaction, we capture 15 flows for each class from interactions of real humans in those 5 Google services. We only use this dataset to test the same model described above. Fig. 3(b) illustrates the performance metrics. Interestingly, accuracy of the Google search and Google document have not changed significantly. However, the accuracy of Google drive, Youtube, and Google music drop up to 7%. This depends on how much human interactions can change the traffic pattern, which is class-dependent. Moreover, there are some actions, such as renaming a file or moving files in Google drive, that our scripts do not

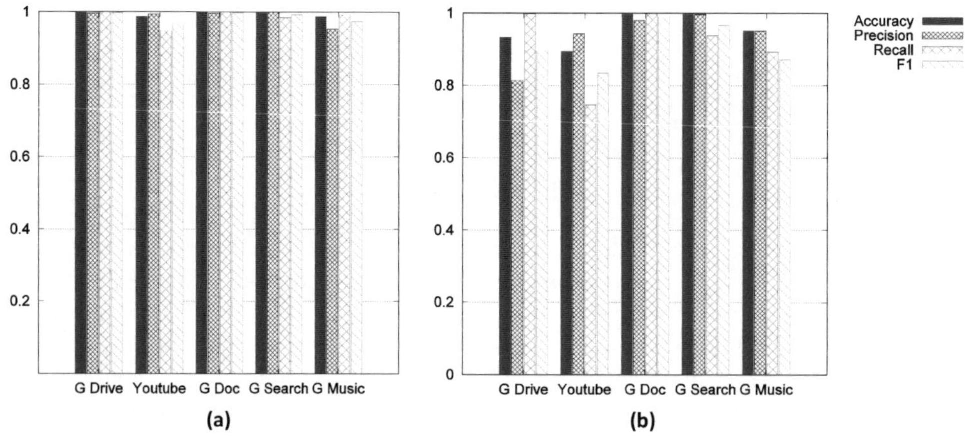

Fig. 3: Per class performance metrics of the model on the test set: (a) generated by the scripts (b) generated by human interactions

Table 3: Accuracy of QUIC dataset with different sampling methods

Pre-trained on Waikato	Fixed step	Random	Incremental
No	74.51%	72.14%	74.35%
Yes	81.50%	81.27%	80.76%

perform. So, these patterns are not available during re-training. This shows the limitations of datasets and studies [14, 8, 3] that only use scripts to capture data.

QUIC protocol has been introduced in 2012 and Chrome browser has had an experimental support for QUIC since 2014. Therefore, Waikato dataset captured before 2014 cannot have QUIC protocol traffic. Our intuition is that a model pre-trained on Waikato dataset can still be useful for the re-training step because it basically learns how to predict statistical features. It can be considered as a naive statistical feature predictor based on sampled data. Table 3 presents the accuracy of our method when Waikato dataset is used for pre-training. Note that sampling method's parameters are different for this experiment. Waikato dataset has many small flows that are not suitable for our previous sampling parameters that covers around 1000 packets. Hence, we change the parameters of sampling methods, similar to the parameter used in next section. That is the reason why the accuracy of even model without pre-training is lower than the experiment shown in Fig. 2. Table 3 clearly shows that the pre-trained model can boost the accuracy even when target traffic does not exist in the pre-training stage. But, the improvement is limited to less than 10% in this case.

5.3 Ariel Dataset

We conduct two additional experiments to evaluate the performance of our semi-supervised learning method on public datasets. In the first experiment, we pre-

Table 4: Accuracy of Ariel datasets with different configurations

Pre-trained on \Sampling	Fixed step	Random	Incremental
-	53.37%	70.76%	40.37%
W	79.76%	75.65%	80.82%
W+A	81.66%	78.54%	84.53%

train a model with the unlabeled Waikato dataset to predict statistical features based on sampled flows. Then, we re-train the model with 5 flows of each class in Ariel dataset. We randomly select 5 flows and use the remainder as a test set and repeat the procedure 10 times[4]. We only show the performance of OS class labels here due to the lack of space. In the second experiment, we pre-train the model with both Waikato and Ariel datasets. Then, we re-train the model similar to the first experiment. When we combine two datasets for pre-training, Ariel flows constitute only around 6% of the entire combined dataset. We deliberately allow the combined dataset to remain imbalanced to mimic real scenarios where only small portion of unlabeled dataset contains the target labels. Additionally, the parameters we use for fixed sampling, incremental sampling and random sampling are 10, $(8, 1.2, 10)$, and 0.15, respectively.

The accuracy of both experiments as well as the one without semi-supervised learning is shown in Table 4. For brevity, we represent Waikato and Ariel datasets with W and A, respectively. When there is no pre-training, random sampling shows the best accuracy. The similar trend is observed with our QUIC dataset as well, in previous section. Interestingly, there is a small but meaningful gap between the two experiments. That shows even if the target classes are only a small portion of dataset during the pre-training step, they can improve the accuracy. This is useful because the percentage of target task's flows might be probably small in real word when data is captured from an operational network.

To measure the performance gap between semi-supervised and fully-supervised learning, we also train the same CNN-based architecture with the entire A dataset in a fully-supervised manner. First, we train the CNN model with augmented sampled flows from A dataset using fixed step sampling. As it shown in Fig. 4, the accuracy is around 89% which can be considered as an upper-bound when sampling is used. To compare how statistical feature prediction degrades the accuracy in comparison with using true statistical features, we perform the following experiment: We feed the true statistical features to the last three layers of the model directly and remove all previous layers. However, the training phase is extremely unstable and high variance with low accuracy. The main reason is that several dense layers of fully connected neural network is too complex to be trained with a small dataset. Recall that when we do sampling, we can sample a single flow multiple times which increases the dataset size. However, in the case of feeding the true statistical features, there is only one set of statistical

[4] The reason we do not perform cross-validation is that if we limit each training folds to only contain 5 flows, the total number of cross validation rounds would be too large to be practically evaluated.

features for each flow leading to small size dataset. Therefore, we use K-Nearest Neighbor (KNN) for a fully-supervised training with statistical features [5].

The performance gap is shown in Fig. 4. We only show results of the fixed step sampling due to the lack of space. The trends of other sampling methods are similar. Interestingly, if a pre-trained model contains the target class labels, it can reach the upper-bound accuracy (fully supervised with sampled flows) with only around 30 labeled flows for each class. This is dramatically smaller than typical datasets used for fully-supervised methods in literature. Moreover, even if the unlabeled dataset does not contain target task's flows, the pre-trained model can act as a general function approximation of statistical features because it has already observed a large number of samples during the pre-training step.

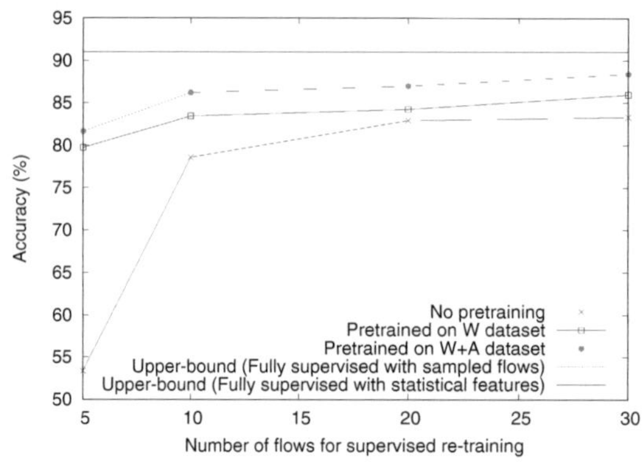

Fig. 4: Effect of labeled dataset size on accuracy

6 Discussion

Typically, network traffic classifiers use one or combination of the following features [12]: statistical features, time series, and header/payload contents. The choice of input features depends on many factors, which are comprehensively explained in [12]. During the pre-training step, our approach takes sampled time series features and outputs statistical features. Hence, our approach does not work on datasets for which time series or statistical features are not good enough for classification. For instance, we also conducted an experiment on ISCX dataset [7] for which the accuracy of model based on statistical and time series features were reported to be around 80% [7]. Our approach failed to produce a model with higher than 68% accuracy when only 20 flows were used from each class

[5] It has shown that it is possible to get a better accuracy with Ariel dataset using some other statistical features [11]. But, we use the same statistical features that we used as regression targets during the pre-training step to have a fair comparison.

during the supervised re-training step. However, a CNN model using payload information achieved above 95% accuracy with fully-supervised learning in [10].

During the pre-training step, the model see most possible traffic patterns, even the patterns that are not similar to any of the target classes. However, it is possible that during the supervised re-training step, some distinctive patterns are missed from labeled dataset which degrades the accuracy dramatically if the model is used in real environment. Hence, the small labeled dataset should be captured carefully. For instance, it has been shown that user actions in certain Android applications, such as Facebook or Twitter can be identified using time series features [3]. These actions are sending message, posting status, etc. This means that if target classes are Android applications, one should ensure that all actions are included in the labeled dataset at least once because the pattern of each action is different from another. This is similar to the experiment we did to test our model on human-triggered data where we realized some actions in some Google services did not exist in our training set, such as renaming a file.

We show that incremental sampling outperforms other sampling methods. Note that we need to choose the parameters appropriately to accommodate the CNN model. CNN uses a set of kernels to cover the entire input. In incremental sampling, the sampling parameter l is increased by α after sampling each β packets. If one chooses a large value for α, distance between the first few sampled packets are significantly smaller that the last few packets. In that case, CNN model is not suitable because the same filter which is supposed to capture certain pattern for close sampled packets will be used on the far apart samples packets. Hence, when using incremental sampling, one should not use large α.

7 Conclusion

In this paper, we propose a semi-supervised learning method that reduces the number of labeled data significantly for network traffic classification. We use 1-D CNN model that takes sampled time series features as input. In the pre-training step, the model is trained to predict statistical features of the entire flow, which does not require human effort for labeling. Then, we transfer the learned parameters to a new model and re-train it with a small labeled dataset. We capture 5 Google services that use QUIC protocol to evaluate our model. We show that with the proposed semi-supervised approach and 20 labeled data from each class the model achieves high accuracy close to a model trained in fully-supervised fashions. We evaluate 3 sampling methods: fixed step, random, and incremental sampling. We also conduct experiments on public datasets to show the generalizability of the proposed approach. We show a model pre-trained on a unlabeled public dataset can improve the accuracy of another labeled dataset. This shows that a model pre-trained with our approach on a large unlabeled dataset can be used as a general traffic classifier that can improve the accuracy of probably any traffic classification tasks if weights are transferred.

References

1. AutoIt: (2006), https://www.autoitscript.com, [Online; accessed 24-Oct-2018]
2. Chen, Z., He, K., Li, J., Geng, Y.: Seq2img: A sequence-to-image based approach towards ip traffic classification using convolutional neural networks. In: Big Data (Big Data), 2017 IEEE International Conference on. pp. 1271–1276. IEEE (2017)
3. Conti, M., Mancini, L.V., Spolaor, R., Verde, N.V.: Analyzing android encrypted network traffic to identify user actions. IEEE Transactions on Information Forensics and Security **11**(1), 114–125 (2016)
4. Dataset, A.U.: (2016), https://drive.google.com/drive/folders/0Bynah7-gERTldG5UZ2NhNkJMMlk, [Online; accessed 24-Oct-2018]
5. Dataset, Q.: (2018), https://drive.google.com/drive/folders/1Pvev0hJ82usPh6d WDlz7Lv8L6h3JpWhE,[Online; accessed 30-Oct-2018]
6. Dataset, W.V.: (2013), https://wand.net.nz/wits/, [Online; accessed 24-Oct-2018]
7. Draper-Gil, G., Lashkari, A.H., Mamun, M.S.I., Ghorbani, A.A.: Characterization of encrypted and vpn traffic using time-related. In: Proceedings of the 2nd international conference on information systems security and privacy (ICISSP). pp. 407–414 (2016)
8. Dubin, R., Dvir, A., Pele, O., Hadar, O.: I know what you saw last minuteencrypted http adaptive video streaming title classification. IEEE Transactions on Information Forensics and Security **12**(12), 3039–3049 (2017)
9. Lopez-Martin, M., Carro, B., Sanchez-Esguevillas, A., Lloret, J.: Network traffic classifier with convolutional and recurrent neural networks for internet of things. IEEE Access **5**, 18042–18050 (2017)
10. Lotfollahi, M., Shirali, R., Siavoshani, M.J., Saberian, M.: Deep packet: A novel approach for encrypted traffic classification using deep learning. arXiv preprint arXiv:1709.02656 (2017)
11. Muehlstein, J., Zion, Y., Bahumi, M., Kirshenboim, I., Dubin, R., Dvir, A., Pele, O.: Analyzing https encrypted traffic to identify user's operating system, browser and application. In: Consumer Communications & Networking Conference (CCNC), 2017 14th IEEE Annual. pp. 1–6. IEEE (2017)
12. Rezaei, S., Liu, X.: Deep learning for encrypted traffic classification: An overview. arXiv preprint arXiv:1810.07906 (2018)
13. Shen, M., Wei, M., Zhu, L., Wang, M.: Classification of encrypted traffic with second-order markov chains and application attribute bigrams. IEEE Transactions on Information Forensics and Security **12**(8), 1830–1843 (2017)
14. Tong, V., Tran, H.A., Souihi, S., Mellouk, A.: A novel quic traffic classifier based on convolutional neural networks. In: IEEE International Conference on Global Communications (GlobeCom). pp. 1–6 (2018)
15. Van Asch, V.: Macro-and micro-averaged evaluation measures [[basic draft]]. Belgium: CLiPS (2013)
16. Velan, P., Čermák, M., Čeleda, P., Drašar, M.: A survey of methods for encrypted traffic classification and analysis. International Journal of Network Management **25**(5), 355–374 (2015)
17. WebDriver, S.: (2015), https://www.seleniumhq.org/, [Online; accessed 24-Oct-2018]
18. Zhou, H., Wang, Y., Lei, X., Liu, Y.: A method of improved cnn traffic classification. In: Computational Intelligence and Security (CIS), 2017 13th International Conference on. pp. 177–181. IEEE (2017)

FAT-DeepFFM: Field Attentive Deep Field-aware Factorization Machine

Junlin Zhang, Tongwen Huang, Zhiqi Zhang

Sina Weibo Inc.
{junlin6, tongwen, zhiqizhang}@staff.weibo.com

Abstract. Click through rate (CTR) estimation is a fundamental task in personalized advertising and recommender systems. Recent years have witnessed the success of both the deep learning based model and attention mechanism in various tasks in computer vision (CV) and natural language processing (NLP). How to combine the attention mechanism with deep CTR model is a promising direction because it may ensemble the advantages of both sides. Although some CTR model such as Attentional Factorization Machine (AFM) has been proposed to model the weight of second order interaction features, we posit the evaluation of feature importance before explicit feature interaction procedure is also important for CTR prediction tasks because the model can learn to selectively highlight the informative features and suppress less useful ones if the task has many input features. In this paper, we propose a new neural CTR model named Field Attentive Deep Field-aware Factorization Machine (FAT-DeepFFM) by combining the Deep Field-aware Factorization Machine (DeepFFM) with Compose-Excitation network (CENet) field attention mechanism which is proposed by us as an enhanced version of Squeeze-Excitation network (SENet) to highlight the feature importance. We conduct extensive experiments on two real-world datasets and the experiment results show that FAT-DeepFFM achieves the best performance and obtains different improvements over the state-of-the-art methods. We also compare two kinds of attention mechanisms (attention before explicit feature interaction vs. attention after explicit feature interaction) and demonstrate that the former one outperforms the latter one significantly.

Keywords: CTR Prediction · Field-aware Factorization Machine · Attention · Squeeze-Excitation Network · Compose-Excitation network.

1 Introduction

CTR estimation is a fundamental task in personalized advertising and recommender systems. Many models have been proposed to resolve this problem such as Logistic Regression (LR) [1], Polynomial-2 (Poly2) [2], tree-based models [3], tensor-based models [4], Bayesian models [5], and Field-aware Factorization Machines (FFMs) [6].

The contributions of our work are summarized as follows:

1) We propose a novel model named FAT-DeepFFM that enhances the DeepFFM model by introducing the CENet field attention to dynamically capture each feature's importance before explicit feature interaction procedure.
2) We compare two different kinds of attention mechanisms(attention on features before explicit feature interaction vs. attention on cross features after explicit feature interaction) and the experiment results demonstrate that the former one outperforms the latter one significantly.
3) We conduct extensive experiments on two real-world datasets and the experiment results show that FAT-DeepFFM achieves the best performance and obtains different improvements over the state-of-the-art methods.

The rest of this paper is organized as follows. Section 2 introduces some related works which are relevant with our proposed model. We introduce our proposed Field Attentive Deep Field-aware Factorization Machine (FAT-DeepFFM) model in detail in Section 3. The experimental results on Criteo and Avazu datasets are presented and discussed in Section 4. Section 5 concludes our work in this paper.

2 Related Work

2.1 Factorization Machines and Field-aware Factorization Machine

Factorization Machines (FMs) [2] and Field-aware Factorization Machines (FFMs) [6] are two of the most successful CTR models. FMs use the dot product of two embedding vectors to model the effect of pairwise feature interactions. FFMs extended the ideas of Factorization Machines by additionally leveraging the field information and won two competitions hosted by Criteo and Avazu. When one feature interacts with other features from different fields, FFMs will learn different embedding vectors for each feature.

2.2 Deep Learning based CTR Models

With the great success of deep learning in many research fields such as Computer Vision and Natural language processing, many deep learning based CTR models have also been proposed in recent years. How to effectively model the feature interactions is the key factor for most of these neural network based models.

Factorisation-Machine Supported Neural Networks (FNN)[13] is a feed-forward neural network using FM to pre-train the embedding layer. However, FNN can capture only high-order feature interactions. Wide & Deep Learning[15] was initially introduced for App recommendation in Google play. Wide & Deep Learning jointly trains wide linear models and deep neural networks to combine the benefits of memorization and generalization for recommender systems. However, expertise feature engineering is still needed on the input to the wide part of Wide & Deep model, which means that the cross-product transformation also requires to be manually designed. To alleviate manual efforts in feature engineering, DeepFM[16] replaces the wide part of Wide & Deep model with FM and shares the feature embedding between the FM and deep component. DeepFM is regarded as one state-of-the-art model in CTR estimation field.

Deep & Cross Network (DCN)[19] efficiently captures feature interactions of bounded degrees in an explicit fashion. Similarly, eXtreme Deep Factorization Machine (xDeepFM) [17] also models the low-order and high-order feature interactions in an explicit way by proposing a novel Compressed Interaction Network (CIN) part.

Our approach is based on neural FFM which was firstly proposed by Yang[20] in Tencent Social Ads contest . It can be regarded as replacing the FM part of DeepFM with FFM and we will describe the model in detail in section 3.

2.3 Attentive CTR Models

Attention mechanism is motivated by human visual attention and it can filter out the uninformative features from raw inputs by reducing the side effects of noisy data. Attention-based model has been widely used and shown promising results on tasks such as speech recognition and machine translation. Attention mechanism is also introduced in some CTR models. For example, Attentional Factorization Machine (AFM)[14] improves FM by discriminating and learning the importance of different feature interactions from data via a neural attention network. DIN[22] represents users diverse interests with an interest distribution and designs an attention-like network structure to locally activate the related interests according to the candidate ad.

3 Field Attentive DeepFFM

3.1 DeepFFM

Our work initially aims at introducing the FFM model into neural CTR systems. However, a similar effort to ours has been reported by Yang etc. [20] in Tencent Social Ads competition 2017. The authors report substantial gains after using neural FFM in their CTR prediction system. Neural FFM was quite successful in that competition: the 3rd place winner solution was based on this single Model and the ensemble version won the 1rd place in the competition. Because its hard to find the detailed technical descriptions about this model, we will firstly introduce the neural FFM which will be called DeepFFM model in this paper.

As we all know, FMs[2] model interactions between features i and j as the dot products of their corresponding embedding vectors as follows:

$$\hat{y}(x) = w_0 + \sum_{i=1}^{m} w_i x_i + \sum_{i=1}^{m} \sum_{j=i+1}^{m} \langle v_i, v_j \rangle x_i x_j \tag{1}$$

An embedding vector $v_i \in R^k$ for each feature is learned by FM, k is a hyper-parameter which is usually a small integer and m is the feature number. However, FM neglects the fact that a feature might behave differently when it interacts with features from other fields. To explicitly take this difference into consideration, Field-aware Factorization Machines (FFMs) learn extra n-1 embedding vectors for each feature(here n denotes field number):

$$\hat{y}(x) = w_0 + \sum_{i=1}^{m} w_i x_i + \sum_{i=1}^{m} \sum_{j=i+1}^{m} \langle v_{ij}, v_{ji} \rangle x_i x_j \tag{2}$$

where $v_{ij} \in R^k$ denotes the embedding vector of the j-th entry of feature i when feature i is interacting with fields j. k is the embedding size.

As depicted in Figure 1, DeepFFM is designed to embody the idea of FFM through neural network. An input instance is firstly transformed into a high-dimensional sparse features via one-hot encoding to denote the raw feature input. The following embedding matrix layer is fully connected with sparse input layer to compress a raw feature to a low dimensional, dense real-value matrix. Specifically, for feature i, a corresponding 2-dimensional embedding matrix

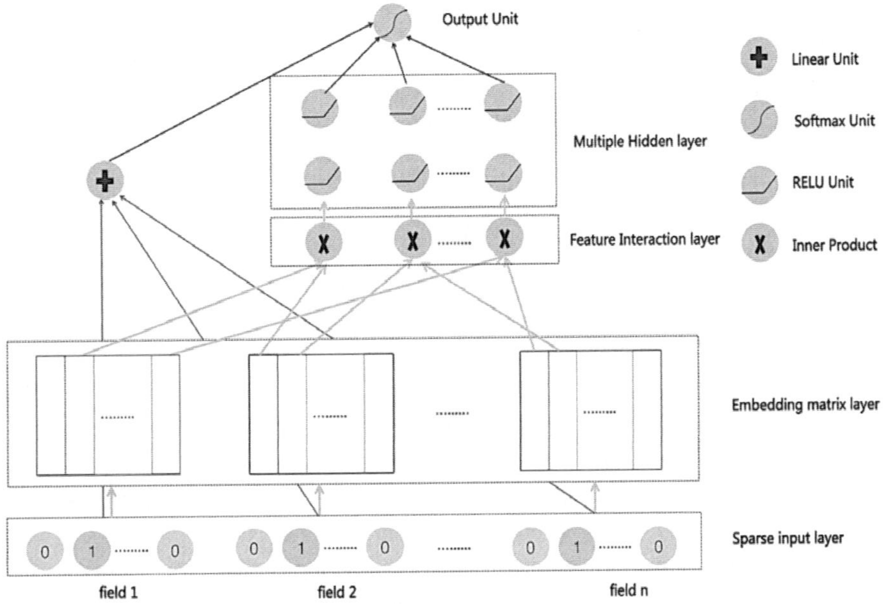

Fig. 1. The Neural Structure of Inner-Product version DeepFFM

$EM_i = [v_{i1}, v_{i2}, \cdots, v_{ij}, \cdots, v_{in}]$ with size $k \times n$ is used to measure its impact of interactions with other features, where $v_{ij} \in R^k$ refers to the j-th embedding vector of field i, n is the number of fields and k is the size of embedding vector. So its obvious that embedding matrix layer EM is a 3-dimensional matrix with size $k \times n \times n$ because we have n fields and each field has one corresponding 2-dimensional embedding matrix.

The following feature interaction layer tries to capture the two way feature interactions between any pair of features from different fields on the embedding matrix EM. Denoting the feature interaction layer as vector A, we have two different types of feature interaction approaches: inner-product version and Hadamard-product version. We can formalize two methods in this layer as follows:

$A = [v_{12} \oplus v_{21}, v_{13} \oplus v_{31}, \cdots, v_{ij} \oplus v_{ji}, \cdots, v_{(n-1)n} \oplus v_{n(n-1)}]$ *Inner Product*

$A = [v_{12} \otimes v_{21}, v_{13} \otimes v_{31}, \cdots, v_{ij} \times v_{ji}, \cdots, v_{(n-1)n} \otimes v_{n(n-1)}]$ *Hadamard Product*

where n is field number, $v_{ij} \oplus v_{ji}$ means the inner product of two embedding vectors as a scalar $\langle v_{ij}, v_{ji} \rangle$ and $v_{ij} \times v_{ji}$ refers to the Hadamard product of two embedding vectors as following vector:

$$v_{ij} \oplus v_{ji} = [v_{ij}^1 \cdot v_{ji}^1, v_{ij}^2 \cdot v_{ji}^2, \cdots, v_{ij}^k \cdot v_{ji}^k]$$

where k is the size of embedding vector v_{ji}. Notice that $j > i$ is required in order to avoid the repeated computation. We can see from here that feature interaction layer A is a wide concatenated vector and the size of this vector is $n(n-1)/2$ if we adopt inner-product version while the size is $kn(n-1)/2$ if the Hadamard product version is adopted.

Multiple hidden layer is a feed-forward neural network on the feature interaction layer to implicitly learn high-order feature interactions. Denote the output of the feature interaction layer as vector and we can feed it into hidden layer of feed-forward neural network. So the forward process is :

$$x^1 = \sigma(W^1 A + b^1) \tag{3}$$

$$x^l = \sigma(W^l x^{1-1} + b^l) \tag{4}$$

where l is the layer depth, σ is an activation function, and x^l is the output of the l-th hidden layer.

Adding the linear part, the output unit of DeepFFM behaves as follows:

$$\hat{y}(X) = \sigma(W_{1inear} x_{linear} + W^{l+1} x^l + b^{l+1}) \tag{5}$$

where σ is the sigmoid function, x_{linear} is the raw features, x^l is the output of multiple hidden layer, W_{1inear}, W^{l+1} and b^{l+1} are learnable parameters.

3.2 CENet like Field Attention on Embedding Matrix Layer

Hu proposed the Squeeze-and-Excitation Network (SENet) [21] to improve the representational power of a network by explicitly modeling the interdependencies between the channels of convolutional features in various image classification tasks. The SENet is proved to be successful in image classification tasks and won first place in ILSVRC 2017 classification task.

Our work is inspired by SENet's success in computer vision field. To improve the representational ability of deep CTR network, we introduce the Compose-Excitation network (CENet) attention mechanism which is an enhanced version of SENet into DeepFFM model on embedding matrix Layer. We aim to dynamically capture each feature's importance by explicitly modeling the interdependencies among all different features before FM's feature interaction procedure. Our goal is to use the CENet attention mechanism to perform feature recalibration through which it can learn to selectively highlights the informative features and suppress less useful ones.

It can be seen from Figure 2 that the CENet like field attention mechanism involves two phases: Compose phase and Excitation phase. The first phase calculates "summary statistics" of each embedding vector of each field by composing all the information of one embedding vector into a simple feature descriptor; the second phase applies attentive transformations to these feature descriptors and then rescales the original embedding matrix using the calculated attention values.

Compose Phase: Let $EM_i = [v_{i1}, v_{i2}, \cdots, v_{ij}, \cdots, v_{in}]$ denotes the 2-dimensional $k \times n$ embedding matrix of field i, where $v_{ij} \in R^k$ refers to the j-th embedding vector of field i, n is the number of fields and k is the size of embedding vector. In this phase we compose the embedding vector v_{ij} into one single number to represent the summary information of the feature. This can be achieved by using 1×1 convolution[23] to generate feature-wise statistics instead of those

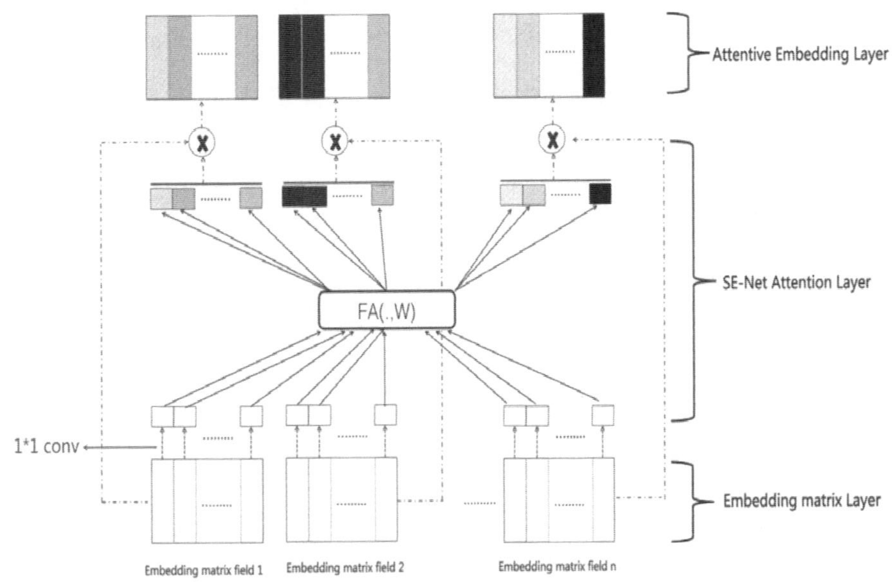

Fig. 2. CENet like Field Attention

squeeze operations such as global max pooling or sum operation commonly used in SENet. The 1×1 convolution, also called a pointwise convolution, is responsible for building new features through computing linear combinations of one input feature embedding. In SENet, we generate a statistic vector $z \in R^n$ for field i by shrinking each embedding vector, where the f-th element of z_i is $z_{if} \in R$ which can be calculated by:

$$z_{if} = F_{sq}(v_{if}) = \max_{1 \le t \le k} v_{if}^t \quad \textit{Global Max Pooling} \tag{6}$$

Here, k means the embedding size of each embedding vector.

The most commonly used squeeze operation is global max pooling in CV field which can capture the strongest feature in corresponding channel. We change the method in this phase by using 1×1 convolution because we posit each position in feature embedding vector is informative in CTR task. So the 1×1 convolution can introduce parameters to learn the composing weight of each position in feature embedding. The 1×1 convolution is calculated as follows:

$$z_{if} = conv1d(U_{if}, v_{if}) = Relu(U_{if} v_{if}) \tag{7}$$

where U_{if} is the convolution weight, the size of convolution kernal is 1×1, the number of filters is 1 and the activation function is set to 'Relu'.

Excitation phase: After the first phase, the embedding matrix of field i $EM_i = [v_{i1}, v_{i2}, \cdots, v_{ij}, \cdots, v_{in}]$ has been transformed into a descriptor vector $DV_i =$

$[z_{i1}, z_{i2}, \cdots, z_{ij}, \cdots, z_{in}]$. We have n different fields, so we summarize all the descriptors by concatenating each descriptor vector as follows:

$$D = concate(DV_1, DV_2, \cdots, DV_n) \tag{8}$$

where the size of vector D is n^2.

To calculate the attention from descriptor vector , two fully connected (FC) layers are used. The first FC layer is a dimensionality-reduction layer with parameters W_1 with reduction ratio r which is a hyper-parameter and it uses ReLU as nonlinear function. The second FC layer increases dimensionality with parameters W_2 , which is equal to dimension of descriptor vector D and it also uses ReLU as nonlinear activation function. Formally, the field attention is calculated as follows:

$$S = F_{ex}(D, W) = \delta(W_2\delta(W_1 D)) \tag{9}$$

where δ refers to the ReLU function, $W_1 \in R^{\frac{n^2}{r} \times n^2}$ and $W_1 \in R^{n^2 \times \frac{n^2}{r}}$,the size of attention vector S is n^2 .

The activation of the ReLU function is used as the final field attention value without softmax normalization operation because we want to encourage multiple features to be important instead of just few of them. Then the values in original embedding matrix EM_i of field i are rescaled by the accordingly calculated field attention vector S_i as follows:

$$AEM_i = F_{scale}(S_i, EM_i) = [S_{i1} \cdot v_{i1}, S_{i2} \cdot v_{i2}, \cdots, S_{ij} \cdot v_{ij}, \cdots, S_{in} \cdot v_{in}] \tag{10}$$

where $F_{scale}(S_i, EM_i)$ refers to vector-wise multiplication between embedding vector v_{ij} and the scalar S_{ij}. The bigger attention value S_{ij} implies that the model dynamically identifies an important feature and this attention value is used to boost the original embedding vector v_{ij}. On the contrary, small attention value S_{ij} will suppress the uninformative features or even noise by decreasing the values in the corresponding embedding vector v_{ij}.

After the compose phase and excitation phase, we have a new 3-dimensional embedding matrix AEM with size $k \times n \times n$, which is equal to the size of the original embedding matrix EM. We call the new embedding matrix attentive embedding layer in our paper.

3.3 Combining the field attention and DeepFFM

As discussed in Section 3.2, the CENet attention mechanism can perform feature recalibration through which it can learn to selectively highlights the informative features and suppress less useful ones. We can enhance DeepFFM model which is described in section 3.1 by inserting the CENet attention module into it. Figure 3 provides overall architecture of our proposed Field Attentive Deep Field-aware Factorization Machine (FAT-DeepFFM). It's similar in neural structure to DeepFFM while the original embedding matrix layer is replaced by the SE-Net like field attention module. We call this newly plugged-in module attentive embedding matrix layer. The other components of FAT-DeepFFM are same as

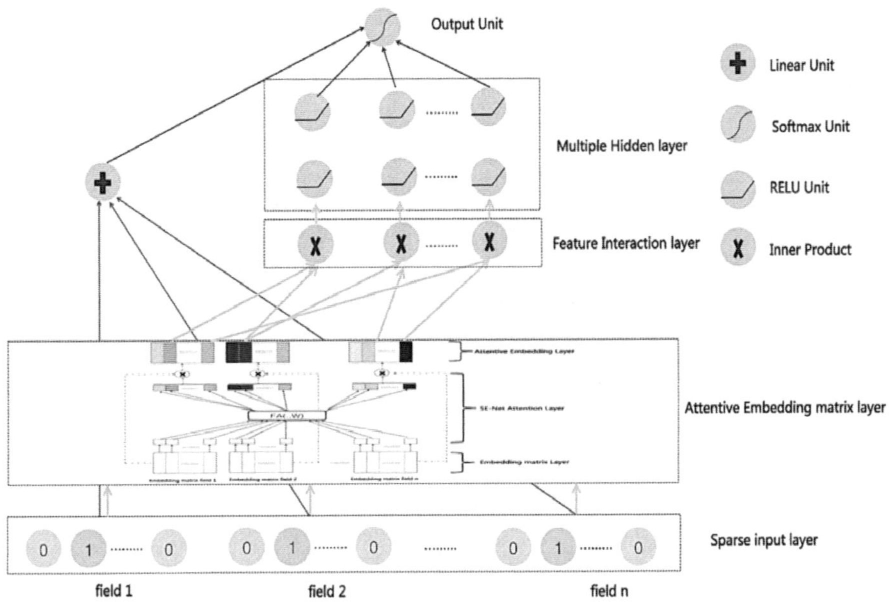

Fig. 3. Neural Structure of Field Attentive DeepFFM (Inner product version)

the DeepFFM model. Similar to the DeepFFM, there are also two versions of FAT-DeepFFM according to the feature interaction type: inner-product version and Hadamard-product version.

We can see from the above-mentioned descriptions that our proposed attention mechanism is a kind of attention before cross features were produced. So a natural research question arises that which one will perform better if we introduce attention on cross features after the explicit feature interaction procedure just like AFM does? To answer this question, we also conduct some experiments to compare the performance difference of two kinds of attention mechanisms. The experimental results demonstrate that the attention before feature interaction outperforms the one after feature interaction consistently. We will discuss these experiments in detail in Section 4.3.

4 Experimental Results

To comprehensively evaluate our proposed method, we design some experiments to answer the following research questions:
RQ1 Can our proposed FAT-DeepFFM outperform the state-of-the-art deep learning based CTR models?
RQ2 Which attention mechanism (attention on features before explicit feature interaction vs. attention on cross features after explicit feature interaction) will perform better on the real world CTR datasets?

RQ3 Which feature interaction method (Inner-Product vs. Hadamard-product) is more effective in neural network based CTR models?

4.1 Experiment Setup

Datasets The following two data sets are used in our experiments:

1. Criteo[1] Dataset. As a very famous public real world display ad dataset with each ad display information and corresponding user click feedback, Criteo data set is widely used in many CTR model evaluation. There are 26 anonymous categorical fields and 13 continuous feature fields in Criteo data set. We split the data into training and test set randomly by 90%:10%.
2. Avazu[2] Dataset. The Avazu dataset consists of several days of ad click-through data which is ordered chronologically. For each click data, there are 24 fields which indicate elements of a single ad impression. We split the data into training and test set randomly by 80%:20%.

Table 1. Statistics of the evaluation datasets

Datasets	#Instances	#Fields	#Features
Criteo	45M	39	2.3M
Avazu	40.43M	24	0.64M

Table 1 lists the statistics of the evaluation datasets. For these two datasets, a small improvement in prediction accuracy is regarded as practically significant because it will bring a large increase in a company's revenue if the company has a very large user base.

Evaluation Metrics AUC (Area Under ROC) and Logloss (cross entropy) are used in our experiments as the evaluation metrics. These two metrics are very popular for binary classification tasks. AUC is insensitive to the classification threshold and the positive ratio. AUC's upper bound is 1 and larger value indicates a better performance. Log loss measures the distance between two distributions and smaller log loss value means a better performance.

Models for Comparisons We compare the performance of the following CTR estimation models as baseline:LR, FM, FFM, FNN, DeepFM, AFM, Deep&Cross Network(DCN) , xDeepFM and DeepFFM, all of which are discussed in Section 2 and Section 3.

---

[1] Criteo http://labs.criteo.com/downloads/download-terabyte-click-logs/
[2] Avazu http://www.kaggle.com/c/avazu-ctr-prediction

Implementation Details We implement all the models with Tensorflow in our experiments. For optimization method, we use the Adam with a mini-batch size of 1000 and a learning rate is set to 0.0001. Focusing on neural networks structures in our paper, we make the dimension of field embedding for all models to be a fixed value of 10. For models with DNN part, the depth of hidden layers is set to 3, the number of neurons per layer is 1600 for FFM-related models and 400 for all other deep models, all activation function are ReLU and dropout rate is set to 0.5. For CENet component, the activation function is ReLU and the reduction ratio is set to 1 in all the related experiments. We conduct our experiments with 2 Tesla K40 GPUs.

4.2 Performance Comparison (RQ1)

Table 2. Overall performance of different models on Criteo and Avazu(the model name with suffix "I" means inner-product version while with suffix "H" means Hadamard product version)

	Criteo		Avazu	
Model Name	AUC	Logloss	AUC	Logloss
LR	0.7808	0.4681	0.7633	0.3891
FM	0.7923	0.4584	0.7745	0.3832
FFM	0.8001	0.4525	0.7795	0.381
FNN	0.8057	0.4464	0.7802	0.38
AFM	0.7965	0.4541	0.774	0.3839
DeepFM	0.8085	0.4445	0.7786	0.381
DCN	0.7977	0.4617	0.768	0.394
xDeepFM	0.8091	0.4461	0.7808	0.3819
DeepFFM-I	0.8087	0.4434	0.7839	0.3783
DeepFFM-H	0.8088	0.4434	0.7835	0.3782
FAT-DeepFFM-I	0.8099	0.4422	0.7857	**0.3763**
FAT-DeepFFM-H	**0.8104**	**0.4417**	**0.7861**	0.3773

The overall performance for CTR prediction of different models on Criteo dataset and Avazu dataset is shown in Table 2. We have the following key observations:

1. FAT-DeepFFM achieves the best performance in general and obtains different improvements over the state-of-the-art methods. As the best model, FAT-DeepFM outperforms FM by 3.64% and 1.80% in terms of Logloss (2.28% and 1.50% in terms of AUC) and outperforms LR by 5.64% and 3.29% in terms of Logloss (3.79% and 2.99% in terms of AUC) on Criteo and Avazu datasets.
2. FAT-DeepFFM consistently outperforms DeepFFM on both datasets. This indicates that CENet field attentive mechanism is rather helpful for learning the importance of raw features.

4.3 Attention Mechanism Comparison (RQ2)

In this subsection, we will discuss the performance of two different kinds of attention mechanisms: one is an attention before explicit feature interaction just like above-mentioned field attention; the other is the attention on cross features after explicit feature interaction procedure just like AFM does.

As for the specific approach for the attention on cross features, two methods are implemented: the similar CENet attention as described in section 3.2 and the MLP based attention just like AFM does, the hyper-parameters are tuned to achieve the best performance. The experimental results is shown in table 3 and the experiments with prefix "MLP" refer to the MLP based attention on cross features while the experiments with prefix "CE" mean the CENet attention is used on cross features.

Table 3 lists the overall performance of two attention mechanisms on Criteo dataset and Avazu dataset. We have the following key observations:

1. No matter which method (CENet or MLP based model as AFM does) is used as the specific attention approach on cross features, attention on features before feature interaction outperforms the attention on cross features after explicit feature interaction consistently, sometimes with a large margin. We infer it's perhaps because the attention on features highlights the important information while suppressed the unimportant features and noise more effectively compared with the attention on cross features.
2. Under some conditions, the attention on cross features is harmful for some real world CTR prediction task. From the results of the inner-product group experiments shown in table 3, we can see that both the MLP-DeepFFM-I and CE-DeepFFM-I model underperform the original DeepFFM model. This result demonstrates that attention on cross features is harmful for CTR prediction task if we use inner-product function as the feature interaction method. The behind reason still needs further investigation.

4.4 Feature Interaction Method(RQ3)

As we discussed in section 3, both the DeepFFM and FAT-DeepFFM model have two kinds of feature interaction approaches: inner product version vs. hadamard product version. So a natural research question arises that which approach will perform better? Table 3 also shows 4 groups of comparable experiments (model names with same prefix and different suffixes form one group such as DeepFFM-I and DeepFFM-H) on two datasets. We have the following key observations:

1. No apparent performance difference is observed if we dont adopt any attention to the DeepFFM model, no matter which feature interaction method is used (DeepFFM-I vs. DeepFFM-H).
2. The Hadamard product function should be preferred to the inner product function if we adopt attention to the DeepFFM model, no matter attention on features or attention on cross features. We can see from table 3 that this conclusion holds in most cases.

Table 3. Overall performance of two attention mechanisms on Criteo and Avazu(the model name with suffix "I" means inner-product version while with suffix "H" means Hadamard product version)

		Criteo		Avazu	
	Model Name	AUC	Logloss	AUC	Logloss
Inner Product Group	DeepFFM-I	0.8087	0.4434	0.7839	0.3783
	MLP-DeepFFM-I	0.8022	0.4499	0.7819	0.3796
	CE-DeepFFM-I	0.808	0.444	0.7816	0.381
	FAT-DeepFFM-I	**0.8099**	**0.4422**	**0.7857**	**0.3763**
Hadamard Product Group	DeepFFM-H	0.8088	0.4434	0.7835	0.3782
	MLP-DeepFFM-H	0.8083	0.444	0.7847	0.3778
	CE-DeepFFM-H	0.8092	0.443	0.7822	0.3786
	FAT-DeepFFM-H	**0.8104**	**0.4417**	**0.7861**	**0.3773**

5 Conclusion

In this paper, we propose a new neural CTR model called Field Attentive Deep Field-aware Factorization Machine (FAT-DeepFFM) by combining the deep field-aware factorization machine (DeepFFM) with CENet field attention mechanism. We conduct extensive experiments on two real-world datasets and the experiment results show that FAT-DeepFFM achieves the best performance and obtains different improvements over the state-of-the-art methods. We also show that FAT-DeepFFM consistently outperforms DeepFFM on both datasets which indicates that CENet field attentive mechanism is rather helpful for learning the importance of raw features when the task has many input features. We also compare two different types of attention mechanisms (attention before explicit feature interaction vs. attention after explicit feature interaction) and the experiment results demonstrate that the former one outperforms the latter one significantly.

References

[1] H. B. McMahan, G. Holt, D. Sculley et al., Ad click prediction: a view from the trenches, in SIGKDD. ACM, 2013, pp. 12221230.
[2] Steffen Rendle. 2010. Factorization machines. In Data Mining (ICDM), 2010 IEEE10th International Conference on. IEEE, 9951000.
[3] Xinran He, Junfeng Pan, Ou Jin, et al. 2014. Practical lessons from predicting clicks on ads at facebook. In Proceedings of the Eighth International Workshop on Data Mining for Online Advertising. ACM, 19.
[4] Yehuda Koren, Robert Bell, and Chris Volinsky. 2009. Matrix factorization techniques for recommender systems. Computer 42, 8 (2009).
[5] Thore Graepel, Joaquin Q Candela, Thomas Borchert, et al. 2010. Web-scale bayesian click-through rate prediction for sponsored search advertising in microsofts bing search engine. In ICML. 1320.

[6] Yuchin Juan, Yong Zhuang, Wei-Sheng Chin, and Chih-Jen Lin. 2016. Field-aware factorization machines for CTR prediction. In Proceedings of the 10th ACM Conference on Recommender Systems. ACM, 4350.
[7] Alex Krizhevsky, Ilya Sutskever, and Geo rey E Hinton. 2012. Imagenet clas-sication with deep convolutional neural networks. In Advances in neural information processing systems. 10971105.
[8] Kaiming He, Xiangyu Zhang, Shaoqing Ren, and Jian Sun. 2016. Deep residual learning for image recognition. In Proceedings of the IEEE conference on computer vision and pattern recognition. 770778.
[9] A. Graves, A. Mohamed, and G. Hinton, Speech recognition with deep recurrent neural networks, in ICASSP. IEEE, 2013, pp. 6645 6649.
[10] H Tang , L Lu , L Kong , K Gimpel and K Livescu. End-to-End Neural Segmental Models for Speech Recognition. IEEE Journal of Selected Topics in Signal Processing (Volume: 11 , Issue: 8 , Dec. 2017)
[11] Kyunghyun Cho, Bart Van Merrinboer, Caglar Gulcehre, Dzmitry Bahdanau, Fethi Bougares, Holger Schwenk, and Yoshua Bengio. 2014. Learning phrase representations using RNN encoder-decoder for statistical machine translation. arXiv preprint arXiv:1406.1078 (2014).
[12] Tomas Mikolov, Martin Kara at, Lukas Burget, Jan Cernocky', and Sanjeev Khu- danpur. 2010. Recurrent neural network based language model. In Eleventh Annual Conference of the International Speech Communication Association.
[13] Weinan Zhang, Tianming Du, and Jun Wang. 2016. Deep learning over multi-field categorical data. In European conference on information retrieval. Springer, 4557.
[14] Heng-Tze Cheng, Levent Koc, Jeremiah Harmsen, Tal Shaked, Tushar Chandra, Hrishi Aradhye, Glen Anderson, Greg Corrado, Wei Chai, Mustafa Ispir, et al. 2016. Wide & deep learning for recommender systems. In Proceedings of the 1st Workshop on Deep Learning for Recommender Systems. ACM, 710.
[15] Jun Xiao, Hao Ye, Xiangnan He, Hanwang Zhang, Fei Wu, and Tat-Seng Chua. 2017. Attentional Factorization Machines: Learning the Weight of Feature Inter- actions via Attention Networks. In Proceedings of the Twenty-Sixth International Joint Conference on Arti cial Intelligence, IJCAI 2017, Melbourne, Australia, August 19-25, 2017. 31193125. https://doi.org/10.24963/ijcai.2017/435
[16] Huifeng Guo, Ruiming Tang, Yunming Ye, Zhenguo Li, and Xiuqiang He. 2017. DeepFM: A Factorization-Machine based Neural Network for CTR Prediction. arXiv preprint arXiv:1703.04247 (2017).
[17] Jianxun Lian, Xiaohuan Zhou, Fuzheng Zhang, Zhongxia Chen, Xing Xie, and Guangzhong Sun. xDeepFM: Combining explicit and implicit feature interactions for recommender systems. In SIGKDD, pp. 17541763. ACM, 2018.
[18] Yanru Qu, Han Cai, Kan Ren, Weinan Zhang, Yong Yu, Ying Wen, and Jun Wang. 2016. Product-based neural networks for user response prediction. In Data Mining (ICDM), 2016 IEEE 16th International Conference on. IEEE, 11491154.
[19] Ruoxi Wang, Bin Fu, Gang Fu, and Mingliang Wang. 2017. Deep & Cross Network for Ad Click Predictions. arXiv preprint arXiv:1708.05123 (2017)

[20] Yi Yang,Shaofeng Shen and Yu liang. Neural Field-aware Factorization Machine. 2017. https://cs.nju.edu.cn/31/60/c1654a209248/page.htm
[21] J. Hu, L. Shen, and G. Sun. Squeeze-and-Excitation networks. arXiv preprint arXiv: 1709.01507(2017).
[22] Guorui Zhou, Chengru Song, Xiaoqiang Zhu, Xiao Ma, Yanghui Yan, Xingya Dai, Han Zhu, Junqi Jin, Han Li, and Kun Gai. 2017. Deep interest network for click-through rate prediction. arXiv preprint arXiv:1706.06978 (2017). [23] Francois Chollet. Xception: Deep learning with depthwise separable convolutions. arXiv preprint, pages 161002357, 2017.

A Proportional Process Mining System

Dinh-Lam Pham[1], Hyun Ahn[1], Minjae Park[2], Kyoung-Sook Kim[1], and Kwanghoon Pio Kim[1]

[1] Collaboration Technology Research Lab.
Division of Computer Science and Engineering
KYONGGI UNIVERSITY
Suwonsi Gyeonggido, 16227, Republic of Korea
e-Mail: {phamdinhlam, hahn, khmjmc, kwang}@kyonggi.ac.kr
http://ctrl.kyonggi.ac.kr

[2] Enterprise Information Systems Research Group
Department of Computer Software
DAELIM UNIVERSITY COLLEGE
Anyangsi Gyeonggido, 13916, Republic of Korea
e-Mail: mjpark@daelim.ac.kr
http://www.daelim.ac.kr

Abstract. This paper defines a novel conceptual framework of business process mining approach and implements a process mining system based upon the framework. The core algorithm of the conceptual framework is named as ρ-Algorithm that is able to completely discover a business process model with its enacted proportions from a process enactment event log dataset. The authors' research group has implemented all the essential components of the framework including the ρ-Algorithm as a proportional process mining system. Especially, the implemented mining system supports a couple of mining-related activities in a fashion of visual and interactive user operations from opening a dataset to visualizing its mined business process model via a series of stepwise and interactive discovering operations. The discovered business process model mined by the system is represented by the mathematical model of proportional information control nets, formally as well as graphically, constructed by an arbitrary number of combinational building blocks of the primitive process patterns such as linear (sequential), disjunctive (exclusive-OR), conjunctive (parallel-AND) and repetitive (iterative-LOOP) process patterns. Finally, in order to prove the correctness of the proportional process mining system, the paper performs an experiment by applying the implemented mining system to the real dataset that contains non-noise and synthetic event logs from the enactment history of 10,000 business process instance event traces of the Large Bank Transaction Process Model, and shows the final discovered outcomes through a visualized screen of a proportional information control net process model captured from the experiment.

1 Introduction

According for the business process (or workflow) automation [1,8] technologies to swiftly grow and be increasingly used by many newly formed process-aware enterprises and organizations, a new branch of requirements and demands has been raised, which is surely a novel concept of business process fidelity. It is eventually related with reengineering and redesigning those deployed business processes and their models running on the process-aware enterprises and organizations. For the sake of deploying business processes and their models onto the enterprises and organizations, it ought to be necessary for any types of the general-purpose business process management systems to be installed on those enterprises and organizations and we name them as the so-called process-aware enterprises and organizations. In general, a business process management system (BPMS) [8,13] is defined as a system that partially or fully automates the definition, creation, execution, and management of work procedures through the use of software that is able to interpret the procedure definition, interact with business-task participants, and invoke their uses of IT tools and applications. Steps of a work procedure are called activities [11,13], and jobs or transactions that flow through the system are called workcases [9,25] or business process instances. Such BPMSs and their related technologies have been constantly deployed and so gradually hot-issued in the IT arena. This atmosphere booming business process modeling and reengineering is becoming a catalyst for triggering emergence of the concept of business process intelligence [1,2,3,4,5,21] and knowledge mining [7,8,9,14,16] that rediscovers several perspectives of business processes such as control flow, data flow, resource allocation planning, social, and organizational perspectives from their execution histories collected at runtime.

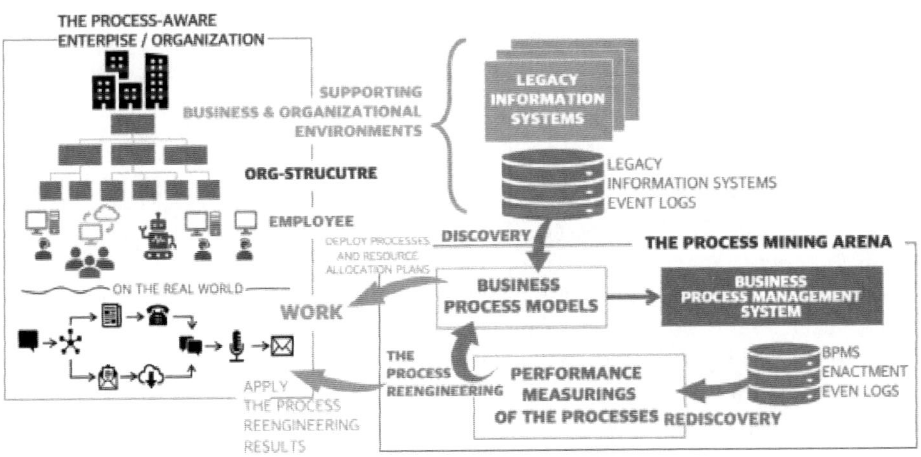

Fig. 1. A Situational View of the Process Mining Concept

Fig. 1 is to illustrate a situational view of the process-aware enterprises and organizations. As you see, the enterprise and organization have been supported from a variety of different information systems that manage all the valuable assets of data, information and knowledge available and produced in the business and organizational environments. One of the recent trends in the traditional business and managerial information systems ought to be the adoption of business process management systems and the deployment of the business process automation methodologies as a means of monitoring and controlling business activities and managements. We call those enterprises and organizations fortified with business process automation and management methodologies, tools and systems as the process-aware enterprises and organizations. The core competitiveness of the process-aware enterprises and organizations ought to be on the process mining functionality that is able to continuously manage as well as repeatedly evolve all the business processes deployed in the corresponding enterprises and organizations. The process mining functionality is mainly composed of the process discovery [7,8,19,20] functionality and the process rediscovery [1,17,24] functionality. The former is to discover business-activity processes from the event logs of the executions of the traditional information systems, while the later is to rediscover the enacted business-activity processes from the event logs stored whenever the corresponding business-activity processes are enacted and executed by their business process management system. Especially, the rediscovered business processes can be re-engineered and re-designed according to their performances measured and mined from the event logs by the process knowledge mining tools and the process intelligence solutions as well. This paper has something to do with the process rediscovery functionality. That is, the paper proposes a process mining framework with its related algorithms for rediscovering a so-called proportional process patterns from the business process enactment event log dataset, implements the process mining framework, and carries out an empirical study based upon a dataset of the specific business process execution event logs particularly delivered from the 4TU.Centre for Research Data.

2 Related Works

The main research challenges of this paper are to devise an algorithmic mining framework for discovering a structured model of information control nets from a business process enactment event log dataset and to propose the process-aware knowledge of enactment proportions on the gateway-activity of the process patterns with thinking out a series of process-aware knowledge discovery algorithms. Therefore, the literature surveys of these challenges are summarized in this section. The most popular approaches of the theoretical modeling methodologies to formally define and graphically represent business process models are the Petri-net model [5,6] of process modeling methodology and the information control net model [11,13] of process modeling methodology. Both of them are based upon the mathematical representation and the graphical representation at the same time. The Petri-net process model has a strong advantage in terms of the mathematical and analytical power, whereas the information control net process model has a much stronger merit in terms of the expressiveness of the business process domain. So far, there have been several business process rediscovery algorithms in the literature. One of the typical rediscovery algorithms for rediscovering the Petri-net process models is the α-Algorithm [4,5], whereas the typical rediscovery algorithm for rediscovering the information control net process models is the σ-Algorithm [1,17]. Note that the name of the rediscovery algorithm proposed in the paper is the ρ-Algorithm, and the naming reason of the ρ-Algorithm will be explained later. The crucial idea and characteristics of these algorithms and their comparisons with the ρ-Algorithm are arranged in this section.

The essential goal of the paper is concerned with the concept of proportional process models, which can be formally represented by the proportional Information Control Net process model, and it can be discovered from the business process enactment event logs. As stated in the previous subsections, for the sake of eventually supporting the model-log comparison, which is the business process fidelity issue, the literature has produced so far the two concepts and theories; one is the Petri-net process modeling methodology and the other is the information control net process modeling methodology. Also, the literature has published the α-Algorithm [4] and the σ-Algorithm [17] for discovering Petri-net process models and information control net process models, respectively. However, all of these discovery approaches have the limitations that they are able to deal with only sequential, parallel and selective process patterns out of all the types of the process patterns such as sequential, parallel, selective and repetitive process patterns. In other words, both of the discovery algorithms have a limitation in dealing with the repetitive-LOOP process patterns. Conclusively speaking, the algorithm (named as the ρ-Algorithm[3]) proposed in the paper is able to appropriately deal with the repetitive-LOOP process pattern.

3 A Proportional Process Mining System

In this section, we implement a proportional process mining system supported a process pattern discovery (from now on, we use the broader term, discovery.) framework. That is, we propose a conceptual framework and implement the proposed framework as a system that is able to eventually discover a proportional and structural information control net model from a business process enactment event log dataset especially formatted in a form of the XES standardized log format [12]. Especially, the core component of the system is the ρ-Algorithm that is firstly introduced and so named by this paper.

[3] In the ρ-Algorithm, the symbol and name of rbo (ρ) comes from the A programming language (APL) firstly released in 1960's. The function rho, coded like ρX in APL, implies that it gives the number of elements in X. The central idea of the discovery algorithm of the framework is exactly same to the implication of the APL function, rho (ρ).

3.1 A Conceptual Framework

In the paper, the emphasis is placed on the quality and reengineering of business process models that are usually built by a combination of the four types of process patterns, such as linear, disjunctive, conjunctive and repetitive process patterns formally defined in the previous section. That is, we used to model a proportional business process model [1,24] by a combination of four types of proportional process patterns, such as linear (sequential), disjunctive (exclusive-OR), conjunctive (parallel-AND), and repetitive (iterative-LOOP) of proportional process patterns. The conceptual framework is to conceptually define a procedural approach to discover a proportional business process model from its enactment event histories logged by executing all the four types of process patterns. After defining the conceptual framework, this section implements the conceptual framework for discovering a proportional business process model from its enactment event histories and logs dataset. Fig. 2 illustrates a series of procedural components of the conceptual framework.

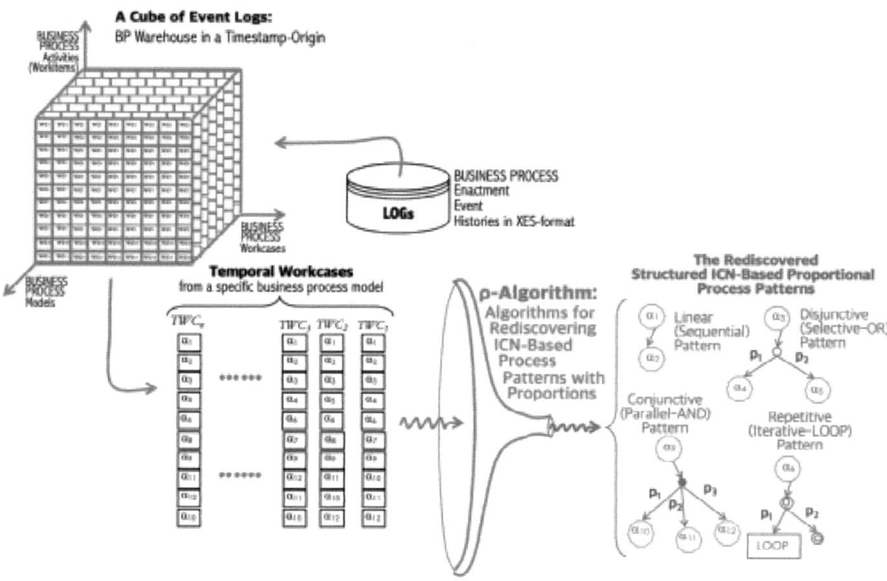

Fig. 2. A Conceptual Framework of the Proportional Process Mining System

The conceptual framework is concretized by a formal framework of discovering a process model of the structured information control nets, and it is composed of a series of formal concepts and their algorithmic formalism such as business process enactment event logs, business process warehouses, temporal workcases, temporal workcase filters and so on. Fig. 2 is to illustrate a series of these procedural concepts and formal implications in the conceptual approach to be used for realizing the discovery framework proposed in the paper. Especially, the figure highlights the conceptual role of the ρ-Algorithm[4]. that is the detailed implementation of the algorithmic discovery approach. Due to the page limitation, this section simply describes only the major components of the framework, such as business process enactment event log dataset as input and proportional process model as output of the conceptual framework and its implemented system.

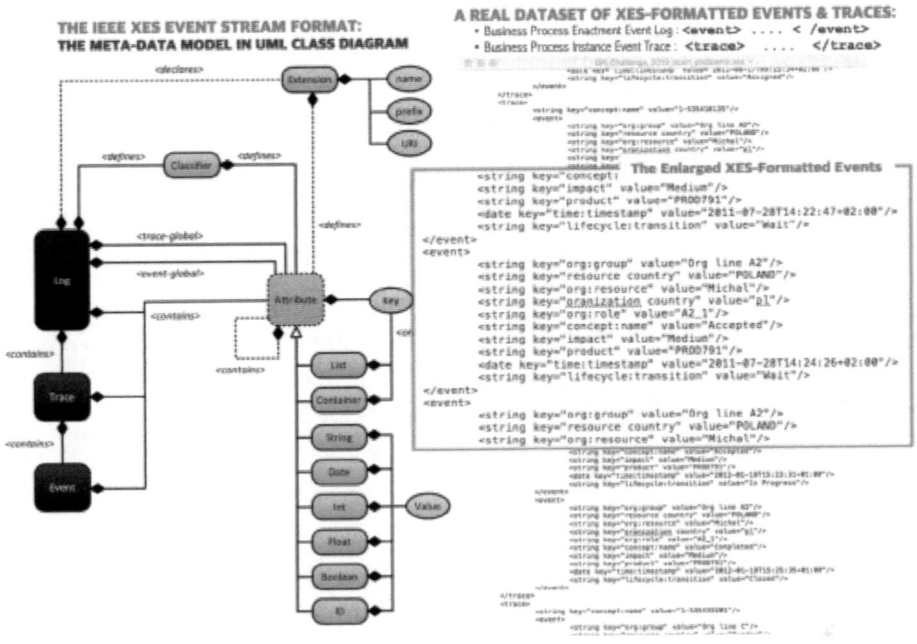

Fig. 3. The IEEE XES Event Log Format

3.2 Preparing the Event Log Format

The algorithmic discovery approach of the framework is mainly for the detailed implementation of the ρ-Algorithm simply stated in the conceptual approach, and it is composed of seven procedural concepts and six transformation algorithms, each of which conducts a transformation from one concept to another concept, one after another, to support the procedural process discovery and

[4] In the ρ-Algorithm, the symbol and name of rho (ρ) comes from the A programming language (APL) firstly released in 1960's. The function rho, coded like ρX in APL, implies that it gives the number of elements in X, from which the concept of ***mass*** comes. The central idea of the discovery algorithm of the framework is exactly same to the implication of the APL function, rho (ρ).

process-aware knowledge mining experiments. These concepts are procedurally listed as business process enactment event log histories in the IEEE XES-format [12]: business process instance event traces, temporal workcase models, pairs of temporally ordered adjacent-activity groups, quantitative adjacent-activity set, proportional process pattern graph, and proportional information control net model, whereas the transformation algorithms are listed as a series of the functional analytics algorithms: event trace mining algorithm, temporal workcase composing algorithm, adjacent-activity fragmentizing algorithm, adjacent-activity quantifying algorithm, proportional process pattern discovering algorithm, and proportional information control net discovering algorithm. Note that the paper needs to axiomatically formalize the procedural discovery approach with its core concepts and algorithms related with the ρ-Algorithm in particular. Due to the page limitation, however, the paper won't describe all of these concepts.

Fig. 3 shows the UML-based meta-data model of the IEEE XES (extensible event stream) format [12] and its samples from a real dataset of the business process enactment event logs recorded at enacting the business process instances of a corresponding business process model. As shown in the lefthand-side of the figure, the XES schema structure has a hierarchical inclusion relationship among Log, Trace and Event classes. Accordingly, in the righthand-side of the figure the real dataset file (BPI-Challenge-2013-open-problems.xes) is corresponding to the Log class, the business process instance event traces in an XML tag form of (`<trace> ... </trace>`) are corresponding to the Trace class, and the business process enactment event logs in an XML tag form of (`<event> ... </event>`) are corresponding to the Event class. The algorithm is to conceptually extract a business process instance event log from the XES-formatted dataset, and the algorithm is also able to conceptually fragmentize a workcase model into a fragment-group of temporally ordered adjacent-activity pairs.

3.3 Mining Proportional Process Patterns in Structured Information Control Nets

In terns of defining the concept of proportions in a business process model, we would adopt a way of formalism for the stochastic information control nets and semantically extend the meaning of stochastic to the concept of proportions. There are a number of AND/OR/LOOP graph models in the business process modeling literature. In particular, we take into account all the process patterns like sequential (linear process pattern), exclusive-OR (disjunctive process pattern), parallel-AND (conjunctive process pattern), and LOOP (iterative process pattern) constructs with holding proportions. Through such constructs, we are able to model decision-making gateway activities in a business process model, and the conceptual approach to be proposed in the paper is able to measure probability (proportion) of each branch of the decision-making choices by rediscovering the observed process patterns and their frequencies from the enactment event logs of a corresponding business process model.

The Proportional Process Patterns For the sake of the formal representation of a proportional business process model, the paper extensively revises the original information control net methodology by supporting the concept of proportions. Fig. 4 shows a series of graphical representations for the primitive constructs of proportional business process patterns, such as linear, disjunctive (OR-open/OR-close), conjunctive (AND-open/AND-close) and iterative (LOOP-open/LOOP-close) process patterns, and their mathematical properties of probabilities holding to the outgoing edges of each of the open gateway nodes.

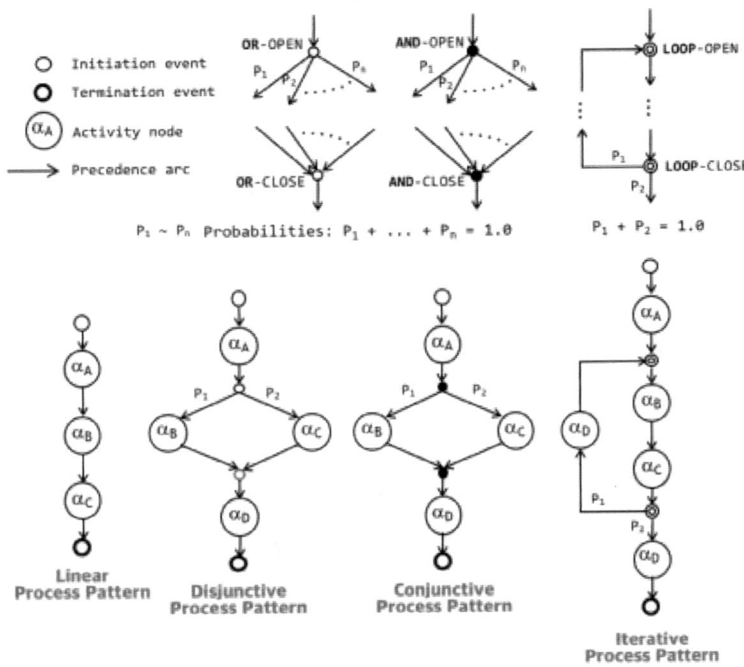

Fig. 4. The Proportional Process Patterns

Based upon these four types of proportional business process patterns, we define a formal representation of proportional business process model, which is named as the Proportional Information Control Net model using the graph theory. That is, the paper conceives the idea of proportional information control nets by extending the classic information control net definition with appending proportions to outgoing arcs of the constructs. Each arc in the graph so has a proportional value after all. In any given node, the sum of all the proportions of the arcs must be one as shown in the Fig. 4. Also, all the activity nodes in a single proportional information control net have to have only one outgoing arc (`out-degree = 1`), the proportion of the activity node's arc so must be one. For convenience, such an activity node's arcs are unlabeled in our graphical representation of the graph. In particular, assume that the iterative-LOOP process pattern is syntactically structured in a similar form of the DO-WHILE pattern in the mediocre programming languages.

The ρ-Algorithm The overall algorithmic approach is a stepwise mining procedure with the functional components to be used for discovering all the types of the proportional process patterns that constitute a structured information control net process model. The approach is named as ρ-Algorithm that consists of three major transformation steps, such as STEP-1, STEP-2 and STEP-3, from forming temporal workcases out of the process enactment event logs to discovering a proportional information control net process model. The first transformation algorithm is to discover the enacted workcases from the event logs, each of which can be modeled into a temporal workcase model. At the same time, it is necessary to count the occurrence of each temporal workcase with its activities. The second transformation algorithm is to discover an activity-driven pattern graph by integrating all the members of the adjacent-activity set and calculating the occurrences of the temporal workcases. In terms of discovering the structured information control net process model from the corresponding activity-driven pattern graph, we develop an algorithm that is able to deal with an any combinational number of AND/OR/LOOP proportional process patterns.

- *STEP-1: Groups of Temporally Ordered Adjacent-Activity Pairs*: The first step of the ρ-Algorithm is to mine a group of temporally ordered adjacent-activities pairs from temporal workcases of the process instance event logs. Also, each of the temporal workcases is formally represented by one of the workcase model types introduced in the conceptual framework. That is, a temporal workcase represents an ordered enactment sequence of activity event logs, each of which is formed with its activity identifier and its time-stamp extracted from its corresponding process enactment event log.
- *STEP-2: Weighted Adjacent-Activity Set and Activity-Driven Pattern Graph*: The STEP-2 of the ρ-Algorithm is to build all the groups of temporally ordered adjacent-activity pairs, each of which corresponds to a process instance event trace. The eventual output of this algorithm is a weighted adjacent-activity set named as adjacencyList β. This set is built from all the groups of temporally ordered adjacent-activity pairs through an internal transformation procedure.
- *STEP-3: Discovering Proportional Process Patterns*: The final step (STEP-3) of the ρ-Algorithm is to discover proportional process patterns of a proportional information control net process model from the activity-driven pattern graph mined from all the groups of temporally ordered adjacent-activity pairs. The eventual goal of the ρ-Algorithm is accomplished through this step. Note that the proportional information control net process model

must be satisfied with the proper nesting as well as the matched pairing properties in forming gateway activities in each process graph pattern.

Summarily, the characteristics of the proportional process mining algorithm proposed and implemented in the paper are as followings: First, the mining system is able not only to discover the process patterns but also to discover the enactment proportions of the process patterns from a dataset of the IEEE XES-formatted enactment event logs of a corresponding business process model. Second, the mining system is theoretically supported by the information control nets modeling methodology of business process models. Third, the essential algorithm of the mining system is named as ρ-Algorithm (rho-Algorithm) that is able to discover a structured information control net model with the enactment occurrences and proportions of the activities associated with an underlying business process model. Fourth, the ρ-Algorithm is firstly developed in the business process management and mining literature as the process mining algorithm that discovers a structured business process model theoretically supported by the information control net modeling methodology. Fifth, the ρ-Algorithm is able to discover all the process patterns such as linear (sequential), conjunctive (parallel-AND), disjunctive (exclusive-OR), and repetitive (iterative-LOOP) process patterns and discover the enactment occurrences and proportions of each branch of the process patterns.

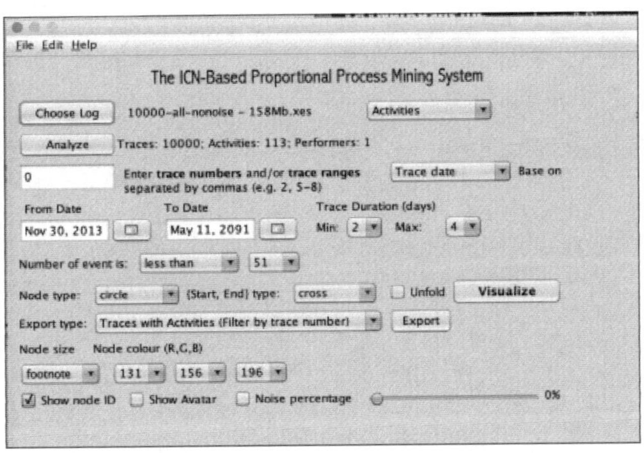

Fig. 5. The Dashboard Screen of the Proportional Process Mining System

3.4 The Implemented Mining System

By implementing the proportional process mining framework, it is necessary for the algorithmic discovery approach to confirm the feasibility and the applicability of the ρ-Algorithm and by applying the implemented system onto a real

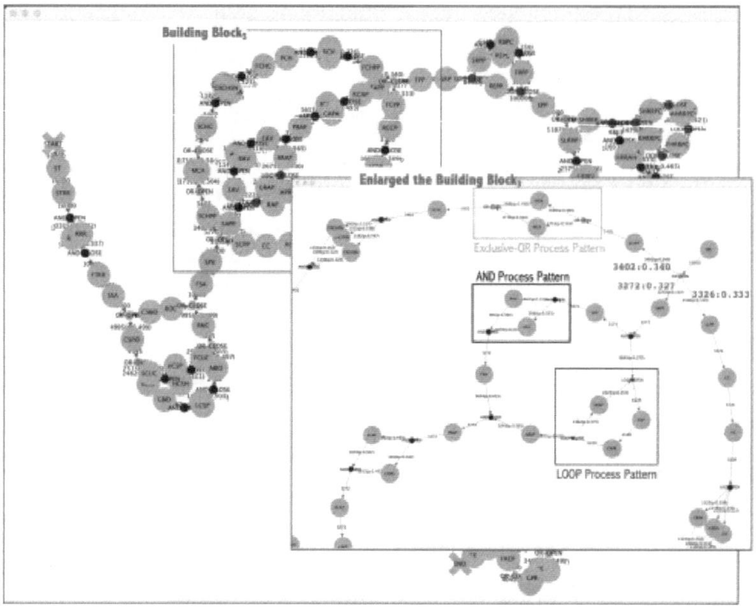

Fig. 6. The Rediscovered Proportional Process Patterns Mined from the Dataset of Large Bank Transaction Process by the System

dataset and proving to ultimately discover all the proportional process patterns in a structural information control net model from a business process enactment event log dataset especially formatted in a form of the XES standardized log format [12]. In other words, the paper implements a proportional process mining system theoretically supported by the ρ-Algorithm-based discovery approach and apply the system to a real dataset of business process enactment event logs, which was released to the public by the 4TU.Centre for Research Data [10]. Fig. 5 is a screen-captured dashboard controlling all the proportional process mining activities through the implemented process mining system. The dashboard represents the current dataset chosen through the Choose Log button, the name of which is 10000-all-nonoise-150MB.xes containing 10,000 business process instance event traces and 113 activities are involved in the enactment of the corresponding business process model, Large Bank Transaction Process Model.

Also, the real dataset of 10000-all-nonoise-150MB.xes is a non-noise and synthetic dataset made by logging the histories of enacting 10,000 business process instances of the Large Bank Transaction Process Model [10]. This feasibility analysis is aiming to prove that the ρ-Algorithm is able to discover all the types of proportional process patterns such as linear, disjunctive, conjunctive and repetitive process patterns and their proportions. According as a business process instance is executed, the logging and auditing component of the business pro-

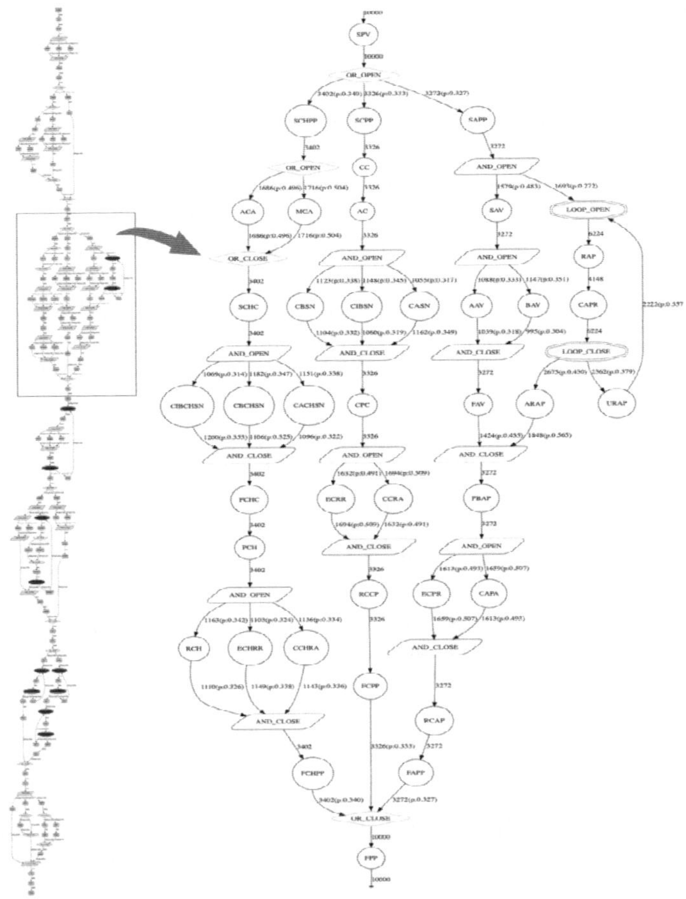

Fig. 7. The Rediscovered Proportional Information Control Net Process Model Generated by the System

cess enactment engine records its workitem execution events on a log repository, and those logged events are arranged in a form of the temporal sequence of events. This execution sequence of a business process instance is forming a business process instance event trace, from which we can extract a business process instance's workitem event trace and its formal representation is specified by a model of temporal workcases. In recent, IEEE has released a standard tag-based language, XES [12], whose aim is to provide designers of information systems with a unified and extensible methodology for capturing systems' behaviors by means of event logs and event streams.

Fig. 6 is the system-made representation and the enlarged representation, respectively, of the proportional process patterns with their proportions, which is the proportional information control net model of the Subprocess Model with holding all the types of process patterns like sequential, disjunctive, conjunctive and repetitive process patterns. These process patterns are perfectly matched paired as well as properly nested. The algorithm so works perfectly. The feasibility analysis for verifying the ρ-Algorithm has been successfully done as presented in this subsections. First of all, discovering the proportional disjunctive process pattern type and the proportional conjunctive process pattern type from the IEEE XES-formatted dataset was successfully fulfilled in the paper. In the next, discovering the proportional repetitive process pattern type has been successfully done in the system, too. Based upon these results of the feasibility analysis, the ρ-Algorithm of the conceptual approach and the algorithmic approach proposed in the paper ought to be reasonable and feasible in terms of their deployments and applications in the real world. Finally, the time complexity of the ρ-Algorithm is $O(N \times M)$, where N is the number of temporal workcases, which implies the number of business process instance event traces in a dataset of business process enactment event logs, and M is the number of activities associated with the underlying business process model. Finally, Fig. 7 is the system-generated proportional information control net process model from the proportional process patterns rediscovered and graphically screen-visualized by the implemented mining system. The left-hand side of the figure is all the proportional information control net process model and the right-hand side is to enlarge a sub-portion of the model.

4 Conclusions

So far, this paper has proposed the proportional process pattern discovery framework and implemented the framework as the proportional process mining system. The theoretical background of the mining system stems from the conceptual rediscovery approach of rediscovering the proportional process patterns such as linear, disjunctive, conjunctive and repetitive process patterns from the process-aware warehouses and data-sets, whereas the implementable background of the mining system is supported by the algorithmic discovery approach of the ρ-Algorithm, by discovering the proportional information control net models from the business process enactment event log data-sets. Based upon these theoretical and algorithmic approaches, the paper devised, implemented and developed these concepts, algorithms and systems, respectively. Based upon the implemented proportional process mining system, the paper carried practically out an experimental analysis by deploying the business process enactment event log data-set, which is name as the Large Bank Transaction Process dataset, provided by the 4TU.Centre for Research Data.

Notes and Comments. This research was supported by the Basic Science Research Program, (Grant No. 2017R1A2B2010697), through the National Research Foundation of Korea (NRF) funded by the Ministry of Education, Republic of Korea. Collaboratively, this work was also supported by the National Research Foundation of Korea (NRF) grant funded by the Korea government (Ministry of Science and ICT, Grant No. NRF-2018R1C1B5086414).

References

1. Kyoungsook Kim, Moonsuk Yeon, Byeongsoo Jeong, Kwanghoon Kim, "A Conceptual Approach for Discovering Proportions of Disjunctive Routing Patterns in a Business Process Model," KSII TRANSACTIONS ON INTERNET AND INFORMATION SYSTEMS, Vol. 11, No. 2, pp. 1148-1161, 2017.
2. Fabio Casati, et al, "Business Process Intelligence," Technical Report, HPL-2002-119, HP Laboratories Palo Alto, 2002.
3. Daniela Grigori, Fabio Casati, Malu Castellanos, Umeshwar Dayal, Mehmet Sayal and Ming-Chien Shan, "Business Process Intelligence," Journal of Computers in Industry, Vol. 53, Issue 3, 2004.
4. W. M. P. van der Aalst, B. F. van Dongena; J. Herbst, L. Marustera, G. Schimm and A. J. M. M. Weijters, "Workflow mining: A survey of issues and approaches," Journal of Data Knowledge Engineering, Vol. 47, Issue 2, pp. 237–267, 2003.
5. W. M. P. van der Aalst and A. J. M. M. Weijters, "Process mining: a research agenda," Journal of Computers in Industry, Vol. 53, Issue 3, 2004.
6. Aalst, W.P.M., Alves de Medeiros, A.K., and Weijters, A.J.M.M., "Process Equivalence: Comparing Two Process Models Based on Observed Behavior," Lecture Notes in Computer Science, Vol. 4102, pp. 129-144, 2006.
7. Minjae Park and Kwanghoon Kim, "Control-path Oriented Workflow Intelligence Analyses," JOURNAL OF INFORMATION SCIENCE AND ENGINEERING, Vol. 24, pp. 343-359, 2008.
8. Kwang-Hoon Kim, "Control-path Oriented Workflow Intelligence Analysis on Enterprise Workflow Grids," The Proceedings of the International Conference on Semantics, Knowledge, and Grid, Beijing, China, 2005.
9. Kwang-Hoon Kim and Clarence A. Ellis, "Workflow Reduction for Reachable-path Rediscovery in Workflow Mining," Series of Studies in Computational Intelligence: the Foundations and Novel Approaches in Data Mining, Vol. 9, pp. 289-310, Springer, 2006.
10. BPI Challenge 2012, 2013, 2014, 2015, 2016, 2017, 2018, 4TU.Centre for Research Data, https://data.4tu.nl/repository/ collection:event-logs-real.
11. Ellis, Clarence A., Kim, K., Rembert, A., Wainer, J., "Investigations on Stochastic Information Control Nets," INFORMATION SCIENCES, Vol. 194, pp. 120-137, 2012.
12. IEEE, "IEEE Standard for eXtensible Event Stream (XES) for Achieving Interoperability in Event Logs and Event Streams," IEEE 1849-2016, 2016. 10.1109/IEEESTD.2016.7740858.
13. Kim, Kwanghoon and Ellis, Clarence A., "Section II / Chapter VII. An ICN-based Workflow Model and Its Advances," HANDBOOK OF RESEARCH ON BUSINESS PROCESS MODELING, pp. 142-172, IGI Global, ISR, 2009.
14. Michael zur Muehlen and Keith D. Swenson, "BPAF: A Standard for the Interchange of Process Analytics Data," Lecture Notes in Business Information Processing, Vol. 66, pp. 170-181, 2011.
15. Kim, Kwanghoon, "A XML-Based Workflow Event Logging Mechanism for Workflow Mining," The Proceedings of the International Workshop on APWeb, pages 132-136, 2006.
16. Minjae Park and Kwanghoon Kim, "XWELL: A XML-Based Workflow Event Logging Mechanism and Language for Workflow Mining Systems," Lecture Notes in Computer Science, Vol. 4707, pp. 900-909, 2007.

17. Kim, Kwanghoon and Ellis, Clarence A., "σ-Algorithm: Structured Workflow Process Mining Through Amalgamating Temporal Workcases," The Proceedings of PAKDD2007, Advances in Knowledge Discovery and Data Mining, Lecture Notes in Artificial Intelligence, Vol. 4426, pp. 119-130, 2007.
18. Ahn, H. and Kim, K., "A Stochastic Activity-to-Performer Affiliation Binding Formalism in ICN-based Workflow Models," ICICI Express Letters, Vol. 9, No. 12, 2015.
19. Kim, H., Ahn, H., and Kim, K., "Modeling, Discovering, and Visualizing Workflow Performer-Role Affiliation Networking Knowledge," KSII TRANSACTIONS ON INTERNET AND INFORMATION SYSTEMS, Vol. 8, No. 2, pp. 691-708, 2014.
20. Kim, Kwanghoon Pio, "Discovering Activity-Performer Affiliation Knowledge on ICN-based Workflow Models," JOURNAL OF INFORMATION SCIENCE AND ENGINEERING, Vol. 29, No. 1, pp. 79-97, 2013.
21. Kim, Kwanghoon Pio, "Human-Centered Workflow Intelligence," Tutorial at the International Conference on Advanced Communications Technology, Phoenix Park, Pyeongchang, South Korea, Feb. 2014.
22. Kim, Kwanghoon Pio, "A Stochastic Workflow Performer-to-Activity Affiliation Network Model," The Proceedings of the 28th Annual Conference of Biomedical Fuzzy System Association (BMFSA2015), Kumamoto, Japan, 21-22 Nov. 2015.
23. Snijders, Tom A.B., Bunt, Gerhard G. van de, Steglich, Christian E.G., "Introduction to Stochastic Actor-Based Models for Network Dynamics," SOCIAL NETWORKS, Vol. 32, pp. 44-60, 2010.
24. Kyoungsook Kim, Youngkoo Lee, Minhyuck Jin, Hyun Ahn, Kwanghoon Pio Kim, "An Experiment on Mining Proportions of Disjunctive Process Patterns from Workflow Logs," The Proceedings of the 13th Asia Pacific International Conference on Information Science and Technology (APIC-IST), pp. 265-268, 2018.
25. Minheak Jin, Hyun Ahn, Dinhlam Pham, Kwanghoon Pio Kim, "Discovering Cardinalities of the Temporal Workcases and Experimental Results from XES-formatted Workflow Logs," The Proceedings of the 13th Asia Pacific International Conference on Information Science and Technology (APIC-IST), pp. 25-28, 2018.
26. Dinhlam Pham, Hyun Ahn, Kwanghoon Pio Kim, "A Temporal Work Transference Discovery Algorithm and Experimental Results on XES-Formatted Workflow Logs," The Proceedings of the 13th Asia Pacific International Conference on Information Science and Technology (APIC-IST), pp. 41-46, 2018.
27. Jaeyoung Yun, Minhyuck Jin, Dinhlam Pham, Kwanghoon Pio Kim, "Algorithmic Generation of Data Sequence Models from Information Control Net Based Workflow Models," The Proceedings of the 13th Asia Pacific International Conference on Information Science and Technology (APIC-IST), pp. 33-35, 2018.
28. Hyun Ahn, Kyoungsook Kim, Minjae Park, Kwanghoon Pio Kim, "A Configurable Treemap Method for Visualizing Process Entity Hierarchies,"The Proceedings of the 13th Asia Pacific International Conference on Information Science and Technology (APIC-IST), pp. 29-31, 2018.
29. Kyoungsook Kim, Minhyuck Jin, Hyun Ahn, Kwanghoon Pio Kim, "Discovering Work Transference Networks on Workflows," The Proceedings of the 19th International Conference on Information Integration and Web-based Applications Services, pp. 568-572. 2017.
30. Kyoungsook Kim, Choongman Lee, Byeongsoo Jeong, Kwanghoon Pio Kim, "An XPDL-Based Structural Analyzer for Verifying Business Process Models," The Proceedings of the 12th Asia Pacific International Conference on Information Science and Technology, pp. 137-144. 2017.

Improving document classification performance by combining resources and integrating word embedding techniques

Kazem Qazanfari and Abdou Youssef

George Washington University, District of Columbia, 20052 Washington, USA
{kazemmit , ayoussef} @gwu.edu

Abstract. Text modeling is a critical step in document classification problems. Word embedding techniques are among the most well-known text modeling methods which recently showed promising results in different applications compared to other text modeling techniques. Word embedding algorithms use repository data to model the words; however, in almost all real-world document classification problems, the distribution of the repository data and the real-world distribution of classes are rarely equivalent. This phenomenon, termed *inadequacy of knowledge,* reduces the accuracy of the document classification methods. Also, *out-of-vocabulary* problem could be considered a subtype of this phenomenon. In this paper, we first address the out-of-vocabulary issue in GloVe embedding, by training this algorithm on n-gram char-level data, instead of words; this version of GloVe is called here C-GloVe. Then we address the issue of inadequacy of knowledge by (1) combining different embedding algorithms and (2) training those embedding hybrids on combined sources of knowledge (universal and domain-specific). The algorithms considered include C-GloVe, GloVe, Word2Vec, ELMo, USE and FastText. Experimental results show that C-GloVe generates more accurate models for documents than GloVe especially when the size of the training dataset is small. More importantly, it is shown that (1) combining universal and local resources and (2) integrating the word embedding techniques resulted in higher F1-Score in document classification, compared to standalone sources of knowledge and standalone word embedding techniques.

Keywords: Document classification, Word embedding, Text modeling.

1 Introduction

Vector space models are an effective way to numerically model the meanings of natural-language terms in a computational system. These models are created using embedding techniques that represent words or phrases as vectors in a high-dimensional space, such that the cosine similarity of any two terms corresponds to their semantic similarity.

These vectors, referred to as the embeddings of the terms in the vector space, can also be used as input to further feed into a machine learning algorithm. Word embedding has been also widely used in many Natural Language Processing (NLP) tasks, such as language modeling [1, 2], named entity recognition and chunking [3, 4, 5]. Recently, the word embedding techniques were also extended to embed queries, documents, phrases, entities, etc. [6, 7], which could play a critical role in industry applications, such as large-scale web search and knowledge mining [8, 9].

In the recent years, dozens of algorithms have been proposed for word embedding. Some well-known representatives are GloVe [10], Continuous Bag-Of-Words (CBOW) and Skip-Gram[11], Fast-Text [12], Deep Contextualized Word Representations (ELMo) [13], and Google's Universal Sentence Encoder (USE) [14].

Depending on the text mining problem, each of these embedding methods should be trained first on a repository dataset. After training, a feature vector $V_i = (f_1^i, f_2^i, \dots, f_n^i)^T$ for a word w_i or document D_i in an n-dimensional real space R^n could be generated [15]. However, in a real-world text mining problem, *L*ocal knowledge *L* (i.e. *repository data*) does not fully and precisely represent the characteristics of the problem –in comparison to the *U*niversal knowledge *U*-. It was shown in [16] that for a classification problem P, the distribution of the data in *L* for each class often does not match the real distribution of the class concept in *U*, and this leads to inaccurate feature values. To demonstrate this problem visually, consider a word w_i that appears in the local knowledge *L*. Let $U(w_i, C_k)$ and $L(w_i, C_k)$ be the relevance of word w_i to the concept of class $C_k$based on the universal knowledge *U* and local knowledge *L*, respectively. In a document classification problem, it is desirable to have $U(w_i, C_k) = L(w_i, C_k)$ or at least $U(w_i, C_k) \cong L(w_i, C_k)$. However, generally the local knowledge *L* suffers from incomplete knowledge about the word w_i which causes difference -and sometimes significant difference, such as *out-of-vocabulary* situation- between $U(w_i, C_k)$ and $L(w_i, C_k)$.

Consider $L(w_i, C_k)$ to be the modeling of the local knowledge *L* about word w_i within class C_k, calculated by Eq. 1:

$$L(w_i, C_k) = \frac{f_{w_i,C_k}}{N_{C_k}} \tag{1}$$

where N_{C_k} is the number of documents in class C_k, and f_{w_i,C_k} is the number of documents (of classC_k) that have word w_i. Therefore, $L(w_i, C_k)$ could be considered as the probability of having word w_i in class C_k.

Consider Fig. 1, which illustrates the likelihood $L(w_i, C_k)$ of having word w_i in different classes C_k, where $w_i \in$ {Paint,Light,Design,Machine,Device,Starter,Across,Bottle,Complex} and $C_k \in$ {"comp.graphics" and "rec.autos"} of the 20-Newsgroups dataset [17]. Based on the general meaning (universal knowledge) of the above words, some words such as "paint" and "design" are more related to the "comp. graphics" class, whereas certain other words such as "device" and "machine" are more related to the "rec.autos" class. However, the calculated likelihoods for these words based on the local knowledge show a different inference: that these words are more related to the other class. Also, by considering the general meaning of words, "across", "bottle" and "complex", which do not have a significant relation to either of these classes, yet we see in the figure that there is a strong connection between these words and one of the classes. Therefore, the accuracy of the document classification algorithms which use the word embedding of these words might be reduced if the word embedding algorithm is trained only on the local knowledge. In this paper, this phenomenon is called *inadequacy of knowledge (IoK)*.

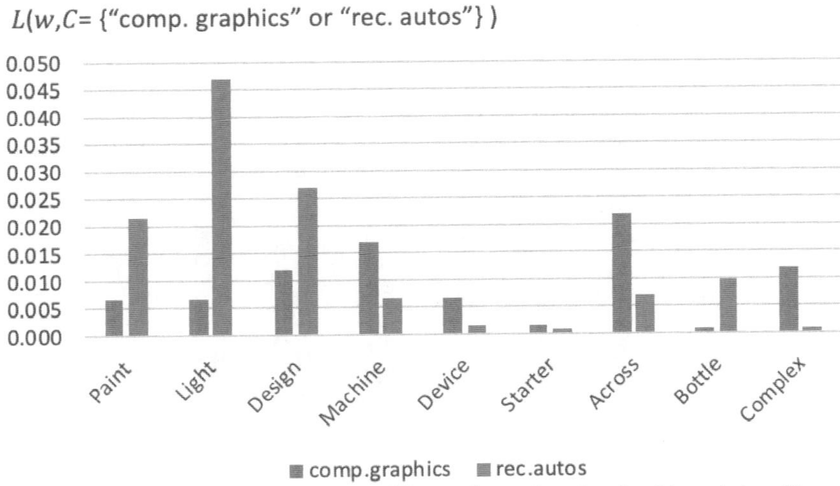

Fig. 1. Relevance of some words to two different classes based on local knowledge -20newsgroups [16].

As another discrepancy between the local and the universal knowledge, consider Fig 2. This figure shows the relatedness between a focus word w_f and two words w_x *or* w_y using a local and universal knowledge.

$$S^L(w_f, w_t) = \frac{V_f^L . V_{x\ or\ y}^L}{\|V_f^L\| . \|V_t^L\|} \quad \text{(where } w_t \text{is } w_x \text{ or } w_y\text{)} \tag{2}$$

$$S^U(w_f, w_t) = \frac{V_f^U . V_{x\ or\ y}^U}{\|V_f^U\| . \|V_t^U\|} \quad \text{(where } w_t \text{is } w_x \text{ or } w_y\text{)} \tag{3}$$

where V_f , V_x and V_y are the feature vectors of word w_f,w_x *and* w_y respectively, generated by Word2Vec (Skip-gram) algorithm, $S(w_f, w_t)$ is the cosine similarity between the feature vectors of the focus word w_f and word w_t, and the superscripts L and U indicate whether the embedding model has been trained on a local source (here Reuters [18]) or universal source of knowledge (here Wikipedia [19]).

As Fig. 2 shows, the universal and local knowledge have different judgments about the relatedness of two words. For example, based on the universal knowledge, the word "sport" is related to both words "health" and "running" with the same weight; however, the local knowledge indicates that the word "sport" is more related to "health" than to "running". More strikingly, with respect to the local knowledge, "love" is completely unrelated to "lovely", and "student" is completely unrelated to "pencil". This is caused by the Out-Of-Vocabulary issue which is an instance of the IoK problem. Out-Of-Vocabulary (OOV) words are unknown words that appear in the testing vocabulary but not in the training vocabulary. They are usually important content words such as names, locations and different forms of pre-known words which contain information crucial to the success of many text mining tasks.

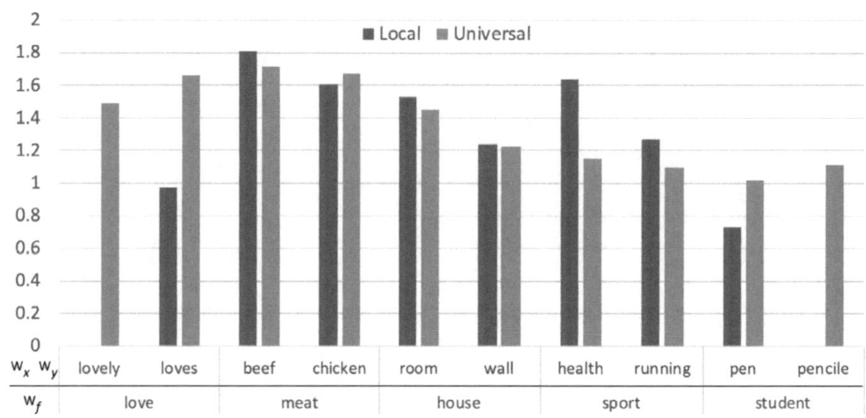

Fig. 2. Relatedness between a focus word w_f and two words w_x or w_y using a local and universal sources of knowledge.

In this paper, to solve the IoK problem:

A. We combine two sources of knowledge for generating the word embeddings:
   i. A universal source of knowledge, which is an external source of knowledge that has the general information about the words.
   ii. A local source of knowledge, which has the domain-specific information of the words for a given problem P.

B. We train different embedding algorithms on both sources of knowledge. The details of the proposed method will come in the next sections.

The rest of this paper is organized as follows: The proposed method for solving specifically the issue of Out-Of-Vocabulary of GloVe word embedding algorithm will be introduced in Section 2. In section 3, the IoK problem will be addressed by combining resources of knowledge and integrating the word embedding techniques. Section 4 covers some document classification experiments and shows how the proposed methods could improve the performance of document classification problem. Finally, a discussion of the achieved results and some suggestions for future directions will be presented in Section 5.

2 C-GloVe: GloVe with no more OOV issue

Glove and Word2Vec are two well-known word embedding algorithms, which suffer from the OOV problem; however, Facebook proposed an algorithm in 2016 to solve the OOV problem in Word2Vec. This method is called FastText, an extension to Word2Vec, in which instead of feeding individual words into the Neural Network, it breaks words into several n-grams and feeds these n-grams to the Neural Network.

As the first contribution of our work, to solve the OOV problem in GloVe, we apply the same extension to GloVe algorithm. The first step of GloVe is collecting word co-occurrence statistics in a form of word co-occurrence matrix X. Each element X_{ij} of the matrix represents how often word i appears in the context of word j. However, in our proposed method, i.e. C-GloVe, instead of computing the word co-occurrences, we compute the co-occurrences of n-grams..

To do so, the n-grams of each word will be substituted for the word. For example, the tri-grams for the word "loves", namely, "lov", "ove", and "ves", take the place of "loves". Then, the n-gram'ed corpus will be scanned in the way that for each n-gram *ng*, we look for context n-grams within an area defined by a parameter window_size before and after *ng*.

After factorizing the calculated co-occurrence matrix using the GloVe algorithm, it will have word embeddings for all the n-grams generated from the training dataset. Rare and OOV words can now be properly represented since it is highly likely that some of their n-grams also appear in other words. Finally, the word embedding vector for each word will be the sum of the embeddings of all n-grams of the word.

3 Solution to the Inadequacy of Knowledge Problem

In this paper, to solve the IoK problem two sources of knowledge are considered for generating the word embeddings: Universal source of knowledge, such as Wikipedia [19], and the local source of knowledge, which has the domain-specific information of the words for a given problem *P*. Figure 3 shows the diagram of the proposed solution for solving the IoK problem.

Depending on the text mining problem, different information about the words could be extracted from the universal source of knowledge, such as similarity and relatedness of the words. As it is shown in Fig 3, once the universal and local sources of knowledge are specified, the word embedding algorithms will be trained on each source of knowledge separately. Such that two models will result for each embedding algorithm: a local knowledge based model and a universal knowledge based model.

Table 1 shows all the experimented models and the abbreviations assigned to them. In the next section we refer to each model by the assigned abbreviation. Note that any other word embedding algorithm could be considered in our approach; however, in this paper, we focused on the well-known and recent word embedding algorithms mentioned in Table 1.

After having all trained models, the next step of the proposed method is to produce all possible pairs of models and to evaluate these pairs using the test sets. The details of generating feature vectors from each pair, and evaluating each pair, are given in the next section. Finally, based on the evaluation results, one or more pair will be identified as the suitable pair/pairs of models for each classification problem.

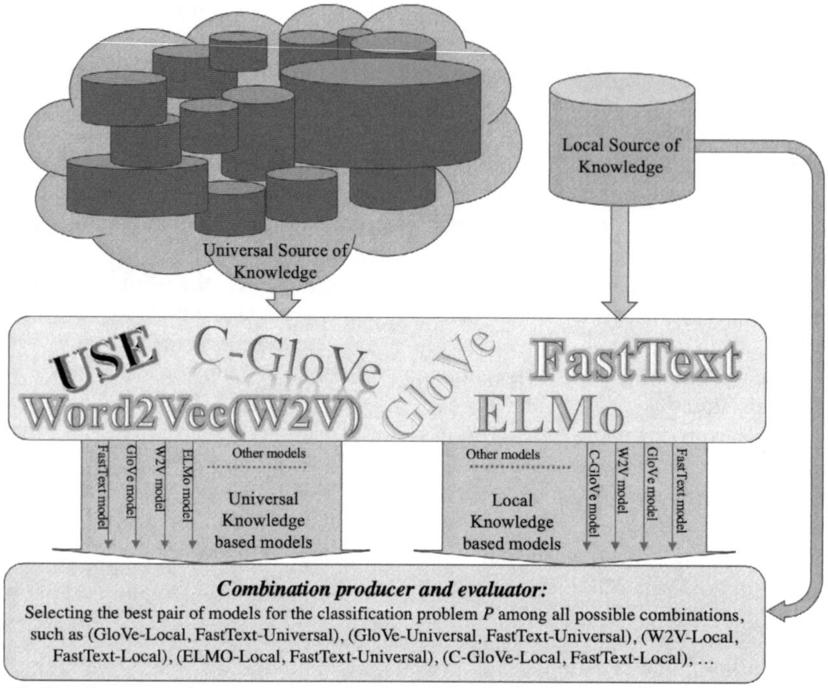

Fig. 3. The diagram of the proposed solution for solving the inadequacy of knowledge problem

Table 1. List of experimented models and their abbreviations

Model name	Abbreviation	Algorithm	Source of Knowledge
GloVe-Local	G-L	GloVe	Local
GloVe-Universal	G-U	GloVe	Universal
FastText-Local	F-L	FastText	Local
FastText -Universal	F-U	FastText	Universal
W2V-Local	W-L	W2V[1]	Local
W2V -Universal	W-U	W2V	Universal
ELMO-Local	E-L	ELMO[2]	Local
ELMO-Universal	E-U	ELMO	Universal
C-GloVe-Local	C-G-L	C-GloVe[3]	Local
USE-Universal	U-U	USE[4]	Universal

[1] The Skip-gram algorithm has been selected, which showed better performance from view point of accuracy and precision.

[2] Embedding from Language Models

[3] The proposed improvement on GloVe in the previous section.

[4] Universal Sentence Encoder

4 Experiments

4.1 Datasets

In our experiment, we use five corpora as local sources of knowledge: 20-Newsgroups [17], Reuters [18], SUBJ [20], TREC [21], and IMDB [22] data sets. Table 2 shows the details of these datasets.

Table 2. Details of the experimented datasets.

Dataset	Number of samples	Number of classes	Description
Reuters	10788	90	Reuters is a benchmark dataset for document classification. To be more precise, it is a multi-class, multi-label dataset
20 Newsgroups	18846	20	The 20 Newsgroups data set is a collection of approximately 20,000 newsgroup documents, partitioned (nearly) evenly across 20 different newsgroups.
SUBJ	10000	2	Subjectivity dataset where the task is to classify a sentence as being subjective or objective.
TREC	5952	6	TREC question dataset - task involves classifying a question into 6 question types (whether the question is about person, location, numeric information, etc.)
IMDB	50000	2	This is a dataset for binary sentiment classification containing substantially more data than previous benchmark datasets.

4.2 Universal Knowledge

Since there is no comprehensive source to be considered as the universal knowledge, instead different available huge datasets such as Wikipedia could be used for training the embedding algorithms to model the words or documents universally. In this paper we used "English wiki dataset 2018 Nov" [19], which includes all the English articles on the Wikipedia website.

4.3 Evaluation

The first experiment shows how C-GloVe could solve the IoK problem, especially when the size of the training set is small. To do so, we train GloVe and C-GloVe with only n% of the samples at a time. For example, if n=1, we first select 1% of the whole samples randomly, then we train both methods using the selected samples. However, in the classification phase, we use all the training samples of the dataset to train a SVM classifier, and we use all testing samples of the dataset to evaluate the trained classifier. For each value of n, this process was performed 10 times and the performance, i.e. Precision, Recall and F1-score, of the classifier was calculated by averaging each metric over these 10 runs.

Table 3. The performance of the SVM classifier on Reuters dataset when C-GloVe and GloVe algorithms are trained on n% of the dataset

Percentage (n)	Precision		Recall		F1-Score	
	GloVe	C-GloVe	GloVe	C-GloVe	GloVe	C-GloVe
1	61.8	72.2	70.6	77.0	65.9	74.5
2	71.0	76.8	75.8	79.0	73.3	77.9
5	75.7	78.5	79.1	80.8	77.4	79.6
10	78.5	80.0	81.5	82.5	80.0	81.2
20	81.0	82.2	83.1	83.8	82.0	83.0
35	82.5	83.2	84.5	85.1	83.5	84.1
50	84.0	84.3	85.9	86.3	84.9	85.3
70	85.6	85.7	87.1	87.2	86.3	86.4
100	86.5	86.6	87.7	87.7	87.1	87.1

Table 4. The performance of the SVM classifier on 20 newsgroups dataset when C-GloVe and GloVe algorithms are trained on n% of the dataset

Percentage (n)	Precision		Recall		F1-Score	
	GloVe	C-GloVe	GloVe	C-GloVe	GloVe	C-GloVe
1	47.80	56.20	56.60	61.00	51.83	58.50
2	57.00	61.80	61.80	63.80	59.30	62.78
5	61.70	64.20	65.10	66.10	63.35	65.14
10	64.50	65.90	67.50	67.70	65.97	66.79
20	67.00	67.50	69.10	69.10	68.03	68.29
35	68.50	68.50	70.50	70.00	69.49	69.24
50	70.00	69.30	71.90	70.70	70.94	69.99
70	71.60	70.50	73.10	71.50	72.34	71.00
100	73.00	71.40	73.80	71.90	73.40	71.65

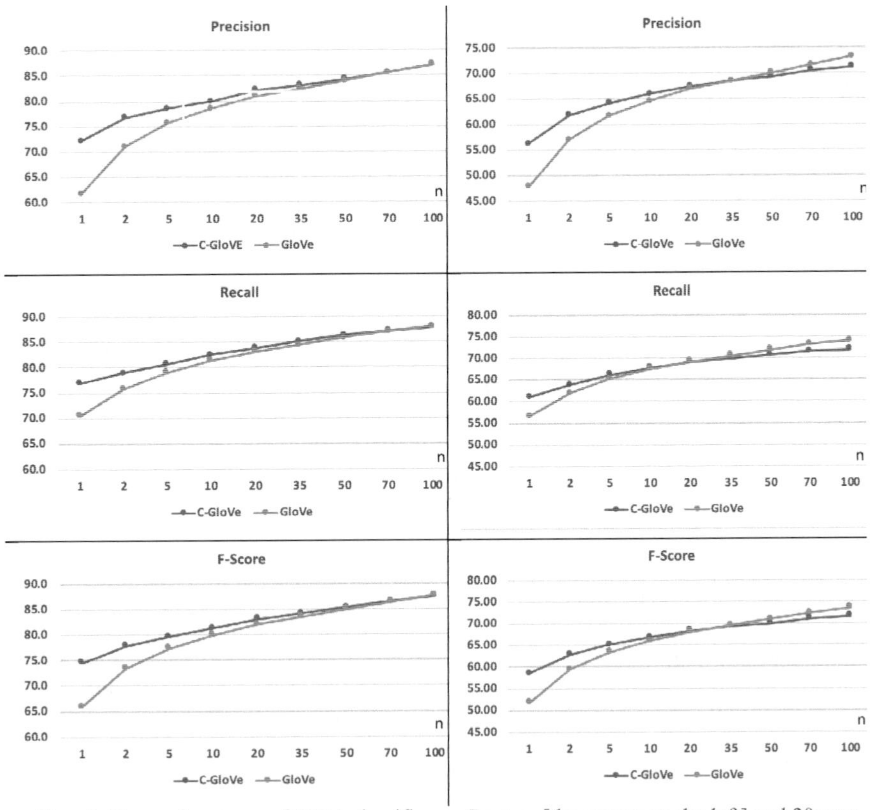

Fig. 4. The performance of SVM classifier on Reuters [the curves on the left] and 20newsgroups dataset [the curves on the right] when C-GloVe and GloVe algorithms are trained on n% of the dataset

This experiment has been performed on two different datasets, Reuters and 20-newgroups. As shown in Table 3 and Fig. 4 [the curves on the left side], the performance of the classifier when C-GloVe is used for generating the samples' models of Reuters dataset are higher than when GloVe is used, specially when the size of the training set is small. Also, considering 20-newsgroups dataset (Table 4 and 2nd column of Fig. 4), although the performance of GloVe is higher than C-GloVe when the whole dataset is used for training, the performance of C-GloVe is higher than GloVe when less than 40% of samples are used for training. Also, it is shown in this figure that the performance of the classifier for both word embedding methods, i.e. GloVe and C-GloVe, converges to almost the same level as more training samples are used for training

In the second experiment, we found that a combined local and universal model mostly resulted in higher F1-Score then standalone models based on either the local knowledge or the universal knowledge. We also found that integrating different word embedding algorithms could result in higher F1-Score than standalone word embedding algorithms. This experiment was performed on five well-known and recent word embedding algorithms, namely, GloVe, Word2Vec, FastText, USE, ELMO, and C-GloVe that we outline above. To do so, two models were generated based on each word embedding algorithm:

- The Local Word Embedding Model: The word embedding algorithm is trained on a local repository. This experiment has been performed on five different datasets: 20-Newsgroups, Reuters, SUBJ, TREC, and IMDB.
- The Universal Word Embedding Model: The word embedding algorithm is trained on the Wikipedia dataset [19].

Tables 5, 6, 7, 8 and 9 show the F1-Score of the SVM classifier using different combinations of the models on Reuters, 20-Newsgroups, SUBJ, TREC, and IMDB respectively. To illustrate, consider the gray cell in the third row and second column of Table 5. This cell shows the F1-Score of the SVM classifier for when the feature vector of each sample of the Reuters dataset is produced by concatenating the following feature vectors:

- F-L embedder based feature vector: a feature vector which has been generated using a trained FastText model on the local source of knowledge which is Reuters here.
- G-U embedder based feature vector: a feature vector which has been generated by a trained GloVe model on the universal source of knowledge.

Regarding the length of the feature vectors, our experimental results showed that having more than 300 features won't improve dramatically the accuracy of C-GloVe, GloVe, FastText and Word2Vvec, and training will be extremely slow. Therefore, the length of the feature set for these algorithms is set to 300, except if the models of a pair are the same, e.g. (G-L and G-L), in which the length of the feature set is set to 600. Also, the length of the feature set based on USE and ELMO models is 512 and1024 respectively. Table 10 shows the length of the feature set for each pair of models.

Table 5. F1-Score of the SVM classifier using different combinations of the models on Reuters dataset.

	G-L	G-U	F-L	F-U	W-L	W-U	E-L	E-U	C-G-L	U-U
G-L	87	-	-	-	-	-	-	-	-	-
G-U	88	85	-	-	-	-	-	-	-	-
F-L	86	87	85	-	-	-	-	-	-	-
F-U	88	87	88	86	-	-	-	-	-	-
W-L	86	87	85	88	84	-	-	-	-	-
W-U	88	87	87	87	87	84	-	-	-	-
E-L	85	86	86	86	85	86	85	-	-	-
E-U	86	86	86	85	86	85	86	85	-	-
C-G-L	87	88	87	88	87	88	87	86	87	-
U-U	88	86	87	87	86	87	87	85	88	80

Table 6. F1-Score of the SVM classifier using different combinations of the models on 20newsgroups dataset.

	G-L	G-U	F-L	F-U	W-L	W-U	E-L	E-U	C-G-L	U-U
G-L	73	-	-	-	-	-	-	-	-	-
G-U	75	68	-	-	-	-	-	-	-	-
F-L	76	75	73	-	-	-	-	-	-	-
F-U	76	73	77	71	-	-	-	-	-	-
W-L	77	76	76	77	74	-	-	-	-	-
W-U	75	72	76	74	76	69	-	-	-	-
E-L	73	72	73	73	73	73	68	-	-	-
E-U	73	71	74	72	73	69	68	67	-	-
C-G-L	77	76	76	77	76	76	73	73	72	-
U-U	77	73	77	74	76	73	74	71	77	69

Table 7. F1-Score of the SVM classifier using different combinations of the models on the SUBJ dataset.

	G-L	G-U	F-L	F-U	W-L	W-U	E-L	E-U	C-G-L	U-U
G-L	87	-	-	-	-	-	-	-	-	-
G-U	91	91	-	-	-	-	-	-	-	-
F-L	97	98	97	-	-	-	-	-	-	-
F-U	92	91	98	91	-	-	-	-	-	-
W-L	87	91	97	92	75	-	-	-	-	-
W-U	92	91	98	91	90	90	-	-	-	-
E-L	90	91	97	92	89	90	90	-	-	-
E-U	91	92	98	92	91	92	91	91	-	-
C-G-L	88	92	97	92	87	91	91	91	87	-
U-U	95	95	99	95	95	95	93	94	95	95

Table 8. F1-Score of the SVM classifier using different combinations of the models on the TREC dataset.

	G-L	G-U	F-L	F-U	W-L	W-U	E-L	E-U	C-G-L	U-U
G-L	88	-	-	-	-	-	-	-	-	-
G-U	80	89	-	-	-	-	-	-	-	-
F-L	88	79	62	-	-	-	-	-	-	-
F-U	85	83	81	80	-	-	-	-	-	-
W-L	87	79	66	79	56	-	-	-	-	-
W-U	88	81	88	85	88	88	-	-	-	-
E-L	90	91	90	90	90	91	92	-	-	-
E-U	91	90	90	91	90	90	93	94	-	-
C-G-L	91	78	84	84	81	87	89	90	80	-
U-U	94	92	93	94	93	94	92	92	94	95

Table 9. F1-Score of the SVM classifier using different combinations of the models on the IMDB dataset.

	G-L	G-U	F-L	F-U	W-L	W-U	E-L	E-U	C-G-L	U-U
G-L	92	-	-	-	-	-	-	-	-	-
G-U	92	88	-	-	-	-	-	-	-	-
F-L	92	91	90	-	-	-	-	-	-	-
F-U	92	89	91	88	-	-	-	-	-	-
W-L	92	91	91	91	90	-	-	-	-	-
W-U	92	90	91	90	91	90	-	-	-	-
E-L	92	89	91	91	90	91	90	-	-	-
E-U	91	90	91	90	91	91	90	89	-	-
C-G-L	92	90	91	90	91	91	91	90	87	-
U-U	93	91	92	91	92	92	91	91	92	91

Table 10. Length of the feature set for each pair of models

	G-L	G-U	F-L	F-U	W-L	W-U	E-L	E-U	C-G-L	U-U
G-L	600	-	-	-	-	-	-	-	-	-
G-U	600	600	-	-	-	-	-	-	-	-
F-L	600	600	600	-	-	-	-	-	-	-
F-U	600	600	600	600	-	-	-	-	-	-
W-L	600	600	600	600	600	-	-	-	-	-
W-U	600	600	600	600	600	600	-	-	-	-
E-L	1324	1324	1324	1324	1324	1324	1024	-	-	-
E-U	1324	1324	1324	1324	1324	1324	2048	1024	-	-
C-G-L	600	600	600	600	600	600	1324	1324	600	-
U-U	812	812	812	812	812	812	1536	1536	812	512

Looking at these tables, one can observe the following:

- A combined local and universal model, in which both models are based on the same embedding algorithm, mostly resulted in higher F1-Score than each standalone model. In most cases, combinations of different embedding algorithms resulted in the highest F1-Score.
- Considering the combination types (i.e. Local-Local, Local-Universal and Universal-Universal), the combination of type Local-Universal mostly resulted in higher F1-Score than other combinations.
- Considering the F1-Score for each individual model (the diagonal of the above tables), the average improvement of combining the model with either local or universal source of knowledge and integrating different word embedding algorithms over all five datasets is 1.4%, 1.2%, 5.66%, 2.48%, 9.73%, 2.17%, 1.26%, 1%, 3.77%, and 2.26% for G-L, G-U, F-L, F-U, W-L, W-U, E-L, E-U, C-G-L, and U-U respectively.
- Also, considering the F1-Score for each individual model (the diagonal of the above tables), the average improvement of combining the model with the second source of knowledge (i.e. if the source of knowledge for the model is local, the second source of knowledge should be the universal source and vise versa) and integrating different word embedding algorithms over all five datasets is

1.52%, 1.12%, 6.28%, 3.12%, 10.44%, 2.64%, 1.28%, 1.2%, 3.96%, and 2.8% for G-L, G-U, F-L, F-U, W-L, W-U, E-L, E-U, C-G-L, and U-U respectively.

- The last two observations show that integrating different word embedding algorithms will produce higher F1-Score if each algorithm of a pair is trained on a different source of knowledge, i.e. one is trained on a local and the other one is trained on a universal source of knowledge.

5 Conclusion

In this paper we identified a phenomenon, termed inadequacy of knowledge, which manifests in many real-world document classification problems, meaning that the distribution of the repository data and the real-world distribution of classes are rarely equivalent. We also showed that the out-of-vocabulary problem could be considered a subtype of this phenomenon. In this paper, first we addressed the issue of out-of-vocabulary caused by the GloVe embedding algorithm, by training this algorithm on a trigram'ed version of the dataset; a solution which we called C-GloVe. Experimental results on C-GloVe and GloVe showed that the performance of the SVM classifier when C-GloVe is used for generating the samples' models is mostly higher than when GloVe is used, especially when the size of the training set is small. Also, to mitigate the IoK problem, we proposed to combine local and universal sources of knowledge and to integrate different word embedding algorithms. Our Experiments showed that a combined model always resulted in higher performance than both a standalone source of knowledge and a standalone word embedding algorithm. It's also observed that integrating different word embedding algorithms will produce higher F1-Score if each algorithm of a pair is trained on a different source of knowledge, i.e. one is trained on a local and the other one is trained on a universal source of knowledge. In this way, the experimental results showed average of 1.52%, 1.12%, 6.28%, 3.12%, 10.44%, 2.64%, 1.28%, 1.2%, 3.96%, and 2.8% improvement for G-L, G-U, F-L, F-U, W-L, W-U, E-L, E-U, C-G-L, and U-U respectively. In these terms, the last letters L and U mean if an embedding algorithm is trained on a Local or a Universal source of knowledge respectively. Also, G, F, W, C-G, E and U stand for GloVe, Fast-Text, Word2Vec, C-GloVe, ELMO and Universal sentence encoder algorithms respectively.

References

1. Bengio, Y., Ducharme, R., Vincent, P., & Jauvin, C.. "A neural probabilistic language model." Journal of machine learning research 3.Feb 1137-1155 (2003)
2. Mnih, Andriy, and Geoffrey Hinton. "Three new graphical models for statistical language modelling." Proceedings of the 24th international conference on Machine learning. ACM, , pp. 641-648, Corvallis, OR, USA (2007)

3. Collobert, Ronan, and Jason Weston. "A unified architecture for natural language processing: Deep neural networks with multitask learning." Proceedings of the 25th international conference on Machine learning. ACM, pp. 160-167, New York, NY, USA (2008).
4. Turian, Joseph, Lev Ratinov, and YoshuaBengio. "Word representations: a simple and general method for semi-supervised learning." Proceedings of the 48th annual meeting of the association for computational linguistics. Association for Computational Linguistics, pp. 384-394, Uppsala, Sweden (2010).
5. Dhillon, Paramveer, Dean P. Foster, and Lyle H. Ungar. "Multi-view learning of word embeddings via cca." Advances in neural information processing systems. pp. 199-207 (2011).
6. Huang, Po-Sen, Xiaodong He, Jianfeng Gao, Li Deng, Alex Acero, and Larry Heck. "Learning deep structured semantic models for web search using clickthrough data." Proceedings of the 22nd ACM international conference on Conference on information & knowledge management. ACM, pp. 2333-2338, San Francisco, CA, USA (2013).
7. Mikolov, T., Sutskever, I., Chen, K., Corrado, G. S., & Dean, J. "Distributed representations of words and phrases and their compositionality." Advances in neural information processing systems. pp. 3111-3119 (2013).
8. Paulheim, Heiko. "Knowledge graph refinement: A survey of approaches and evaluation methods." Semantic web 8(3) pp. 489-508 (2017).
9. Cheng, Y., Chen, K., Sun, H., Zhang, Y., & Tao, F. "Data and knowledge mining with big data towards smart production." Journal of Industrial Information Integration 9, pp. 1-13 (2018).
10. Pennington, Jeffrey, Richard Socher, and Christopher Manning. "Glove: Global vectors for word representation." Proceedings of the 2014 conference on empirical methods in natural language processing (EMNLP). pp. 1532-1543, Doha, Qatar (2014).
11. Mikolov, T., Chen, K., Corrado, G., & Dean, J.a. "Efficient estimation of word representations in vector space." arXiv preprint arXiv:1301.3781 (2013).
12. Bojanowski, P., Grave, E., Joulin, A., & Mikolov, T. "Enriching word vectors with subword information." Transactions of the Association for Computational Linguistics 5, pp. 135-146 (2017).
13. Peters, M. E., Neumann, M., Iyyer, M., Gardner, M., Clark, C., Lee, K., &Zettlemoyer, L. (2018). Deep contextualized word representations. arXiv preprint arXiv:1802.05365.
14. Cer, D., Yang, Y., Kong, S. Y., Hua, N., Limtiaco, N., John, R. S., Sung, Y. H. (2018). Universal sentence encoder. arXiv preprint arXiv:1803.11175.
15. K Qazanfari, A Youssef, "Contextual Feature Weighting Using Knowledge beyond the Repository Knowledge", International Journal of Computer and Communication Engineering 7 (3), pp. 45-57, (2018).
16. K. Qazanfari, and A. Youssef. "Document Clustering Using Local and Universal Knowledge." International Conference on Machine Learning and Data Mining in Pattern Recognition. Springer, New York, NY, USA (2018).
17. T. Joachims. “A probabilistic analysis of the Rocchio algorithm with TFIDF for text categorization”, Computer Science Technical Report CMU-CS-96-118. Carnegie Mellon University, (1996)
18. D.Lewis, Reuters-21578, Distribution 1.0, 1987
19. https://dumps.wikimedia.org/enwiki/20181001/
20. B. Pang and L. Lee. A sentimental education: Sentiment analysis using subjectivity summarization based on minimum cuts. In Proceedings of the 42nd annual meeting on Association for Computational Linguistics, page 271. Association for Computational Linguistics, 2004

21. E. M. Voorhees and D. M. Tice. Building a question answering test collection. In Proceedings of the 23rd annual international ACM SIGIR conference on Research and development in information retrieval, pp. 200–207. ACM, (2000)
22. Maas, A. L., Daly, R. E., Pham, P. T., Huang, D., Ng, A. Y., & Potts, C. "Learning word vectors for sentiment analysis." Proceedings of the 49th annual meeting of the association for computational linguistics: Human language technologies-volume 1. Association for Computational Linguistics, pp. 142-150, Portland, Oregon (2011).

A Hybrid Model on Learning Cross Features for Transaction Fraud Detection

Han Wu and Guanjun Liu

Department of Computer Science, Tongji University, Shanghai, China
{wuhan2017,liuguanjun}@tongji.edu.cn

Abstract. Feature engineering is one of the important factors to produce an effective prediction model using a machine learning method. For transaction fraud detection models, their feature engineering was often manual based on expertise and experience, which is not only time-consuming and laborious but also loses many predictive cross features since the transaction data is discrete, sparse and high-dimensional. Therefore, it is necessary and meaningful to automatically learn cross features from complex data. In this paper, we propose an embedding-based hybrid method to learn cross features for fraud prediction. With the design of embedding, we use DNN (Deep Neural Network) to automatically learn the implicit cross features and GBDT (Gradient Boosting Decision Tree) to extract the explicit cross features from the raw data. We then combine them into a new feature vector as the input of LR (Logistic Regression) and finally produce a prediction model for transaction fraud detection. A set of experiments on two real transaction datasets show that our method outperforms nine state-of-the-art ones.

Keywords: Finance · Transaction fraud detection · Machine learning · Feature mining · Deep Neural Network · Gradient Boosting Decision Tree

1 Introduction

E-commerce and mobile finance have boosted the economic development and brought convenience to people. However, transaction fraud events occur frequently and result in a lot of losses for companies or individuals [1]. Therefore, it is essential to establish an online monitoring system in order to judge the risk of every transaction and prevent the occurrence of high-risk transactions.

The current popular methods are data-driven rules that can utilize supervised learning models to learn the features from all previous labelled transactions, and then mathematically determine the possibility of a standard fraudulent transaction. These models including Logistic Regression (LR) [1], Support Vector Machine (SVM) [2], and Random Forests (RF) [3] are often used. However,

[1] David Roberson. The Nilson Report on Historical Non-Cash Payment. (2016/10/07).https://nilsonreport.com/upload/content_promo/The_Nilson_Report_10-172016.pdf

these early models only used the original transaction information as their input, such as amount, location, and equipment number. It is challenging for them to model highly variable and heterogeneous patterns since they ofen require costly development, maintenance, and revision of handcrafted features. At present, a relatively effective method is to construct some aggregated statistical features of users within a time interval so as to describe users' spending habits [4].

Such a feature construction is still not enough, because it only depicts the spending habits of a user at the individual level. Some cross features are also necessary to more accurately distinguish legal and fraud transactions. Cross features refer to the cartesian product of categorical features. For example, the two raw feature fields (age, education background) can be transformed to several 2-order cross features after cartesian product between different feature values, e.g. (old people, junior high school graduate degree) and (youth, master degree). These cross features are very useful and distinctive accordding to data analysis for different consumer groups. However, it is hard for those manual designs to capture the subtle, high-order and predictive cross featuress hidden behind fraud behaviours, especially in a high-dimensional feature space. Moreover, there is no doubt that this is a time-consuming and laborious operation, relying on a large amount of prior knowledge. Without a proper understanding of the business, this is likely to backfire, since it possibly introduces a lot of irrelevant noise features so that the performance of the model becomes worse.

In recent years, Neural Networks (NN) have achieved remarkable success in many fields such as computer vision, speech, and natural language processing [5]. Literature [1] shows that deep neural networks (DNN) are of a good performance for fraud detection under a feasible number of parameters. These successful applications have established the effectiveness of DNN-based feature learning that involves pattern extraction from unstructured tabular data collected in transactions logs [6]. One of the biggest advantages of NN are that the specific representation is calculated autonomously and representation or feature learning also improves the capacity of a model to extract unseen patterns that are not well represented in the raw data, which is a major problem for other data-driven models [6].

Deep learning is more like a black box, however, due to its highly non-linear properties. We hardly understand the meaning of the parameters in a NN and its importance with very solid basis of statistical hypothesis [7]. For the problem of fraud detection, it is not completely enough to ensure that these feature representation can reveal the correlation between the raw feature and the target. Moreover, we believe it is crucial to supercharge a fraud detection system with informative reasons like the cross feature (age, education background). Thus the following questions are important: (1) How to effectively extract those explicit cross features so as to distinguish legal and fraud transactions more accurately? (2) How to estimate feature-label score in an explainable way? (3) How to integrate these cross features with the powerful NN?

Our Contribution: We combine the strong feature representation ability of NN with the tree-based model that can automatically extract cross features.

Therefore, we can get interpretable higher-order feature representations with strong predictability. In the gradient boosted decision trees (GBDT) part of our hybrid model, we use the stage-wise learning to extract richer and more complex features and introduce a multi-level architecture. There is a factorization machine (FM) [8] over the GBDT [9] to learn higher order and deeper interpretable cross features, integrating the attention mechanism to make feature presentation more robust.

Additionally, we face a huge search space that makes model training time-consuming extremely. For example, in our experiment on Ant dataset (see Section 3), every record contains 299 fields (attributes) and then can be encoded into more than 1 millon features. Obviously, it is very difficult to process these high-dimensional and high-volume data from the perspectives of the usefulness of features and the feasibility of computation. Thus the challenge relies on how to encode and represent cross features instead of the traditional approach such as one-hot encoding [8].

The embedding design is popular in natural language processing and NN to learn word vectors [10], and it is also applicable to other entities apart from words [11] such as users and items [12]. We use the embedding design to map discrete, sparse and high-dimensional categorical features into low-dimensional dense vectors, aiming to learn cross features from raw data effectively. It provides us an efficient parameter estimation for the sparse and high-dimensional data and guarantees the effectiveness of capturing the relations among features in a low feature vector space.

In this paper we propose a deep learning based transaction fraud detection approach for the high-dimensional and sparse data generated in electronic transactions. The embedding-based network combines two components: one is DNN that is based on embedding representations of categorical features and can learn non-linear, high-order cross features, and another is GBDT that can mine those interpretable and explicit cross features. High order features are learned by FM. An attention network is also incorporated in order to learn robust representations. The proposed method is a supervised end-to-end classification model. The experiments on two real financial datasets demonstrate a good performance.

2 Hybrid Model

In this section, we describe the overall structure of our hybrid model. As depicted in Fig.1, it consists of two parts: the GBDT part and the DNN part. They are followed by a final layer which combines the outputs from the two parts. The final estimated target of the hybrid model is:

$$\hat{y} = \rho\left(\widehat{y}_{\overline{GBDT}} + \widehat{y}_{\overline{DNN}}\right) \tag{1}$$

where $\widehat{y}_{\overline{DNN}}$ and $\widehat{y}_{\overline{GBDT}}$ are the outputs of DNN and GBDT parts, respectively. ρ is the sigmoid function.

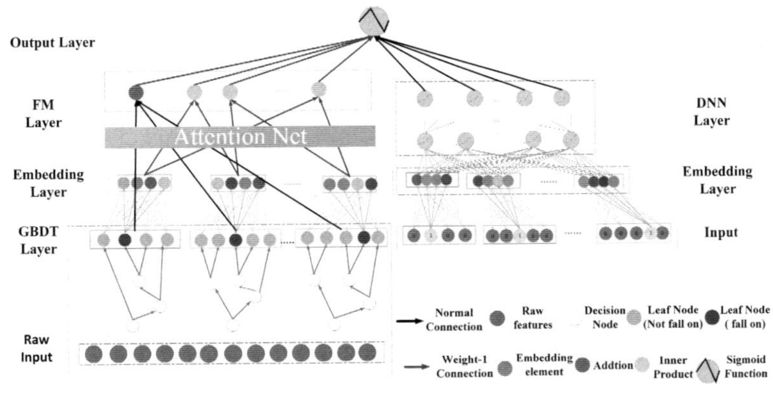

Fig. 1: **The structure of our Hybrid model**

2.1 Embedding layer

We assume that our data $D = \{(x_i, y_i)\}$ consists of n labelled samples. Each sample has m features, $x_i \in \mathbb{R}^m$, and label $y_i \in \{0, 1\}$ indicates whether a transaction is fraudulent. The raw input feature can be classified into two types: continuous features (e.g., age, transaction amount) and categorical features (e.g., gender, transaction location). Continuous features can be input into the model directly. Typically, each categorical feature is encoded as a group of one-hot vectors. For example, one transaction record $[user\_id = a101, gender = male, ..., organization = tju, city = shanghai]$ is usually transformed into a high-dimensional space feature vector via the field-aware one-hot encoding:

$$\underbrace{[0,1,0,0,...,0,0]}_{user\_id}\ \underbrace{[0,1]}_{gender}\ ...\ \underbrace{[0,1,0,...,0,0]}_{organization}\ \underbrace{[0,0,1,...,0,0]}_{city}$$

Obviously, the above multi-field binary vector space is huge. Therefore, we employ the embedding layer to project them into a dense, low-dimensional real-value feature space:

$$e_i = W_{embed,i} x_i \tag{2}$$

where $e_i \in \mathbb{R}^{n_e}$ is the embedding vector of the i-th field binary input $x_i \in \mathbb{R}^m$, and $W_{embed,i} \in \mathbb{R}^{n_e \times n_v}$ is the parameter matrix of the corresponding embedding layer which will be optimized during the training process as well as the whole network. n_e and n_v are the embedding size and vocabulary size, respectively.

The specific transformation process is shown in Fig.1. Actually, we only need to consider the embedding vectors for the non-zero features in the multi-field binary input. This can greatly reduce computation cost.

The raw high-dimensional and sparse input features are finally transformed into a dense concatenated vector:

$$e = [e_1, e_2, ..., e_m] \tag{3}$$

where m denotes the number of fields in the raw feature space. It is worth mentioning that even though the lengths of one-hot vectors for different fields are different, the lengths of their embedding vectors are the same: $n_e \times m$.

2.2 GBDT Part

The prior work by Facebook [13] feeds the leaf nodes of GBDT into an LR model. The cross features extracted by GBDT have the following four advantages besides of saving a lot of manual work: (1) high-order and unobservable, (2) interpretable and explicit by nature, (3) strongly predictive for the last prediction under the mechanism of decision tree, and (4) for continuous features, the optimal segmentation point can be selected automatically and the nonlinear relation is introduced at the same time. It avoids a lot of work that would be done with prior knowledge. For example, the feature (age), as a continuous feature, is divided into the young and the old after data statistics and analysis.

We denote the structure of a decision tree model as Q, and the i-th leaf node as N_i. Fig.2 shows the structure of decision trees: each decision node in white refers to $[x_t < v_t]$ or $[x_t = v_t]$ that divides samples into two part. For continuous features (e.g., age), a decision node chooses the most appropriate threshold [14] v_t to split the features into $[x_t < v_t]$ and $[x_t \geq v_t]$. For categorical features, it determines whether the feature equals to a certain value, e.g., $[x_t = v_t]$ or $[x_t \neq v_t]$. Each leaf node has a score ω_i, representing the prediction value of the corresponding decision tree.

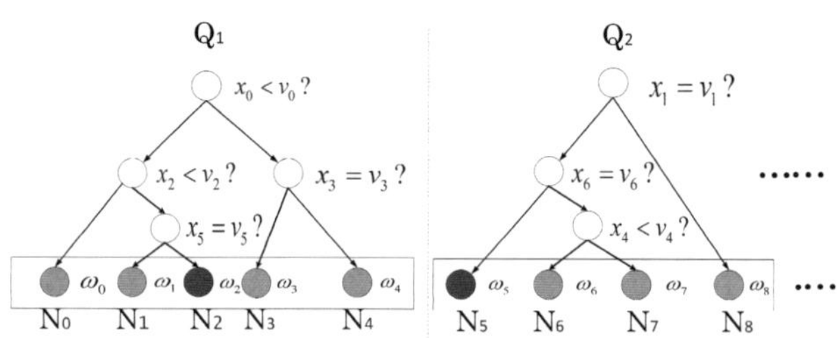

Fig. 2: **The structure of GBDT (with two subtrees).**

A path from the root node to a leaf node represents a decision rule on the splitting features along the path and also indicates a cross feature. For example, the leaf node N_2 in Fig.2 represents cross feature $[x_0 < v_0]$ & $[x_2 \geq v_2]$ & $[x_5 \neq v_5]$.

Every leaf node categorize samples as much as possible, therefore, tree-based models are inherently self-explanatory and a path from the root to a leaf node can be considered as the most prominent cross feature for prediction under this splitting mechanism.

A single decision tree with complex data generally falls into the problem of insufficient generalization. GBDT can settle this problem in an ensemble fashion. Specifically, GBDT uses a boosting strategy to train multiple trees iteratively and minimize the loss in each iteration. In each iteration, the ensemble trees give each sample a prediction, which is the sum of the scores of all created subtrees. Then all samples are re-labelled with the corresponding difference between the prediction and the original label, which can pay more attention to those samples with poor predictions. Thus, a new decision tree trained in the next iteration can try to correct the previous error. As a result, GBDT can make more accurate predictions [9]. Formally, after the t-th round iteration, the objective function is as follows:

$$\ell^t = \sum_{i=1}^{n} \ell\left(y_i, y_i^{t-1} + f_t(x_i)\right) \tag{4}$$

where the subtree generated in the t-th iteration is represented as a function $f_t \in \Gamma$ and $\Gamma = \left\{ f\left(x\right) = \omega_{Q_{(x)}} \right\}$. $Q_{(x)}$ represents the tree structure that maps a sample x to the index of the corresponding leaf node, and the score of the decision tree is ω. The final prediction function is in the form of an additive function with a learning rate η_t:

$$\hat{y} = \sum_{t=1}^{T} \eta_t \cdot f_t\left(x\right) \tag{5}$$

Therefore, when a new tree is built, the remaining features are used to optimize the prediction results and seek more explicit cross features for a better final prediction. Thus it is reasonable to think that all leaf nodes in GBDT trees represent more useful and in-depth cross features.

In our application, we employ the GBDT to learned not only some simple cross-over features such as (Transaction Completed Time=03:00a.m.; Transaction amount=10k$), also learned such characteristics as (Transaction Completed Location=Kunming, Account Registration Location=Shanghai, Transaction Amount=10k$, Account Balance = 10.5k$, Merchant Tag=Virtual&electronics), which is complex and difficult to construct manually. But they are helpful for evaluating a risky transaction.

Use GBDT to Extract Explicit Cross Features Therefore, the speciality of this design is that every single tree can be considered as a categorical feature field, and the index value of the leaf node in which a sample falls can be taken as the feature value of the sample. Given a sample x, iteratively generating multiple decision trees means multiple such categorical features, and thus all of them can form a new feature vector :

$$q = \left[Q_1\left(x\right), Q_2\left(x\right), Q_3\left(x\right), \ldots, Q_T\left(x\right)\right]$$

Normally, we express q as a binary vector transformed by the one-hot encoding. For example, as depicted in Fig.2, if the sample x falls into the third leaf node of the first tree and into the first leaf node of the second tree respectively, then the corresponding new feature vector is:

$$[\underbrace{0,0,1,0,0}_{Q_1}\underbrace{1,0,0,0}_{Q_2},\ldots,\underbrace{\ldots\ldots}_{Q_T}]$$

Use Attention Net to Identify Key Cross Features and Use FM to Mine More Cross Features Using new features to fit a linear model is to learn the weights of these cross features or rules of dividing samples essentially. He et al. [13] built a model in this way and took a global weighting mechanism. The newly transformed features are directly put into LR for prediction. However, the contribution of different cross features to the final prediction should be different. Therefore, their method can be improve since the weights of these cross features are all identical in their method. A cross feature with a high predictive power should be assigned a higher weight before it is fed into LR.

We use Attention Network [15] to learn an attention score for each embedding field of the whole embedding vector in order to select those useful cross features. Let $q = \{q_1, q_2, \ldots, q_n\}$, $q_i \in \mathbb{R}^{1 \times n_e}$, be a set of features. First of all, we feed each element of this embedding vector into a fully connected layer, which is followed by a ReLU layer for activations. The bias term is dropped for simplcity. The output of the activation function is a set of learnt attention activations:

$$\mathrm{C} = \{c_1, c_2, ..., c_T\}, \qquad c_i = \mathrm{Re}LU\left(q_i W_{attention}\right) \tag{6}$$

where $q_i \in \mathbb{R}^{1 \times n_e}$, $c_i \in \mathbb{R}^{1 \times n_e}$, and $W_{attention} \in \mathbb{R}^{n_e \times n_e}$ denotes the weight matrix of the hidden layer.

Secondly, we choose softmax as the normalizaion operation across all the elements of the embedding vector, computing a set of attention scores $S = \{s_1, s_2, ..., s_N\}$:

$$s_i = \left[{s_i}^1, {s_i}^2, {s_i}^3, ..., {s_i}^D\right], \quad {s_i}^d = \frac{\exp\left(c_i^d\right)}{\sum\limits_{i=1}^{n_e} \exp(c_i^d)} \tag{7}$$

where ${c_i}^d$ is the d-th entry of c_i.

Thirdly, the calculated attention scores S are multiplied by the corresponding original embedding vector q and then generate a new set of weighted features: $O = \{o_1, o_2, ..., o_T\}$, where

$$o_i = q_i \cdot s_i \tag{8}$$

The above is the attention mechanism to capture the different importance of cross features for prediction by assigning attention scores for each element of the embedding vector. In addition, since these cross features almost are low-order, we still need to explore the cross features in a higher level. Next step, we feed these new features into FM to get higher-level cross features.

As shown in Fig.1, real-valued embedding vectors are transformaed into a new feature vector $O \in \mathbb{R}^T$, where T denotes the numbers of trees.

As a linear model, FM is often used to learn the pair-wise cross features. This limits its ability of feature representation. With transformed input of GBDT, it is feasible for FM to learn non-linear relationships and complex patterns in real-world transaction data. Then the FM layer learns pari-wise cross features in the way of inner product of each pair of embedding vectors [8]:

$$\hat{y}_{GBDT} = w_0 + \sum_{i=1}^{n} w_i o_i + \sum_{i=1}^{n} \sum_{j=i+1}^{n} < V_i, V_j > o_i o_j \tag{9}$$

where $\hat{y}_{GBDT}$ is the output of the GBDT part, w_0 is the global bias, and w_i is the weight of the one-order features transformed by GBDT. $< V_i, V_j >$ denotes the pair-wise (2-order) cross features, where $V_i \in \mathbb{R}^{n_e}$ and n_e is the size of embedding vectors. These 2-order factorized interactions represents higher level of implicit cross features.

2.3 DNN Part

In the DNN part, its inputs are the embedding vectors transformed from the original features. As shown in Fig.1, the dense field-aware embedding vectors are fed into the hidden layers in order to capture the implicit and highly nonlinear cross features.

We denote an embedding vector as $e = [e_1, e_2, ..., e_m]$. Then the output of each fully-connected layer is:

$$x_1 = \alpha(W^1 e + b_1) \tag{10}$$

$$x_l = \alpha(W^l x_{l-1} + b_l) \tag{11}$$

$$\hat{y}_{DNN} = \alpha(W^L x_{L-1} + b_L) \tag{12}$$

α is an activation function such as ReLU and Tanh. l is the layer depth. x_l and x_{l-1} are the outputs of the l-th and $(l-1)$-th hidden layers, respectively. b_l is the bias of the l-th layer. W_l is the parameter matrix for the l-th layer. L is the number of hidden layers.

2.4 Combination layer

GBDT part and DNN part can be complementary since the former focuses on explicit cross features and the latter on implicit cross features. Our hybrid model combine the two parts. The final estimated target of the hybrid model is:

$$p = \rho\left(\widehat{y}_{GBDT} + \widehat{y}_{DNN}\right) \tag{13}$$

where $\widehat{y}_{DNN}$ and $\widehat{y}_{GBDT}$ are the outputs of DNN part and GBDT part, respectively. ρ is the sigmoid function. The objective function is the sum of the loss function and the regularization term:

$$\ell = -\frac{1}{N} \sum_{i=1}^{N} y_i \log(p_i) + (1 - y_i) \log(1 - p_i) + \lambda \sum_{t} \|w_l\|^2 \tag{14}$$

where p_i is the prediction probability of the i-th sample computed by Equation 13, N is the number of all the trained samples, λ is the L2 regularization parameter, and w denotes all the parameters in the model.

3 Expriment and Result

The main contribution of our work is to produce a predication model for fraud detection in e-commerce based on the above cross features in a huge, multiple-discrete and sparse feature space. In this section, we illustrate a series of experiments done on a public dataset and a private one, respectively. We answer the following questions:

1. Q1: whether GBDT part has a positive effect on the overall performance of the model?
2. Q2: Can our hybrid model get a competitive performance compared with the state-of-the-art supervised learning methods of fraud detection?
3. Q3: How do hyper-parameter settings affect the performance of the model?

3.1 Datasets

We conduct experiments in the following two data sets and Table 1 shows the statistics of the two data sets. We divide the data set into training set and test set in a ratio of 8 to 2. Note that these data have been desensitized.

Table 1: Statistics of the evaluation datasets

Datasets	Instances	Fields	features(sparse)
Ant	0.99M	299	1.1M
Bank	5.12M	64	170K

1. Ant Financial Service Group Dataset[2]: Ant Financial Service Group is a company that provides online payment services. This open dataset contains about one million labelled transaction records and each record has 299 features. For simplicity, we call it Ant dataset.
2. Dataset from a financial company in China: Through cooperation with the company, the company provides us about 5 million transaction records including user demographics, transaction behaviour records, and context features. The dataset is mostly composed of categorical features. For simplicity, we call it Bank dataset.

[2] ATEC ant developer competition: https://dc.cloud.alipay.com/

3.2 Expriment Settings

Evaluation Metrics We use four common evaluation indicators: **recall**, **precision**, **F1 score** and **AUC**. Positive corresponds to Fraud cases and Negative corresponds to legal ones.

Sampling strategy Fraud detection is a typical sample class imbalance problem [1][16], a high degree of imbalance between the minority class (fraudulent transactions) and the majority class (legal transactions). We use a simple down-sampling method [17] to obtain the samples from the majority class, so that the ratio of positive and negative samples is about 20:1.

Model Comparison We compare our model with the most commonly used machine learning methods in the industry such as LR, SVM, FM and DNN. Two tree-based models are also used: RF and GBDT. GBDT2LR, GBDT+NN, and Deepfm are also used. For those classical machine learning algorithms, the state-of-the-art feature engineering [4] be performed first and then input them to the model for the binary classification. All models are fine-tuned using grid search. We employ equivalent hyper-parameter searches for all methods.

1. embedding2DNN: We use embedding vector as its input in order to testify whether our GBDT part can improve the overall performance. We set the dimension of the embedding vector from 5 to 30, which is the same as the hybrid model. As for other parameters in DNN part: the number of hidden layers is from 1 to 4, and the number of neural nodes in each layer is from 32 to 256. The learning rate is from 0.0001 to 0.001. For each parameter, we set up early stopping to avoid overfitting. We choose ReLU as the activation function. For fairness, our model and other deep models share the same settings with grid search.
2. GBDT2LR[13]: We first train a GBDT on the whole training dataset using LightGBM, then convert a real-valued feature vector into a binary-valued vector and lastly feed them into LR for final prediction without embedding.
3. GBDT+NN: We remove the upper part of the GBDT part of our hybrid model. The purpose of this comparison model is to verify that FM and attention mechanisms extract richer features and improve the performance of overall model, rather than redundant structures.
4. Deepfm [18]: This model is the state-of-the-art embedding-based model. It applies DNN to learn cross features automatically and uses FM to learn low-order cross features. However, the cross features generated by this model lack a high-level interpretability. Therefore, the aim of comparing this method with ours is to show the usefulness of high-level interpretable cross features.
5. Our Hybrid Model: Our hybrid model is basically implemented with tensorflow[19], and the GBDT part is implemented via LightGBM. For the data preprocessing, the continuous features of the original features is normalized through mean removal and variance scaling. For the optimization method, we apply the Adam [20] with a mini-batch size of 2048, and Batch normalization is

also used for the optimization of deep networks. We use L2 Regularization to avoid overfitting of deep networks.

3.3 Performance Comparision

Table 1 stand for the best results on testing data after the hyperparameter tuning. We use cross-validation on training data and the parameters with the best performance are selected. For Q1, we want to figure out whether the GBDT part and FM layer can improve the overall performance, respectively. Therefore, we compare our model with embedding2DNN and GBDT+NN. As shown in Table 2, the predictions based on these implicit features are quite competitive but not as good as our hybrid model. Furthermore, the GBDT+DNN model without FM layer and attention mechanism yields much better results than the embedding2DNN model, but less than our hybrid model since our model uses the FM layer. **In summary, explainable and explicit cross features transformed by GBDT are helpful for prediction in a high-dimensional and sparse feature space. The FM layer and attention does further enrich the representation of these cross features.**

Table 2: Performance Comparison on Ant and Bank respectively

	Ant				*Bank*			
	R(%)	*P*(%)	*F*1(%)	*AUC*(%)	*R*(%)	*P*(%)	*F*1(%)	*AUC*(%)
LR	53.3	41.3	46.5	66.1	62.1	71.3	66.3	70.1
SVM	59.3	65.1	62.1	41.6	73.1	71.4	67.2	60.3
FM	67.6	42.4	52.1	55.3	73.6	39.3	51.2	67.2
RF	74.5	70.3	72.3	70.3	87.3	70.9	78.2	77.1
GBDT	74.4	76.1	75.2	71.0	80.5	69.3	74.5	74.9
embedding2DNN	72.1	78.5	75.2	66.1	86.0	49.7	63.0	65.1
GBDT2LR	76.9	74.6	75.7	70.8	78.1	70.0	73.8	76.3
Deepfm	73.5	78.9	76.1	72.9	92.4	78.8	85.6	79.0
GBDT+NN	77.8	83.2	80.7	73.4	92.1	80.7	86.0	79.6
Our Model	**78.5**	**84.1**	**81.2**	**73.8**	**93.2**	**83.6**	**88.1**	**80.1**

Q2 is that whether our method is competitive compared to the commonly used supervised learning methods for fraud detection. As shown in Table 2, our model has achieved the best results. Compared with Deepfm that is the state-of-the-art embedding-based model to learn cross features, our model achieves a better performance on both Ant dataset and Bank dataset. Meanwhile, we have the following observations:

We classified the representarion of cross features into four types: high-order, low-order, explicit and implicit. The more types are considered, the better performance is obtained for a model. Learning more comprehensive cross features can lead to more abundant feature representation and more accurate predictions. This observation is from the fact that FM (which only models low-order cross features explicitly) and DNN (which only models high-order cross features implicitly) obtain lower performance than GBDT+DNN and our Hybrid model (since GBDT+DNN and Hybrid model can learn not only implicit and explicit cross features but also extract high-order and low-order ones). The features learned by Deepfm include low-order and high-order ones, but all are implicit and unexplained. Obviously, the performance of Deepfm is lower than GBDT+DNN and ours.

3.4 Hyper-Parameter Study (Q3)

In this section, we review the effects of different hyper-parameter settings to the performance of our hybrid model.

Hyper-Parameter in DNN part For the DNN part, hyper parameters includes (1) activation functions; (2) the number of neurons per layer; and (3) the number of hidden layers.

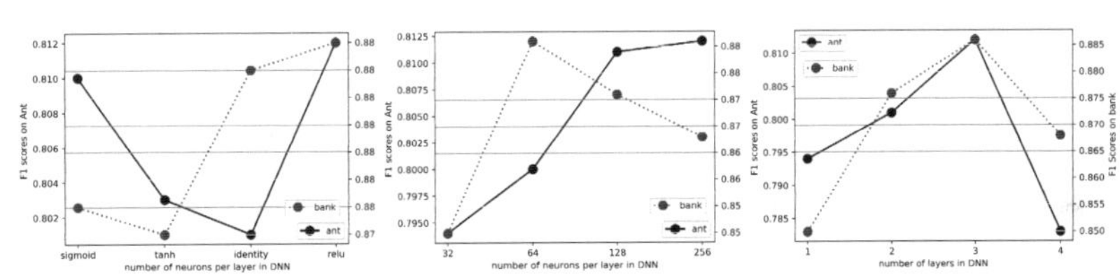

(a) Activation units. (b) Number of neurons. (c) Number of layers.

Fig. 3: F1 Scores comparison of different hyper-parameters for DNN part

Activation Function: Activation functions play an important role in learning and understanding the complex and non-linear functions. We use four different activation functions including sigmoid, tanh, identity, and ReLU to figure out which activation function works best. As shown in Fig.3 (a), ReLU is best for the DNN part.

The number of neurons per layer: When increasing the number of neurons per layer and keeping the other settings unchanged, we find the following phenomenon, as shown in 3 (b): for the performance on the Ant dataset, the generalization ability of our model is improved gradually. However, on the Bank dataset, setting 40 neurons per layer would bring the performance to the peak, but the performance gradually declined after that. The reason is that the characteristics of the two data sets are different: the data structure of the Ant dataset is more complex than that of the Bank dataset. The increased number of neurons per layer satisfies the requirement of Ant dataset for more powerful expression and represents more complex dependencies. But for the Bank dataset, it is a step towards overfitting.

The number of hidden layers: Fig.3 (c) shows the impact of the number of hidden layers. The performance changes on the two datasets are quite similar. The performance of our model is enhanced with the the increasing of depth of the network. However, when the network depth is greater than 3, the performance of the model decreases. Therefore, 3 is a more suitable setting for the depth of the neural network.

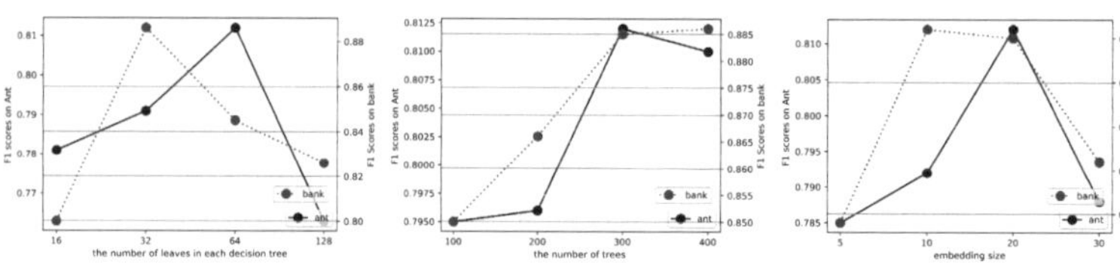

(a) Number of leaves. (b) Number of trees. (c) Embedding Size

Fig. 4: F1 Scores comparison of different hyper-parameters for the GBDT part

Hyper-Parameters in GBDT part In the GBDT part, we measure the impact of different hyper-parameters in GBDT by the predictive results of the whole hybrid model, including: (1) the number of leaves in each decision tree, (2) the number of the tree, and (3) the embedding size. We conduct experiments by using the best settings for the DNN part while changing the settings for the GBDT part.

The number of leaves in each decision tree: Adding the number of leaves in each tree means enriching the information contained in the newly transformed features, but meanwhile make the new feature vector more sparse. The number of leaves in each decision tree has a huge impact on overall performance, as shown in Fig.4(a): the difference between the best and worst performance on the Bank dataset (resp. the Ant dataset) is eight percentage points (resp. five percentage points). Different tree structures greatly affect how we get information from the original data through the tree. Therefore, this is a key hyper-parameter that determines the overall performance.

The number of the tree: The number of trees in the GBDT part represents how many new feature fields are transformed by GBDT and how much predictive information are extracted from data. From Fig.4(b), we can see that as the number increases, the performance on Ant dataset slightly increases. Using a small learning rate with a large number of trees can enhance the accuracy slightly. However, it has to spend a large amount of time. For the performance on Bank dataset, when the tree number exceeds the optimal setting (300), the F1 Score drops sharply, which should suffer from the overfitting problem.

Impact of Embedding Size We set four different values for the embedding size. The results are shown in Fig.4(c). It has a huge impact to our hybrid model. Expanding the embedding size, the model has a more powerful representation to learn cross features. However, a too long embedding size possibly causes overfitting and lows the performance of the model.

4 Conclusion

In this paper, we propose an embedding-based hybrid method to solve the prediction problem in the field of transaction fraud detection. Our method makes full use of the effectiveness of the embedding-based design, the strong generalization ability of neural networks, and the explainability of tree-based models in order to learn various types of cross features. It is good at dealing with those high-dimensional sparse electronic transaction data. To the best of our knowledge, we first propose this hybrid method for the transaction fraud detection and obtain a good performance.

Acknowledgment

Authors would like to thank reviewers for their constructive comments and also thank Professor C.J. Jiang for his help of experiments. The paper was supported by the National Nature Science Foundation of China (grant no. 61572360) and Shanghai Shuguang Program (grant no. 15SG18). G.J. Liu is the corresponding author.

References

1. S. Bhattacharyya, S. Jha, K. Tharakunnel, and J. C. Westland, "Data mining for credit card fraud: A comparative study," *Decision Support Systems*, vol. 50, no. 3, pp. 602–613, 2011.
2. N. Cristianini and Shawe-Taylor, *An introduction to support vector machines and other kernel-based learning methods*. Cambridge University Press, 2000.
3. S. Xuan, G. Liu, Z. Li, L. Zheng, S. Wang, and C. Jiang, "Random forest for credit card fraud detection," in *2018 IEEE 15th International Conference on Networking, Sensing and Control (ICNSC) ,Zhuhai, China*, 2018, pp. 1–6.
4. C. Whitrow, D. J. Hand, P. Juszczak, D. Weston, and N. M. Adams, "Transaction aggregation as a strategy for credit card fraud detection," *Data Mining & Knowledge Discovery*, vol. 18, no. 1, pp. 30–55, 2009.
5. Y. Lecun, Y. Bengio, and G. Hinton, "Deep learning." *Nature*, vol. 521, no. 7553, p. 436, 2015.
6. Y. Bengio *et al.*, "Learning deep architectures for ai," *Foundations and trends® in Machine Learning*, vol. 2, no. 1, pp. 1–127, 2009.

7. A. Oztekin, D. Delen, A. Turkyilmaz, and S. Zaim, "A machine learning-based usability evaluation method for elearning systems," *Decision Support Systems*, vol. 56, pp. 63–73, 2013.
8. S. Rendle, "Factorization machines," in *IEEE International Conference on Data Mining, Sydney, NSW*, 2011, pp. 995–1000.
9. J. H. Friedman, "Greedy function approximation: a gradient boosting machine," *Annals of Statistics, Vol. 29, No. 5*, pp. 1189–1232, 2001.
10. T. Mikolov, K. Chen, G. Corrado, and J. Dean, "Efficient estimation of word representations in vector space," *arXiv preprint arXiv:1301.3781*, 2013.
11. G. Cheng and F. Berkhahn, "Entity embeddings of categorical variables," 2016.
12. O. Barkan and N. Koenigstein, "Item2vec: neural item embedding for collaborative filtering," in *Machine Learning for Signal Processing (MLSP), 2016 IEEE 26th International Workshop on.* IEEE, 2016, pp. 1–6.
13. X. He, J. Pan, O. Jin, T. Xu, B. Liu, T. Xu, Y. Shi, A. Atallah, R. Herbrich, S. Bowers *et al.*, "Practical lessons from predicting clicks on ads at facebook," in *Proceedings of the Eighth International Workshop on Data Mining for Online Advertising*, New York, NY, USA, 2014, pp. 1–9.
14. G. Ke, Q. Meng, T. Finley, T. Wang, W. Chen, W. Ma, Q. Ye, and T.-Y. Liu, "Lightgbm: A highly efficient gradient boosting decision tree," in *Advances in Neural Information Processing Systems 30 (NIPS 2017), Long Beach, CA, USA.*, 2017, pp. 3146–3154.
15. J. Xiao, H. Ye, X. He, H. Zhang, F. Wu, and T.-S. Chua, "Attentional factorization machines: Learning the weight of feature interactions via attention networks," in *Proceedings of the Twenty-Sixth International Joint Conference on Artificial Intelligence, (IJCAI-17), Melbourne, Australia*, 2017, pp. 3119–3125.
16. F. Zhang, G. Liu, Z. Li, C. Yan, and C. Jiang, "Gmm-based undersampling and its application for credit card fraud detection," in *the 32nd International Joint Conference on Neural Network (IJCNN'2019)*, Budapest, Hungary., 03 2019.
17. X.-Y. Liu, J. Wu, and Z.-H. Zhou, "Exploratory undersampling for class-imbalance learning," *IEEE Transactions on Systems, Man, and Cybernetics, Part B (Cybernetics)*, vol. 39, no. 2, pp. 539–550, 2009.
18. H. Guo, R. Tang, Y. Ye, Z. Li, and X. He, "Deepfm: a factorization-machine based neural network for ctr prediction," *arXiv preprint arXiv:1703.04247*, 2017.
19. M. Abadi, P. Barham, J. Chen, Z. Chen, A. Davis, J. Dean, M. Devin, S. Ghemawat, G. Irving, M. Isard, M. Kudlur, J. Levenberg, R. Monga, S. Moore, D. G. Murray, B. Steiner, P. Tucker, V. Vasudevan, P. Warden, M. Wicke, Y. Yu, and X. Zheng, "Tensorflow: A system for large-scale machine learning," in *Proceedings of the 12th USENIX Conference on Operating Systems Design and Implementation (OSDI'16), Savannah, GA, USA*, 2016, pp. 265–283.
20. D. P. Kingma and J. Ba, "Adam: A method for stochastic optimization," *arXiv preprint arXiv:1412.6980*, 2014.

Efficiency assessment of event-based predictive maintenance in Industry 4.0

Athanasios Naskos[1] and Anastasios Gounaris[2]

[1] Atlantis Engineering, Thessaloniki, Greece
naskos@abe.gr
[2] Aristotle University of Thessaloniki, Greece
gounaria@csd.auth.gr

Abstract. Predictive maintenance has evolved from a vision to reality for several industries. Notwithstanding, there is not yet a clear view on the behavior of the algorithmic tools proposed. The aim of this work is to fill this gap and perform an insightful comparison and sensitivity analysis of the main representatives for event-based predictive maintenance, which typically rely on pattern mining and machine learning. We provide a publicly available environment to compare techniques and we perform extensive experiments. The results of our work show that fine tuning is required and judicious feature generation and selection are two important aspects in efficiently predicting faults.

Keywords: predictive maintenance, sequential pattern mining, multiple instance learning, Industry 4.0

1 Introduction

The key goal of Industry 4.0 is towards personalized products, zero defects and breakdowns along with lot size one. Not surprisingly, it has altered the daily operation of factories, something that is commonly referred to as the fourth industrial revolution [1].

Smart factories come with several features. Their cornerstone is data collection and analysis to be employed at different levels and for complementary objectives: from reducing operation expenses and equipment downtime through predictive maintenance (PdM) to the support of new business models and after-sales services. In this work, we focus on PdM, which involves continuous sensor-based inspection managed by both reliability engineers and data scientists; the latter are called to effectively apply proactive analytics.

According to a recent survey of 268 companies in Belgium, Germany and the Netherlands[3], PdM has departed from its early infancy and hype stages and has been transformed into a powerful widely-spread technology that is capable of yielding *"tremenous"* benefits. The above findings are supported by other

[3] https://www.pwc.nl/nl/assets/documents/pwc-predictive-maintenance-beyond-the-hype-40.pdf

surveys as well. For example, another survey predicts 11% growth in industry due to AI-based applications, with PdM being the key one.[4]. Overall, the market for PdM applications *"is poised to grow from 2.2B in 2017 to 10.9B US dollars by 2022, a 39% annual growth rate.*[5] In addition, PdM is supported by and has attracted great interest from numerous big IT vendors, such as SAP, Siemens and Microsoft.

Broadly, PdM can be either *model-driven* or *data-driven*. In the former case, the maintenance prediction is based on expert knowledge captured in the form of mathematical equations or rules derived by experts. In practice, such an approach is applicable to small-scale static systems only, as reported in [14]. In the latter case, events or logs are subject to intensive processing in order to automatically derive patterns of machine failure and then leverage such patterns in order to plan or advise on maintenance actions in a timely manner before a failure occurs but not much earlier, e.g., [10,14,6]. Event- or log-based PdM solutions rely on applied data mining concepts, and more specifically on pattern mining, feature selection and machine learning [2]. The main assumption is that equipment failures are preceded by patterns, the early detection of which can be leveraged by sophisticated PdM techniques. The solutions can be regarded as application independent higher-level methodologies consisting of a series of techniques, as explained hereafter.

The contribution of this work is threefold: (i) to decompose state-of-the-art data-driven PdM methodologies into their main building blocks; (ii) to develop a tool that can simulate realistic settings, where the relevant events are a small minority in all reported events (as, for instance, typically occurs in aviation industry [10]), in order to assess the behavior of each methodology in a repeatable, controllable and configurable manner; and (iii) to compare existing methodologies and perform insightful sensitivity analysis regarding the main parameters of each methodology under investigation.

The remainder of this paper is structured as follows. In the next section, we provide a concise overview of data-driven predictive maintenance. Section 3 elaborates on the main methodologies and the techniques they employ. In Sections 4 and 5, we describe the setting emulating a real industrial environment and we conduct our thorough experiments. We conclude in Section 6.

2 Related Work

Data-driven techniques, where the data refer to past events, commonly in the form of log entries, are widely used in PdM. One such approach applied to aviation industry is presented in [10], where past events (i.e. post-flight logs) are used to predict a specific *target event* (i.e., fault). The proposed approach penalizes rare (more rare than the *target event*) and frequent events (implicitly performing feature selection) and amplifies the strength of the events closer to the *target*

[4] https://www.elektroniknet.de/international/ai-achieves-over-11-percent-growth-in-industry-158062.html

[5] https://iot-analytics.com/top-20-companies-enabling-predictive-maintenance/

event, using a Multi-Instance Learning (MIL) technique. Such preprocessed log data form the training set, which is then fed into a regression analysis algorithm for the prediction of the *target event*. In our work, we further elaborate on this approach as a key representative of the state-of-the-art; further technical details are provided in Section 3.2.

Another event-based approach is presented in [13], where historical and service data from a ticketing system are combined with domain knowledge to train a binary classifier for the prediction of a failure. As in the previous work, a feature selection [4] and an event amplification technique (i.e. MIL) is used to enhance the effectiveness of the SVM-based classifier. In [10] evidence is provided that the work in [13] is less suitable in a real-world scenario with a sparse feature set and rare interesting targeted events. Event-based analysis, based on event and failure logs, is also performed in [14], where it is assumed that the system is capable of generating exceptions and error log entries that are inherently relevant to significant failures. This work relies on pattern extraction and similarity between patterns preceding a failure, while emphasis is posed on feature selection. We further discuss this technique in Section 3.3.

The work in [15] proposes a correlation-driven approach between different sensor signals and fault events to guide the PdM process. This approach tries to identify correlations between detected anomalies in different sensor signals, which are mapped to specific faults. Here, we focus on log event processing.

Predicting a fault in the equipment is in-directly similar to estimating its Remaining Useful Lifetime (RUL). The authors in [9] propose a RUL estimation approach based on vibration analysis. Their approach uses domain experts knowledge for the creation of a training set of health ranking of specific equipment, which is used by a regression analysis approach for the estimation of RUL of other equipment. A more general and domain-agnostic approach for the estimation of the RUL is proposed in [8]. Data-driven PdM is also related to online frequent episodes mining; research works [3] and [12] propose techniques in this topic. A good overview of the the data-driven PdM is presented in [11].

3 Details of the state-of-the-art event-based PdM methodologies

Life data analysis is a traditional process in the industry, which provides important estimates about product life characteristics, such as reliability or probability of failure at a specific time, the mean life and the failure rate of the product and other useful statistical results. Fitting a statistical distribution (most commonly the Weibull distribution) to life data from a representative sample of the products population, the process attempts to make predictions about the life of all the products in the population. The effectiveness of the life data analysis, is affected by the volume of the gathered life data for the product, the selected lifetime distribution to fit the data and model the life of the product, and the estimated parameters that will fit the distribution to the data. Although useful to some degree, the life data analysis is attempting to use a single number

Algorithm 1 Sequential pattern mining for PdM

procedure PATTERN EXTRACTION
  $nof \leftarrow$ number of failures
  $min\_support \leftarrow \alpha \cdot nof,\ 0 < \alpha \leq 1$
  $constraints \leftarrow$ set constraints on the pattern period and the gap between events
  Extract frequent sequential patterns given *min_support* and *constraints*
  Keep only the partners ending in the *target event* $E_1E_2E_3 \dots E_nX$
  $Result \leftarrow \emptyset$
  for each subset S of $E_1E_2E_3 \dots E_n$ **do**
    if $support(S) \leq (1+\varepsilon) \cdot support(E_1E_2E_3 \dots E_nX),\ \varepsilon \geq 0$ **then**
      $Result \leftarrow Result \bigcup S$

procedure PATTERN USAGE
  Continuously check whether any pattern in *Result* applies

(e.g. Mean Time to Failure (MTTF)) to describe an entire lifetime distribution, which can be misleading and may lead to poor business decisions especially when a non-exponential lifetime distribution appears in reality. To overcome this pitfall, more versatile and powerful data-driven techniques, which are able to adapt in dynamic environments, are progressively adopted.

3.1 Sequential pattern mining

A data-driven technique with a wide range of applications is the sequential pattern mining (SPM). SPM consists of discovering useful patterns in the data, such as frequent itemsets, associations, sequential rules, or periodic patterns. In PdM, SPM can provide useful information about associations between fault events as a sequence of minor faults or other events can potentially lead to a major failure. Traditionally, SPM does not integrate the notion of time between the provided associations [14]. However, there are research works like [7] that allow the specification of time constraints for the identification of the patterns, or works like [3] and [12] that provide solutions for an extension of SPM for online processing of temporal data sequences[6].The combination of such techniques with Complex-event processing (CEP) can predict failures in a variety of complex systems, such as the ones encountered in the industry. In this work, we will examine the prediction efficiency of a system that uses SPM with time constraints between events. An outline is presented in Algorithm 1, where the main input parameters consist of the constraints on the pattern period and the gap between events, the α parameter, which sets the support threshold in relation to the occurrence of faults in the training set, and ε, which keeps patterns not generating many false alarms.

[6] Open-source implementations are provided in libraries such as [5].

3.2 Event-driven machine learning for PdM focusing on log preprocessing

An advanced data-driven predictive maintenance approach is presented in [10]. The objective of this research work is to develop an alerting system that provides early notifications to aviation engineers for upcoming aircraft failures, providing the needed time for the maintenance actions. The aviation is a well-documented field, as all the maintenance and flight data are systematically logged. Hence, event-based techniques can leverage this special characteristic and provide effective predictive solutions. The main challenge is to cope with the large set of log entries that are essentially irrelevant to the main failures.

In [10], the emphasis is placed on log preprocessing; therefore, we will refer to this methodology as LP_{PdM}. The post flight logs are partitioned in ranges defined by the occurrences of the fault that PdM targets. These ranges are further partitioned into time-segments, which may correspond to a day or to a single usage of the equipment. The idea is that the segments that are closer to the end of the range may contain fault events that are potentially indicative of the main event. The goal is to learn a function that quantifies the risk of the targeted failure occurring in the near future, given the events that precede it. Hence, a sigmoid function is proposed, which maps higher values to the segments that are closer to the *target event*. The steepness and shift of the sigmoid function are configured to better map the expectation of the time before the *target event* at which correlated events will start occurring. The segmented data in combination with the risk quantification values are fed into a Random Forests algorithm as a training set to form a regression problem, which is based on the minimization of the mean squared error.

In order to increase the effectiveness of the approach standard preprocessing techniques are applied: (1) Rare events (more rare than the *target event*), are considered as extremely rare, hence they are removed to reduce the dimensionality of the data. (2) Multiple occurrences of the same event in the same segment can either be noise or may not provide useful information. Hence, multiple occurrences are shrank into a single one. (3) Most frequent events usually do not contain significant information since they correspond to issues of minor importance. A tf-idf (term-frequency - inverted document frequency) or a simple threshold-based approach can be used to remove most frequent events. (4) Events of minor importance occur and appear in every segment until their underlying cause is treated by the technical experts. Hence, the first occurrence of events that occur in consecutive segments is maintained. (5) A statistical feature selection technique, based on the distance of the fault events with the *target event* is applied, to filter out fault events, which are far from the *target event.* Finally, to deal with the imbalance of the labels (given that the *target event* is rare) and as several events appear shortly before the occurrence of the *target event*, but only a small subset of them is related to the *target event*, the authors use Multiple Instance Learning (MIL) bagging the events. A single bag contains fault events of a single day. Using MIL, the data closer to the *target event* (a threshold is specified), are over-sampled.

aspect	LP_{PdM} [10]	FS_{PdM} [14]
event aggregation	period between targeted failures	fixed period
ML technique	random forests	random forests, XGBoost
features	event type occurrence	event type frequencies, statistics, relevant event combinations and similarities to failure patterns
feature selection	implicit or explicit through Wiebull distribution fitting	explicit through ReliefF/InfoGain
rare event pruning	explicit	implicit through pattern mining
risk quantification	sigmoid function	binary

Table 1. Main differences between the techniques in [10] and [14]

3.3 Event-driven machine learning focusing on feature selection

The PdM approach proposed in [14], although it is evaluated over a use case of automated teller machines (ATMs), is general enough to be applied on any industrial scenario, where error and failure logs are available. It follows a similar rationale as [10], but implicitly assumes that the log types recorded are more commonly related to the targeted failure (e.g., generated from software exceptions) and puts more emphasis on feature generation and selection. We will refer to this approach as FS_{PdM}. Its main drawback is that it cannot scale in the number of event types that are present in the logs.

The authors propose a configurable approach for the creation of the training and testing datasets and the formation of a binary classification problem. More specifically, the dataset is divided into partitions (named *Observation Windows (OW)*) and each *OW* is further divided into daily segments. Every *OW*, is followed by a *Prediction Window (PW)* (i.e. partition with daily segments), in which a fault is predicted to take place. The range from the beginning of each OW up to the end of the related PW defines a training or testing instance. The labelling of an instance (i.e. classes: likely to fail, or not to fail) depends on the existence of a ticket report inside the *PW* (i.e. if there is a ticket in the PW, the instance is considered positive (i.e. likely to fail)).

Each created instance is comprised by five feature categories. (1) Basic Features: A frequency vector for each error type inside an *OW*. (2) Advanced Statistical Features: A vector of statistics like, minimum, maximum and mean distance of an error type inside the *OW*, from the beginning of the corresponding PW and mean and standard deviation of the distance between instances of the same error type inside the *OW*, for each error type. (3) Pattern-based Features: A binary vector of error type patterns, which is created based on a confidence threshold on the relative frequency of each pattern in all the *OWs*. The initial set of patterns is created based on the power set (excluding the null set) of the error types inside each *OW*. (4) Failure Similarity Features: The Jaccard similarity of two consecutive failures (tickets) of the same type, computed based on the error types of each corresponding OW. (5) Profile-based Features: Consider equipment specific features, like the model and the installation date of a ATM machine.

The research work examines the predictive effectiveness of the five feature types and their combinations, four feature ranking algorithms (i.e. InfoGain, GainRatio, ReliefF, SymmetricalUncert) and four prediction algorithms (i.e. XGBoost, Random Forests, Ada Boost M1 and LibSVM). Based on the evaluation, the usage of all the statistical features, the ReliefF and InfoGain feature ranking algorithms and the XGBoost and Random Forest prediction algorithms produced the higher performance. Table 1 summarizes the main differences between the two methodologies.

4 Event Dataset Generation

To enable a fair, repeatable, extensible and realistic experimentation of event-based PdM approaches, we develop a configurable generator, in line with the environments in works such as [10,14]. An outline of the generator is presented in Algorithm 2. The generator is publicly available [7]. The parameters are summarized in Table 2.

Algorithm 2 Events Dataset Generator

```
procedure EventsGeneration
    ft ← number of fault event types
    dataset_size ← s_tr + s_te (s_tr, s_te ← training/testing set size)
    day_events_map ← ∅
    p ← number of points to generate (can be set to a large integer)
    for each event from 1 to ft do
        Ŵ_dist ← Random_Weibull_Dist(p)
        day ← 0
        for each p of Ŵ_dist do
            day ← day + p
            day_events_map[day] ← day_events_map[day] ⋃[event]
            if day ≥ dataset_size then
                break
    day_events_map ← add_pattern(day_events_map)
    day_events_map ← remove_target_events(day_events_map)
    return day_events_map

procedure Random_Weibull_Dist(p)
    s ← random(0, 20)
    mdbe ← max distance between events
    W_dist ← Weibull(shape = s, points = p)
    Ŵ_dist ← normalize(W_dist, [0, mdbe])
    return Ŵ_dist
```

[7] `http://interlab.csd.auth.gr/anaskos/ebp_icdm.git`

```
24:
25: procedure ADD_PATTERN(DAY_EVENTS_MAP)
26:     pl ← pattern length
27:     min_t, max_t ← min/max distance of the pattern from the target event
28:     min_p, max_p ← min/max distance between pattern events
29:     min_f, max_f ← min/max forms of each pattern event
30:     s ← shuffle the order of the events of the pattern
31:     pattern_events ← get_pattern_events(ft, pl)
32:     p_forms ← generate_pattern_forms(pattern_events, min_f, max_f)
33:     for each day of day_events_map do
34:         if target_event ∈ day then
35:             pt_dist ← random(min_t, max_t)
36:             p_forms ← shuffle(p_forms, s)
37:             if 0 ≤ day ≤ s_tr then
38:                 p_forms ← partial_pattern(p_forms)
39:             for each pe of p_forms do
40:                 pe_dist ← random(min_p, max_p)
41:                 p_day ← day − pt_dist − (pe_index * pe_dist), 0 ≤ pe_index ≤ pl
42:                 day_events_map[p_day] ← day_events_map[p_day] ⋃[pe]
43:     return day_events_map
44: procedure PARTIAL_PATTERN(p_forms)
45:     pc ← pattern clarity
46:     pps ← partial pattern size (percentage of the original pattern size)
47:     p_forms ← mapping of each pattern event to more event types
48:     if random.uniform() < (1 − pc) then
49:         return p_forms * pps
50:     else
51:         return p_forms
52:
53: procedure REMOVE_TARGET_EVENTS(DAY_EVENTS_MAP)
54:     for each day of day_events_map do
55:         if target_event ∈ day ∧ ¬partial_pattern then
56:             if random.uniform() < (1 − pc) then
57:                 day_events_map[p_day] ← day_events_map[p_day] − [target_event]
58:     return day_events_map
```

The dataset produced by the generator is an array of sets of event log identifiers; the identifiers range from 1 to ft, where ft is the size of the event dictionary, and are going to be referred as *events* for the rest of the paper. An event might indicate a specific maintenance process that has taken place or a specific fault. The array size is $s_{tr} + s_{te}$, where s_{tr} and s_{te} are the number of the daily segments of the training and test sets, respectively.

In lines 6-13, for each event type, a random normalized Weibull distribution is produced (lines 7,18-23). Then, we choose random points from this distribution. Each point is used to compute, the daily segment where the event of the specific type is going to be placed. This is the main extensibility point of our generator; although the Weibull distribution is widely used to map early-life, random or

Parameter	Description
ft	number of different event/fault types
s_{tr}	size of training dataset (in days)
s_{te}	size of testing dataset (in days)
pl	pattern length
min_t/max_t	min./max. distance (in days) of the last pattern event from the target event
min_p/max_p	min./max. distance (in days) between pattern events
min_f/max_f	min./max. pattern event forms
pc	pattern clarity
pps	the percentage of the missing events in the distorted patterns

Table 2. Main dataset generator parameters.

wear-out failures and produce life-usage statistics, someone can implement her own event occurrence distribution function.

Then, to test the accuracy of the PdM techniques, specific patterns of events of length *pl* from the ft dictionary that precede the *target event* are infused (lines 14,25-43). The goal of the PdM techniques is to effectively discover and learn such patterns, so that they can predict the *target events*. Furthermore, the clarity of the pattern is distorted in order to emulate the real world cases, where the preceding indications of a prominent failure are not always exactly the same or clear (lines 38,44-51). More specifically, a clarity percentage (*pc*) is specified along with a partial pattern size (*pps*), where the former defines the percentage of partial patterns (i.e. pattern instances that are missing some of the events of the original pattern), while the latter defines the percentage of the missing events. For example, $pc = 0.9$ and $pps = 0.5$, means that 10% of the pattern instances (i.e. $1 - pc$) are going to include only the half (i.e. $1 - pps$) of the events of the original pattern. *pc* also defines the percentage of the full patterns (i.e. patterns that include all the events) that are not followed by a *target event* (i.e. the *target events* that follow these patterns are removed from the dataset). E.g. $pc = 0.9$ specifies that 10% of the 90% of the *target event* instances are going to be removed (lines 15,53-58).

To better map real world cases, the patterns are not deterministic, but each of the *pl* elements is linked to $min_f - max_f$ specific events (lines 29,32). This corresponds to the situation, where there are families of faults (event types) that might precede the target event. In addition, the distances of the pattern and the *target event* and between pattern events are also configurable (lines 27,32,35,41). All these are taken into account when generating the preceding pattern through the $generate\_pattern\_forms$ function. Finally, the order of the events of the pattern can also be shuffled (line 36), to allow for higher flexibility of the supported scenarios.

Dataset	ft	$shuffle$	pl	min_f	max_f	s_{tr}	s_{te}	min_t	max_t	min_p	max_p	pc	pps
DS1	150	no	6	1	3	1094	730	1	5	1	2	90%	50%
DS2			4	3	4								
DS3	1500	same as DS1											
DS4		same as DS2											
DS5	150	yes											
DS6													

Table 3. Dataset generator parameters. $DS1$ to $DS5$ contain approx. 50 target events, whereas $DS6$ contains 25 target events.

5 Experiments

The experimental section comprises three parts: (i) dataset description, (ii) comparison of the approaches in Section 3, and (iii) sensitivity analysis. For the SPM approach, we are experimenting with two different implementations: with and without the pre-processing and over-sampling specified in Section 3.2.

5.1 Datasets

Table 3 presents the parametrization used for the generation of six synthetic datasets that are used for the evaluation of the PdM approaches. All the datasets are separated into training and testing sets of sizes 3 and 2 years, respectively. The distance of the pattern from the *target event* ranges from 1 to 5 days, while the distance between the events of the pattern ranges from 1 to 2 days. The pattern clarity is set to 90%, while the partial patterns include only the half of the events of the full pattern (i.e. *pps* = 50%). The number of *target events* is set to $\approx$ 50, as such, with the specified *pc* value, there are approximately 5 cases of partial patterns and 5 cases of patterns that are not followed by *target events* out of the 30 cases of *target events* that correspond to the training set.

There are two main datasets, namely, DS1 and DS2 and four datasets (DS3-6) that are slightly altered versions of the former ones. More specifically, DS3 is the same as DS1 and DS4 the same with DS2, with the difference that 10X more event types are used (i.e. 1500 instead of 150). DS5 is the same as DS2 with the difference that the sequence of the events of the pattern is shuffled. Finally, DS6 is the same as DS5 with the difference that there are fewer *target events* (i.e. $\approx$ 25 instead of $\approx$ 50), making the training process more challenging.

In the experiments, ten instances of each dataset are produced. The presented results are the average values out of ten executions. For the reproduction of the results, all the necessary code is provided [8]. For the evaluation of the efficiency of predictions, we have specified a range of days before the target event in which the prediction should be made. Predictions that are inside this range are considered as true positives and are counted once. Too early predictions occurring before

[8] `http://interlab.csd.auth.gr/anaskos/ebp_icdm.git`

PdM	DS1			DS3			DS2			DS4		
	P	R	**F1**	P	R	**F1**	P	R	**F1**	P	R	**F1**
LP_{PdM}	0.54	0.99	0.70	0.77	0.93	**0.83**	0.55	0.69	0.60	0.68	0.25	0.31
FS_{PdM}	0.83	0.85	**0.84**	0.78	0.88	0.82	0.63	0.88	**0.73**	0.70	0.74	**0.71**
SPM	0.51	1.00	0.66	0.55	0.87	0.66	0.36	0.88	0.50	0.22	0.46	0.29
$SPM_{LP_{PdM}}$	0.22	0.30	0.26	0.34	0.99	0.49	0.39	0.80	0.50	0.16	0.98	0.27

Table 4. PdM approaches comparison of the best achieved results for DS1-DS3 and DS2-DS4 (P: precision, R: recall).

PdM	DS2			DS5			DS6		
	P	R	**F1**	P	R	**F1**	P	R	**F1**
LP_{PdM}	0.55	0.69	0.60	0.56	0.65	0.59	0.28	0.75	**0.40**
FS_{PdM}	0.63	0.88	**0.73**	0.66	0.69	**0.68**	0.48	0.30	0.35
SPM	0.36	0.88	0.50	0.00	0.00	0.00	0.43	0.40	0.37
$SPM_{LP_{PdM}}$	0.39	0.80	0.50	0.40	0.66	0.49	0.18	0.86	0.29

Table 5. PdM approaches comparison of the best achieved results for DS2-DS5-DS6 (P: precision, R: recall).

the range trigger unnecessary maintenance actions, which result in time and monetary loses and are counted as false positives. If no prediction is made before a *target event* or the prediction is delayed, the case is considered a false negative. For DS1,3 the range is set to [1,30] and for DS2,4,5,6 to [1,22]. It is straightforward to adapt the techniques and experiments for ranges not starting from 1 day, which correspond to a buffer window between the prediction and the predicted fault (details are omitted due to lack of space).

5.2 Comparison

Here, we present only the best achieved result of each approach after experimenting with different parameterizations using DS1 and DS2; we re-use the best performing parameters in DS3-5. Extra parameters were tested for DS6. The sensitivity analysis is deferred to the next subsection. The best performing results in terms of the F1-score are summarized in Tables 4 and 5.

Regarding the first dataset, the FS_{PdM} approach achieved the best F1-score (i.e. 0.84), followed by the LP_{PdM} and SPM approaches (i.e. 0.7 and 0.66, respectively). Interestingly, combining the preprocessing of LP_{PdM} with SPM degraded the performance, since less rules were generated. The increase in the number of fault types from 150 to 1500 in DS3, not only did not cause any negative effects in the results, but in some cases there were increases in the F1-score as in the LP_{PdM} (0.83 best score) and $SPM_{LP_{PdM}}$ (0.49) approaches. This is due to the fact that LP_{PdM} inherently targets sparse sets, where most of the event types are non-related to the *target event*. In DS2, where the pattern length is lower (i.e. 4) and there are more alternative event types for each pattern element, FS_{PdM} is still the best performing technique but with lower F1-scores. The increase of the number of the event types in DS4 had negative impact on all the approaches, which is largely attributed to the sensitivity of the LP_{PdM}-based techniques to their parameters.

In the next set of experiments, summarized in Table 5, we examine the effect of the shuffling of the order of the events of the pattern and the combination of the shuffling with the reduction in the *target event* instances. Table 5 also contains the DS2 scores for comparison. Regarding DS5, FS_{PdM} achieved the best F1-score (i.e. 0.68), followed by the LP_{PdM} approach (i.e. 0.59). SPM was not able to produce any rule that lead to the *target event*. However, the application of the MIL oversampling helped $SPM_{LP_{PdM}}$ approach to achieve a good F1-score (i.e. 0.49). In DS6, the parametrization of the approaches was re-evaluated. FS_{PdM} and $SPM_{LP_{PdM}}$ approaches achieved higher recall, while the LP_{PdM} and SPM achieved higher precision. This led to very similar F1-scores, with LP_{PdM} achieving the best one (i.e. 0.4).

The key observation is that, in general, the FS_{PdM} approach, which employs more statistical features coupled with feature selection, pays off in practice. Overall, FS_{PdM} and LP_{PdM} approaches achieved the best score in all the cases compared to the SPM implementations. FS_{PdM} seems to be more robust than the LP_{PdM} approach, as it achieved better or almost the same score in all the cases, where the parametrization kept the same (i.e. DS1-DS3 and DS2-DS4,5). The preprocessing and the MIL process applied on the $SPM_{LP_{PdM}}$ help the latter to achieve better results in some cases than the SPM approach, however in all the cases the results from both the implementations were inferior to the other two more advanced approaches.

5.3 Sensitivity Analysis

This section focuses on the sensitivity analysis of the LP_{PdM} and FS_{PdM} approaches using DS2. The number of possible combinations is apparently exhaustive, thus we focus on the most important parameters.

Regarding the LP_{PdM} approach, a key issue is to understand the impact of the parameters of the underlying sigmoid function, as defined in Figure 1(a). Adjusting the shift (or midpoint) parameter m, the steepness s and the threshold leads to different trade-offs between precision and recall.

The first experiment, presented in Figure 1(b), considers the shift of the sigmoid function, which in our case is defined as the distance of the middle point of the sigmoid function from the target event. As shown, higher shift values increase the recall of the approach lowering its precision, while lower values have the opposite effect.

The next experiment, presented in Figure 1(c), examines the effect of the steepness parameter for three different parameter values (i.e. 0.5 (green square, 0.7 (red circle) and 0.9 (blue triangle))). As it is depicted in the figure, setting the lower of the three value (i.e. 0.5), the recall of the approach is negatively affected as more events obtain closer values from the sigmoid function. The two higher values achieve similar results.

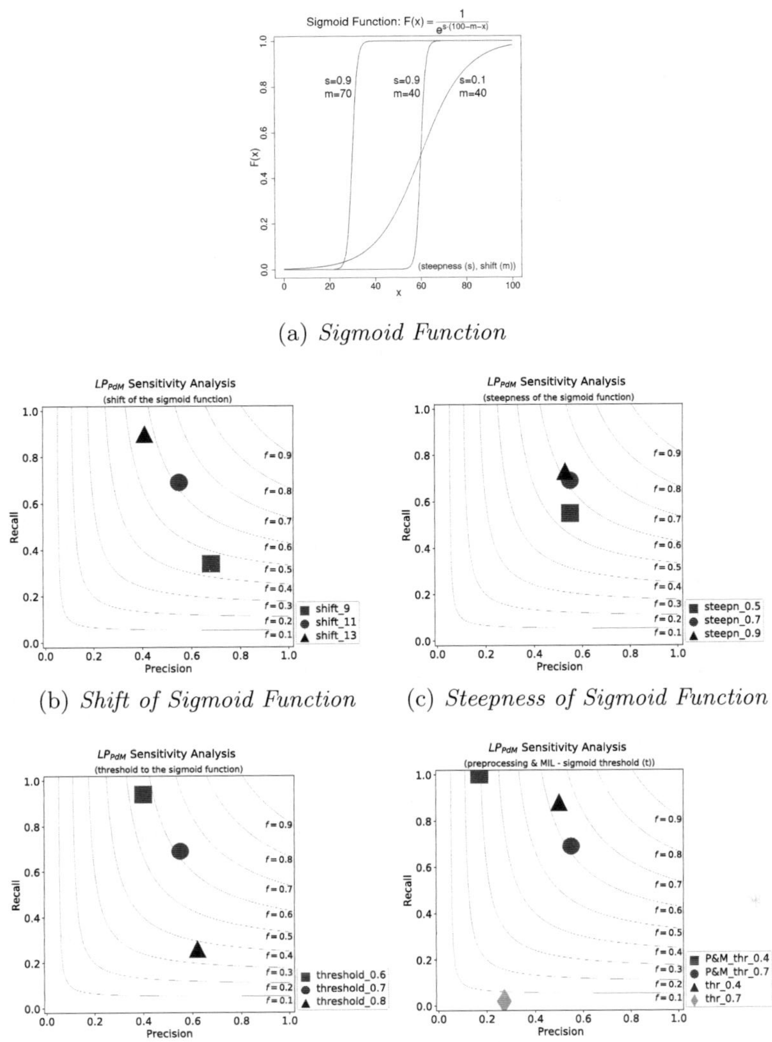

(a) *Sigmoid Function*

(b) *Shift of Sigmoid Function* (c) *Steepness of Sigmoid Function*

(d) *Threshold on Sigmoid Function* (e) *Preprocessing & MIL*

Fig. 1. Sensitivity analysis of the LP_{PdM} PdM approach.

For the threshold impact on the prediction efficiency (Figure 1(d)), we have examined three parameters (0.6 , 0.7, and 0.8) keeping the steepness high. The threshold parameter, as shown in the figure, highly affects the recall of the approach (i.e. lower values increase the recall score) and more slightly the precision (i.e. higher threshold values lead to higher precision).

In the last experiment regarding LP_{PdM}, we examine the effect of the application of the preprocessing and the MIL process on the approach efficiency (Figure 1(e)). Four cases are depicted: (i) preprocessing and MIL enabled setting the

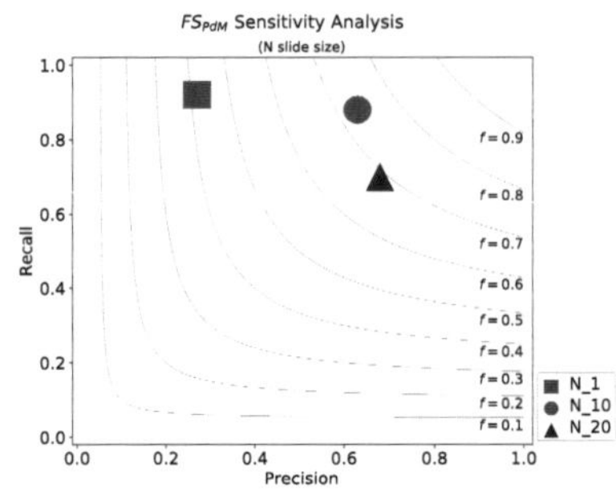

Fig. 2. Impact of OW slide in FS_{PdM}

threshold parameter to 0.4 (green square *P&M_thr_0.4*), (ii) preprocessing and MIL enabled setting the threshold parameter to 0.7 (red circle *P&M_thr_0.7*), (iii) disabled preprocessing and MIL with threshold parameter equal to 0.4 (blue triangle *thr_0.4*) and (iv) disabled preprocessing and MIL with threshold equal to 0.7 (yellow diamond *thr_0.7*). There are two cases, one with preprocessing and MIL enabled and one with both disabled, which both achieved similarly high F1-scores (i.e. *P&M_thr_0.7* (F1=0.6), *thr_0.4* (F1=0.62)). This might be erroneously interpreted as that there is no point in applying the expensive tasks of preprocessing and MIL; however, if we consider the other two cases, we observe that applying the preprocessing and MIL process provides more robust behavior, as for the same change in the threshold, the F1-score is drastically reduced in the case without preprocessing and MIL.

FS_{SPM} is more robust to its parameters. We have experimented with different segmentation and OW size values, but these parameters seemed to play a small role. An important parameter is the slide of the window, which defines the OW movement. Setting the slide lower than the OW size causes over-sampling. As it is shown in Figure 2, the lowest possible value of the slide (i.e. 1 (green square)) has negative impact on the precision of the approach. Setting the slide size equal to the half of the OW size (red circle) achieves better results than setting it to the size to the OW (blue triangle).

6 Conclusion

In this work, we targeted event-based predictive maintenance. We presented the main state-of-the-art approaches to date, we developed a publicly available, extensible comparison framework and we conducted repeatable experiments. The main lessons learnt are twofold: first, employing statistical features on the logged events coupled with feature selection is the best performing technique in our experiments, and second, when using regression, parameter tuning is a key issue in achieving configurable trade-offs between precision and recall.

Our work can be extended in several ways. Combining feature expansion, feature selection and log preprocessing is a promising avenue. Also, more thorough experiments need to be conducted. However, we believe that an important issue is to transfer the event-based techniques to a setting where the input data is raw time series signals from Industry 4.0 sensors.

Acknowledgement. This research work is funded by the BOOST4.0 project (funded by European Unions Horizon 2020 research and innovation program under grant agreement No 780732).

References

1. Industry 4.0: A survey on technologies, applications and open research issues. Journal of Industrial Information Integration **6**, 1 – 10 (2017)
2. Aggarwal, C.C.: Data Mining - The Textbook. Springer (2015)
3. Ao, X., Luo, P., Li, C., Zhuang, F., He, Q.: Online frequent episode mining. In: IEEE 31st Int. Conf. on Data Engineering (ICDE). pp. 891–902 (2015)
4. Bach, F.R.: Bolasso: model consistent lasso estimation through the bootstrap. In: Proc. of the 25th Int. Conf. on Machine learning. pp. 33–40. ACM (2008)
5. Fournier-Viger, P., Lin, J.C.W., Gomariz, A., Gueniche, T., Soltani, A., Deng, Z., Lam, H.T.: The spmf open-source data mining library version 2. In: Joint European conference on machine learning and knowledge discovery in databases. pp. 36–40. Springer (2016)
6. Giobergia, F., Baralis, E., andTania Cerquitelli, M.C., Melliaz, M., Neriy, A., Tricaricoy, D., Tuninettiy, A.: Mining sensor data for predictive maintenance in the automotive industry. In: IEEE 5th Int. Conf. on Data Science and Advanced Analytics (DSAA). pp. 351–360 (2018)
7. Hirate, Y., Yamana, H.: Generalized sequential pattern mining with item intervals. JCP **1**(3), 51–60 (2006)
8. Hu, C., Youn, B.D., Wang, P., Yoon, J.T.: Ensemble of data-driven prognostic algorithms for robust prediction of remaining useful life. Reliability Engineering & System Safety **103**, 120–135 (2012)
9. Jung, D., Zhang, Z., Winslett, M.: Vibration analysis for iot enabled predictive maintenance. In: Data Engineering (ICDE), 2017 IEEE 33rd International Conference on. pp. 1271–1282. IEEE (2017)
10. Korvesis, P., Besseau, S., Vazirgiannis, M.: Predictive maintenance in aviation: Failure prediction from post flight reports. In: IEEE Int. Conf. on Data Engineering (ICDE). pp. 1414–1422 (2018)
11. Kovalev, D., Shanin, I., Stupnikov, S., Zakharov, V.: Data mining methods and techniques for fault detection and predictive maintenance in housing and utility infrastructure. In: 2018 International Conference on Engineering Technologies and Computer Science (EnT). pp. 47–52 (2018)
12. Li, H., Peng, S., Li, J., Li, J., Cui, J., Ma, J.: Once and once+: Counting the frequency of time-constrained serial episodes in a streaming sequence. arXiv preprint arXiv:1801.09639 (2018)
13. Sipos, R., Fradkin, D., Moerchen, F., Wang, Z.: Log-based predictive maintenance. In: Proceedings of the 20th ACM SIGKDD international conference on knowledge discovery and data mining. pp. 1867–1876. ACM (2014)
14. Wang, J., Li, C., Han, S., Sarkar, S., Zhou, X.: Predictive maintenance based on event-log analysis: A case study. IBM Journal of Research and Development **61**(1), 11–121 (2017)
15. Zhu, M., Liu, C.: A correlation driven approach with edge services for predictive industrial maintenance. Sensors (Basel, Switzerland) **18**(6) (2018)

Sliding Window Based Weighted Periodic Pattern Mining over Time Series Data

Redwan Ahmed Rizvee[1], Md Shahadat Hossain Shahin[1], Chowdhury Farhan Ahmed[1], Carson K. Leung[2][0000-0002-7541-9127] (✉), Deyu Deng[2], and Jiaxing Jason Mai[2]

[1] University of Dhaka, Dhaka, Bangladesh
farhan@du.ac.bd
[2] University of Manitoba, Winnipeg, MB, Canada
kleung@cs.umanitoba.ca

Abstract. Sliding windows have been crucial in mining time series. Many existing studies focus on reconstruction of the underlying structure (e.g., suffix tree) for each new window. However, when the window size is large or when the window slides frequently, reconstruction may perform poorly. In this paper, we propose a solution that dynamically updates the structure (rather than reconstruction for each modification or sliding). Moreover, many existing studies rely on the weight of maximum weighted item in the database to avoid testing unnecessary patterns when mining weighted periodic patterns from time series, but it may still require lots of weight checking to determine whether a pattern is a candidate. In this paper, we also propose an additional solution to address this problem by discarding unimportant patterns beforehand so as to speed up the candidate generation process. Evaluation results on real-life datasets show the effectiveness of our two solutions in handling sliding window and pruning redundant candidate patterns.

Keywords: Time series · Weighted periodic pattern mining · Dynamic database · Sliding window · Pruning.

1 Introduction

Discovering an efficient approach for mining frequent patterns has always been an important issue in knowledge discovery [5, 10, 12, 13, 16]. The idea of generating patterns has evolved over time and flooded a huge set of new domains. Sequential pattern mining [9, 14, 17, 19] is one of the popular areas in the field of pattern mining, and *time series pattern mining* [6, 7] is a very renowned and widely discussed topic in sequential pattern mining. The core input of time series pattern mining is data stream (e.g., a stream of sequence of events or items found with respect to time interval). A popular structure to represent time series is a *suffix tree* [18], from which *frequent patterns* can be mined on different thresholds and conditions. Data streams are *continuous, unbounded*, and *not necessarily uniformly distributed* [3, 11]. This creates the challenge of *dynamicity*, which is also the core of *sliding window problem* [1] in numerous real-life applications (e.g., weather forecast, natural disasters prediction, etc.) [21]. To solve this sliding window problem, many existing studies rely on reconstructing the data structure to represent a modified window. However, this approach can be very expensive, especially in case of large window size or frequent sliding of windows. In this paper, we propose a *dynamic tree based solution to handle sliding window in time series* (*DTSW*), which focuses on (i) updating the data structure dynamically, (ii) maintaining (rather than reconstructing) a dynamic tree for each modified window, and (iii) keeping the tree suitable for various kinds of pattern mining.

In addition to DTSW, our second contribution centers around mining *weighted periodical patterns* [6] from time series. The introduction of weight to patterns helps in mining more interesting patterns when compared with its unweighted counterpart [1]. Weighted periodical patterns in time series are weighted sequences that periodically occur at least a certain amount of times along with a weight satisfying the user-specified threshold. Weighted pattern mining can be very useful in time series to discover interesting features. For example, if analyzing the transactions of a sports kit shop, the sold products may vary with many parameters (e.g., time, event, etc.). Selling rate of football jersey increases after every four years when the World Cup hits. A main challenge in weighted pattern mining is how to avoid testing *undesired candidates* so as to speed up the candidate generation process. Note that the *downward closure property* (*DCP*) cannot be applied directly in weighted versions of pattern mining. To speed up candidate generation, many existing works use the *Max Weight* concept, but they need to test a large number of unnecessary patterns for candidacy which in turn degrades performance. Hence, our second contribution in this paper is an efficient pruning solution—called *maximum possible weighted support* (*MPWS*) *pruning*—to significantly reduce the number of patterns to be tested for candidacy. To recap, *our key contributions* of this paper is our following two solutions:

- DTSW, a dynamic tree based solution to handle sliding window in time series (Section 3).
- MPWS pruning, an efficient solution to speed up the candidate generation process in weighted periodic pattern mining (Section 4).

The remainder of this paper is organized as follows. The next section gives background and related works. Sections 3 and 4 present our two proposed solutions. Section 5 shows evaluation results. Finally, conclusions are drawn in Section 6.

2 Background and Related Works

2.1 Sliding Window Problem

Discretization is a technique to represent a group of data with a single symbol. As time series is basically information gathered with respect to time interval, it can be represented as a string or sequence of characters from a given set by

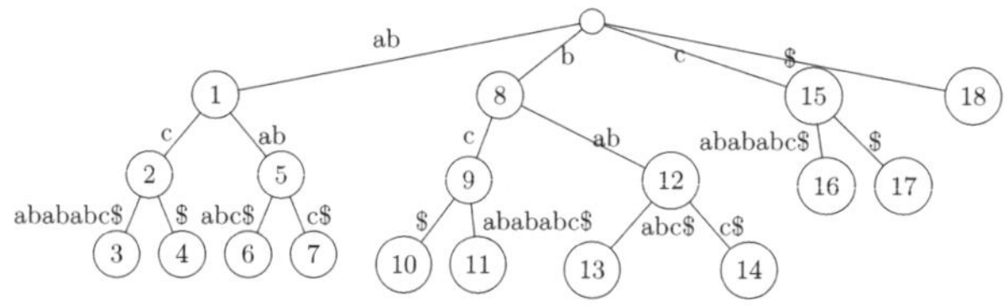

Fig. 1: Explicit suffix tree for string "abcabababc$"

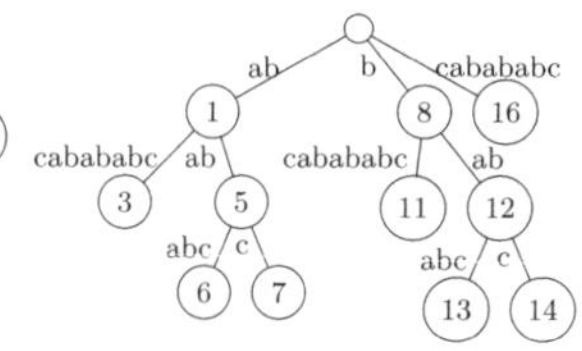

Fig. 2: Implicit suffix tree for string "abcabababc".

discretizing the values. For example "abcabababc$" is a discretized time series sequence.

As the suffix tree has been shown [18] to be an efficient data structure to represent time series and for frequent periodical pattern mining, we use it as our data structure. We use *Ukkonen's algorithm* [20], which a fast linear-time algorithm to construct suffix tree. To elaborate, a suffix tree represents all the suffixes of a string. If all the suffixes can be found by traversing from root to leaf nodes, then the suffix tree is in its *explicit* form. On the other hand, if all the suffixes do not end in leaves but rather embedded in the paths, then the tree is in its *implicit* form. Fig. 1 shows an explicit suffix tree of string "abcabababc$", and Fig. 2 shows an implicit suffix tree of string "abcabababc". An important concept in the Ukkonen's algorithm for constructing a suffix tree is *suffix link*, which helps to traverse the tree efficiently. According to Ukkonen's proposal, each and every internal node of the tree points to another internal node (or the root) as its suffix link. Suffix link of a node A with path "$\alpha\beta$" from root where (i) 'α' is exactly one symbol and (ii) 'β' can contain zero or more symbols will point to another (internal or root) node B as its suffix link if and only if node B has the path 'β' from the root. For example, in Fig. 1, Node 1 points to Node 8 as its suffix link. Each pass of Ukkonen's algorithm for adding symbol starts from an *active point*, which represent the position of largest implicit suffix in the tree at the current moment. The active point consists of (i) an *active node* representing the node position from which new pass will start), (ii) an *active edge* providing the information about the edge from active node where suffixes overlapping is being occurred, and (iii) an *active length* representing the number of symbols been overlapped in the direction of active edge from active node. Ukkonen proposed *rule extensions* in his algorithm. For instance, to add a new symbol to the end of all the existing suffixes in the tree, one does not have to traverse all the leaves. One can use a global reference. The extensions ensure maximization of suffixes overlapping in the tree. Moreover, Ukkonen also used *edge label compression* in the algorithm by not saving the exact symbols for edge labels. Instead, it stores only pointers to the starting and ending position of the input sequence. Each pass inserts a new symbol to the tree. Before each pass, every existing node must have a suffix link to some other node, and active point must be maintained accordingly.

However, many existing works in time series do not give solution for handling the data structure in a dynamic environment. To handle sliding window problem

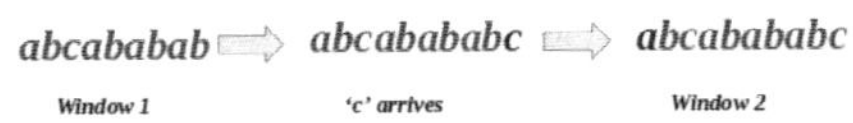

Fig. 3: Sliding window

in time series, many existing works build the structure from scratch for each new window. Let us illustrate the sliding window problem by Fig. 3, in which the window size is considered to be 9 (symbols). Window 1 contains the sequence "abcababab". After the arrival of new discretized input symbol 'c', the window slides and we get new modified window with (i) symbol 'a' is deleted from the beginning of the old window and (ii) symbol 'c' is inserted at the end. When the time series is represented by a suffix tree, if we have a sequence S and a suffix tree T for S, we need to be able to *efficiently* update T in case of (i) insertions of new symbols at the end of S or (ii) deletion of symbols from the beginning of S.

As a preview, to alleviate this problem, we propose DTSW, which is a framework for handling *both insertion and deletion* of events in a *single* framework. The basis of our solution is to keep the tree consistent so that, any time insertion or deletion of events is possible. The idea of making a data structure consistent for batch events was inspired by Leung and Khan's work on the DSTree [11], which aims to keep the tree consistent for future updates and makes only necessary modifications to reflect the current data under consideration.

2.2 Pruning for Weighted Periodical Pattern Mining

Introduction of weight has been an important concept in pattern mining because it helps to find patterns with more important features [1, 2] and is popular in time series. Many existing studies [7, 18] mine (unweighted) periodic patterns from time series by using the downward closure property to speed up the candidate generation process. Related works [6] for mining *weighted* periodic patterns from time series use the weight of maximum weighted character/item in the time series to reduce the number of unnecessary patterns tested, and thus to speed up the candidate generation.

As a preview, we propose the MPWS pruning solution. It provides a much tighter bound so as to reduce the number of candidates to be tested by using a heuristic value for the patterns.

3 Our Dynamic Tree Based Solution to Handle Sliding Window in Time Series (DTSW)

Our dynamic tree based solution to handle sliding window in time series (DTSW) consists of two modules: (i) A module for *handling deletion events*, which updates suffix tree if we delete some symbols from the starting of the sequence; and (ii) a module for *handling insertion events*, which updates our tree if we insert new symbols to the end of the sequence.

3.1 Handling Deletion Events

Deleting a symbol from the starting of a sequence means deletion of the largest suffix from the sequence. For example, if we have sequence "abcabababc", then removing the first symbol 'a' from the sequence means deleting the largest suffix "abcabababc" from the sequence resulting in sequence "bcabababc". So, the problem centers around how we can delete a suffix from the suffix tree. Hence, we define our Condition 1.

Condition 1. *Before deleting any suffix from the suffix tree, the tree must be in its explicit form.* Main reasoning behind this is, if the tree is in explicit form, then it is always enough to remove a leaf node from the tree to delete a suffix. For example, if we want to remove suffix "abcabababc$" from the explicit tree of Fig. 1, it is sufficient to remove Node 3 from the tree. Moreover, by definition, deletion of suffixes from a sequence goes from larger to smaller suffixes. Let us discuss some possible scenarios resulted from the deletions nodes and the ways to tackle them. We will state them as propositions.

Proposition 1 (Conversion from internal to leaf node). If the parent of a node V (say, U) loses all of its child nodes after removing V from an explicit suffix tree, then if U is not root, we will (i) convert U to a leaf node from an internal node and (ii) if any node W was pointing to U as its suffix link, then the suffix link of W will be redirected to root node. Reasoning behind this redirection lies in definition of suffix links that point from an internal node to another internal node. Path symbols from the root to any node X is unique because of the tree structure. So, suffix link of W must be redirected to the root.

Proposition 2 (Merging a splitted path). Suppose we remove node V for deletion from an explicit suffix tree. After the deletion, if (i) parent of V (say, U) becomes a node having a single child node W and (ii) U is not the root and has a parent node X, then we will (i) delete node U, (ii) merge the split path between X to U and U to W, and (iii) redirect the suffix link to root if any internal node Y was pointing to U as its suffix link. For example, from Fig. 1, after removing Node 3, Node 2 will only have a single child Node 4. Then, we will remove Node 2, and merge the path between Node 1 to Node 2 and the path between Node 2 to Node 4. Here, no node was pointing to Node 2 as its suffix link. Otherwise, we would have redirected to the root because path symbols "abc" (from the root to Node 2) would not have repeated elsewhere in the tree (from the root). This proposition is essential to maintain our Condition 1 and insertion module.

3.2 Handling Insertion Events

Our proposed solution DTSW is a complete framework for maintaining a dynamic suffix tree to handle sliding window, where our algorithm considers both *insertion* and *deletion* as two independent modules. Our solution is capable to (i) update the suffix tree for multiple insertion or deletion events and (ii) keep the structure consistent for future updates.

To *convert an implicit suffix tree to an explicit suffix tree*, a unique symbol is added to the tree. A symbol that does not exist in the sequence (upon which suffix tree is built) is considered as a unique symbol. This addition creates many nodes, splits many paths, and converts every implicit suffix explicit. Fig. 1 is the explicit suffix tree of string "abcabababc$", where main string is "abcabababc" and '$' is the unique symbol; implicit suffix tree of "abcabababc" is shown in Fig. 2. Although both figures represent the same suffixes, Fig. 1 has an advantage of ending all suffixes in leaves and ignoring the last symbol from each suffix we can extract the main suffixes to work with.

The main goal of our *insertion module* is to convert the tree to such an extent that the Ukkonen's algorithm can be used to insert symbols to the tree. Key steps include:

1. Conversion from explicit to implicit: We will revert back the tree from explicit to implicit form, which means we will remove the unique symbol and erase all the effects created due to it.
2. Finding new active point: Each pass of the Ukkonen's algorithm starts from the largest implicit suffix of the tree. After Step 1, some explicit suffixes will become implicit, then we need to find the largest implicit suffix's position and update the *active point* for the new pass.

There exists many reasons behind Step 1: (i) As unique symbol is not part of the input, this symbol has to be removed from the tree before any new addition. If we keep unique symbol, then adding new input and extracting the main suffixes will be costly. (ii) Addition of unique symbol creates some extra nodes and split paths in the tree. If we do not revert back the effect before new insertion, maximization of overlapping suffixes will not be ensured. The compact nature of the tree will be violated. Consider '$' as our unique symbol. Let us discuss cases which can occur due to addition of '$' and we have to revert back those effects:

1. *Child node V created from an existing node for '$'.* In this case, we have to remove the child node V. Because of deletion, if parent of V (say, U) loses all its children and U is not the root, then we have to convert U to a leaf node following Proposition 1 and if U remains with only one single child node, then we have to delete U and merge the path following Proposition 2.
2. *Child node V created by splitting an existing path for '$'.* This case can be explained from Figs. 2 and 1. Due to addition of '$' path between Node 1 and Node 3 gets split. New node 2 is inserted in between them, and then Node 4 is created for '$'. To revert back this case, we will first delete node V and then merge the split path by following Proposition 2. Here, in our example, we will first delete Node 4, then delete Node 2 and merge the path between Nodes 1 to 2 and Nodes 2 to 3. We would also have redirected the suffix link if any suffix link was pointing to Node 2 to the root.

Step 2 is find active point for the new pass. The whole process and reasoning can be provided as follows:

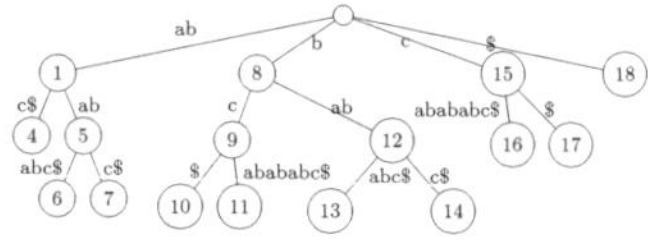

Fig. 4: Deletion

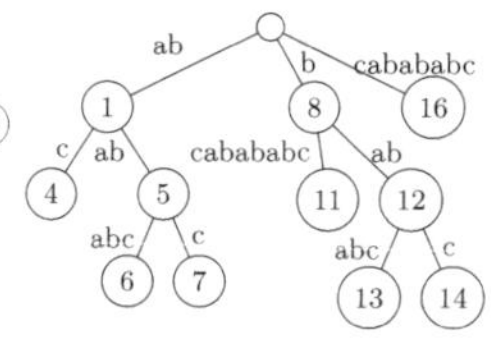

Fig. 5: Conversion

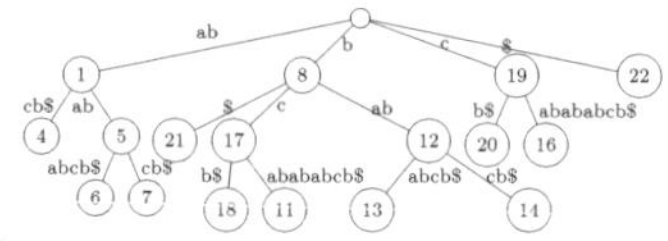

Fig. 6: Insertion

- In Step 1, we convert explicit suffixes to its implicit form. So, we can actually count the number of suffixes that have been converted. This number denotes the length of the largest implicit suffix at the moment after conversion. Suppose the number is l. So, all the suffixes present at most 1 distance from the end of the sequence will be implicit now, because a suffix becomes implicit along with all of its smaller sub suffixes. Moreover, suffix deletion is also sequential, larger suffixes will be effected first before its smaller sub-suffixes.
- Then, we will revert back the effects in reverse order by which the nodes were created or paths were split due to addition of '\$'. So, while erasing the effects, if we encounter a node which has been modified, we stop reverting because all of the previous effects created due to addition of '\$' have been compromised. So, we already found the largest implicit suffix of the tree. Now, by traversing the tree, we can find its position and update active point (aka *active Node*), *active Edge* and *active Length*. These information can also be saved while erasing the effects. As an example, if we want to have the tree of Fig. 2 from Fig. 1, we will revert back the effects of Nodes 18, 15, 9 and 2, respectively. Removing child for '\$' from the root does not help determining the largest implicit suffix because it is a dummy node.

Let us consider a simulation of our algorithm. Suppose we had a window of string "abcabababc" (the explicit tree for this window is shown in Fig. 1) and then we get a new symbol 'b' and our window slides. Fig. 4 shows the tree after deletion of 'a', Fig. 5 shows the tree after conversion and from explicit to implicit with the largest implicit suffix "bc", and Fig. 6 shows the resultant explicit tree after addition of 'b'.

4 Our Maximum Possible Weighted Support (MPWS) Pruning

Checking every pattern if they are weighted frequent (or weighted periodic) pattern is impractical. In unweighted version of pattern mining, the downward closure property (DCP) is used. As trivial DCP does not work in weighted pattern mining, most used technique is to use the weight of the maximum weighted character ($MaxW$) of the database to reduce the number of patterns tested. Testing a pattern means evaluating if that pattern can be a candidate pattern.

In this section, we propose a maximum possible weighted support (MPWS) pruning solution, which provides a tighter bound than the use of $MaxW$. In the remainder of this section, we will use 0.8, 0.1, 0.2 and 0 as the weights of characters 'a', 'b', 'c' and '$', respectively.

Definition 1. ***sumW(N)*** *is defined as the sum of all the characters from the root to node N.*

Definition 2. ***weight(X)*** *is defined as the average weight of the characters of pattern X.*

Definition 3. ***min_sup*** *is defined as a user-specified support threshold with a real number between 0 and 100, and* $\boldsymbol{\sigma}$ *is defined as its corresponding normalized threshold:*

$$\sigma = \frac{min\_sup \times (MaxW \times length\_of\_dataset)}{100.0} \tag{1}$$

With the maximum weight of a character in the dataset be MaxW, no pattern can have weighted support greater than $MaxW \times length\_of\_dataset$.

Definition 4. ***weightedSupport(X)*** *is defined as a product of the average weight of the character of pattern X and the actual periodicity support(X) of the pattern X:*

$$weightedSupport(X) = weight(X) \times support(X) \tag{2}$$

A pattern X is defined as **weighed periodic** *if* $weightedSupport(X) \geq \sigma$.

Definition 5. ***cnt(A, B)*** *is defined as the number of characters encountered on the path from node A to node B.*

Definition 6. ***maxW(A, B)*** *is defined as the weight of the character having the maximum weight among the characters on the path from node A to node B.*

Definition 7. ***sizeV(N)*** *is defined as the size of the occurrence of vector of node N. In other words, it captures the number of occurrence of the pattern that ends at node N.*

Definition 8. ***subStr(A, B)*** *is defined as the substring of the time series encountered on the path from node A to node B.*

For example, in Fig. 1, $sumW(Node\ 14)$ is the sum of weight of the characters 'b', 'a', 'b' and 'c', which is $0.1 + 0.8 + 0.1 + 0 = 1.2$. If X is "abac", then $weight(X) = \frac{0.8+0.1+0.8+0.2}{4} = 0.475$. In Fig. 1, $cnt(8, 13) = 6$, meaning that 6 characters are encountered on the path from Node 8 to Node 13. $maxW(8, 13) = 0.8$ means that the maximum weight among all 6 characters on the path from Node 8 to Node 13 is 0.8. $subStr(8, 13)$ is "ababc$", which is the substring of the time series encountered on the path from Node 8 to Node 13.

Definition 9. *Let (i) node P be the parent of node N, (ii) E be the edge between nodes N and P, and (iii) R be the root. Then,* ***nodeW(N)*** *is defined as the* *maximum possible weighted support of a pattern ending exactly above node N (between nodes N and its parent P):*

$$nodeW(N) = \max\{A, B\} \times sizeV(N) \tag{3}$$

where

$$A = \frac{sumW(P) + maxW(P, N)}{cnt(R, P) + 1} \tag{4}$$

$$B = \frac{sumW(P) + maxW(P, N) \times cnt(P, N)}{cnt(R, P) + cnt(P, N)} \tag{5}$$

Definition 10. *Let (i) node P be the parent of node N, (ii) E be the edge between nodes N and P, and (iii) R be the root. Then,* ***S*** *is defined as a representative of all the patterns that end between some node N and its parent P:*

$$S \leftarrow S_1 + S_2 \tag{6}$$

where

$$S_1 \leftarrow subStr(root, P) \tag{7}$$

$$S_2 \leftarrow \text{any nonempty prefix of } subStr(P, N) \tag{8}$$

Lemma 1. *$nodeW(N) \geq weightedSupport(S)$ always holds.*

Proof. By Eq. (3), $nodeW(N) = \max\{A, B\} \times sizeV(N)$ where values of A and B can be computed by Eqs. (4) and (5), respectively. And, by Eq. (2), $weightedSupport(S) = weight(S) \times support(S)$. Here, $\max(A, B)$ gives the maximum possible value of $weights(S)$ under any circumstances. Consider the following three cases:

1. $weight(S_1) > maxW(P, N)$: In this case, even if all the characters in E has the same weight as $maxW(P, N)$, $weight(S)$ cannot be greater than A. Because Eq. (4) assumes that S_3 has length 1. If we increase length of S_3, $weight(S)$ will gradually decrease. So, A is the maximum possible value of $weight(S)$ in this case.
2. $weight(S_1) < maxW(E)$: We need an upper bound for $weight(S)$. So, let us assume all the characters in E has weight equal to $maxW(P, N)$. Then, $weight(S)$ will gradually increase with the increasing length of S_3. We get the value of B (see Eq. (5)) by assuming S_3 has maximum possible length. So, B is the maximum possible value of $weight(S)$ in this case.
3. $weight(S) = maxW(P, N)$: In this case, the length of S_3 does not matter.

So, $\max\{A, B\} \geq weight(S)$, and $sizeV(N) \geq Support(S)$. Hence, $nodeW(N) = \max\{A, B\} \times sizeV(N)$, and thus $nodeW(N) \geq weightedSupport(S)$. □

Definition 11. ***MPWS(N)*** *is defined as the maximum value among $nodeW()$ of all the nodes in the subtree of node N. Subtree of node N includes itself. Let $nodeW(N)$ be the maximum possible weighted support pattern S. Then, $MPWS(N)$ is the maximum of $nodeW$ of all the nodes in the subtree, and it is the maximum possible weighted support any pattern can achieve that has S_1 as a prefix.*

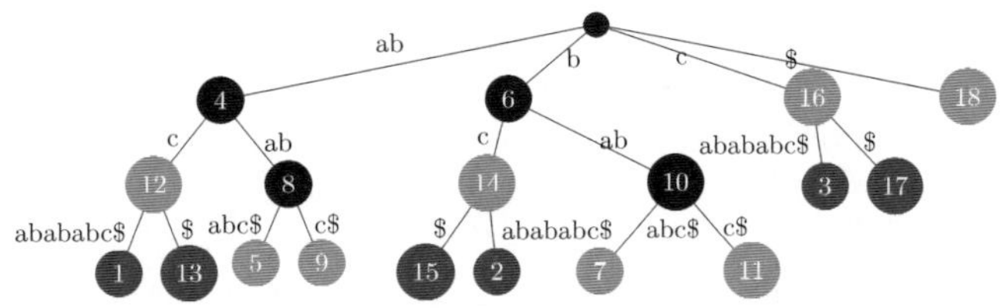

Fig. 7: Example of our MPWS pruning solution

Table 1: MPWS pruning necessary values calculated for Fig. 7

Node	sizeV	A	B	nodeW	MPWS
1	1	0.48	0.68	0.68	0.68
2	1	0.37	0.67	0.67	0.67
3	1	0.50	0.73	0.73	0.73
4	4	0.80	0.80	3.20	3.20
5	1	0.52	0.62	0.62	0.62
6	4	0.10	0.10	0.40	1.13
7	1	0.45	0.60	0.60	0.60
8	2	0.57	0.62	1.25	1.25
9	1	0.40	0.37	0.40	0.40

Node	sizeV	A	B	nodeW	MPWS
10	2	0.45	0.57	1.13	1.13
11	1	0.30	0.28	0.30	0.30
12	2	0.37	0.37	0.73	0.73
13	1	0.28	0.28	0.28	0.28
14	2	0.15	0.15	0.30	0.67
15	1	0.10	0.10	0.10	0.10
16	2	0.20	0.20	0.40	0.73
17	1	0.10	0.10	0.10	0.10
18	1	0.00	0.00	0.00	0.00

Candidate generation. Candidate patterns can be generated by a breadth first search (BFS) in the suffix tree. Following Definition 10, when we reach node N in the breadth first search, for every S, if $weight(S) \times sizeV(N) \geq \sigma$, then we will consider S as a *candidate pattern*.

Pruning condition. In the suffix tree for a string of size L, the number of nodes will be around N. However, the sum of the number of characters in the edges can be close to L^2. Thus, there can be around L^2 possible patterns in the dataset.

The candidate generation process mentioned above tests every pattern and makes that a candidate if it passes the test. However, checking every pattern is time consuming. So, we have to find a better pruning condition that reduces the number of patterns checked. The most commonly used technique is to use the weight of the maximum weighted character ($MaxW$) of the database. If $MaxW \times support(P) < \sigma$, any super pattern of P cannot be weighed frequent. So, those patterns cannot be periodic patterns either.

Lemma 2. *For any child C of node N, if $MPWS(C) < \sigma$, then we can ignore the whole subtree of C. This means that we do not need to visit any node in the subtree during the candidate generation of BFS.*

Proof. It can be easily proved because any node U in the subtree of C will not have $nodeW(U) \geq \sigma$ according to the definition of $MPWS(N)$. □

All the candidate patterns are actually *weighted frequent subsequence* of the current time series. To check if they are also periodic patterns, we can test the occurrence vector of each candidate pattern with different period values using known periodicity detection algorithms.

An example of our MPWS pruning solution is shown in Fig. 7 and Table 1. Here, the figure shows a suffix tree of string "abcabababc$" with $min\_sup = 10\%$. Detailed calculation of MPWS and other associated values is shown in Table 1. There are 3 types of nodes in Fig. 7:

1. Any pattern that has a *blue node* (e.g., Nodes 4, 6, 8 and 10) in its subtree is tested. For example, only patterns "a","ab","aba","abab","b","ba","bab" has a blue node in their subtree. So, only these patterns are tested for candidacy.
2. A *green node* N means that, starting from N, its whole subtree is unimportant and can be ignored during candidate generation BFS. Nodes 5, 7, 9, 11, 12, 14, 16 and 18 are green nodes.
3. All the nodes having a green node as an ancestor are *red nodes* (e.g., Nodes 1, 2, 3, 13, 15 and 17).

In this example, according to MPWS pruning, only seven patterns are tested for candidacy. Five of them eventually become candidate patterns. There are 50 patterns in total that had to be tested if we did not use any pruning. If we used the traditional *MaxW* pruning, we had to test 10 patterns.

Additional complexity for pruning. If we build a suffix tree for a string of size L, there can be at most $2 \times L$ nodes in the suffix tree. During candidate generation, we first determine the MPWS value for all the nodes, which can be done by a depth first search (DFS) on the tree. We need the *MaxW* value for each edge during that DFS. We have determined it using range minimum query (RMQ) in static data. As the query complexity for each edge is O(1), the added complexity by MPWS pruning becomes O(L).

5 Evaluation Results

We have used several data sets taken from UCI Machine Learning Repository [8] to compare our solutions with existing approaches. As all of them show consistent results, we will be showing the results of the following three datasets, which were discretized into string of characters:

1. Individual household electric power consumption dataset, which consists of 50000 events discretized into 13 types;
2. Appliances energy prediction dataset, which consists of 19735 events discretized into 12 types; and
3. Diabetes dataset, which consists of 2400 events discretized into 37 types.

All the codes were written using the C++ programming language. We used a machine having AMD Ryzen 5 machine with 1600 CPU (3.2 GHz) and 8 GB RAM for evaluation.

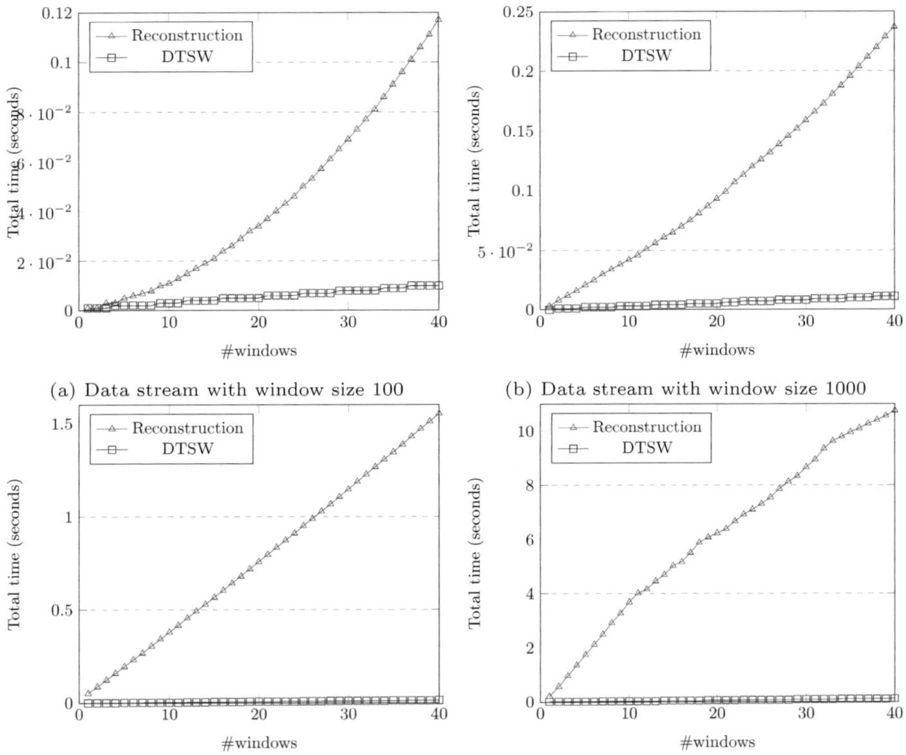

(a) Data stream with window size 100

(b) Data stream with window size 1000

(c) Data stream with window size 10000

(d) Data stream with window size 30000

Fig. 8: Sliding window with window sizes 100, 1000, 10000 and 30000

5.1 Evaluation on the DTSW Algorithm

Existing works on time series do not handle the sliding window based problem. Hence, they build the data structure from scratch for every window sliding, which can be inefficient. We show a comparison of the experimental result between DTSW and reconstruction of the tree for every window. Building the tree again for each new window performs poorly when the window size is large or the number of windows is large. In these scenarios, DTSW is very useful.

In Fig. 8, we show four graphs for four different window sizes from the individual household electric power consumption dataset. (As results for the other three datasets are similar, we omit them.) In the figures, the x-axis shows the number of windows passed and the y-axis shows the total time taken from the beginning. With the increasing window size, the performance of reconstruction gets worse, but DTSW runs very efficiently.

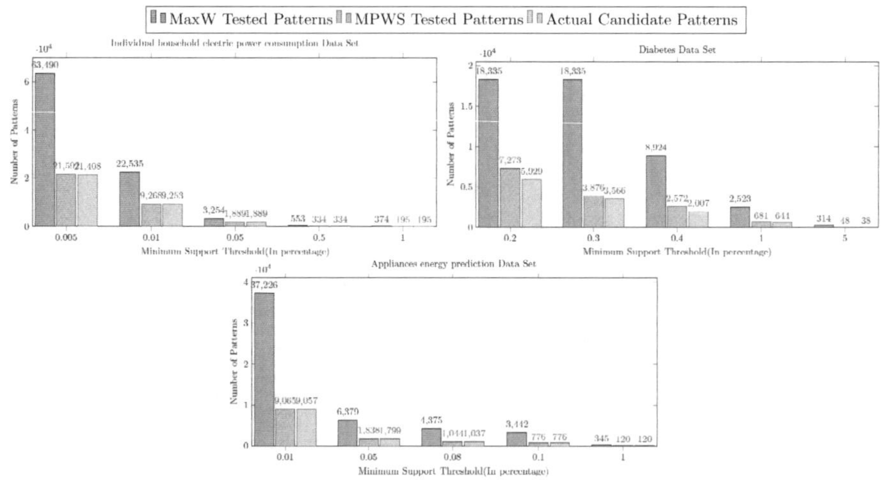

Fig. 9: MPWS pruning vs. MaxW pruning on varying minimum weighted support threshold

5.2 Evaluation on the MPWS Pruning

In the candidate generation process without any pruning, every pattern has to be tested to check if it can be a candidate. However, this is not practical as there can be many unnecessary patterns. Our main goal in the MPWS pruning is to avoid testing patterns that will not become a candidate pattern eventually.

For all the datasets, we have discretized them and assigned each unique character a weight that follows a normal distribution (μ=0.5 and σ=0.2). For different weighted support thresholds, we have compared our MPWS pruning with the traditional *MaxW* pruning on all the databases. Fig. 9 shows that our MPWS pruning tests much fewer patterns when compared with the traditional *MaxW* pruning. For example, in the individual household electric power consumption dataset, when the minimum support threshold is 0.005%, if we try to optimize the candidate generation process by using only *MaxW* in the database, it checks 63, 490 patterns. In contrast, mining with our MPWS pruning checks only 21, 592 patterns. With only 21, 408 actual candidate patterns, our MPWS pruning significantly reduces the number of tested patterns to close to the number of actual candidate patterns. Moreover, our MPWS pruning is observed not to test more patterns than the traditional *MaxW* pruning. In fact, our MPWS pruning is guaranteed to test no more patterns than the traditional *MaxW* pruning.

6 Conclusions

In this paper, we solved two important problems in time series pattern mining. Our *dynamic tree based solution to handle sliding window in time series* (*DTSW*)

is an algorithm for solving the sliding window problem. Our *maximum possible weighted support* (*MPWS*) *pruning* is a technique that reduces the number of patterns to be tested for candidacy. Both solutions are shown to be more efficient than existing approaches. Note that both of these solutions are independent of each other and can be used as two separate modules. Specifially, our first contribution—namely, *DTSW*—is an algorithm to dynamically update suffix tree. It is adaptable to run time dynamic window size, and is applicable for both weighted and unweighted framework. It solves the challenge of dynamic time series data. Our second contribution—namely, *MPWS*—can be used in different kinds of weighted pattern mining (with necessary modifications) in place of traditional *MaxW* because of its unique style for approximating an upper bound. As ongoing and future work, we are extending our solutions using dynamic weights in time series.

Acknowledgements

This project is partially supported by NSERC (Canada) and University of Manitoba.

References

1. Ahmed, C.F., Tanbeer, S.K., Jeong, B.S., Lee, Y.K.: An efficient algorithm for sliding window-based weighted frequent pattern mining over data streams. IEICE TIS E92-D(7), 1369–1381 (2009)
2. Ahmed, C.F., Tanbeer, S.K., Jeong, B.S., Lee, Y.K.: Handling dynamic weights in weighted frequent pattern mining. IEICE TIS E91-D(11), 2578–2588 (2008)
3. Almusallam, N., Tari, Z., Chan, J., AlHarthi, A.: UFSSF - an efficient unsupervised feature selection for streaming features. In: PAKDD 2018, Part II. LNCS (LNAI), vol. 10938, pp. 495–507 (2018)
4. A'yun, K., Abadi, A., Saptaningtyas, F.: Application of weighted fuzzy time series model to forecast Trans Jogja's passengers. IJAPM 5(2), 76–85 (2015)
5. Braun, P., Cuzzocrea, A., Leung, C.K., Pazdor, A.G.M., Souza, J.: Item-centric mining of frequent patterns from big uncertain data. Procedia Computer Science 126, 1875–1884 (2018)
6. Chanda, A.K., Ahmed, C.F., Samiullah, M., Leung, C.K.: A new framework for mining weighted periodic patterns in time series databases. ESWA 79, 207–224 (2017)
7. Chanda, A.K., Saha, S., Nishi, M.A., Samiullah, M., Ahmed, C.F.: An efficient approach to mine flexible periodic patterns in time series databases. EAAI 44, 46–63 (2015)
8. Dheeru, D., Karra Taniskidou, E.: UCI machine learning repository (2017), `http://archive.ics.uci.edu/ml`
9. Kane, A., Shiri, N.: Multivariate time series representation and similarity search using PCA. In: ICDM 2017. LNCS (LNAI), vol. 10357, pp. 122–136 (2017)
10. Leung, C.K., Hoi, C.S.H., Pazdor, A.G.M., Wodi, B.H., Cuzzocrea, A.: Privacy-preserving frequent pattern mining from big uncertain data. In: IEEE BigData 2018, pp. 5101–5110 (2018)

11. Leung, C.K., Khan, Q.I.: DSTree: a tree structure for the mining of frequent sets from data streams. In: IEEE ICDM 2006, pp. 928–932 (2006)
12. Leung, C.K., Zhang, H., Souza, J., Lee, W.: Scalable vertical mining for big data analytics of frequent itemsets. In: DEXA 2018, Part I. LNCS, vol. 11029, pp. 3–17 (2018)
13. Mantuan, A.B., Fernandes, L.A.F.: Spatial contextualization for closed itemset mining. In: IEEE ICDM 2018, pp. 1176–1181 (2018)
14. Morris, K.J., Egan, S.D., Linsangan, J.L., Leung, C.K., Cuzzocrea, A., Hoi, C.S.H.: Token-based adaptive time-series prediction by ensembling linear and non-linear estimators: a machine learning approach for predictive analytics on big stock data. In: IEEE ICMLA 2018, pp. 1486–1491 (2018)
15. Mozaffari, L., Mozaffari, A., L. Azad, N.: Vehicle speed prediction via a sliding-window time series analysis and an evolutionary least learning machine: a case study on San Francisco urban roads. JESTech 18(2), 150–162 (2015)
16. Phan, H., Le, B.: A novel parallel algorithm for frequent itemsets mining in large transactional databases. In: ICDM 2018. LNCS (LNAI), vol. 10933, pp. 272–287 (2018)
17. Rahman, M.M., Ahmed, C.F., Leung, C.K.: Mining weighted frequent sequences in uncertain databases. Inf. Sci. 479, 76–100 (2019)
18. Rasheed, F., Alshalalfa, M., Alhajj, R.: Efficient periodicity mining in time series databases using suffix trees. IEEE TKDE 23(1), 79–94 (2011)
19. Singh, R., Graves, J.A., Talbert, D.A., Eberle, W.: Prefix and suffix sequential pattern mining. In: ICDM 2018. LNCS (LNAI), vol. 10933, pp. 309–324 (2018)
20. Ukkonen, E.: On-line construction of suffix trees. Algorithmica 14(3), 249–260 (1995)
21. Yan, X., Wang, Z., Yu, S., Li, Y.: Time series forecasting with RBF neural network. In: ICMLC 2005, pp. 4680–4683 (2005)

A Symmetry of the Data Pattern Structure

Alexey Myachin[1,2][0000-0003-4578-0736]

[1] National Research University Higher School of Economics
20 Myasnitskaya street, Moscow 101000, Russia
[2] Institute of Control Science of Russian Academy of Science
65 Profsoyuznay street, Moscow 117997, Russia
amyachin@hse.ru

Abstract. We present a method of finding clusters with the property of mutual symmetry of the data pattern structure in parallel coordinates. The description of the method and the implementing algorithm is given. Clear-cut examples of identifying the symmetry of the data structure are considered using the examples of “Balance Scale Data Set”, “Car Data Set”, and “Pollen Data Set” on the one hand, as well as the capabilities and specific aspects of the method for Visual Data Mining purposes on the other hand. The conclusion contains the main results obtained in the course of experimental verification with regard to the properties of the analyzed objects, reflected by the structure of their data.

Keywords: Visual Data Mining; Pattern Analysis; Ordinal-Invariant Pattern Clustering; Cluster Analysis; Symmetry of Data Structure

1 Pattern Analysis

1.1 Introduction

The need to analyze multi-factor objects in difficult to formulate areas as sociology, political science, economics, and others contributed to the active development of tools and individual areas of Visual Data Mining. One of these already proven directions is the method of parallel coordinates [5, 6]. Its main idea consists of having some set of objects under study: each object is characterized by a set of m parameters written in a vector form as $p_i = (p_{i1}, p_{i2}, \ldots, p_{ij}, \ldots, p_{im})$ where p_{ij} is the value of the j-th parameter of the i-th object. For the purpose of data analysis, a graphical representation of the object in parallel coordinates is used. This representation uses m parallel, usually vertical and uniformly distributed coordinate axes, each of which reflects one of the selected parameters. The object is depicted as polylines with vertices on the coordinate axes. Such a graphical representation of the data allows to study and visually analyze polylines, and in particular, combining objects into separate groups (clusters), based on the monotony of polylines [6]. This method has successfully established itself in solving applied problems of macroeconomics, banking, political science [1-3]. However, it should be noted that the type of polylines significantly depends on the order of the coordinate axes, which in some cases leads to ambiguity of the clustering results [7].

This paper focuses on the search for clusters with polylines of mutual symmetry, which should not be violated with a change in the order of the coordinate axes. Therefore, further, the analysis relies on the clustering method that provides this property. The semantic content reflected in each individual case by the property of mutual symmetry represents separate interest.

1.2 Ordinal-Invariant Pattern Clustering

The main idea of ordinal-invariant pattern clustering is to search and merge objects that do not change their affiliation to the cluster (i.e., keep the polylines monotonous) for any change in the sequence of coordinate axes when the object is displayed in parallel coordinates [8, 9].

The clustering procedure, the result of which does not depend on the sequence of coordinate axes of the indicators of the objects under study, will be called "ordinal-invariant pattern clustering". The clusters obtained as a result of its use, respectively, are fairly ordinal-invariant pattern-clusters. The theorem presented below formulates an important property of ordinal-invariant pattern-clusters.

Theorem. Ordinal-invariant pattern-clusters do not intersect. In other words, one data line cannot belong to two different ordinal-invariant pattern-clusters. The proof of the theorem is presented in [9].

The theorem actually determines the uniqueness of ordinal-invariant pattern clustering, and therefore has an important application both for the construction of an algorithm for its implementation and for the development of individual applications.

2 Ordinal-Invariant Pattern-Clusters with Mutually Symmetric Structure

The purpose of this section is to demonstrate (by the example of widely known, practically, "academic" data sets) the existence of clusters with a symmetrical structure of patterns, on the one hand, and certain aspects of the proposed method for Visual Data Mining purposes, on the other. For these purposes, the following data sets have been used:

- "Balance Scale Data Set" [11, 14];
- "Car Data Set" [15]; and
- "Pollen Data Set" [16].

2.1 Balance Scale Data Set

The Balance Scale Data Set was generated to simulate psychological experiments described by Robert Siegler [11]. The source data table contains 625 rows. Each line reflects the values of five parameters $(p_0, p_1, p_2, p_3, p_4)$, which characterize the parameters and state of the balance scale apparatus (see Fig. 1).

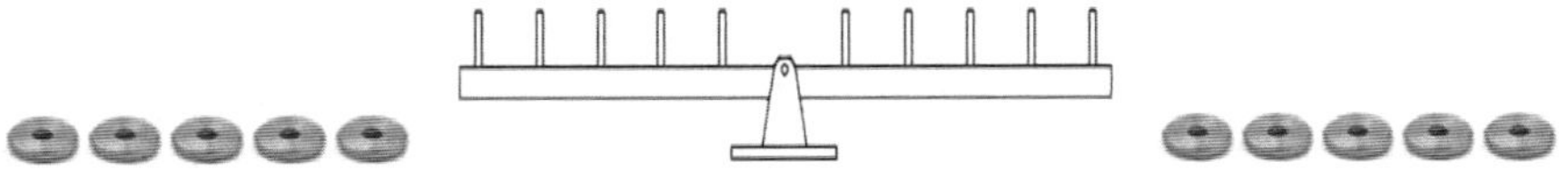

Fig. 1. The balance scale apparatus (adapted to text from [11]).

The parameter p_0 = {"B", "L", "R"} characterizes the state of the apparatus: balance (B); downward deviation of the left (L) or right (R).

The remaining parameters p_1, p_2, p_3 and p_4 take integer values from one to five and characterize:

- $p_1 = \{1, 2, 3, 4, 5\}$ – the number of weight units of the left side;
- $p_2 = \{1, 2, 3, 4, 5\}$ – the distance from the fulcrum to the left;
- $p_3 = \{1, 2, 3, 4, 5\}$ – the number of weight units of the right side;
- $p_4 = \{1, 2, 3, 4, 5\}$ – the distance from the fulcrum to the right.

The source data set contains 49 lines corresponding to the state "B" (balance); 288 - state "L" (deviation to the left); and 288 - the state of "R" (deviation to the right).

The purpose of the experiment: demonstrate the individual capabilities of the ordinal-invariant pattern clustering for visual analysis of data when solving the Data Mining problem and identify clusters that have the symmetry property of data patterns, using the "Balance Scale Data Set".

The result of the ordinal-invariant pattern clustering procedure was the division of the original "Balance Scale Data Set" into a plurality of ordinal-invariant pattern-clusters with a number of visually distinctive features that allow them to be divided into three groups.

First of all, the group of ordinal-invariant pattern-clusters is distinguished, for which the absolute symmetry of the right and left parts of the polylines is characteristic (see Fig. 2). In total, this group combines 45 out of 49 lines corresponding to the state "B" (balance).

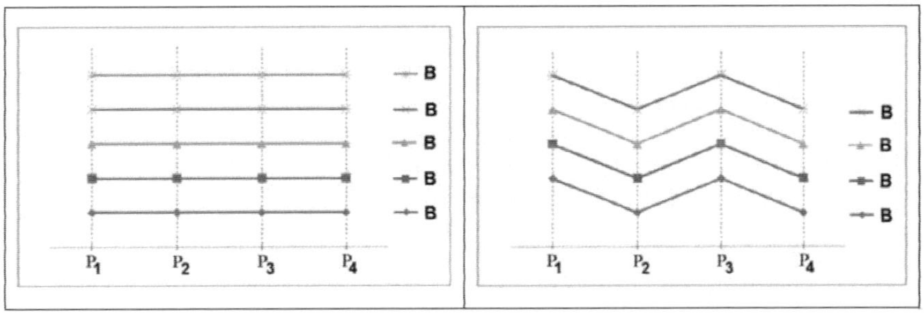

Fig. 2. Examples of polylines of ordinal-invariant pattern-clusters corresponding to the state of "Balance" (B). They are characterized by a symmetrical shape of the right and left parts of polylines.

The remaining set of clusters is visually subdivided into four groups with the following distinct feature: each cluster of one group can indicate its corresponding clusters of the other three groups that have a mirror-symmetric form of polylines relative to vertical and horizontal axes (see Fig. 3).

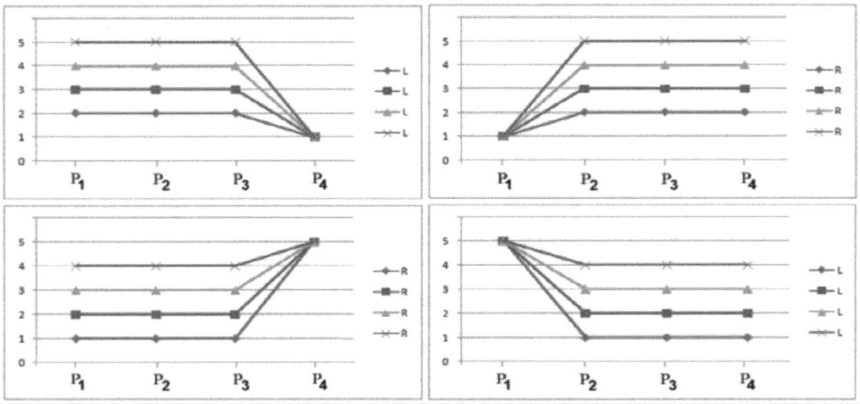

Fig. 3. Four ordinal-invariant pattern-clusters characterized by a mirror-symmetric form of polylines.

It is important to note that almost all ordinal-invariant pattern-clusters contained objects of only one type: “B”, “L” or “R”. The exception was made only by four objects of group "B" (Balance). Unlike other objects of this group, they were ranked as clusters containing objects with a mirror-symmetric form of polylines (see Fig. 4).

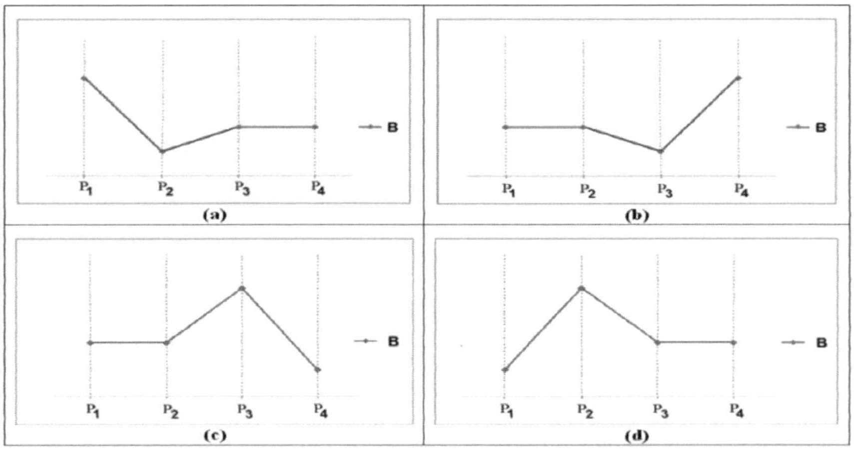

Fig. 4. Four objects of the group "B" are characterized in pairs mirror-symmetrical form of polylines (a) - (b) and (c) - (d).

Thus, the application of the procedure of the ordinal-invariant pattern clustering to the Balance Scale Data Set made it possible to divide the total amount of data into three groups corresponding to three different states of the original object (the balance scale apparatus): balance, deviation to the left, and deviation to the right. The appearance of the polylines allows us to make an assumption about the presence of certain symmetric properties of the original object.

2.2 Car Data Set

This dataset contains the technical specifications of automobiles produced by various companies in the USA, Europe, and Japan from 1970 to 1982. The dataset was created by Ernesto Ramos and David Donoho and first presented at the American Statistical Association Data Exposition in 1983.

Description of the source dataset. The source data table contains 406 rows. Each line reflects the values of 9 parameters (p_0, p_1, p_2, p_3, p_4, p_5, p_6, p_7, p_8), which characterize the following vehicle parameters:

Parameter p_0 reflects the car model. The parameters p_1, p_2, p_3, p_4, p_5 and p_6 take numerical values and describe the technical characteristics of the car:

- p_1 – MPG (fuel consumption: miles per halon);
- p_2 – number of cylinders;
- p_3 – engine displacement: cubic feet;
- p_4 – horsepower (power in hp);
- p_5 – car weight (lbs);
- p_6 – acceleration time from 0 to 60 miles per hour (sec.).

Parameters p_7 and p_8 characterize:

- p_7 – model year of release;
- p_8 – origin (USA, Europe or Japan).

Background experimental research. Visual analysis of large amounts of information and the identification of individual groups with similar features in it is substantially harder due to the presence of clutter in the image when displaying a significant amount of data. As an example, we present a graphical representation of the "Car Data Set" in parallel coordinates (Fig. 5).

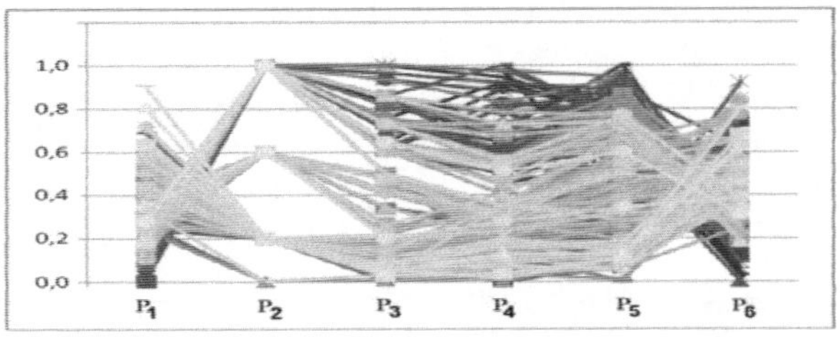

Fig. 5. Graphical representation of the normalized "Car Data Set" in parallel coordinates.

The article [10] is dedicated to image clutter reduction with the aim of facilitating visual analysis using the example of the “Car Data Set”. However, clutter reduction does not completely solve the problem, since the very presence of clutter is primarily due to the display and interposition of large amounts of different types of graphic data.

The purpose of the experiment: demonstrate the capabilities of the considered method to reduce the clutters of data visualization and identify mutually symmetric structures, using "Car Data Set".

The results of the experiment. Clustering was carried out according to the technical characteristics of cars p_1, p_2, p_3, p_4, p_5 and p_6, expressed in normalized values in the range [0-1]:

$$p_{in} = \frac{p_{ij} - p_{i\,min}}{p_{i\,max} - p_{i\,min}}, \qquad (1)$$

where: $p_{i\,min} = min_j(p_{ij})$, $p_{i\,max} = max_j(p_{ij})$ | $i = 1, \ldots, 6; j = 1, \ldots, 406$.

The result was a partition of the original set into a number of clusters, examples of which are shown in the Fig. 6.

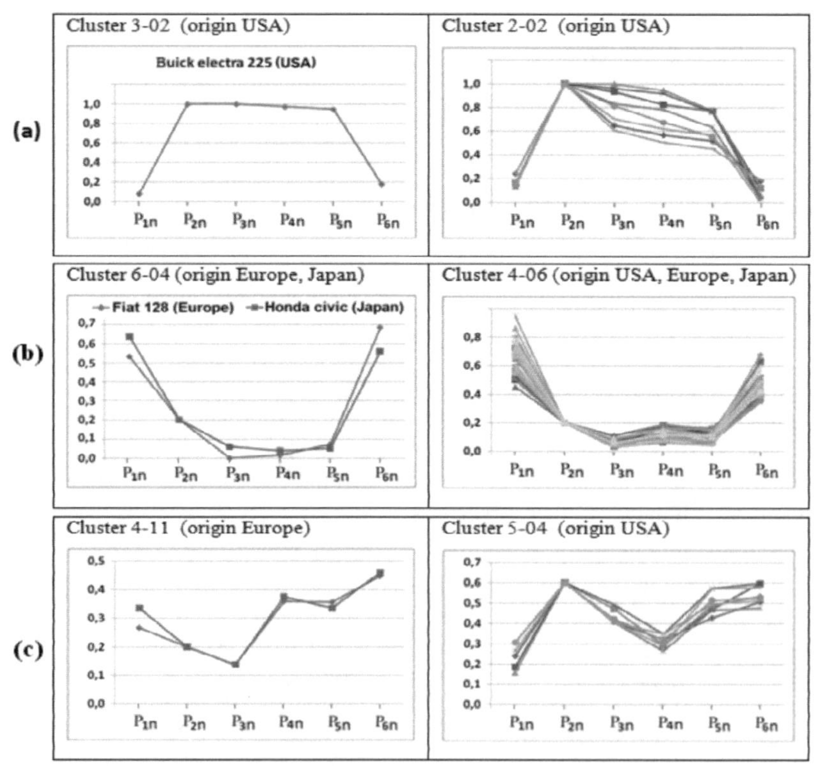

Fig. 6. Visually distinct types of patterns: (a) polylines, convex upwards and their variations; (b) polylines, convex down and their variations; (c) “intermediate” types of polylines.

These figures demonstrate a significant clutter reduction in image, which is a consequence of two factors:

- division of the initial set into a number of clusters containing structurally similar data;
- relatively small (compared to the initial set) number of data in each cluster.

Assessing the possibility of using the results of ordinal-invariant pattern clustering for the purposes of Visual Data Mining, it should be noted that the following typical types of patterns are highlighted (see Fig. 6):

- patterns of allocated clusters have the form of polylines, convex upwards. These clusters are typical for the early 1970s USA cars. Modification of individual parameters of cars produced in subsequent years reflected in the variation of the pattern, as shown in Fig. 6a;
- another type of visually distinguished pattern has the character directly opposite to the previous one and is represented by a polyline, convex downwards. Allocated clusters are typical for a number of car models produced in Europe, Japan, and the USA since the second half of the 1970s. As in the previous case, the modification of individual parameters of cars produced in subsequent years was reflected in the variation of the pattern, as shown in Fig. 6b.
- the third type of pattern is "intermediate" between those considered above. It is characterized both by clusters containing data of automobiles produced only in the USA, and clusters in which automobiles of various countries are represented (Fig. 6c).

The observed symmetry of the data structure (polylines convex up and down) reflects various approaches in creating individual car models in the USA, Europe, and Japan of that time. In the USA, with high energy resources, powerful and heavy car models were actively produced, requiring the use of 8 (in some models, 6) cylinder engines, high fuel consumption, and low acceleration during gaining speed. Such models are characterized by polylines, convex upwards (Fig. 6a). In Europe and Japan, preference was given to lighter and more "nimble" car models, using 4 (in some models, even 3) cylinder engines that do not require such high fuel consumption. They are characterized by polylines, convex down (Fig. 6b). The development of the automotive industry led to the convergence of these various approaches, reflected in the form of patterns (Fig. 6c).

2.3 Pollen Data Set

Pollen Data Set is a synthetic data created by David Coleman at RCA Laboratories in Princeton, New Jersey.

Description of the source dataset. The source data table contains 3,848 rows. Each line reflects the values of six parameters (p_1, p_2, p_3, p_4, p_5, p_6), the last of which, p_6, is an additional parameter, reflecting the line number in the data set. According to the description of the variables p_1 – p_5, given by the author, "the variables were given entirely fictitious names" and they conditionally characterize the geometric dimensions along the x, y, z axes, the mass and density of pollen grains:

- p_1 – ridge;
- p_2 – nub;
- p_3 – crack;
- p_4 – weight;
- p_5 – density;
- p_6 – observation number (for convenience).

The purpose of the experiment: demonstrate the capabilities of the considered method for large amounts of data, using Pollen Data Set.

Background experimental research. The "Pollen Data Set" is synthetic, i.e. belongs to the class of artificially formed sets for which it is difficult to expect the presence of clusters with a mutually symmetric data structure. We also note the complexity of visual analysis in parallel coordinates, which is associated with a large volume and high density of data (see Fig. 7a). The use of grayscale intensities in the image proposed in [13], allowed to partially solve this problem and improve the visual presentation (see Fig. 7b).

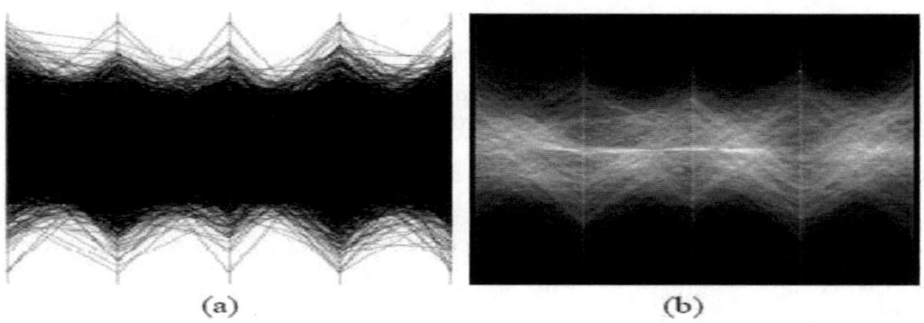

Fig. 7. a) Visualization of *Pollen* data set; b) Visualization of the same data set, with the intensity of the grey levels set proportionally to the superimposition of the polylines over a black background [13].

The method was further developed in [4], where the authors proposed interactive algorithms "Interactive Parallel Coordinates Frequency Plot" and "Interactive Parallel Coordinates Density Plot", in which the gray intensity levels are determined by analyzing the frequency and density of image areas. An example of applying the Interactive Parallel Coordinates Density Plot algorithm to the Pollen Data Set is shown in Fig. 8.

A visual analysis of Fig. 7b and Fig. 8b allows us to assume that there are clusters with a symmetrical structure of patterns in the Pollen Data Set.

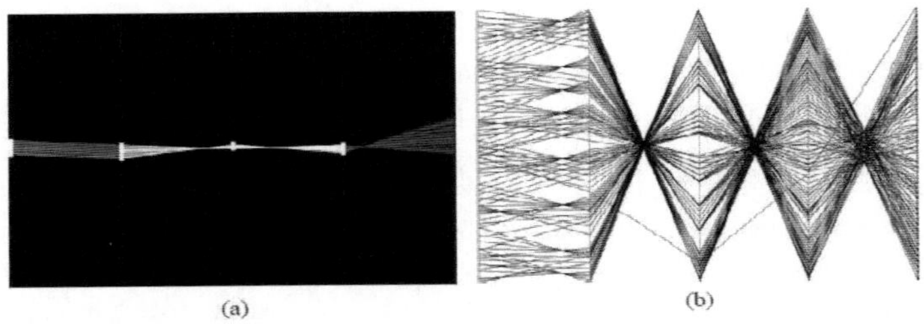

Fig. 8. a) Visualization of *Pollen* data using the *IPC Density Plot* with the intervals along the axes being selected by the user; b) Zoom of the selected records [4].

The results of the experiment confirmed the presence in the considered set of clusters with a mutually symmetric structure of data patterns, which is reflected in Fig. 9.

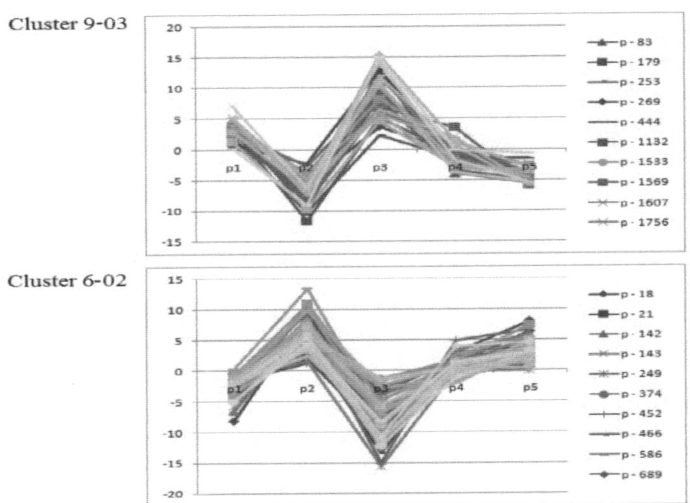

Fig. 9. Examples of mutual symmetry of the pattern structure of ordinal-invariant pattern-clusters in Pollen Data Set.

The presence of such structures with a sufficiently large number of elements is due to the method used to form the Pollen Data Set. According to the description, one of the stages was that after forming part of this set (part A), its second (part B) was obtained by inverting the sign in three of the five variables of part A, which in fact meant mirroring this parameter relative to the zero point of the corresponding axis.

2.4 Finding Patterns with a Mutually Symmetric of Data Structure

Let us consider the selection of clusters with a mutually symmetric structure of patterns for a given order of coordinate axes. The solution of the problem consists of two stages. At the first stage, the ordinal-invariant pattern clustering of the initial data set is performed. Each cluster, in this case, contains data that is graphically represented in parallel coordinates by monotonous polylines. By virtue of the ordinal invariance of clusters, co-monotonicity is preserved for any sequence of coordinate axes. A detailed description of the ordinal-invariant pattern clustering algorithm, which is necessary for the implementation of the first stage, is given in [9].

At the second stage, the cluster is searched, having the property of mutual symmetry of the structure of their polylines. For a small number of formed clusters, the search can be performed visually. For large sets, it is advisable to use the automatic search. We take into account that each cluster formed at the first stage contains a set of data graphically represented in parallel coordinates in the form of co-monotone polylines. A general view of the polylines of each cluster can be described by a code sequence, where each parameter ("A", "B" or "C") characterizes slope category on a separate interval [7], see Fig. 10.

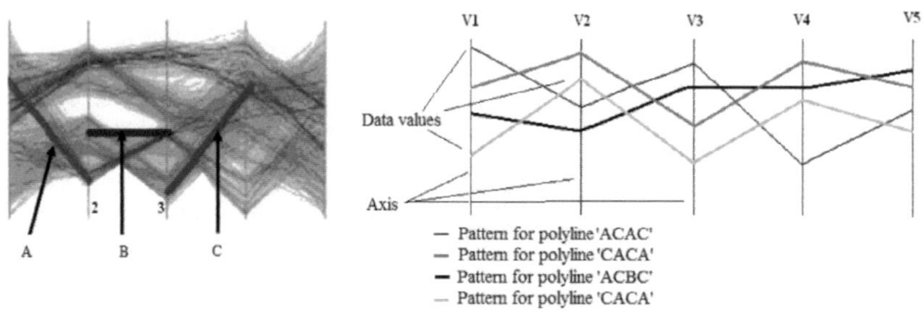

Fig. 10. (a) Slope category A, B, and C of data sets in Parallel coordinates; (b) Polylines representing various patterns [7].

To search for a cluster containing an inverse (relative to the horizontal axis) form of a polyline, we should form the "inverse" code sequence of parameters that characterizes it, replacing the symbols "A" with "C", and "C" with "A" (leaving the symbol "B" without change).

We turn to the question of finding clusters that retain the mutual symmetry property, regardless of the order of the coordinate axes. For this purpose, we choose an arbitrary object of the first ordinal-invariant pattern-cluster (Cluster 1), and arrange its parameters in a non-decreasing sequence. Let us set the given sequence for coordinate axes. In this case, the polylines of the objects will have the form of a non-decreasing graphic and is described by a code sequence containing only the parameters "B" and "C" (due to the co-monotonicity of the polylines, all other objects of this cluster are also described by this sequence). Constructing an "inverse" code sequence, as described above (i.e., changing the "C" symbol to "A" and leaving the "B" symbol unchanged), we obtain a code sequence describing Cluster 2 objects. The form of the graphs of these objects will have non-increasing polyline. We show that the inverse character of the code sequence will be preserved for any other sequence of coordinate axes. Indeed, consider two objects $e_1 = (a_1, a_2, a_3, \ldots, a_n)$ and $e_2 = (b_1, b_2, b_3, \ldots, b_n)$ belonging to, respectively, Cluster 1 and Cluster 2.

According to the condition, the object's parameters are arranged in a non-decreasing sequence:

$$a_1 \leq a_2 \leq a_3 \leq \cdots \leq a_n,$$

whence it follows that for any values of k, l, and m $(k, l,\ m \in [1, 2, \ldots, n])$, the inequalities hold:

$$a_k \leq a_m \ if\ k < m;$$
$$a_l \geq a_m \ if\ l > m.$$

For the parameters of the object e_2, the nature of inequalities is the opposite:

$$b_1 \geq b_2 \geq b_3 \geq \cdots \geq b_n,$$

whence it follows that:

$$b_k \leq b_m \ if\ k < m;$$
$$b_l \geq b_m \ if\ l > m.$$

It can be seen that the nature of the inequalities described above is of an opposite nature for any values of k, l, and m $(k, l,\ m \in [1, 2, \ldots, n])$which means the presence of this property for any arrangement of the coordinate axes.

As an illustration, Fig.11a shows four two ordinal-invariant pattern-clusters with a mutually symmetric structure. Changing the order of the coordinate axes changes the shape of the graphs, but does not violate their symmetry, see Fig. 11b.

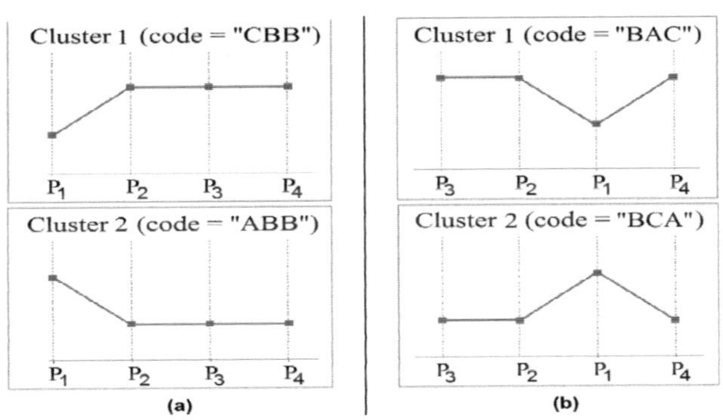

Fig. 11. (a) Two ordinal-invariant pattern-clusters with a mutually symmetric structure; (b) Changing the order of the coordinate axes changes the appearance of the graphs, but does not change their symmetry.

We note the following features of the method described above.

1. Unambiguity. This property is ensured by the uniqueness of the results of the ordinal-invariant pattern clustering, on the one hand, and the uniqueness of the procedure for finding symmetric structures of data patterns, proved above, on the other.

2. The number of clusters (at the first stage of the algorithm) is not predetermined in advance and is determined automatically during the operation of the clustering procedure. The number of clusters with a symmetric structure of data patterns (outlined in the second stage) is determined by the presence of such structures in the initial set, properties of the studied objects, reflected in the structure of the source data.

3. The data should be presented in numerical form. If individual parameters are specified in different metric units or ranges, it is advisable to present them in a normalized form, defined by expression (1).

3 Conclusion

This work lies in the general course of work related to the study of the properties and applications of the ordinal-invariant pattern clustering [8, 9]. The article deals with the search and selection of clusters with the property of mutual symmetry of the structure of their patterns. The proposed algorithm allows you to select a mirror or visually symmetric structure in a large amount of data and high image clutter. At the same time, the symmetry of the patterns is preserved for any order of coordinate axes.

The results of applying the described method are given using the examples of the Balance Scale Data Set, Car Data Set, and Pollen Data Set. It is noted that in each considered example, the symmetry of the patterns had a certain semantic content:

- for Balance Scale Data Set, the mirror symmetry of the patterns reflected the symmetry of the object itself - the balance scale apparatus;
- for Car Data Set, symmetry of patterns reflected two different trends of the 70s when creating cars: heavy and powerful prestigious cars with high fuel consumption (USA), and less powerful, but lighter and "nimble" cars with relatively low fuel consumption (Europe, Japan, USA). The data set reflected the presence of "intermediate" models, partially incorporating features of both trends;
- for Pollen Data Set, the presence of clusters with a symmetrical structure reflected the features of the data set generation algorithm.

The considered examples demonstrate the potential for extracting additional information about objects based on an analysis of the structure of the data generated by them. Note also that the visually distinguishing features are close to those with which a person operates. This feature allows you to consider the possibility of using the described method, for example, in systems modeling "human" choice.

Acknowledgements

The article was prepared within the framework of the Basic Research Program at the National Research University Higher School of Economics (HSE) and supported within the framework of a subsidy by the Russian Academic Excellence Project '5-100'.

References

1. Aleskerov, F., Alper, C.: A clustering approach to some monetary facts: a long-run analysis of cross-country data. In: The Japanese Economic Review, vol. 51, No. 4, pp. 555–567 (2000).
2. Aleskerov, F., Ersel, H., Yolalan, R.: Multicriterial Ranking Approach for Evaluating Bank Branch Performance. In: International Journal of Information Technology and Decision Making, vol. 3, No. 2, pp. 321–335 (2004).
3. Aleskerov, F., Nurmi, H.: A method for finding patterns of party support and electoral change: An analysis of British general and Finnish municipal elections. In: Mathematical and Computer Modelling, vol. 48, pp. 1385–1395 (2008).
4. Artero, A. O., de Oliveira, M. C. F., Levkowitz, H.: Uncovering Clusters in Crowded Parallel Coordinates Visualizations. In: Proc. of IEEE Symposium on Information Visualization, pp. 81-88, Austin, Texas, USA (2004).
5. Inselberg, A.: The plane with parallel coordinates. In: The visual computer, vol. 1, No. 2, pp. 69-91 (1985).
6. Few, S.: Multivariate analysis using parallel coordinates. In: Perceptual edge, pp.1-9 (2006).
7. Makwana, H., Tanwani, S., Jain, S.: Axes Re-ordering in Parallel Coordinate for Pattern Optimization. In: International Journal of Computer Applications, vol. 40, No.13, pp. 43-48 (2012).
8. Myachin, A.: New methods of pattern analysis in the study of Iris Anderson-Fisher Data. In: Computers Communications and Control (ICCCC), 2016 6th International Conference, IEEE, pp. 97-102 (2016).
9. Myachin, A.: Pattern Analysis in Parallel Coordinates Based on Pairwise Comparison of Parameters. In: Automation and Remote Control, Vol. 80, No. 1, pp. 112-123 (2019).
10. Peng, W., Ward, M., Rundensteiner, E.: Clutter reduction in multi-dimensional data visualization using dimension reordering. In: Proceedings of the Symposium on Information Visualization, pp. 89–96, Los Alamitos, USA. IEEE Computer Society (2004).
11. Siegler, R.S.: Three Aspects of Cognitive Development. In: Cognitive Psychology, 8(4), pp.481S520 (1976).
12. Wegman, E.J., Luo, Q.: High Dimensional Clustering using Parallel Coordinates And The Grand Tour. In: Conf. German Classification Society, Freiburg, Germany, pp. 93-101 (1996).
13. Zhou, H., Yuan, X., Qu, H., Cui, W., & Chen, B.: Visual clustering in parallel coordinates. In: Computer Graphics Forum, vol. 27, No. 3, pp. 1047-1054 (2008).
14. UCI Machine Learning Repository: Balance Scale Data Set, http://archive.ics.uci.edu/ml/datasets/balance+scale, last accessed 2019/01/15
15. UCI Machine Learning Repository: Car Data Set, https://archive.ics.uci.edu/ml/datasets/automobile, last accessed 2019/01/15
16. Pollen Data Set, http://lib.stat.cmu.edu/datasets/pollen.data, last accessed 2019/01/15

The Use of Frequent Subgraph Mining to Develop a Recommender System for Playing Real-Time Strategy Games

Isam A. Alobaidi[1], Jennifer L. Leopold[1], and Ali A. Allami[2]

[1] Missouri University of Science & Technology
Department of Computer Science
Rolla, MO, USA
[2] University of Missouri
Electrical Engineering & Computer Science Department
Columbia, MO, USA
iaahgb@mst.edu, leopoldj@mst.edu, aaaw46@mail.missouri.edu

Abstract. Machine learning and computational intelligence have facilitated the development of recommendation systems for a broad range of domains. Such recommendations are based on contextual information that is explicitly provided or pervasively collected. Recommendation systems often improve decision-making or increase the efficacy of a task. Real-time strategy (RTS) games are one domain where computationally determined recommendations for moves that a player should, and should not, make can provide a competitive advantage. The goal of our research is to develop an accurate predictive recommendation system for multiplayer strategic games that is based on frequent subgraph mining. Herein we present that approach and validate it using the historical data of one RTS game.

Keywords: Graph mining · Game mining · Recommendation system.

1 Introduction

The ever-increasing expansion of information and communications technology has initiated a new era for the development of recommendation systems for a wide variety of application domains (e.g., entertainment, E-commerce, E-Health, etc.); see Fig. 1. Recommendations could be for products or services that a customer might consider purchasing, treatments that a doctor might consider prescribing for a patient, or a sequence of actions that a robot should perform in a certain situation. Typically, the recommendations are based on an analysis of historical data, often characterized as positive and negative examples for the recommendation scenario. In order to be of value, recommendation systems must have high predictive accuracy.

Another venue where recommendation systems can be valuable is strategic games. Players have long been interested in studying previously played games to try to discern which moves are advantageous to make and which moves should be

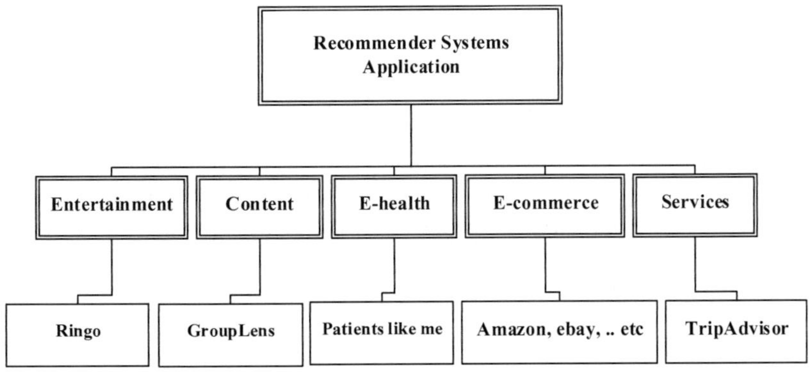

Fig. 1: Recommender System Classification.

avoided. With the current widespread interest in online, real-time strategy (RTS) games, which can involve a diverse and complex set of entities and functionality, determining which moves to make (and which not to make) can be extremely challenging. Fortunately, there are several databases of played games that can be analyzed to glean some insight.

In this study, we develop a predictive recommendation system for strategic multiplayer games that is based on graph mining. Using a database of played games, we model each of those games as a directed graph, and use frequent subgraph mining to look for patterns of moves that occurred frequently in winning games; these form the basis of our recommendations for moves that a player should make. Similarly, we look for patterns of moves that occurred frequently in losing games; those become the basis of our recommendations for moves that a player should not make. We test the accuracy of our method by repeatedly partitioning our database of played games into training and test datasets, and testing for the occurrence of true positives, true negatives, false positives, and false negatives. We also compare our method to an alternative approach, frequent sequence mining.

The organization of this paper is as follows. Section 2 provides a brief discussion of the main topics in this paper: game data mining, frequent subgraph mining, and frequent sequence mining. The particular algorithm that we used for frequent subgraph mining is explained in more depth in Section 3. A description of the RTS game data that we used for testing our method is provided in Section 4. Our experimental method and results are discussed in Section 5. A summary of this research and consideration of future work is discussed in Section 6.

2 Background

In this section we briefly discuss some of the related work that has been done in the fields of game data mining, frequent subgraph mining, and frequent sequence mining.

2.1 Game Data Mining

One objective of game data mining is to analyze a collection of played games and find patterns of moves that were made in winning (and possibly losing) games. Game data mining was the main focus of research in [1,2,3]. In [2] a method, Playtracer, for game analysis and improvement was proposed. A multidimensional scaling strategy was applied to cluster players and game states, and a detailed visual representation of the paths taken by players during the game was provided. Specifically, Classical Multidimensional Scaling (CMDS) [4] was used in order to visualize the paths. The Playtracer method showed mutual ways that players succeeded and failed, and enabled tracking a specific player's progress across multiple levels.

Two widely used data mining techniques, Classification and Regression Trees (CART) and artificial neural networks, were utilized in [3] to analyze a collection of game data (i.e., STEAM) for predictive purposes. CART is a decision tree algorithm that aims to build a predictive model based on the values of several inputs. Artificial neural networks also attempt to discover new patterns from inputs by subjecting them to a repetitive learning process. The aim of this study was to predict what should be followed as accurately as possible. Their method relied on the analysis of the online reviews (e.g. number of screenshots, number of reviews of a specific action) to achieve their objectives.

2.2 Frequent Subgraph Mining

Given a single (directed or undirected) graph, it can be useful to know which subgraphs occur at least n times where n is a user-specified threshold for frequency. Similarly, given a collection of graphs and a frequency threshold n, it may be important to know which subgraphs occur in at least n of those graphs. The process of answering this question is called frequent subgraph mining.

Several methods for frequent subgraph mining were presented in [5,6,7,8]. An algorithm that finds only maximal frequent subgraphs from a collection of graphs was given in [5]. This method consists of two basic steps: (1) from a collection of graphs, all frequent trees (i.e., undirected graphs in which any two vertices are connected by exactly one path) are first found; (2) from the mined trees, maximal subgraphs then are constructed. This strategy can significantly reduce the size of the result set.

Another method was proposed in [6] to only find closed frequent graph patterns instead of mining all subgraphs. The main idea behind this method was to consider the graph g closed when it is not possible to find a proper supergraph of g with the same support (i.e., frequency) as g.

An algorithm named Fast Frequent Subgraph Mining (FFSM) was developed in [7]. The strategy in that work was to reduce the number of redundant candidate subgraphs that are examined by utilizing specialized operations (called FFSMJoin and FFSM-Extension) to generate the candidate subgraphs.

A technique for finding frequent subgraphs in a large sparse graph was proposed in [8]. In that work, two approaches for exploring the search space of subgraphs were examined. A breadth-first approach was employed in their first algorithm, HSI-GRAM, examining the search space for frequent subgraphs in a horizontal way. A depth-first approach was employed in their second algorithm, VSIGRAM, to explore the search space in a vertical fashion when looking for frequent subgraphs.

Amongst many of the frequent subgraph mining algorithms that have been developed, computationally expensive extension/joining operations (to create larger candidate subgraphs from smaller frequent subgraphs) and false positive pruning (to reduce the search space) have been the biggest challenges that researchers have tried to address. Unfortunately, most methods have been limited to only working on a single graph or a collection of graphs, but not being applicable to both settings.

Frequent subgraph mining is a reasonable approach to consider for game mining. Each played game can be represented as a directed graph, wherein a vertex represents a move made by a player in that game and an edge represents two consecutive moves. It then could prove useful to identify subgraphs (i.e., sequences of moves) that frequently occur in the collection of graphs (i.e., played games).

2.3 Frequent Sequence Mining

Frequent sequence mining is used to find a set of patterns amongst a collection of instances that specify a sequence (e.g., a list) of items. This methodology can be used for diverse types of data; in [9] it was used to look for patterns in sequences of speech and bio-signals based on methods proposed in [10].

In [11], researchers proposed an algorithm called Sequential Pattern Discovery using Equivalence classes (SPADE). It starts by computing the frequencies of single-item sequences. In the next step, it counts the frequency of two-item sequences using a bi-dimensional matrix to count the number of sequences for each pair of items. Subsequent n-item sequences are processed by joining $(n-1)$-item sequences using lists of *ids* representing other objects. The size of those *ids* lists is the number of sequences in which an item appears.

A disadvantage to frequent sequence mining algorithms is that the results (i.e., the most frequently occurring sequences) do not list the items in the same order that they may have appeared in an instance's sequence in the dataset; the method does not care about the order in which an item appeared in an instance's sequence, it simply cares about whether or not the item occurred in the instance's sequence. Nonetheless this method can potentially provide some predictive recommendations from a strategic game dataset where each game can be viewed as sequences of moves by a winner and a loser.

3 Methodology: Frequent Subgraph Mining

The primary data mining technique that we used to develop a predictive recommendation system for strategic games was frequent subgraph mining. As mentioned in the previous section, we modeled each played game as a graph where a vertex represented a move in the game and an edge represented two consecutive moves. A game graph was not a strictly linear sequence of edges because some moves in turn generated multiple moves (e.g., a move could create a monster that would in turn propagate additional monsters, each of which would result in a new vertex and edge). We then analyzed the collection of graphs (a dataset of played games) to find frequent subgraphs: sequences of moves that were common to several winners' games and sequences of moves that were common to several losers' games.

In this section we start by briefly providing some basic graph terminology that will facilitate discussion of the particular frequent subgraph algorithm that we utilized for our study.

3.1 Preliminaries

Let $\mathcal{G} = \{G_1, G_2, ..., G_n\}$ be a set of linear directed graphs which represents the historical data in our case. Each G_i represents a single game's moves, such that $G_i = (V_i, E_i)$ where V_i represents a node labeled as an action code of a player's move, while an edge in E_i represents two consecutive moves. A graph $T = (V_T, E_T)$ is a subgraph of $G_i = (V_i, E_i)$ iff $V_T \subseteq V_{G_i}$, $E_T \subseteq E_{G_i}$.

Definition Let $T = (V_T, E_T)$ be a subgraph of a graph $G_i = (V_i, E_i)$. A subgraph isomorphism of T to G_i is an injective function $f : V_T \rightarrow V_{G_i}$ satisfying $(f(u), f(v)) \in E_{G_i}$ for all edges $(u, v) \in E_T$. Intuitively, a subgraph isomorphism is a mapping from V_T to V_{G_i} such that each edge in E_{G_i} is mapped to a single edge in E_T and vice versa.

Problem (1) Given a set of graphs $\mathcal{G}$, the frequent subgraph isomorphism mining problem is defined as finding all subgraphs T in G such that $t_G(T) \geq \tau$, where $t_G(T)$ is the number of graphs in G that contain T and τ is the user-specified threshold.

Problem (2) Given a set of graphs $\mathcal{G}$ such that each G_i is divided into three phases G_{i1}, G_{i2}, G_{i3} and a frequent subgraph T, the frequent phase mining problem is defined as finding all subgraphs T in G_{ij} such that $t_{G_{ij}}(T) \geq \tau$, where τ is the user-specified threshold.

In our case, problem (2) counts the actual frequency (i.e., occurrences) of each subgraph provided that it is greater than or equal to τ. However, this may not be useful in various cases [12,8], while others necessitate the exact number of occurrences (like graph indexing in [13]).

3.2 GraMi Algorithm

For the purpose of generating candidate subgraphs, a variety of frequent subgraph mining and subgraph extension algorithms have been developed, as discussed in previous work [14,8,15]. In particular, GraMi [15] is one of the most efficient methods and is the foundation for the work presented in this paper. The key ideas behind GraMi are briefly outlined here.

Algorithm 1 is used to find a set of all frequent edges $fEdges$ in the collection of graphs $= \{G_{i=1,...,n}\}$. All of these frequent edges have support greater than or equal to the assigned threshold τ. Because of the anti-monotone property, only frequent edges will be considered when finding the frequent subgraphs. Algorithm 2 is given each frequent edge to extend it to a new frequent subgraph. This is done by incorporating that edge with another subgraph. All extensions created in previous iterations are excluded by utilizing the $DFScode$ canonical form that was introduced for gSpan [14]. The set $Candidate$ in Algorithm 2 will include all the new subgraph extensions that had not been considered in prior iterations. In subsequent steps, any new subgraph extension within the set $Candidate$ that does not meet the support threshold τ requirement will be discarded. If any of those subgraphs had been extended, they would produce a new non-frequent subgraph according to the anti-monotonic property.

Algorithm 1 Frequent Subgraph Mining - FSM

Input $\mathcal{G} = \{G_{i=1,\ldots,n}\}$ and frequency threshold τ
Output All $fSubgraphs$ $S(G_i)$ with the support $\geq \tau$
$fSubgraphs \leftarrow \emptyset$
$Count = 0$
for each edge e_{G_i} **do**
  if $e_{G_i} = e_{G_{i+1}}$ **then**
    $Count++$
  end
  if $Count \geq \tau$ **then**
    $fEdges \leftarrow fEdges \cup e_{G_i}$
  end
end
for each $e \in fEdges$ **do**
  $fSubgraphs \leftarrow fSubgraphs \cup SubE(e, \mathcal{G}, \tau, fEdges)$
  Remove e from $\mathcal{G}$ and $fEdges$
end
return $fSubgraphs$

3.3 Using Frequent Subgraphs to Make Recommendations

In this section we discuss the algorithms that we utilized in order to mine the game dataset for frequent subgraphs and build a recommendation system. The task of finding the number of occurrences for each subgraph was carried out using Algorithm 3. The mechanism for node-finding was used for matching the first node of a candidate subgraph with its occurrence in the original dataset. The objective of this process was to determine the starting point for conducting a depth-first search ($DFSearch$) to find all similar subgraphs in the winner (or loser) graph collection. These results were stored temporarily in a $temp$ set to compute their replication in the subsequent steps, and then the final result was placed within $ExactFSG$ set.

Algorithm 2 Subgraph Extension - *SubE*

```
Input fSubgraph S, fEdges, and threshold τ
Output All fSub_new with the support ≥ τ
fSub_new ← ∅
Candidate ← ∅
for each e ∈ fEdges and n ∈ fSubgraph do
  if e fit to extend n then
   Generate a new subgraph ExtS
    if ExtS exist in 𝒢 and not generated before then
     Candidate ← Candidate ∪ ExtS
    else
     remove ExtS
    end
  end
for each ExtS ∈ Candidate do
  if ExtS count in 𝒢 ≥ τ then
  fSub_new ← fSub_new ∪ SubE(ExtS, 𝒢, τ, fEdges)
end
 return fSub_new
```

It was decided that the recommendation system might be more useful if the moves were analyzed for three phases of the game: the beginning of the game, the middle of the game, and the end of the game. This is traditionally being done for strategic games (i.g. chess) with the aim of analysis. Hence each game was divided into the first third number of moves, the second third number of moves, and the last third number of moves. Our work is not fixed to three phases; the number of phases can be easily modified by making a small change in Algorithm 4 to handle k phases. The objective of Algorithm 4 was to determine the number of occurrences of each individual subgraph considering in which phase of the game the sequence of moves was made. Algorithm 4 takes the $ExactFSG$ set that was introduced by Algorithm 3 and facilitates the node-finding and $DFSearch$ process to determine the phase of each individual frequent subgraph in this set. The node-finding mechanism was used a second time in subsequent steps, but only to identify the first node identity, $node_{ID}$, of the candidate subgraph assigned to it from the original dataset this time. It is worth mentioning that we consider the majority of appearances to decide the phase of the frequent subgraph. It should be noted that the subgraph nodes may straddle two consecutive phases. If so, we report that subgraph as it appeared in two phases.

4 Data Description

Interloper is an online multiplayer real-time strategy (RTS) game [16]. The game allows the creation and deployment of entities, and the destruction of an opponent's entities. A player wins the game when the other player's entities/assets have been destroyed or the other player cannot create any more assets. A dataset

Algorithm 3 Exact Subgraph Frequency

```
Input 𝒢 = {G_{i=1,...,n}}, fSubgraphs, and τ
Output All the Exact Frequent Subgraph with their frequency
 count = 0
 for i = 1 → all graphs in (fSubgraphs) do
  frq = 0
  for j = 1 → all graphs in (𝒢) do
   if findnode(G_j, fSubgraphs_i) ≠ 0 do
    temp ← dfsearch(G_j, fSubgraphs_i)
    if temp ≥ size(fSubgraphs_i) & isisomorphic(fSubgraphs_i, G_j) do
     frq++
    end
   end
  end
  if frq ≥ τ do
   count++
   ExactFSG(count) ← fSubgraphs_i
  end
 end
return ExactFSG
```

of 19 played games involving 2 players was obtained for this study. Each player's move in the dataset was encoded with 15, 7, or 6 digits. The first two digits in a code of length 15 or 7 represented the type of action (i.e., move); only the first digit was used in a code of length 6 to represent the type of action. The last four digits in all codes were used to represent a counter of each specific action. The purpose of the counter was to produce a unique data item for each move in the game. The middle eight digits in a code of length 15 was used to represent the source and destination location when moving an entity. The player ID was represented with the third digit in codes of lengths 15 and 7, and with the second digit in codes of length 6.

For this study the dataset was separated into the winner's moves and the loser's moves for each game. Because of the limited size of the dataset we obtained (i.e., 19 games), a program was written to increase the number of games to 90 and 120 by randomly duplicating games. Our method was tested on both the original dataset of size 19 and the larger datasets of sizes 90 and 120.

5 Experimental Evaluation

In this section we discuss the criteria by which we evaluated the performance of our recommendation system. As noted above, we analyzed the game in terms of three phases (i.e., beginning game, middle game, and end game) by dividing each game into three equal parts; the total number of moves in a game (by both the winner and the loser) ranged from 183 to 5,338. For each of the 3 phases analyzed, 60% of the data were used for training and the remaining 40% were

Algorithm 4 Majority of Subgraph Appearance

```
Input 𝒢 = {G_{i=1,...,n}} and ExactFSG
Output Display each ExactFSG and the locate phase
count_1 = 0, count_2 = 0, count_3 = 0
phase_1 = 0, phase_2 = 0, phase_3 = 0, phase1&2 = 0, phase2&3 = 0
for i = 1 → all graphs in (ExactFSG) do
  frq = 0
  for j = 1 → all graphs in (𝒢) do
  phase = ⌈size(G_j)/3⌉
   if findnode(G_j, ExactFSG_i) ≠ 0 do
    temp ← dfsearch(G_j, ExactFSG_i)
    if temp ≥ size(ExactFSG) & isisomorphic(fSubgraphs_i, G_j) do
      for k = 1 → size(ExactFSG) do
       node_ID = findnode(G_j, ExactFSG_i)
       if node_ID ≤ phase do
        count_1 + +
       elseif node_ID > phase & node_ID ≤ phase * 2 do
        count_2 + +
       else
        count_3 + +
       end
      end
    end
   end
    if count_1 ≠ 0 do
       if count_1 > count_2 do
        phase_1 + +
       elseif count_1 < count_2 do
        phase_2 + +
       else do
        phase_{1&2} + +
       end
    elseif count_2 ≠ 0 do
       if count_2 > count_3 do
        phase_2 + +
       elseif count_2 < count_3 do
        phase_3 + +
       else do
        phase_{2&3} + +
       end
    else
        phase_3 + +
    end
  end
end
return phase result
```

used for testing with k-fold cross-validation [17]. We measured precision and recall, which are viewed as metrics of exactness and completeness of testing, respectively. Equations 1 and 2 are the mathematical formulas for precision and recall, respectively.

$$Precision = \frac{True\ Positive}{True\ Positive + False\ Positive} \tag{1}$$

$$Recall = \frac{True\ Positive}{True\ Positive + False\ Negative} \tag{2}$$

The trade-off between precision and recall was measured by using for another metric named F-measure [17], which represents the harmonious mean between precision and recall. The accuracy scale was applied to measure the closeness of the measured value to the true value. Equations 3 and 4 are the mathematical formulas of F-measure and accuracy, respectively.

$$F - measure = 2 * \frac{Recall * Precision}{Recall + Precision} \tag{3}$$

$$Accuracy = \frac{True\ Positive + True\ Negative}{True\ Positive + False\ Positive + False\ Negative + True\ Negative} \tag{4}$$

5.1 Experiment and Results

In this section we present the results of analyzing the Interloper game dataset using both frequent subgraph mining and frequent sequence mining. The algorithms presented in Section 3 were (collectively) implemented in Matlab and Java. SPADE (discussed in Section 2.3) was implemented in R. Our experiments were executed on an Intel(R) Core(TM) i7-6700 CPU@3.40GHz computer with 32GB memory.

Tables 1 and 2 show some of the experimental results of frequent subgraph mining using a threshold of 2 for the winner and loser datasets consisting of 19 games. The first and second columns show the actions in the frequent subgraphs with their number of occurrences from the entire dataset, respectively. The tables also list the phase of the game in which each frequent subgraph most often was found. The fourth column in each table is a classification of the majority of that subgraph's actions; we classified that game's actions as either offensive, defensive, or movement (of an entity in the game space).

Table 1: Winner Data

Winner Subgraph	Frequency	Majority of Appearance	Classification
2810040 2810041 2810042	3	Second phase	offensive
2810035 2810036 2810037	4	First phase	offensive
2300171 2300172 2300173 2300174	3	Second and Third phase	move
2300171 2300172 2300173	6	Second phase	move
2810084 2810085 2810086 2810087	3	First and Second phase	offensive
2810084 2810085 2810086	3	Third phase	offensive
2500010 2500011 2500012	2	Third phase	offensive

Table 2: Loser Data

Loser Subgraph	Frequency	Majority of Appearance	Classification
2710003 2810015 2810017	3	First phase	offensive
2810003 2810005 2710001	2	First phase	offensive
2810024 2810026 2810028	6	First phase	offensive
2810008 2810010 2810012	3	Third phase	offensive
2510000 2510001 2510002	3	Third phase	offensive
2310187 2310188 2310189	3	Second phase	move
2310419 2310420 2310421	4	Third phase	move

These results were obtained by performing 3-fold cross-validation, repeated five times. Each time, for the 19-game dataset, 12 games were selected randomly (without duplication) for training, and the remaining 7 games were used for testing. The size of the resulting frequent subgraphs ranged from two nodes with one edge to four nodes with three edges. All of the two-node subgraphs were ignored because of the limited information they provide for the recommendation objective (i.e., only two moves) compared to larger subgraphs.

Frequent subgraphs that were found in the winner graphs indicate actions that are recommended for a player to do, whereas frequent subgraphs that were found in the loser graphs indicate actions that are recommended that a player should not do. The benefit of the counter attached to each action reflects the relative number of times the player had made that type of move in that game. Characterizing the actions, such as offensive or defensive, gives a general notion of the strategy the player is employing in that sequence and would facilitate mapping one game's actions to another's (e.g., mapping Interloper's offensive actions to StarCraft's offensive actions).

Fig. 2 shows the precision, recall, and F-measure scores obtained for each phase of the game that was analyzed. In order to ensure the fineness of the results, three different sizes of datasets were tested: 19, 90, and 120 games. All of these tests were subject to the same conditions of the 3-fold cross-validation with five repetitions. Averages for these five repetitions were calculated to determine the final results of these metrics. Precision and recall can be affected when the size of the input dataset increases. Despite this, our system did not experience a significant difference in those results. Fig. 3 shows the comparison of average accuracy for the different sized datasets.

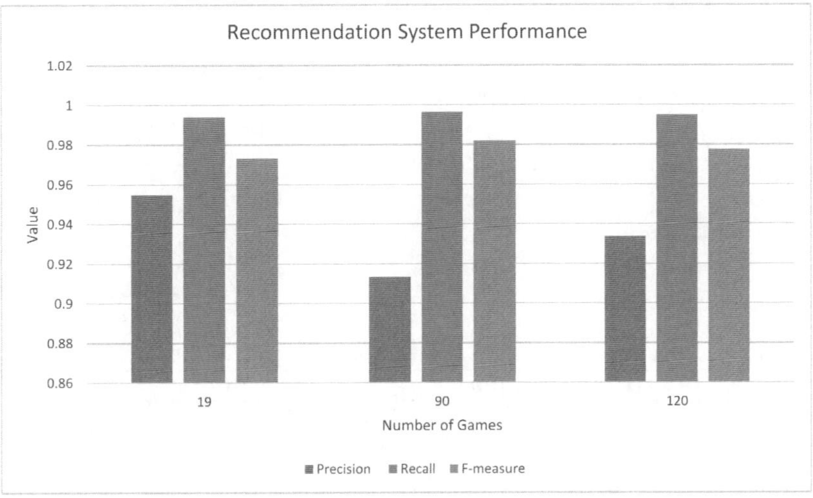

Fig. 2: Comparison of Average Precision, Recall and F-measure for Different Number of Games.

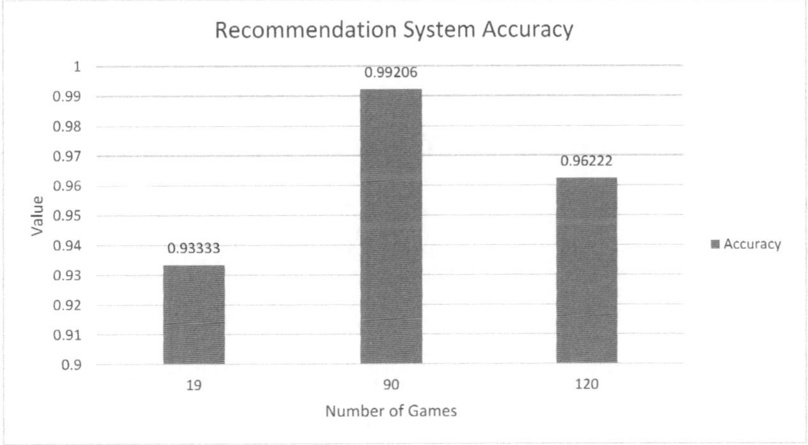

Fig. 3: Comparison of Average Accuracy for Different Number of Games.

We also utilized frequent sequence mining to analyze the Interloper game data; specifically, we used an implementation of the SPADE algorithm discussed in Section 2.3. The majority of the SPADE results (some of which are shown in Table 3 for the 19-game dataset) were not consecutive sequences of actions from games; they were simply lists of individual actions that had occurred in some order in a majority of winners' or losers' games. While this was somewhat informative, it was equivalent to if we had limited our frequent subgraph mining to subgraphs of single vertices (no edges). Unfortunately, the highest support for the results returned by SPADE was 0.5, meaning that only 50% of the games in the tested dataset contained the reported list of actions. This was the case for not only the 19-game dataset, but also the larger 90- and 120-game datasets. Consequently, we did not feel that the predictive accuracy of the recommendations we could make from these results would be high, and did not pursue cross-validation testing.

Table 3: Portion of the SPADE Output for the 19-Games Dataset

Dataset	Phase	Support	Subgraph
Winner	1	0.5	2300005 2300006 2300000 2300005 2300006 2300000 2300004 2300005 2300006
Winner	2	0.3	2700018
Winner	3	0	No result
Loser	1	0.4	2810003 2710007 2810003
Loser	2	0.2	2710017 2810064 2810066 2710017 2810064 2810066
Loser	3	0.2	600011 500010 600011 500010 600009 600011

6 Conclusion and Future Work

The use of recommendation systems has become widespread in our society. In general, they examine historical data and try to predict what should be done in the future. Herein we have applied a graph data mining technique, frequent subgraph mining, to a strategy game dataset to develop a system that can provide recommendations about moves that a player should and should not make in order to improve his/her chances of winning the game. As proof of concept, we tested our system on a real-time strategy (RTS) game dataset, and achieved very accurate results when we tested our recommendations. We also attempted to apply another technique, frequent sequence mining, but did not find that it provided as useful or accurate recommendations.

In the future we plan on testing our approach on other RTS games such as StarCraft, and will try to develop a generalized mapping scheme for action types that will be applicable for the broader genre of RTS games. We then hope to apply this approach to other problem domains that can map their entities and actions to those of a strategic game in a broad semantic sense, where resources are effectively created and destroyed, and where it would be beneficial to have recommendations for optimal management of those resources.

References

1. A. Drachen, C. Thurau, J. Togelius, G. N. Yannakakis, and C. Bauckhage, "Game Data Mining," in *Game Analytics: Maximizing the Value of Player Data*, (London, UK), pp. 205–253, Springer, 2013.
2. E. Andersen, Y.-E. Liu, E. Apter, F. Boucher-Genesse, and Z. Popović, "Gameplay Analysis Through State Projection," in *Proceedings of the 5th International Conference on the Foundations of Digital Games*, (Monterey, CA, USA), pp. 1–8, ACM, 2010.
3. H.-N. Kang, H.-R. Yong, and H.-S. Hwang, "A Study of Analyzing on Online Game Reviews using a Data Mining Approach: STEAM Community Data," *International Journal of Innovation, Management and Technology*, vol. 8, no. 2, p. 90, 2017.
4. M. A. A. Cox and T. F. Cox, *Multidimensional Scaling*, pp. 315–347. Berlin, Heidelberg: Springer, Berlin Heidelberg, 2008.
5. J. Huan, W. Wang, J. Prins, and J. Yang, "SPIN: Mining Maximal Frequent Subgraphs from Graph Databases," in *Proceedings of the 10th ACM SIGKDD International Conference on Knowledge Discovery and Data Mining*, KDD '04, (Seattle, WA, USA), pp. 581–586, ACM, 2004.
6. X. Yan and J. Han, "CloseGraph: Mining Closed Frequent Graph Patterns," in *Proceedings of the 9th ACM SIGKDD International Conference on Knowledge Discovery and Data Mining*, KDD '03, (Washington DC., USA), pp. 286–295, ACM, 2003.
7. J. Huan, W. Wang, and J. Prins, "Efficient Mining of Frequent Subgraphs in the Presence of Isomorphism," in *Proceedings of the 3rd IEEE International Conference on Data Mining*, ICDM '03, pp. 549–552, IEEE, 2003.
8. M. Kuramochi and G. Karypis, "Finding Frequent Patterns in a Large Sparse Graph," in *Proceedings of the 2004 SIAM International Conference on Data Mining*, pp. 345–356, SIAM, 2004.
9. H. P. Martínez and G. N. Yannakakis, "Mining Multimodal Sequential Patterns: A Case Study on Affect Detection," in *Proceedings of the 13th International Conference on Multimodal Interfaces*, ICMI '11, (Alicante, Spain), pp. 3–10, ACM, 2011.
10. R. Agrawal and R. Srikant, "Mining Sequential Patterns," in *Proceedings of the 11th International Conference on Data Engineering*, (Taipei, Taiwan), pp. 3–14, IEEE, 1995.
11. M. J. Zaki, "SPADE: An Efficient Algorithm for Mining Frequent Sequences," *Machine Learning*, vol. 42, no. 1, pp. 31–60, 2001.
12. W.-T. Chu and M.-H. Tsai, "Visual Pattern Discovery for Architecture Image Classification and Product Image Search," in *Proceedings of the 2nd ACM International Conference on Multimedia Retrieval*, ICMR '12, (Hong Kong, China), pp. 1–27, ACM, 2012.

13. X. Yan, P. S. Yu, and J. Han, "Graph Indexing: A Frequent Structure-based Approach," in *Proceedings of the 2004 ACM SIGMOD International Conference on Management of Data*, SIGMOD '04, (Paris, France), pp. 335–346, ACM, 2004.
14. X. Yan and J. Han, "gSpan: Graph-based Substructure Pattern Mining," in *Proceedings of the 2002 IEEE International Conference on Data Mining*, ICDM '02, (Maebashi City, Japan), pp. 721–724, IEEE, 2002.
15. M. Elseidy, E. Abdelhamid, S. Skiadopoulos, and P. Kalnis, "GraMi: Frequent Subgraph and Ppattern Mining in a Single Large Graph," *Proc. VLDB Endowment*, vol. 7, no. 7, pp. 517–528, 2014.
16. "Interloper Game Description." `http://interlopergame.com/`. Accessed: 2018-18-12.
17. P.-N. Tan, M. Steinbach, and V. Kumar, *Introduction to Data Mining*. Pearson Education India, 2006.

Anomaly Detection in Univariate Time Series: An Empirical Comparison of Machine Learning Algorithms

Sina Däubener[1], Sebastian Schmitt[2], Hao Wang[3][0000-0002-4933-5181], Peter Krause[1], and Thomas Bäck[3][0000-0001-6768-1478]

[1] divis intelligent solutions GmbH, Joseph-von-Fraunhofer-Str. 20, 44227 Dortmund, Germany daeubener@divis-gmbh.de

[2] Honda Research Institute Europe GmbH, Carl-Legien-Strasse 30, D-63073 Offenbach/Main, Germany sebastian.schmitt@honda-ri.de

[3] LIACS, Leiden University, Niels Bohrweg 1, 2333 CA Leiden, Netherlands {h.wang,t.h.w.baeck}@liacs.leidenuniv.nl

Abstract. This paper presents an empirical comparison of common machine learning and statistical methods applied to univariate time series with the purpose of detecting anomalies. Based on the assumption that anomalies are infrequently observed and non predictable states, we use regression algorithms to identify these points. In particular we applied random forests, support vector machines, k-nearest neighbour regression, artificial neural networks, Gaussian Processes, Twitter's anomaly detection method AdVec and an ARIMA model. Each algorithm is trained on the complete dataset to learn normal behaviour where the default hyperparameters are used. To dismantle the unpredictable states the generalized extreme studentized test is applied on the residuals. We compare this method on publicly available data sets with labeled anomalies covering a total of 419 time series. Even though the training process of the anomaly detection systems is unsupervised, the labels are available in the datasets, so that well-established measures of classification accuracy are applicable for evaluating the performance of the applied algorithms. The results demonstrate that all algorithms show comparable performance with a slight favor for Gaussian processes and support vector machines. The simple method used here delivered an F1 score higher or equal to 0.8 in 36% of the time series data sets.

Keywords: Anomaly detection · univariate time series · machine learning

1 Introduction

Anomaly detection has received increasing attention with the progress of digitization in private life and Industry 4.0. There are multiple application areas ranging from detecting unusual user behaviour in social media or network intrusion detection to industrial applications, e.g. in production process control. These diverse fields offer different definitions of anomalous data. What is common for many of them is that anomalies are defined as **observations which occur infrequently and are significantly different from other observations** [13]. We differentiate between two groups of methods for finding anomalies:

1. Direct approaches like clustering, classification or distance/density based methods: Anomalies are roughly considered to be either far away from cluster centers, to form a very small class/cluster of its own, to be at far distance from their nearest neighbours [12], or to have a high probabilistic distance [18].
2. Indirect or more precisely residual based approaches: The normal behavior is learned and modeled. Based on these models, predictions are made and the deviation between observed and predicted value is used to decide whether an observation is anomalous.

Many direct anomaly detection methods are described in [13]. In addition, there are some newer methods like hybrid isolation forests [21], which is a combination of separating data points while simultaneously using the density of the data distribution. Another method is based on robust principal component analysis [23], which is for example used for network intrusion detection. However, within this paper we focus on residual based methods, where the creation of a prediction model comes before the anomaly detection task. We use standard regression methods and apply them on univariate time series where previously observed points serve as input parameters [22]. The characteristics of a time series is that it is "a sequence of observation consecutive in time", which leads to the formal description of a time series [9] as a vector $\mathbf{y} = (y_{t_1}, y_{t_1}, ..., y_{t_n})$ of n discrete observations at consecutive time points $t_i < t_{i+1}\ \forall i \in \{1, ..., n\}$. In the following, we will write y_i instead of y_{t_i} for simplicity of the notation. A popular method for time series regression is based on auto regressive models and dates back to the 1960s. These models use previous observed data points and assume a linear relationship to the next instance. Autoregressive (integrated) moving average (AR(I)MA) regression [9] is an extension for additional feature generation. As an alternative, machine learning approaches can be applied to time series by generating features for classification models [4] or using previous (transformed) values as input variables [2,7].
There are a few other algorithms which are based on an residual approach and are explicitly designed for anomaly detection in time series. Prominent examples are Twitter's AdVec algorithm [17] and Numenta's anomaly detection method based on hierarchical temporal memory [1]. We found that in industry the first obstacle in anomaly detection is to label anomalous instances in existing data. Therefore, the approach presented here is relevant for real world applications by highlighting possible anomalies without extensive data pre-processing.
The remainder of this paper is structured as follows: The modeling algorithms are introduced in section 2. Section 3 describes the data sets used for testing and comparing algorithms. In section 4, the experimental results are presented and discussed, and section 5 provides our conclusions and an outlook for future research.

2 Modelling Algorithms

In this paper, we follow the assumption that anomalies are unpredictable states and therefore punctual and collective anomalies can be detected with a regression model. When learning a regression model based on a fixed small window w of consecutive previous points with the goal to predict the next instance, each regression method learns indirectly the small pattern of this window. A point anomaly can be detected if the predicted value is significantly different from the observed one. It is possible to detect collective anomalies if the small input pattern has not been observed multiple times and therefore the prediction is expected to deviate from the real observation. Because of the limitation of the window size, deviations in pattern length which exceed the input window can not be detected. Without analyzing and adapting to each time series this is a compromise to make. In the simplistic approach used here we set $w = 10$, with which the computations are still feasible. Given the time series $y = (y_1, ..., y_n)$ with window $w = 10$, we use $\{y_i, ..., y_{i+w-1}\}$ as input to predict y_{i+w} for all $i \in \{1, ..., n - w\}$. This way we use all the data to fit a regression model in the first step. Next, this model is used to predict the data it was fitted on. Each method thereby fits the training data to its best of capabilities regarding its default hyperparameter settings. Even though this is regarded as learning by heart associated with overfitting, and normally cross-validation, separate test- and training data set or leave-one-out approaches are common to prevent this overfitting, we utilize this to detecting anomalies. We want the data to be learned as much as possible by each algorithm and then thes the ability to detect unsupervised anomalies without any pre-processing of the data set. After the model is fit we obtain the predictions $\hat{y}_{w+1}, \hat{y}_{w+2}, ..., \hat{y}_n$. For flagging possible anomalies we use the residuals $r_i = y_i - \hat{y}_i$ (difference between observed value y_i and model prediction $\hat{y}_i$). We assume that the residual are approximately asymptotically normal distributed. Given the set of residuals $\mathcal{D} = \{r_i\}_{i=w+1}^{n} = \{y_i - \hat{y}_i\}_{i=1}^{n}$, the generalized extreme studentized deviate test (ESD) [25] is applied to detect statistical outliers in $\mathcal{D}$. The hypotheses of ESD are:

$$H_0 : \text{There are no anomalies in the data.}$$
$$H_a : \text{There are up to } k \text{ percent of anomalies.}$$

In ESD, only an upper bound is required for the suspected number of outliers and not the exact number of outliers. The test is performed in an iterative manner: in each step, the extreme value $r^* = \arg\max_{r_i \in \mathcal{D}} |r_i - \bar{r}|$ with sample mean $\bar{r}$ is checked against the null hypothesis. The test statistic is:

$$R = \frac{\max\{|r_i - \bar{r}| : r_i \in \mathcal{D}\}}{s} = \frac{r^*}{s}, \tag{1}$$

where s is the sample standard deviation. At the significance level α, the test statistic R is tested against the critical value:

$$\lambda = \frac{(n-1)t_{p,n-2}}{n\sqrt{(n-2+t_{p,n-2}^2)}}, \; p = 1 - \frac{\alpha}{2n}, \; n = |\mathcal{D}|, \tag{2}$$

with n denoting the size of the data set and $t_{p,n-2}$ denoting the $100 \cdot p$ percentage point of the t-distribution with $n-2$ degrees of freedom [25]. The null hypothesis H_0 is rejected when $R > \lambda$. Regardless of the decision on H_0, the current extreme value r^* is removed from $\mathcal{D}$ and the same procedure is repeated on the remaining $n' = n - 1$ data points. The iteration stops when at most k percent of the data points have been removed from the initial $\mathcal{D}$. Outliers are the removed data points on which the null hypothesis is rejected. The ESD procedure is summarized in Alg. 1. In the following subsections, we will give a brief description to the regression models used in our approach.

Algorithm 1 Generalized Extreme Studentized Deviate

procedure ESD($k, \mathcal{D}$) ▷ k: maximal percentage of anomalies; $\mathcal{D}$: set of residuals
  $N \leftarrow \lceil k|\mathcal{D}| \rceil$, $n \leftarrow |\mathcal{D}|$
  for $i = 1, 2, \ldots, N$ **do**
    $\bar{r} \leftarrow \text{MEAN}(\mathcal{D})$, $s \leftarrow \text{STD}(\mathcal{D})$
    $R_i \leftarrow \max\{|r - \bar{r}| : r \in \mathcal{D}\}/s$
    Compute λ_i according to Eq. (2)
    $r_i^* \leftarrow \arg\max\{|r_j - \bar{r}| : r_j \in \mathcal{D}\}$
    $\mathcal{D} \leftarrow \mathcal{D} \setminus \{r_i^*\}$, $n \leftarrow n - 1$
  end for
  Set q to the last index where $R_i > \lambda_i$ is true
  return $\{r_1^*, r_2^*, \ldots, r_q^*\}$
end procedure

2.1 Random Forest

Random Forest [10] is an ensemble of classification or regression trees [11], where the tree is randomized to reduce the modeling variance as follows: 1) Each tree is trained on bootstrap samples from the data and 2) only a random subset of input features are chosen for the splitting procedure when growing each tree. As for the overall prediction, the predictions from all trees are averaged for regression tasks and a majority vote is taken for classification tasks.

2.2 Support Vector Machine

The support vector machine (SVM) [15] is originally proposed to perform a binary classification task, where the optimal separating (hyper-)plane is obtained by maximizing the distance between sharp linear boundaries of two classes. If the problem is not linearly separable, the well-known kernel trick [8] is applied to map the input into the high dimensional feature space (through the so-called feature map), where the linearly separability is again attained.

2.3 k-Nearest Neighbour Regression

k-Nearest Neighbour Regression (kNN regression) [3] is a proximity based algorithm where the target value of a data point is estimated by the average value of its k nearest neighbours. The proximity between data points is determined by some distance metric, e.g., the Euclidean distance which is used in this paper. In addition, a weighting scheme is commonly used in averaging target values of the neighbours and the weight is scaled with respect to the proximity.

2.4 Artificial Neural Networks

Artificial Neural Networks (ANN) are structural machine learning algorithms that are inspired by biological nervous systems [6]. The so-called feedforward neural network model is adopted here. The feedforward neural network [26] consists of multiple layers of artificial neurons which take inputs from the preceding layer and feeds the output of some activation function to the next layer. A feedforward neural network (with more than two layers) is able to approximate any continuous function, according to the Universal Approximation Theorem [16].

2.5 Gaussian Processes

The formal definition of Gaussian processes is that it is a "collection of random variables, any finite number of which have a joint Gaussian distribution" [24]. This Gaussian distribution is completely defined by its mean vector and its covariance matrix, which are calculated based on the training data with applying the kernel trick. However, the prediction is not solemnly based on this joint Gaussian distribution results but also the minimization of the expected loss. Through the covariance matrix this algorithm directly incorporates a uncertainty measure for every prediction.

2.6 ARIMA

Auto Regressive Integrated Moving Average (ARIMA) [9] uses previously observed data (AR) and the moving average (MA) of previous data points to model not directly the output, but the d-th differenced output value (integrated). This is done to derive a stationary time series, which is needed for being able to extrapolate information gained on one section of the time series to the next.

2.7 AdVec

This algorithm developed by Twitter, also commonly referred to as AdVec based on its R command *AnomalyDetectionVector*, decomposes the time series using the seasonal-trend decomposition procedure based on LOESS regression (STL) [14] and applies a form of the generalized ESD on the calculated residuals on a time frame. Instead of taking the mean value the evaluation here uses the median in the ESD test for a more robust estimation against outliers [17].

Table 1. Summary of the Data sets

Data sets		Number of Observations	Value range	Number of Anomalies
Yahoo				
A1 (67)	min	741	0	0
	max	1,461	7,845,760	12
A2 (100)	min	1,421	-2,204	1
	max	1,421	128,420	3
A3 (100)	min	1,680	-7,988	1
	max	1,680	7,006	16
A4 (100)	min	1,680	-6,171	1
	max	1,680	6,324	16
Numenta				
Artificial w. Anomaly (6)	min	4,032	-22	1
	max	4,032	165	1
realAdExchange (6)	min	1,538	0	1
	max	1,643	16	4
realAWSCloudwatch (16)	min	4,032	0	0
	max	4,730	863,964,000	3
realKnownCause (7)	min	1,882	0	2
	max	22,695	39,197	5
realTraffic (5)	min	1,127	0	1
	max	2,500	5,578	4
realTweets (10)	min	15,831	0	2
	max	15,902	13,479	5

2.8 Ensemble Method

To use all aforementioned algorithm as an ensemble, the simple majority vote method is taken, which predicts an anomaly if at least three of the methods introduced in subsections 2.1-2.7 do so.

3 Data Sets

We use two publicly available anomaly detection data sets as benchmark, namely the Yahoo S5 data set [19] and the Numenta data set [20]. These two main data sets are divided into different classes, where each class contains multiple not necessary related time series, which vary in length, value range and anomalies contained as summarized in Table 1. They are briefly described in the following sections.

3.1 Yahoo S5 Data Set

This data set is divided into four classes, named A1, A2, A3 and A4. While A1 consists of 67 real time series from computational services, the other three data sets include each 100 artificially created time series with inserted anomalies and of increasing difficulty. The value range and frequency is not comparable within a class, so that each time series in a class is considered a separate data set. The number of anomalies in each time series is between 0 and 16.

3.2 Numenta Data Set

The Numenta time series benchmark consists of 58 labeled data sets from different domains with multiple anomalies. The domains range from social media chatter to network utilization and also artificially generated data sets. The anomalies are labeled as such and an anomaly window is defined around them. We did not include the artificial time series where no anomalies were present, and excluded one of the network utilization data sets where the labeling was not clear. It is also important to mention that either the root cause for the anomalies in the Numenta benchmark is known, or anomalies were labeled according to "a result of the well-defined NAB labeling procedure" [20]. As in the Yahoo S5 data set each time series in a domain is considered a separate data set with number of anomalies ranging from 0 to 5.

4 Experimental Results

We used standard R packages for all algorithms and the default parameter settings where possible[4].

4.1 Pre-processing Techniques

There are several different approaches for the setup of time series prediction (e.g., see [7]). One approach is to decompose the time series into pattern and features [4]. Therefore some kind of window size needs to be set. This parameter can be optimized based on the precision of a model. But since the goal in this paper is to find unsupervised anomalies and not to create a good prediction model we did not apply these approaches. However, since time series are often incorporated with seasonality, we used the partial auto correlation [9] to automatically determine a window size. We chose a value for the window size which was slightly higher than the highest correlated value at least 11 points away. Because especially in the artificial Yahoo data set some periods lasted longer than 200 points we chose equidistantly 10 points in such a period for the input values of our regression model. However the F1 scores were a lot worse than the ones presented in Table 2. Next to data operations like scaling, detrending, log-transformation and normalization [2,5,29] we conducted another experiment where we computed the first order differences of the time series and used these as inputs. However, this did not improve the F1 scores so no pre-processing was applied for our final results in Chapter 4.

To analyze the sensitivity of the approach based on w, we tested the window sizes $w \in \{5, 10, 15, 20\}$ and found that the results are insensitive to a choice from those four values. However, to provide a consistent learning window, we use $w = 10$ in the following.

[4] More precisely: "ranger" for Random Forests with `mtry` set to 5, "e1071" for SVM, "FNN" for k-nearest neighbours with k equals 10, "nnet" for the neural network with 20 nodes, "kernlab" for Gaussian Processes, "forecast" for ARIMA and `github("twitter/AnomalyDetection")` for AdVec with periodicity of 40, which was found most useful in [27].

4.2 Performance Metrics and Tests

After the regression models were trained and again used to predict the time series, we calculated the residuals $r_i = y_i - \hat{y}_i \ \forall i = 1, ..., n$ and applied the ESD test on them. The ESD test here uses a significance level of $\alpha = 0.05$ to find at most 0.5% of the data set as anomalous. This small ratio of anomalies is the same for all data sets and algorithms. In the AdVec algorithm a modified version of ESD is already encoded, so that it is not reapplied.
In case of the Numenta data set not only punctual anomalies are given, but also an anomaly window. This has an impact on the evaluation: The exact anomaly does not necessarily have to be found; instead an anomaly is considered to be detected if at least one observation in the anomaly window is labeled as an anomaly. Furthermore, multiple points labeled as an anomaly in the same anomaly window do not affect the performance measure, whereas each point which is labeled as an anomaly but is not within the window is considered as a false positive.

The following performance measures are used in our study:

1. True positives (TP): The number of anomalies correctly detected as such.
2. False positives (FP): The number of data points labeled by the underlying algorithm as anomalies even though they are normal instances.
3. False negatives (FN): The number of anomalies that are not detected.
4. Precision: The ratio of correctly labeled anomalies over all anomalies which are detected, i.e.: $\text{precision} = \frac{\text{TP}}{\text{TP}+\text{FP}}$.
5. Recall: The ratio of all correctly labeled anomalies over all actual anomalies, i.e.: $\text{recall} = \frac{\text{TP}}{\text{TP}+\text{FN}}$.
6. F1 score: The harmonic mean between precision and recall, i.e. $\text{F1} = 2 \cdot \frac{\text{precision} \cdot \text{recall}}{\text{precision}+\text{recall}}$. This is the most reliable score since maximizing precision and recall are often conflicting goals.

4.3 Results

The results are summarized in Table 2 where the average values of precision, recall and F1 score are shown for all data sets divided into their sub-classes.

For the Numenta benchmark the results are quite satisfactory in terms of the recall measure, implying that almost all anomalies are found. In contrast, the precision values are in general very low and never exceed 0.4, which indicates high rates of false alarms. Consequently, the F1 score is rather low for the Numenta data set. One reason for this observation is posed by the anomaly labels provided by the data set. In Figure 1 a time series from the Numenta data set is shown which has only two labeled anomalies. No algorithm we tested was able to detect those anomalies, but instead false positive detection of peak values can be observed. In case of univariate time series one would assume that anomalies should be understandable. However, without additional information on the nature of the time series it is currently unclear why these anomalies are actually labeled as such, whereas all the clearly visible spikes and peaks are not labeled as anomalies. Therefore, the observed behaviour is actually more or less expected

Table 2. Average performance on the data set groups using the lagged method with window size $w = 10$.

Data set	Measure	RF	GP	SVM	kNN	ARIMA	AdVec	ANN	Ens
Yahoo									
A1 (67)	P	0.4	**0.48**	0.46	0.44	0.41	0.44	0.43	**0.48**
	R	0.77	0.72	0.76	0.76	0.75	0.48	0.55	**0.79**
	F1	0.52	0.58	0.58	0.56	0.53	0.46	0.49	**0.6**
A2 (100)	P	0.48	0.67	0.82	0.48	0.4	1	**0.84**	0.62
	R	**0.98**	**0.98**	**0.98**	**0.98**	0.97	0.29	0.54	**0.98**
	F1	0.65	0.79	**0.9**	0.65	0.57	0.45	0.66	0.76
A3 (100)	P	0.84	0.86	0.83	0.87	0.66	**1**	0.9	0.89
	R	**0.69**	**0.69**	0.64	0.68	0.54	0.02	0.21	0.67
	F1	0.75	**0.77**	0.72	0.76	0.6	0.03	0.34	0.76
A4 (100)	P	0.69	0.71	0.71	0.68	0.57	0.28	**0.81**	0.77
	R	**0.61**	0.6	**0.61**	0.59	0.49	0.06	0.2	0.6
	F1	0.65	0.65	0.66	0.63	0.53	0.1	0.32	**0.67**
Numenta									
Artificial w.	P	0.04	0.06	0.06	0.06	0.04	0.05	**0.07**	0.05
Anomaly (6)	R	0.83	0.83	**1**	**1**	0.67	0.67	**1**	**1**
	F1	0.08	0.11	0.11	0.11	0.07	0.09	**0.12**	0.1
realAd	P	0.26	0.27	0.28	0.26	0.29	**0.38**	0.24	0.26
Exchange (6)	R	0.71	0.71	0.71	0.71	0.71	0.71	0.71	0.71
	F1	0.38	0.39	0.4	0.38	0.42	**0.5**	0.36	0.38
realAWS	P	0.11	0.11	0.1	**0.12**	**0.12**	0.09	**0.12**	0.11
Cloudwatch	R	**0.93**	0.82	**0.93**	**0.93**	0.89	0.79	**0.93**	**0.93**
(16)	F1	0.19	0.19	0.19	**0.21**	**0.21**	0.17	**0.21**	0.2
realKnown	P	0.06	0.07	0.07	0.05	0.11	0.06	**0.15**	0.07
Cause (7)	R	**0.63**	0.58	0.63	0.58	0.58	0.42	0.37	0.58
	F1	0.11	0.12	0.13	0.1	0.19	0.11	**0.21**	0.13
realTraffic	P	0.22	0.28	0.24	0.28	**0.3**	0.21	0.21	0.23
(5)	R	0.79	0.79	0.79	0.79	**0.93**	0.64	0.71	0.79
	F1	0.34	0.41	0.37	0.41	**0.45**	0.32	0.33	0.35
realTweets	P	0.05	**0.06**	0.05	0.05	**0.06**	**0.06**	**0.06**	0.05
(10)	R	**1**	0.97	0.94	0.97	0.97	0.91	0.97	0.97
	F1	0.1	**0.11**	0.1	0.1	0.1	**0.11**	**0.11**	0.1

from unsupervised anomaly detection algorithms. With additional information, the number of false positives could be reduced if, for example, all peak values above 0.2 should not be considered abnormal.

Concerning the Yahoo data sets, we frequently observe a better balance between precision and recall than for the Numenta data sets and, consequently, a much higher value of the F1 score.

We illustrate an exemplary time series from the Yahoo benchmark in Figure 2 with the corresponding anomalies marked in red but without anomaly windows. This artificially created time series reveals a general problem of our unsupervised anomaly detection method. The anomaly detection algorithms learn the overall statistics of a complete dataset, and anomalies are detected by inspecting the difference between prediction and actually observed value. Therefore, a change in the average statistics and of the overall scale of the time-series is not well-captured by the detection method and the anomalies in the first third of the dataset are masked by the last part, where the amplitude increased. As a result, no method used here can capture the anomalies within the initial low amplitude signal. Such cases would benefit strongly from employing an online algorithm where, for example sliding analysis windows or forgetting factors are used to adjust to qualitative changes of the time series.

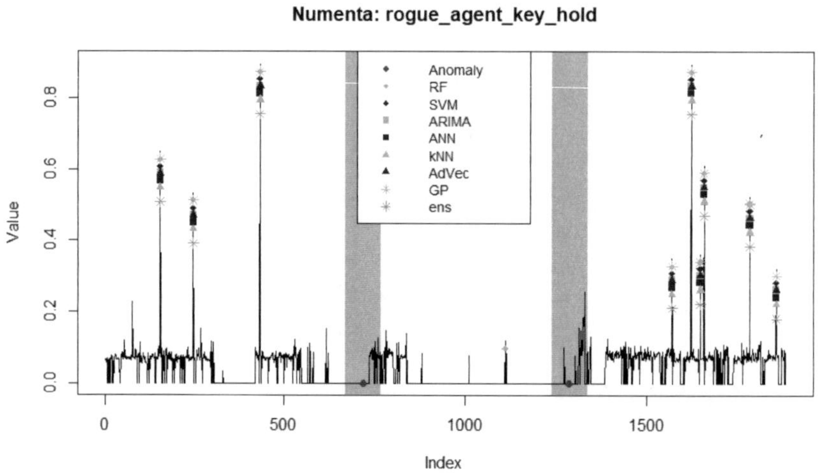

Fig. 1. A Numenta time series with two anomaly windows marked in grey, where the two red dots indicate the actual anomalies. None of the algorithms tested has been able to identify the true anomalies, but all marked the high peak values as anomalies. Indeed, it seems difficult to derive the characteristics of the two labeled anomalies from the underlying time series.

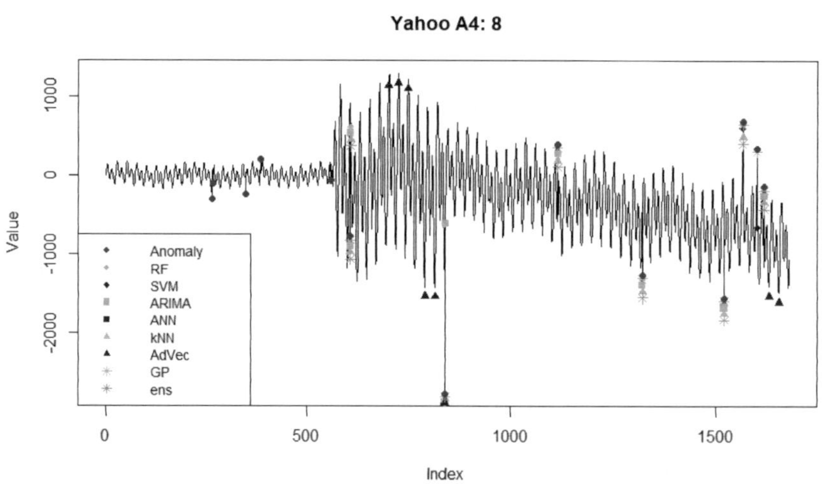

Fig. 2. Yahoo time series A4: 8, with 13 labeled true anomalies (red dots). None of the algorithms tested can correctly identify the first five anomalies, while the next 8 are correctly identified by gaussian processes, and 7 by four other methods. AdVec generates seven false positives.

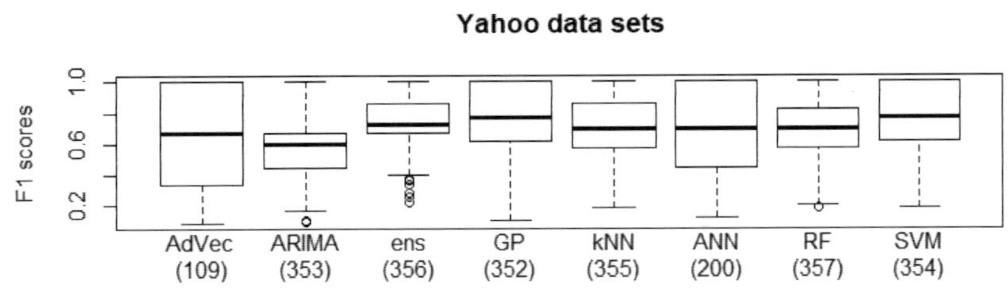

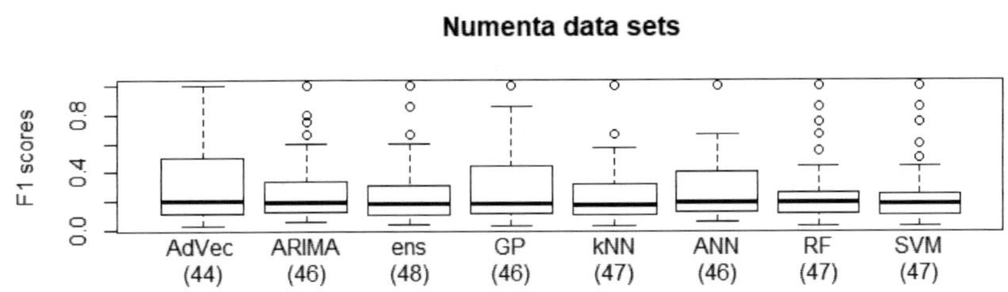

Fig. 3. F1 scores represented as boxplots for the corresponding algorithm and divided by data set affiliation. The thick horizontal line indicates the median and the box corresponds to the 25% and 75% quantile. The number on the x-axis corresponds to the number of time series where the F1 score was successfully calculated. Unsuccessful calculations are those where the algorithm could not calculate the F1 score because of a division by 0, i.e. if no true positives were found.

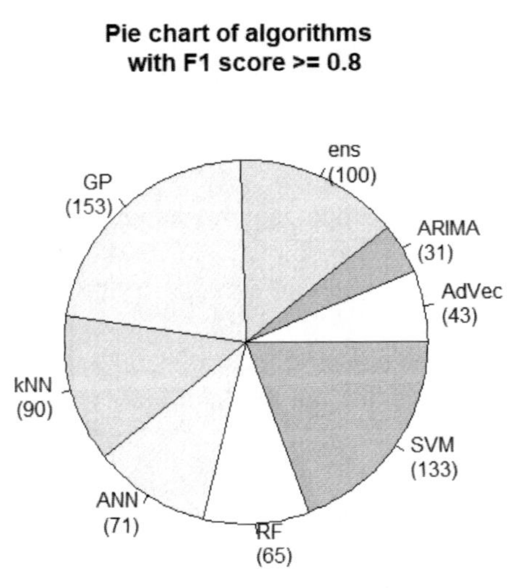

Fig. 4. Distribution of algorithms with the highest F1 score for scores larger than 0.8. The number under each algorithm's name is the number of time series where this algorithm could reach the maximal F1 score. Because multiple algorithms can have the same maximal F1 score for one time series the cumulative numbers exceed the number of time series.

Table 3. Mean correlation based on block wise sampled test data.

Data set	Algorithm						
	RF	GP	SVM	kNN	ARIMA	AdVec	ANN
Yahoo							
A1 (67)	0.75	0.60	0.70	0.74	**0.82**	0.80	0.40
A2 (100)	**0.98**	**0.98**	**0.98**	**0.98**	**0.98**	**0.98**	0.56
A3 (100)	**0.97**	**0.97**	**0.97**	**0.97**	**0.97**	0.95	0.71
A4 (100)	**0.97**	0.96	**0.97**	0.96	0.96	0.94	0.75
Numenta							
Artificial w. Anomaly (6)	0.82	0.76	0.67	0.80	**0.90**	0.78	0.81
realAdExchange (6)	**0.64**	0.60	0.28	0.26	0.29	0.38	0.24
realAWSCloudwatch (16)	0.11	0.11	0.1	**0.12**	0.12	0.09	**0.12**
realKnownCause (7)	0.06	0.07	0.07	0.05	0.11	0.06	**0.15**
realTraffic (5)	0.22	0.28	0.24	0.28	**0.3**	0.21	0.21
realTweets (10)	0.05	0.06	0.05	0.05	**0.06**	**0.06**	**0.06**

Figure 3 shows the statistics of the F1 scores for each algorithm over each time series. Generally, there is a substantial variation in the F1 scores for all methods and data set. As already observed, the performance on the Yahoo data set is generally acceptable where the majority results are located in the upper half of performance scores, i.e. between 0.5 and 1. For AdVec the bulk of the results is distributed over the complete score scale and an anomaly label could only be calculated for about one third of time series due to no anomaly detections at all. The minimum (i.e. worst) F1 score generated by all algorithms is between 0 and 0.2, but at the same time all methods reach once or multiple times a score very close to 1. While for the Numenta data set the minimal and maximal F1 score are comparable, the general performance is much worse where the median values are found around an F1 score of about 0.2. This indicates that many anomalies labeled in time series of the Numenta data set are much more difficult to find.

Even though the prediction accuracy is not the main interest here, we analyzed how well the algorithms perform on the given data sets. In order to divide the time series in training and test set, we choose a block-wise sampling where in total 20% of the data was sampled in 10 equidistantly distributed blocks to function as the test data. (We decided against using 80% of the first part of the data for training and the remaining last 20 % to test, since the time series contain trends, concept drifts, different seasonality pattern and anomalies at the end of the observation period. We also did not use random sampling, since for time series data this leads to no reliable prediction accuracy because of the natural link between two consecutive points is lost.) Because of the strong variation in the range of values (cf. Table 1), the averaged correlation was used instead of the average mean squared error. In Table 3 we observe, that the prediction capability of models trained on the Yahoo S5 data set are better than for those in the Numenta data set. Interestingly, a good prediction capacity does not necessarily be connected with the best anomaly score, compare Numentas realAdExchange, where random forests provided the highest correlation but AdVec the best F1 score.

From the above presented results we can conclude that none of the studied anomaly detection methods significantly outperforms any other approach. All algorithms performed similarly, except for AdVec where the F1 score was often not calculable (due to zero detected anomalies) and showed more variation if calculable. The reason for this is very likely found in the target application scenario for which AdVec was designed and the implicit assumptions about the data made there. Presumable, with fine tuning the periodicity hyperparameter according to each time series AdVec would perform better. The simple ensemble method we applied is a bit more robust against the variation of an individual algorithm and thus can achieve good overall performance. Analyzing the frequencies with which the algorithms achieve F1 scores equal or higher than 0.8 in Figure 4, we find that Gaussian processes and support vector machine provide the most high F1 scores.

5 Conclusions and Future Work

A total of seven machine learning algorithms and one simple ensemble method were compared on a large number of univariate time series data sets commonly used in anomaly detection. The evaluation criteria used here were precision, recall and F1 score. A central finding of this work is that all methods perform comparably, with a slight favor for gaussian processes, support vector machine and the ensemble method. On the Numenta data sets, all methods show reasonably good recall performance while they all perform poorly with respect to the precision and consequently also the F1 measure, which is due to a high rate of false detections. For the Yahoo data set the precision and recall measures are much more balanced and therefore the F1 scores are usually much larger. Our results show a tendency that an ensemble method will yield a more constant performance than an individual algorithm. This is intuitive as it reflects the usual insight that it is beneficial to combine many weak learners into a strong learner. Put differently, individual algorithms failing on some time series will not affect the average ensemble performance much as long as there is no systematic reason for many algorithms to fail simultaneously. In the current approach, we did not do any hyperparameter tuning and also did not use any a priori information about the types and characteristics of the data sets. This was done to achieve an unbiased comparison of the algorithms for situations where not much knowledge about the data is available and uniformed analysis of real-world data is targeted. However, it can be expected, that the performance will improve when a priori information about the data is utilized. There are many routes to improving the performance of the anomaly detection approach presented in this paper. One such improvement could be realized by utilizing an online approach so that the algorithms are not trained globally on all available data. Instead, the algorithm could adjust constantly to the recently observed data by, for example, using a sliding window approach or introducing a forgetting factor. With this, the algorithms would be able to adapt to seasonality, concept drift or other global changes in the time series. Additionally, more advanced data pre-processing and feature detection could be employed. Especially the development of automated data pre-processing techniques should further be investigated. The approach presented here can be applied without intensive data processing to get anomalies flagged in an industrial use case where many different time series are present and no labeling information exists. As in [28], these anomaly suggestions are to be verified by the process expert and pre-studies performed on a network use case nurture the hope that this investigation method contributes to an increased process understanding. These options are left for further research studies.

References

1. Ahmad, S., Purdy, S.: Real-time anomaly detection for streaming analytics. CoRR **abs/1607.02480** (2016), http://arxiv.org/abs/1607.02480
2. Ahmed, N.K., Atiya, A.F., Gayar, N.E., El-Shishiny, H.: An empirical comparison of machine learning models for time series forecasting. Econometric Reviews **29**(5-6), 594–621 (2010)
3. Altman, N.S.: An introduction to kernel and nearest-neighbor nonparametric regression. The American Statistician **46**(3), 175–185 (1992)
4. Bagnall, A., Lines, J., Bostrom, A., Large, J., Keogh, E.: The great time series classification bake off: A review and experimental evaluation of recent algorithmic advances. Data Min. Knowl. Discov. **31**(3), 606–660 (May 2017). https://doi.org/10.1007/s10618-016-0483-9, https://doi.org/10.1007/s10618-016-0483-9
5. Balkin, S.D., Ord, J.K.: Automatic neural network modeling for univariate time series. International Journal of Forecasting **16**(4), 509–515 (2000)
6. Bishop, C.M.: Pattern recognition and machine learning. Information Science and Statistics, Springer, New York (2006). https://doi.org/10.1007/978-0-387-45528-0, https://doi.org/10.1007/978-0-387-45528-0
7. Bontempi, G., Ben Taieb, S., Le Borgne, Y.A.: Machine learning strategies for time series forecasting. In: Aufaure, M.A., Zimányi, E. (eds.) Business Intelligence: Second European Summer School, eBISS 2012, Brussels, Belgium, July 15-21, 2012, Tutorial Lectures, pp. 62–77. Springer Berlin Heidelberg, Berlin, Heidelberg (2013). https://doi.org/10.1007/978-3-642-36318-4_3, https://doi.org/10.1007/978-3-642-36318-4_3
8. Boser, B.E., Guyon, I.M., Vapnik, V.N.: A training algorithm for optimal margin classifiers. In: Proceedings of the fifth annual workshop on Computational learning theory. pp. 144–152. ACM (1992)
9. Box, G.E., Jenkins, G.M., Reinsel, G.C., Ljung, G.M.: Time series analysis: forecasting and control. John Wiley & Sons (2015)
10. Breiman, L.: Random forests. Machine learning **45**(1), 5–32 (2001)
11. Breiman, L., et al.: Classification and Regression Trees. Chapman & Hall, New York (1984)
12. Breunig, M.M., Kriegel, H.P., Ng, R.T., Sander, J.: Lof: Identifying density-based local outliers. SIGMOD Rec. **29**(2), 93–104 (May 2000). https://doi.org/10.1145/335191.335388, http://doi.acm.org/10.1145/335191.335388
13. Chandola, V., Banerjee, A., Kumar, V.: Anomaly detection: A survey. ACM computing surveys (CSUR) **41**(3), 15 (2009)
14. Cleveland, R.B., Cleveland, W.S., McRae, J.E., Terpenning, I.: Stl: A seasonal-trend decomposition procedure based on loess. Journal of Official Statistics **6**(1), 3–73 (1990)

15. Cortes, C., Vapnik, V.: Support-vector networks. Machine Learning **20**(3), 273–297 (Sep 1995). https://doi.org/10.1007/BF00994018, https://doi.org/10.1007/BF00994018
16. Csáji, B.C.: Approximation with artificial neural networks. Faculty of Sciences, Etvs Lornd University, Hungary **24**, 48 (2001)
17. Hochenbaum, J., Vallis, O.S., Kejariwal, A.: Automatic anomaly detection in the cloud via statistical learning. arXiv preprint arXiv:1704.07706 (2017)
18. Kriegel, H.P., Kröger, P., Schubert, E., Zimek, A.: Loop: local outlier probabilities. In: CIKM. pp. 1649–1652. ACM (2009), "http://dblp.uni-trier.de/db/conf/cikm/cikm2009.html#KriegelKSZ09"
19. Laptev, N., Amizadeh, S.: Yahoo anomaly detection dataset S5 (2015), available under https://webscope.sandbox.yahoo.com/catalog.php?datatype=s&did=70
20. Lavin, A., Ahmad, S.: Evaluating real-time anomaly detection algorithms–the numenta anomaly benchmark. In: Machine Learning and Applications (ICMLA), 2015 IEEE 14th International Conference on. pp. 38–44. IEEE (2015)
21. Marteau, P.F., Soheily-Khah, S., Béchet, N.: Hybrid isolation forest - application to intrusion detection. CoRR **abs/1705.03800** (2017), http://arxiv.org/abs/1705.03800
22. Muller, K., Smoła, A., Rätsch, G., Schölkopf, B., Kohlmorgen, J., Vapnik, V.: Predicting time series with support vector machines. In: Lecture Notes in Computer Science (including subseries Lecture Notes in Artificial Intelligence and Lecture Notes in Bioinformatics). Lecture Notes in Computer Science (including subseries Lecture Notes in Artificial Intelligence and Lecture Notes in Bioinformatics), vol. 1327, pp. 999–1004. Springer Verlag (1997)
23. Paffenroth, R., Kay, K., Servi, L.: Robust PCA for anomaly detection in cyber networks. CoRR **abs/1801.01571** (2018), http://arxiv.org/abs/1801.01571
24. Rasmussen, C., Williams, C.: Gaussian Processes for Machine Learning. Adaptive Computation and Machine Learning, MIT Press, Cambridge, MA, USA (Jan 2006)
25. Rosner, B.: Percentage points for a generalized esd many-outlier procedure. Technometrics **25**(2), 165–172 (1983)
26. Schmidhuber, J.: Deep learning in neural networks: An overview. Neural Networks **61**, 85 – 117 (2015). https://doi.org/https://doi.org/10.1016/j.neunet.2014.09.003, http://www.sciencedirect.com/science/article/pii/S0893608014002135
27. Thill, M., Konen, W., Bäck, T.: Online anomaly detection on the webscope s5 dataset: A comparative study. In: 2017 Evolving and Adaptive Intelligent Systems (EAIS). pp. 1–8 (May 2017). https://doi.org/10.1109/EAIS.2017.7954844
28. Vercruyssen, V., Meert, W., Verbruggen, G., Maes, K., Baumer, R., Davis, J.: Semi-supervised anomaly detection with an application to water analytics. pp. 527–536 (11 2018). https://doi.org/10.1109/ICDM.2018.00068
29. Zhang, G.P., Qi, M.: Neural network forecasting for seasonal and trend time series. European Journal of Operational Research **160**(2), 501–514 (2005), https://EconPapers.repec.org/RePEc:eee:ejores:v:160:y:2005:i:2:p:501-514

Predictive Analysis of Real-Time Strategy Games Using Discriminative Subgraph Mining

Jennifer L. Leopold[1], Isam A. Alobaidi[1], and Nathan W. Eloe[2]

[1]Missouri University of Science & Technology
Department of Computer Science
Rolla, MO, USA
[2]Northwest Missouri State University
School of Computer Science and
Information Systems
Maryville, MO, USA
leopoldj@mst.edu, iaahgb@mst.edu, nathane@nwmissouri.edu

Abstract. Real-Time Strategy (RTS) video games are not only a popular entertainment medium, they also are an abstraction of many real-world applications where the aim is to increase your resources and decrease those of your opponent. An obvious application is a military battle; yet another example is a person's physical health where it is advantageous to increase the number of healthy cells in the body and destroy cancerous cells (wherein cancer is your opponent). Using predictive analytics, which examines past examples of success and failure, we can learn how to predict positive outcomes for such scenarios. Herein we show how discriminative subgraph mining can be employed to analyze a collection of played RTS games, and make recommendations about sequences of actions that should, as well as should not, be made to increase the chances of winning future games. As proof of concept, we present the results of an experiment that utilizes our strategy for one particular RTS game.

Keywords: Graph mining, Game Mining, Predictive Analytics.

1 Introduction

Real-Time Strategy (RTS) games are a subgenre of strategy video games wherein the participants position and maneuver units (e.g., troops, robots, and drones) and structures under their control to secure areas and destroy their opponent's assets. In some games, the created entities can in turn create and destroy other entities. Hence the focal points of such games are: resource generation and destruction, and indirect control of units and structures (via other units and structures). RTS games typically have a diverse set of resources which the player can deploy, basically offensive or defensive in nature, and a large variety of environments/storylines from which to select, often with a military science fiction theme; a popular and sophisticated example is StarCraft. The games are usually multi-player, with the winner determined by some criterion such as the player with the most assets at the end of a certain time period or by the last player remaining after all other players' assets have been depleted. Although the RTS game scenario is used for entertainment purposes, it can be abstracted as a model for real-world applications such as military battles, cyberinfrastructure networks that may need to be managed as they come under malicious attack, and even disease history/diagnosis systems which track a patient's symptoms, treatments, and disease progression over time.

Herein we test the hypothesis that predictive analytics can be employed to examine a collection of played games and make recommendations as to what a player should do and what a player should not do in order to increase the chances of winning the game the next time s/he plays. As proof of concept, this method will be tested for one particular RTS game; however, the method that we employ should be applicable to any multi-player RTS game and possibly could be generalized to sequences of categorically offensive versus defensive moves for any RTS game. Specifically, we will model the moves of each played game as directed graphs for the winner's and loser's moves, respectively, and apply discriminative subgraph mining to identify our game strategy recommendations.

The organization of this paper is as follows. Section 2 provides a brief overview of game data mining, data mining techniques used in predictive analytics, and discriminative subgraph mining. Section 3 explains the discriminative subgraph mining algorithm that we utilized for our study. Section 4 outlines the experiment that we conducted to test our hypothesis and the results that we obtained. A summary and conclusions of our research are given in Section 5. Future work is discussed in Section 6.

2 Related Work

2.1 Game Data Mining

For years there has been interest in analyzing games played by others in order to become a more competitive player. In its earliest form, people sought to identify the moves in the game that led to desirable, rather than undesirable, outcomes. For many games it is not only the quantity of assets, but particular features of the assets in the game that must be considered (e.g., an asset's functionality and location). For example, in the game of chess, given the choice, it is usually better to have one bishop than three pawns; position of a piece on the game board is also important as a bishop that is blocked by other pieces may not be able to attack. A number of studies have been conducted wherein a database of played games is analyzed to determine the winning percentage under various scenarios such as games in which one player has two bishops and no knights and the other player has two knights and no bishops after some point in a chess game; see [1, 2] for examples of such studies.

Contemporary genres of games, such as RTS video games, have a much more sophisticated collection of assets (e.g., game pieces) than traditional games such as chess and the characteristics of the assets can be much more diverse. Accordingly, analysis of desirable asset acquisition and deployment throughout a game has become more complex and computationally expensive.

Another branch of game data mining, also known as game telemetry, involves analysis of the people who play the game and/or the personas they may create. There are databases of this information for various online games and mining software to analyze data such as the players' skill level and time spent having played the game; see [3] for an example of such software. Some analyses may try to relate features from a player's profile to his/her winning percentage and odds of winning future games. This area of study is not the focus of the research pursued herein; we do not consider any data related to a player's profile.

As is discussed in [4], the intentions of game data mining should be made clear. *Description* describes patterns found in the game data; similarly, *characterization* is a summation of some general features associated with the data. These patterns could be independent of whether they occurred in the winners' games or the losers' games, or whether the patterns occurred in a majority or a minority of the games in the dataset. Description and characterization are the fundamental, general goals of most data mining efforts. *Classification* (and *clustering*) are used to compare and organize some features of the data into classes; with game data this usually isn't necessary since we are most interested in classifications as winning and losing games, information which is already known. *Discrimination* seeks to identify the differences between groups of instances in the game data beyond just the classification of winning and losing. *Prediction* has the goal of providing a rule (or some form of guideline) that can be used as guidance for playing or forecasting the outcome of future games. The work presented in this study focuses on discrimination and prediction of game data.

2.2 Data Mining Techniques Used in Predictive Analytics

Utilizing mathematical modeling, the field of predictive analytics examines past examples of success and failure to determine the variables that lead to successful outcomes and can be used to make predictions about future events. It has been used widely in the financial and insurance sectors. Here we briefly discuss some of the most common types of data mining methods used for predictive analytics.

Regression analysis: Linear regression is one type of regression analysis commonly used for predictive analytics. This method analyzes the relationship between a dependent variable and a set of independent variables. The relationship is expressed as an equation that predicts the value of the dependent variable as a linear function of the independent variables. For game data the dependent variable is typically the outcome of the game (i.e., win or lose) and the independent variables can be the various possible moves. Given the number of possible moves in an RTS game and the number of possible sequences of moves, this method could be computationally prohibitive.

Rule induction: Rule induction methods such as association rule mining seek to find relationships between variables in the dataset. For example, it could be determined that when the player does actions A and B, s/he also does actions C and D. By applying association rule mining on only the winners' games, we could identify some actions that winning players did. Similarly, by mining the losers' games, we could find some actions common to losing players. However, we then would have to examine the differences between those rule sets to gain knowledge about what winners did that losers did not do, and vice-versa. It should be noted that rule mining typically generates a considerable number of rules because of its combinatorial approach; typically, only rules meeting a certain support threshold are retained.

Decision trees: Decision trees are most often used for classification and can be thought of as a graphical depiction of a rule; each branch of a decision tree can be thought of as a separate rule consisting of a conjunction of the attribute predicates of nodes along that branch. One approach would be to construct decision trees from the winning games and losing games, respectively. Resultingly, the issues previously mentioned for association rule mining of the RTS game data would apply for decision tree methods as well.

Clustering: Clustering is a way to categorize a collection of instances in order to look for patterns; groups are formed to maximize similarity between the instances within a group and to maximize dissimilarly between instances in different groups. Game data are already clustered into two groups: winners and losers. For the purpose of analyzing successful (and unsuccessful) actions, we would likely attempt to form clusters of action sequences. As with linear regression, given the number of possible moves in an RTS game and the number of possible sequences of moves, this method would be computationally prohibitive, and likely would result in an uninformative number of clusters, unless some type of feature reduction mapping method was employed (i.e., mapping specific actions and their time of occurrence in the game to more generalized representations).

Neural networks: Neural networks are composed of a series of interconnected nodes that map a set of inputs into one or more outputs. The interconnections between inputs (which, for the game data, could be actions in the game) are determined based on an analysis of the played games. As with clustering, this method likely would be computationally prohibitive, and would probably not yield useful results, for the RTS game data unless we employed some type of data reduction mapping, which subsequently could result in loss of useful, specific information.

2.3 Discriminative Subgraph Mining

Many problems can be modeled with graphs, wherein entities are represented as vertices and relationships between entities are represented as edges. When the relationship between two vertices has some semantic distinction of a predecessor and a successor, the edges are directed and hence the graph is considered directed. A played RTS game can be modeled as a directed graph where each action (e.g., move) is represented by a vertex and an edge represents two consecutive actions that were made in the game. By necessity, each vertex also must be identified by which player performed that action. The moves for one player do not form a strictly linear sequence because an action can generate multiple actions; for example, the player may create a drone which in turn simultaneously spawns 5 more drones, each of which becomes a new vertex, and 5 edges are created from the propagating drone vertex.

Finding interesting patterns in graphs (both directed and undirected) has been well-researched and is applicable to many problem domains in fields such as bioinformatics, cheminformatics, and communication networks. An 'interesting' pattern in a graph could be a subgraph that appears frequently over a collection of graphs or could be a subgraph that has a particular topography (e.g., a clique). Another type of interesting pattern is a discriminative subgraph.

Discriminative subgraph mining seeks to find a subgraph that appears in one collection of graphs, but does not appear in another collection of graphs. This approach has been used to study several problems including identifying chemical functional groups that trigger side-effects in drugs [5], classifying proteins by amino acid sequence [6], and identifying bugs in software [7, 8, 9]. Here we briefly discuss some of the strategies that have been employed for discriminative subgraph mining.

In [10] the authors define global-state networks, a collection of graphs that represent a series of snapshots taken over a period of time and model some event. Each snapshot graph has the same topology, but the nodes and/or edges in each graph may have different values. The authors' technique, MINDS, is specifically designed to find minimally discriminative subgraphs in large global-state networks. The network graph search space is organized as a set of decision trees to scrutinize the changes from one snapshot to the next in the collection. To reduce an exponential subgraph search space, they employ a Monte Carlo Markov sampling strategy. While the strategies employed in MINDS were found to work well for the global-state networks, they would not be appropriate for the RTS game dataset where each game, and hence each graph's topology, can differ significantly from other games. Additionally, as will be discussed in Section 3, game data mining should not necessarily be limited to just finding minimally discriminative subgraphs.

Discriminative subgraph mining was used in [11] to find subgraphs that would cover as many positive examples and as few negative examples as possible. The test dataset contained protein structures possessing a specific function and proteins not having that function. Each graph contained approximately 1,000 edges and was very dense (i.e., in terms of the number of edges relative to the number of vertices in the graph). Two heuristics were employed to reduce the computational complexity of the mining process. Together these heuristics were used to assign a score to each candidate discriminative subgraph; the score considered the number of positive graphs minus the number of negative graphs in which the subgraph was found. Only the smallest such subgraphs with high scores were returned in the results; any (larger) subgraph that contained one of these (smaller) subgraphs was not further examined, thereby reducing the search space. This algorithm could have been adapted for the predictive game strategy study, but would have had to have been run for both the cases of the winning games being the positive examples and the losing games being the negative examples, and the winning games being the negative examples and the losing games being the positive examples in order to find recommendations for what should and should not be done to win the game.

Another strategy for dealing with the large search space normally incurred with discriminative subgraph mining was presented in [12]. As discussed above, a scoring scheme was used to evaluate the discrimination potential of candidate subgraphs. However, The Learning To Search (LTS) algorithm of [12] differed from the work of [11] by combining the scoring scheme with a sampling strategy to select candidate subgraphs. Candidates deemed promising (in terms of their score) were added to a list and further extended with edges for additional consideration; non-promising candidates were discarded, thereby implementing a branch-and-bound search. This method was tested on protein datasets with good prediction accuracy and a faster runtime than some other discriminative mining methods. As with the algorithm in [12], this approach possibly could be used to analyze a strategy game dataset.

Discriminative subgraph mining also has been used to find bugs in software in [7, 8, 9]. For this application, a program is modeled as a graph based on its control flow graph. In brief, a control flow graph is a directed graph made up of nodes representing basic blocks. Each basic block contains one or more statements from the program. There is an edge from basic block Bi to basic block Bj if program execution can flow from Bi to Bj. Traces through the control flow graph for inputs that produce correct results forms one collection of graphs and traces for inputs that produce incorrect results forms a second collection of graphs. The idea is to look for a discriminative subgraph between the two collections of graphs; this represents the lines of code that are, or are not, being executed when the bug occurs. The algorithm presented in [7] utilizes the LEAP algorithm [13] as a branch-and-bound heuristic on the search space of graphs that it examines; it is based on the observation that subgraphs with higher frequency are more likely to be discriminative. This algorithm was modified slightly to specifically scrutinize certain programming constructs and subsequently was tested in [8, 9]. This general approach to discriminative subgraph mining is applicable to the RTS game dataset and is discussed in more detail in the next section.

3 Methodology: Discriminative Subgraph Mining

The algorithm we employed for discriminative subgraph mining is similar to the approach taken in [8, 9], but does not employ any heuristics specific to game data. Although we ran it sequentially, it easily lends itself to parallel or distributed processing.

Let C^+ and C^- represent two sets of (undirected or directed) graphs for which we want to find a discriminative subgraph; that is, we want to find a subgraph that appears in the graphs in C^- and does not appear in the graphs in C^+, or vice-versa. We shall refer to C^+ as the positive graphs and C^- as the negative graphs although this naming convention has no direct semantic correlation to the classification of the graphs in those respective sets (e.g., 'winner' does not necessarily mean positive). The function *FindDiscriminativeGraph* (Fig. 1) first removes non-discriminative edges from the graphs in both sets; since such edges appear in the graphs in both sets, they cannot be used to differentiate the graphs in the those sets. *FindDiscriminativeGraph* then calls *CreateDiscriminativeGraph* (Fig. 2) to try to find a subgraph that is common to all graphs in C^-, but not common to all the graphs in C^+. If we are unable to find such a graph, then the function *RelaxedCreate-DiscriminativeGraph* (Fig. 3) is called, which relaxes the requirement that the subgraph we seek not be present in all of the C^+ graphs; instead the subgraph only has to not be present in $\alpha * |C^+|$ of the C^+ graphs, where α is a user-specified parameter (our default is $\alpha = 0.5$).

FindDiscriminativeGraph and *CreateDiscriminativeGraph* use a function called *Augment*; this function takes a subgraph G and adds to it an edge (and possibly a node) such that the source vertex exists in G, and the edge (and destination node) exists in all graphs in subgraph collection S1. In this way, a subgraph with an additional edge that exists in all elements of S1 is created and considered by the algorithm.

If we still fail to find a discriminative subgraph, then the difference likely does not involve edges that are in all graphs in C^- and not in graphs in C^+, but rather involves edges in the C^+ graphs that are not in the C^- graphs. Thus, we again call *CreateDiscriminativeGraph*, but reverse the order of the parameters (C^+ and C^-) from our previous call. If we still fail to find a discriminative subgraph, we again call *Relaxed-CreateDiscriminativeGraph* and look for a subgraph that only has to not be present in $\beta * |C^-|$ of the C^- graphs, where β is a user-specified parameter (our default is $\beta = 0.5$).

It is possible that the resulting discriminative graph will be disconnected. Additionally, it could be the case that multiple subgraphs could qualify as a discriminative subgraph. The algorithm addresses both of these cases by returning the maximal discriminative subgraph; this result may be disconnected and will include all possible discriminative edges. It should be noted that it also is possible that our algorithm will not find any subgraph that meets the discriminative conditions. This could occur if the requirement that at least α (β) of the graphs in C^- (C^+) must have at least one edge in common has not been satisfied.

The computational complexity of the process is dependent upon the number of graphs in each collection and the number of edges in each graph. As specified in line 1 of *CreateDiscriminativeGraph,* we begin by examining each single edge from each graph in one of the graph collections. However, in lines 7-9 of that algorithm, we potentially build larger subgraphs that must be searched for; this is the subgraph isomorphism problem, which is NP-complete.

```
Algorithm: FindDiscriminativeGraph(C+, C-, α, β)
C+: set of positive graphs
C-: set of negative graphs
α: percentage of graphs that discriminative subgraph need not be present in C+ when
relaxing conditions
β: percentage of graphs that discriminative subgraph need not be present in C- when
relaxing conditions
remove non-discriminative edges from graphs in C+ and C-;
G = CreateDiscriminativeGraph(C-, C+);
if G is empty then
  G = RelaxedCreateDiscriminativeGraph(C-, C+,
                                        |C+| * α);
  if G is empty then
    G = CreateDiscriminativeGraph(C+, C-);
    if G is empty then
      G = RelaxedCreateDiscriminativeGraph(C+, C-,
                                            |C-| * β);
    end-if;
  end-if;
end-if;
return G
```

Fig. 1. Algorithm for *FindDiscriminativeGraph*

```
Algorithm: CreateDiscriminativeGraph(S1, S2)
S1: set of graphs
S2: set of graphs
FreqSG = queue of 1-edge subgraphs in S1;
while FreqSG is not empty do
   G = FreqSG.dequeue();
   if G is not in any graph in S2 then
     return(G);
   end-if;
   NewGraphs = Augment(G);
   for each graph G' in NewGraphs do
     FreqSG.enqueue(G');
   end-for;
end-while;
return(empty graph)
```

Fig. 2. Algorithm for *CreateDiscriminativeGraph*

Algorithm: *RelaxedCreateDiscriminativeGraph(S1, S2, γ)*

```
S1: set of graphs
S2: set of graphs
γ: threshold for number of graphs discriminative subgraph must be present in
FreqSG = queue of 1-edge subgraphs in S1;
while FregSG is not empty do
   G = FreqSG.dequeue();
   if G is in < γ graphs in S2 then
     return(G);
   end-if;
   NewGraphs = Augment(G);
   for each graph G' in NewGraphs do
     FreqSG.enqueue(G');
   end-for;
end-while;
return(empty graph)
```

Fig. 3. Algorithm for *RelaxedCreateDiscriminativeGraph*

4 Experiment and Results

In this section we discuss the details of an experiment we conducted to test the hypothesis that predictive analytics, specifically discriminative subgraph mining, can be employed to examine a collection of played strategy games and make recommendations as to what a player should do, and should not do, in order to increase the chances of winning the game in the future.

4.1 Experimental Setup

The game that we selected is an online, multi-player RTS game called Interloper [14]. Interloper was chosen over more sophisticated RTS games like StarCraft because of its relatively limited set of action types which include: creating territory tiles, spawning drones, spawning blockades, creating units (e.g., sentinels, drones, defenders, destroyers, markers, bombs, blockades, and snipers), building structures, destroying targets, moving and positioning characters, removing characters, hitting characters, and exploding characters. We obtained a database of 19 played Interloper games from the game's developer. Each of these games contained the sequence of actions performed by each of two players, with a designation of which player won the game. Each action type in the data file had a documented integer encoding. The total number of moves (for both players) in a game in the dataset ranged from 183 to 5,338.

For each game in the dataset we created two individual files: one for the winner's moves and one for the loser's moves. The format for each of the data files that we created was modeled as a directed graph, one edge per line, where each vertex was an action, and an edge represented a consecutive sequence of (two) actions made in that game. As with games such as chess, we thought it would be interesting to analyze (and make recommendations for) the game in three phases: the beginning game, the middle game, and the end game. In chess there is no clear definition of when the middle game begins and ends, or when the end game begins. Similarly, we had no such guidelines for Interloper. Therefore, we simply divided each game file into the first third number of moves, the middle third number of moves, and the last third number of moves, and referred to these as phases 1, 2, and 3 of the games, respectively. Each phase was analyzed separately.

As described in the previous section, our discriminative subgraph mining algorithm would not find a discriminative subgraph unless a certain percentage of the graphs in each (C^- or C^+) "collection" had at least a certain percentage of edges in common. Therefore, we had to test small groups of games at a time. To make sure that we did not miss any possible common edges, we tested every combination of two winning and two losing graphs; that is, a pair of winning graphs played the role of C^+ in *FindDiscriminativeGraph* and a pair of losing graphs played the role of C^-. We then reversed the roles (i.e., a pair of losing graphs played the role of C^+ and a pair of winning graphs played the role of C^-). Depending on whether the discriminative subgraph was found in C^+ or C^- for the particular assignment to those parameters told us whether the moves should be recommended as something that should be done in order to increase the chance of winning (because it was a difference found in the winning graphs) or something that should not be done (because it was a difference found in the losing graphs).

To test the predictive accuracy of our method, we performed cross validation on the dataset of 19 played games. For phase 1, we used 5-fold cross validation. Five partitions were created, 4 of which contained 4 games and 1 of which contained 3 games; by 'game' we mean both the winner and loser for that game. A random number generator (www.random.org/lists/) was used to determine which games were assigned to each partition (with no duplication). For each of the 5 iterations of the 5-fold cross validation, the "training" dataset was formed from 4 of the partitions and the "test" dataset was the remaining partition; the roles of the partitions were rotated through each iteration of the 5-fold cross validation. Discriminative subgraphs were determined from all possible pairs of winning and losing games in the "training" dataset (i.e., 4 of the 5 partitions). This resulted in a set of subgraphs that formed the recommendations for actions that should be done and a set of subgraphs which formed the recommendations for actions that should not be done in order to win the game.

The error rate was calculated as follows. If a recommendation for what should be done (subgraph) was found in one of the winning graphs in the test partition, it was counted as a true positive (TP); if instead that recommendation (subgraph) was found in one of the losing graphs in the test partition, it was counted as a false positive (FP). If a recommendation for what should not be done (subgraph) was found in one of the losing graphs in the test partition, it was counted as a true negative (TN); if instead that recommendation (subgraph) was found in one of the winning graphs in the test partition, it was counted as a false negative. The error rate was calculated as 1 – ((TP + TN) / (TP + TN + FP + FN)), and was averaged over the five iterations of the 5-fold cross validation.

For phases 2 and 3 of the game, significantly fewer discriminative subgraphs were found than for phase 1; this will be discussed in the next section. Therefore, instead of creating 5 partitions for cross-validation, we only created 3 partitions: 2 partitions contained 6 games and 1 partition contained 7 games. Consequently, only 3 iterations were run in those cross validations instead of 5. As was done for phase 1, games still were randomly chosen for each partition for each test. All cross-validation tests (for all phases) were repeated 5 times.

It should be noted that the discriminative subgraph mining algorithm was implemented in Python 3.7. A combination of Python programs and bash scripts were created for data file conversions and batch program executions. All programs were executed on a Dell Intel i7-7700 3.60 GHz 64 GB RAM Windows 10 PC.

4.2 Experimental Results

Each of the three phases of the game was analyzed separately using cross-validation, with each cross-validation test repeated 5 times with randomized data (game) assignment for training and test data from the 19-game dataset. Table 1 shows the average error rate for each of the cross-validation tests for each phase, as well as the average error rate over each phase's 5 tests. The resulting predictive accuracy was good, considering that, in general, discriminative subgraphs can have very low frequencies. The collective recommendations (for moves that should be made and moves that should not be made) were accurate approximately 86.5%, 92.4%, and 98.7% of the time for phases 1, 2, and 3 of the game, respectively. It should be noted that the accuracy for phases 2 and 3 were likely much higher than for phase 1 in part because 3-fold (rather than 5-fold) cross validation testing was used for those phases and because there were significantly fewer discriminative subgraphs to test in those phases.

Table 1. Cross-Validation Test Results

Test No.	Phase 1 Avg. Error Rate	Phase 2 Avg. Error Rate	Phase 3 Avg. Error Rate
1	14.40%	10.60%	1.00%
2	13.40%	0.08%	1.60%
3	13.00%	9.10%	0.70%
4	13.50%	9.80%	2.00%
5	13.30%	8.50%	1.40%
Avg.	**13.52%**	**7.62%**	**1.34%**

For phase 1 of the game, when testing all pairs of 2 winning and 2 losing graphs, 2,333 discriminative subgraphs were found that constituted "should do" recommendations and 2,270 discriminative subgraphs were found that represented "should not do" recommendations. The average size of the "should do" recommendation subgraphs was 28 edges; the smallest had 1 edge and the largest had 170 edges. The average size of the "should not do" recommendation subgraphs was 22 edges; the smallest had 1 edge and the largest had 168 edges.

Of the ten most frequently recommended "should do" subgraphs, 3 contained 3 edges (i.e., 4 moves) and 4 contained 4-5 edges (i.e., 5-6 moves). In contrast, 5 of the 10 most frequently recommended "should not do" subgraphs contained only 1 edge (i.e., 2 moves) and 5 contained 2-3 edges (i.e., 3-4 moves). Thus, for this phase of the game, we are not able to provide quite as much information about what a player should not do as we can say about what a player should do.

The types of actions in the phase 1 discriminative subgraphs were predominantly only two types: creation of territory tiles and (fast) moves of a game character. In the Interloper game, creation of territory files can be considered an offensive action against one's opponent. Movement of a game character could be either an offensive or defensive action; the player's intent (e.g., moving away from danger versus moving to a more strategic position in the game space) cannot be deduced from the game data. Another observation that can be made from these particular discriminative subgraphs is a counter that is associated with both of these types of moves. For each game, the counter for each type of action begins at 1 and is incremented by 1 each time that type of action occurs. The phase 1 discriminative subgraphs differed not only in sequences of territory tile creation and character movement, but also in how relatively early (or late) those actions occurred and in what succession. For example, an edge (2800029, 2800030) represents two tile creations with counters 29 and 30, indicating that these were tile creations that occurred well after the game had started (i.e., they were the 29th and 30th tile creations that this player made). Their occurrence in a discriminative subgraph would indicate that it either is or is not advisable to create so many tiles (back to back) in the first phase of the game.

For phase 2 of the game, when testing all pairs of 2 winning and 2 losing graphs, 250 discriminative subgraphs were found that represented "should do" recommendations and 213 discriminative subgraphs were found that characterized "should not do" recommendations. These were about 90% less than the respective numbers of subgraphs found in phase 1. This is not surprising as the number (and order) of different moves that a player could (and likely did) make increased at this point in the game, thereby reducing the number of graphs that had edges in common and could meet the criteria of *FindDiscriminativeGraph*. The average size of the "should do" recommendation subgraphs was 25 edges; the smallest had 1 edge and the largest had 274 edges. The average size of the "should not do" recommendation subgraphs was 14 edges; the smallest had 1 edge and the largest had 155 edges.

The most frequently recommended "should not do" subgraphs in phase 2 only contained a single edge (i.e., 2 moves); thus, there was a further decrease in the amount of information we could provide a player in terms of what not to do in order to win the game. In contrast, 3 of the top 6 most frequently recommended "should do" subgraphs contained at least 11 edges (i.e., 12 moves). Overall, compared to phase 1, this can be seen as the ability to provide much more information about what a player should do in order to win the game during this phase. Unfortunately, again the types of actions that occurred in the discriminative subgraphs were limited, mostly moving a game character (although now at a slower speed than in phase 1); we had anticipated seeing more offensive actions during this phase of the game.

For the final phase of the game, 68 discriminative subgraphs were found that characterized "should do" recommendations; this was a 97% decrease from the number found in phase 1 and a 72% decrease from the number found in phase 2. In this phase, 36 discriminative subgraphs were found that represented "should not do" recommendations; this was a 98.4% decrease from the number of such subgraphs found in phase 1 and an 83% decrease from the number found in phase 2. As mentioned previously, the moves in this phase of the game likely varied more from game to game, and, as such, it became more difficult to meet the criteria stipulated in *FindDiscriminativeGraph*. The average size of the "should do" recommendation subgraphs was 22 edges, which was only slightly smaller than what had been seen in the other two phases; the smallest had 1 edge and the largest had 115 edges, which was by far the smallest of the three phases. The average size of the "should not do" recommendation subgraphs was 18 edges, which is the average size between what was seen for phases 1 and 2; the smallest had 1 edge and the largest had 145 edges, which was slightly smaller than in phase 2. There were 92% fewer discriminative subgraphs found in phase 3 than had been found in phase 1.

For phase 3, we finally saw some of the most frequently recommended "should not do" subgraphs have multiple edges (i.e., more than 2 moves); of the top 7 such subgraphs, 3 contained more than 4 edges, and 2 of those contained 9-10 edges. Amongst the top 7 most frequently recommended "should do" subgraphs, only 1 had a single edge; the average number of edges for the others in this list was 7 edges (i.e., 8 moves). Although we could provide more recommendations about what 'not to do' in phase 3 than for phases 1 and 2, we still could provide much more information about what 'to do' during this phase of the game.

The majority of the actions in the "should do" subgraphs still involved (slow) movement of a game character whereas the actions in the "should not do" subgraphs predominantly involved territory tile creation, removal of a game character, and/or positioning of a game character. Territory tile creation and removal of a game character can be considered offensive actions in Interloper; as mentioned previously, positioning of a game character could be for offensive or defensive purposes, which cannot be determined from the game data. We were surprised that none of the discriminative subgraphs (for any of the phases) included any defensive actions (e.g., spawning a blockade); however, there are by far more offensive types of actions in the game than defensive actions.

Of all the pairs of 2 winner and 2 loser graphs tested, only a few failed to produce a discriminative subgraph. There were no contradictory results; that is, it was never the case that a sequence of actions in essence would be both recommended and not recommended. Some test pairs produced the same results as other pairs; duplicates were not included in the counts of discriminative subgraphs reported for each phase. Some test pairs produced discriminative subgraphs that were subgraphs of other reported discriminative subgraphs; this was not unexpected since some test (game) pairs had edges in common.

5 Summary and Conclusions

Herein we tested the hypothesis that a form of predictive analytics, namely discriminative subgraph mining, can be used to examine a set of played strategy games and generate a set of recommendations that could be used to predict the chances of winning the game in the future. Using a dataset of played games of a multi-player, Real-Time Strategy (RTS) video game, Interloper, we modeled each game as a graph and found a collection of subgraphs that specified sequences of actions that players should, and should not, make in each of three phases of the game. Although the dataset only contained 19 games, the experimental results showed that the accuracy of our recommendations was high. Overall, our recommendations for our test game, Interloper, were more informative in terms of what a player should do at each of three phases of the game in order to win; however, we also were able to provide some information about what the player should not do. Most importantly, this study has served as a proof of concept that this approach may be a promising strategy for not only game predictive analytics, but also for other problem domains that involve direct and indirect resource generation and destruction.

6 Future Work

We plan to test our discriminative subgraph mining approach on other types of RTS games. If we have the success that we had with Interloper, we hope to establish a mapping between action types and assets in this genre of games so that a more generalized recommendation system can be developed. We also hope to explore ways to make the algorithms more efficient, perhaps applying some heuristics to reduce the search space that are inherent to the nature of game data. Ultimately, we intend to abstract this strategy to other problem domains such as a health care disease tracking and prediction systems using the same foundation of analyzing examples of success and failure in order to make recommendations for future positive outcomes.

References

1. Kaufman, L.: "The Relative Value of the Pieces", Computer Chess Reports, 4:2, pp. 33-34 (1994).
2. Sturman, M.: "Beware the Bishop Pair", Computer Chess Reports, 5:2, pp. 58-59 (1995).
3. Braun, P., Cuzzocrea, A., Keding, T., Leung, C., Padzor, A., and Sayson, D.: "Game Data Mining: Clustering and Visualization of Online Game Data in Cyber-Physical Worlds", International Conference on Knowledge Based and Intelligent Information and Engineering Systems, pp. 2259-2268, Marseille, France (2017).
4. Drachen, A., Thurau, C., Togelius, J., Yannakakis, G., and Bauckhage, C.: Game Data Mining, Springer-Verlag, Heidelberg, Germany (2011).
5. Shao, Z., Hirayama, Y., Yamanishi, Y., and Saigo, H.: "Mining Discriminative Patterns from Graph Data with Multiple Labels and Its Application to Quantitative Structure-Activity (QSAR) Models", Journal of Chemical Information Models, 55(12), pp. 2519-2527 (Dec. 2015).
6. Jin, N. and Wang, W.: "Discriminative Subgraph Mining for Protein Classification", Computational Knowledge Discovery for Bioinformatics Research, pp. 279-295 (2012).
7. Cheng, H., Lo, D., Zhou, Y., Wang, X., and Yan, X.: "Identifying Bug Signatures Using Discriminative Graph Mining", ISSTA, pp. 141-151, Chicago, IL (2009).
8. Leopold, J., Eloe, N., and Taylor, P.: "BugHint: A Visual Debugger Based on Graph Mining", Proceedings of the 24th International Conference on Visualization and Visual Languages, pp. 109-118, San Francisco, CA (2018).
9. Leopold, J., Eloe, N., Gould, J., and Willard, E.: "A Visual Debugging Aid Based on Discriminative Graph Mining", Journal of Visual Languages and Computing, (to appear February 2019).
10. Ranu, S., Hoang, M., and Singh, A.: "Mining Subgraphs from Global-State Networks", KDD, pp. 509- 517, Chicago, IL (2013).
11. Fuksova, A., Kuzelka, O., and Szaboova, A.: "A Method for Mining Discriminative Graph Patterns", Proceedings of NIPS Machine Learning in Computational Biology Workshop (2013).
12. Jin, N. and Wang, W.: "LTS: Discriminative Subgraph Mining by Learning from Search History", Proceedings of IEEE International Conference on Data Engineering (ICDE), pp. 207-218, Hannover, Germany (2011).
13. Yan, X., Cheng, H., Han, J., and Yu, P.: "Mining Significant Graph Patterns by Leap Search", SIGMOD 2008, pp. 433-444, Vancouver, BC, Canada (2008).
14. Interloper Game, http://interlopergame.com, last accessed 2019-12-01.

Interpretable detection of unstable smart TV usage from power state logs

Tamir Mazaev[1], Olivier Janssens[1], Dirk Van Gheel[2], Lieve Lanoye[2], Guillaume Crevecoeur[1], and Sofie Van Hoecke[1]

[1] Ghent University - imec, Department of Electronics and Information Systems, IDLab, Ghent, Belgium,
{tamir.mazaev@ugent.be,odjansse.janssens@ugent.be,
guillaume.crevecoeur@ugent.be,sofie.vanhoecke@ugent.be}
[2] TP Vision Belgium NV, Ghent, Belgium,
{lieve.lanoye@tpv-tech.com,dirk.vangheel@tpv-tech.com}

Abstract. Power state logs from smart TVs are collected in order to construct a time-series representation of their usage. Time-series that belong to a TV exhibiting instability problems are classified accordingly. To do so, an automated feature extraction approach is used, together with linear classification methods in order to realize interpretable classification decisions. A normalized true positive rate of 0.84 ± 0.10 is obtained for the classification. The normalized true negative rate equals 0.80 ± 0.03. The final model returns a regularity statistic called the Approximate Entropy as its most important feature.

Keywords: user profiling · smart TV · time-series · feature extraction · TSFRESH · logistic regression · approximate entropy

1 Introduction

Gartner has predicted that over 25 billion "things" will be connected by 2020. In today's smart home, there are already a variety of connected devices that we interact with on a daily basis, including thermostats, home lighting, security systems, music speakers and smart TVs [4].

This rise of the Internet of Things (IoT) and Big Data enables companies to make better-informed business decisions by collecting and properly exploiting massive sets of data from every aspect of their organization.

By exchanging information over the network, collected by (virtual) sensors attached to these IoT devices, the devices become more context-aware as they aggregate knowledge on their surroundings [5]. Applying machine learning on the collected data may lead to the optimization of operational processes, or a better understanding of a company's customer base. In this paper, we focus on the analysis of smart TV usage. When a customer experiences problems with his TV, he may file a claim describing the problem and bring the device in for repair. We focus on a particular subclass of anomalous behavior called "instability"

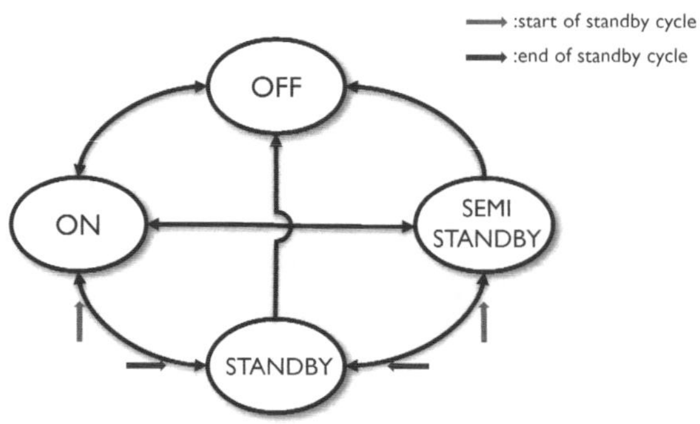

Fig. 1: Simplified power state transition diagram of a smart TV. Circles are possible states of the TV, and the black arrows indicate how the different states can be reached. Colored arrows define the concept of a "standby cycle". If a TV enters a state through a transition indicated by a green arrow, this marks the beginning of the cycle. The red arrows indicate its termination.

problems. In Section 3 we will explain in more detail what this umbrella term entails.

Overall, TPVision collects the smart TV data to detect stability issues in TVs at the customers' home. This way, we want to identify which features are linked to instability and hence need to be avoided in software or, when seen in test, which need to be fixed with highest priority. As part of this overall investigation, smart TV power cycle data are collected. These records specify when individual TVs are switching between different power collection states (see Figure 1). Obviously among devices and even among power cycles on each unique device, variations in timing of these parameters are observed, making it difficult to detect anomalies in this behavior.

We proceed in the rest of the paper as follows: Section 2 describes how we construct time-series representing the usage of a TV based on its power state logs. Section 3 describes the classification methodology applied to detect unstable devices. In Section 4, we describe the results and discuss them. Section 5 concludes this paper.

2 Constructing Time-series of Smart TV Usage

The power state logs were collected in the summer of 2017. In Figure 1, a simplified diagram is given of the logged power states of the smart TVs:

- *On* state: TV screen is on;
- *Off* state: the TV is completely inactive;
- *Standby* state: low power state where the screen is off and CPU is inactive;
- *Semi-standby* state: low power state where the screen is off but CPU is still active.

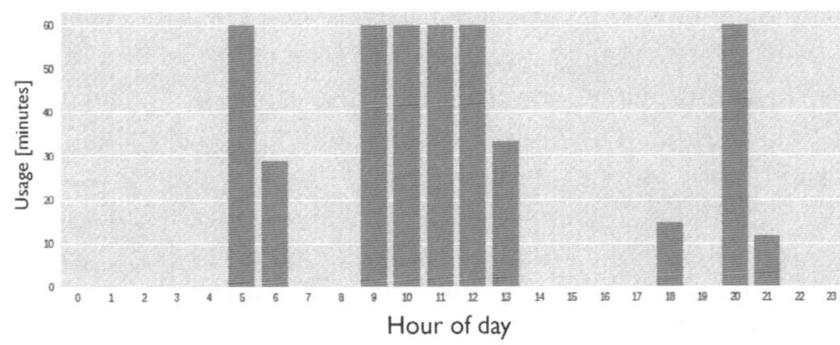

Fig. 2: Example of smart TV usage per hour on one day.

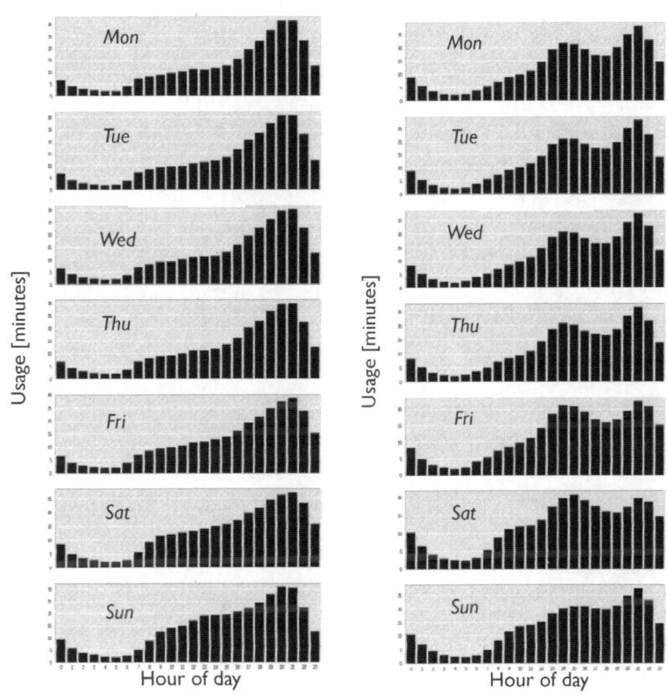

(a) The Netherlands (b) Spain

Fig. 3: Smart TV usage per hour for each day of the week. Averages for two countries are shown (N = 1000 for each country).

Different cycles can be defined on the smart TV power state transition diagram. For example, a "boot cycle" starts with a transition from the *Off* state to the *On* state, and ends with a transition to the *Off* state from any other state.

For this paper, the "standby cycle" is of interest to us because it leads to a representation of the usage of the TV. The corresponding transitions are indicated on the figure; green arrows indicate the start of the cycle, and red arrows indicate its termination. As an extra constraint, we may require that the *On* state must be reached during the standby cycle. This way, we limit the standby cycles to "user sessions" where the TV is actually being used by a human. Standby cycles that are not user sessions are, for example, power cycles where updates are being pushed to the operating system of the smart TV. For these cases, the device is never in the *On* state during the standby cycle.

The logging system of the TVs keeps a timestamp of every transition in the power cycle diagram. This way, the initiation and termination of every user session is known. The intermediate time interval then represents the device being used. Using the logs and timestamps, time-series showing the usage history of a device can be constructed. For example, in Figure 2 we visualize for how many minutes a smart TV has been used per hour throughout the day.

In Figure 3, the average usage profile per day of the week is shown for the Netherlands and Spain (N = 1000 each). As can be seen, these two countries' profiles differ clearly. One can see that there is much more activity in the early afternoon in Spain than in the Netherlands. This is just one example, more additional insights can be discovered from the data other than the identification of instability issues. Note that many other data representations could be considered starting from the smart TV log files as, for example, system states other than those describing TV power cycles are also logged. For this paper, the choice of constructing the TV usage history was made since this particular view on the data is very straightforward to interpret. We will discuss in the following sections how the time-series are used to detect unstable behavior.

3 Instability Detection

The following list describes a range of problems that may occur for a smart TV:

- (Re)boot issues;
- Operating system locks out / crashes / hangs;
- Picture disappearing.

All of these issues are called "instability" problems. Consequently, devices, brought in for repair under these claims, are labeled as being unstable.

We will now formulate the detection of instabilities in a TV as a predictive modeling problem. A schematic overview of our instability detection approach is given in Figure 4. We start by constructing a pair $(\mathbf{x}, y)$ per smart TV with $\mathbf{x} = (x_1, x_2, ..., x_n)$ the time-series associated with the usage of the TV as described above in Section 2 and y a binary target vector describing whether the device was brought in for repair for instability problems during the workweek right after $\mathbf{x}$ (stable $= 0$, unstable $= 1$).

We always consider a period of two week starting on a Monday. Since we look at the TV usage binned per hour of the day, we always have $n = 24 \times 14 = 336$. We call $\mathbf{X}$ the set of all time-series $\mathbf{x}$.

We train a classifier to predict the target label y from its associated $\mathbf{x}$. Our total dataset consists of 91 unstable and 1000 stable devices. The set consists of German and Dutch devices combined in order to get enough unstable examples. We hold out 30% of this set as a test set, and train (and cross-validate) on the remaining samples.

After constructing the time-series $\mathbf{X}$, we apply an automated feature extraction algorithm called TSFRESH [3]. TSFRESH stands for "*Time-Series Feature extraction based on Scalable Hypothesis tests*". Its development was motivated by industrial big data applications as predictive maintenance or production line optimization, but its use also applies to our classification goal.

TSFRESH characterizes time-series by first calculating a large number of well-established feature mappings (e.g. mean, kurtosis, Fourier coefficients, ...). In total, 788 features are calculated. A feature selection step follows. Each feature vector is evaluated with respect to its dependence on the target label. If the feature is deemed significant for predicting the target, it is kept as input for the ensuing prediction algorithm. The significance of a feature is addressed by statistical hypothesis testing.

In our case the target label is binary, and the calculated features non-binary. The following hypothesis is tested by a Kolmogorov-Smirnov test:

$$H_0^{\phi} = \{f_{x_\phi|y=0} = f_{x_\phi|y=1}\}, \tag{1}$$

$$H_1^{\phi} = \{f_{x_\phi|y=0} \neq f_{x_\phi|y=1}\}. \tag{2}$$

Here x_ϕ stands for a calculated feature based on $\mathbf{x}$. $f_{x_\phi|y}$ denotes the conditional density function of x_ϕ given y. Further details on the independence tests may be found in [3].

Features that pass the previous feature selection step are Z-normalized before the next step.

Two different supervised learning methods are used for classifying the extracted features. Logistic regression is a binary linear classifier where a logistic sigmoid is applied to a linear function of the feature vector $\mathbf{x}_\phi$ confining the output between 0 and 1. Logistic regression is based on the following probability model:

$$p(y = 1 \mid \mathbf{x}_\phi) = \sigma(\mathbf{w}^T \mathbf{x}_\phi) = \frac{1}{1 + \exp(-\mathbf{w}^\mathbf{T} \mathbf{x}_\phi)} \tag{3}$$

where $\mathbf{w}$ is the weight vector that needs to be learned. Computing the classification model of linear support vector machine (SVM) classifier amounts to minimizing an expression of the form

$$\left[\frac{1}{n}\sum_{i=1}^{n} \max(0, 1 - y_i(\mathbf{w}^T \mathbf{x}_{\phi,i}))\right] + C||\mathbf{w}||^2, \tag{4}$$

where C indicates the importance assigned to maximizing the classification boundary margin between the two classes versus classifying the classes correctly, which makes it a regularization parameter [1]. We also use L1 and L2 regularization in order to improve the generalization performance of the logistic regression model. On all classifiers 3-fold stratified cross validation is performed on the training set as a hyperparameter optimization step for the regularization term. We are dealing with imbalanced classes, so the Area Under the Receiver Operating Characteristic (AUROC) curve is chosen as the validation metric. This metric is insensitive to disparities in the class proportions.

Next we apply another feature selection step. In order to further reduce the number of features, recursive feature elimination is used. First the linear estimators are trained on the original set of features and the weights of each feature are ranked according to their value. Then the least important weights are excluded from the current set of features. This process is recursively repeated on the pruned set until the optimal number of features to select is reached. Each recursive step is performed within a cross validation loop, again with the AUROC score as the validation metric. In short, we call this *recursive feature elimination with cross validation* (RFECV). For the evaluation of the final classification, we look at the normalized true positive and true negative rate.

We also apply a nonlinear classification method (SVM with Radial Basis function (RBF) kernel) on the full feature set. These SVMs are able to represent a wide range of nonlinear decision boundary classes by setting the appropriate hyperparameters [1]. We set these parameters by using the same validation procedure as mentioned above, and compare the result with the linear classifiers.

The feature selection method used in this work is only directly applicable to linear models. We note that different feature selection methods exist other than the one used in this work [2]. For example, note that for a SVM with a RBF kernel the weights $\mathbf{w}$ can not be explicitly computed, so they are not directly available for ranking. Hence another approach is required.

The class distribution of the dataset is unbalanced, so the class weights for all classifiers are balanced.

For the final classification model we focus on linear models only, since these offer the most straightforward interpretation of the relation between the feature values and their corresponding classification outputs.

4 Results

After the calculation of the 788 features by TSFRESH, only 217 features are deemed relevant by the algorithm. The normalized true positive rate (unstable class) and normalized true negative rate (stable class) of the trained classification models after applying RFECV on these remaining features are shown in Table 1. The averages and standard deviations for both classes are shown for ten runs with a different train-test set splitting seed. Before the application of RFECV, the linear classifiers perform better on the positive class and worse on the negative class than the SVM with a RBF kernel. After the application

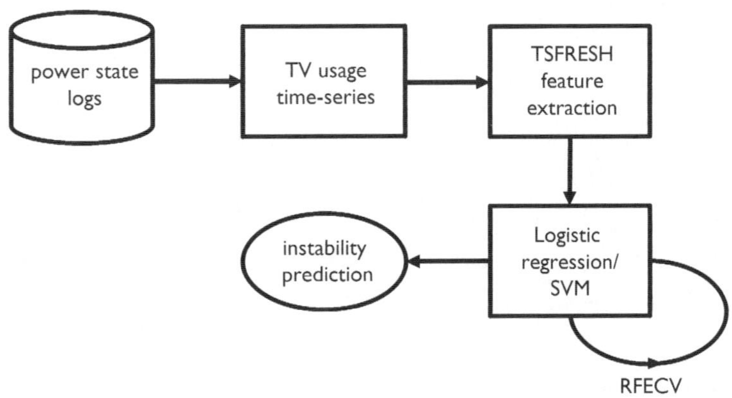

Fig. 4: Schematic representation of instability detection approach

Table 1: Test set result of the trained classification models. The normalized true positive rate (unstable class) and normalized true negative rate are shown (stable class). Ten runs with a different train-test split seed where performed.

(a) Before RFECV

	L1 LR	L2 LR	SVM LIN	SVM RBF
unstable	0.72 ± 0.1	0.74 ± 0.06	0.66 ± 0.08	0.60 ± 0.09
stable	0.79 ± 0.02	0.73 ± 0.02	0.79 ± 0.02	0.83 ± 0.02

(b) After RFECV

	L1 LR	L2 LR	SVM LIN
unstable	0.84 ± 0.10	0.83 ± 0.07	0.79 ± 0.08
stable	0.80 ± 0.03	0.80 ± 0.02	0.80 ± 0.03

weight	TSFRESH feature name
3.48	approximate_entropy__m_2__r_0.1
1.92	change_quantiles__f_agg_"var"__isabs_False
-0.84	fft_coefficient__coeff_70__attr_"real"
-0.79	fft_coefficient__coeff_28__attr_"real"
0.79	fft_coefficient__coeff_24__attr_"abs"
0.58	fft_coefficient__coeff_61__attr_"abs"
0.57	fft_coefficient__coeff_74__attr_"abs"
0.53	fft_coefficient__coeff_29__attr_"abs"
0.53	agg_linear_trend__f_agg_"mean"__chunk_len_5
0.49	sum_of_reoccuring_data_points

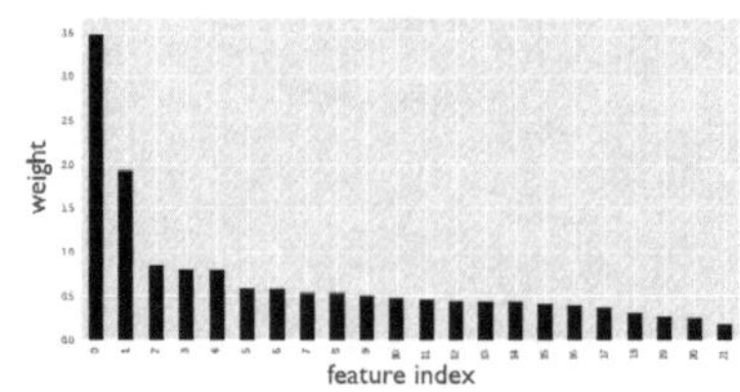

(a) For L1 logistic regression

weight	TSFRESH feature name
0.70	approximate_entropy__m_2__r_0.1
-0.51	value_count__value_0
0.44	fft_coefficient__coeff_24__attr_"abs"
-0.44	fft_coefficient__coeff_28__attr_"real"
0.43	fft_coefficient__coeff_54__attr_"abs"
0.40	fft_coefficient__coeff_38__attr_"abs"
-0.39	number_cwt_peaks__n_1
0.39	range_count__max_1__min_-1
0.38	sum_of_reoccuring_data_points
0.37	agg_linear_trend__f_agg_"max"__chunk_len_50

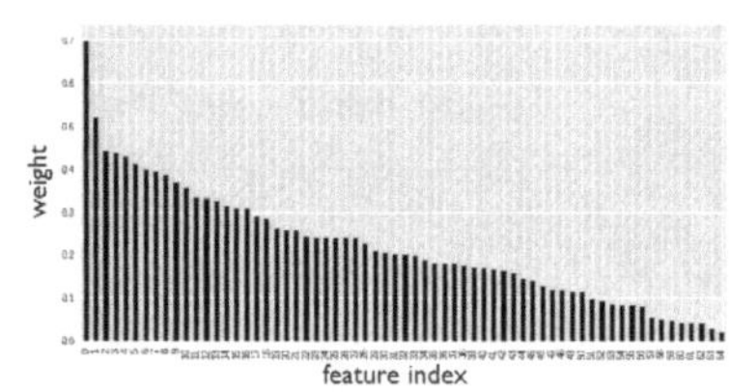

(b) For L2 logistic regression

weight	TSFRESH feature name
0.38	approximate_entropy__m_2__r_0.1
-0.23	fft_coefficient__coeff_28__attr_"real"
0.21	fft_coefficient__coeff_52__attr_"abs"
0.20	sum_of_reoccuring_data_points
0.19	fft_coefficient__coeff_54__attr_"abs"
-0.18	fft_coefficient__coeff_70__attr_"real"
-0.18	mean_second_derivative__central
0.17	fft_coefficient__coeff_24__attr_"abs"
0.16	fft_coefficient__coeff_38__attr_"abs"
-0.16	agg_autocorrelation__f_agg_"var"

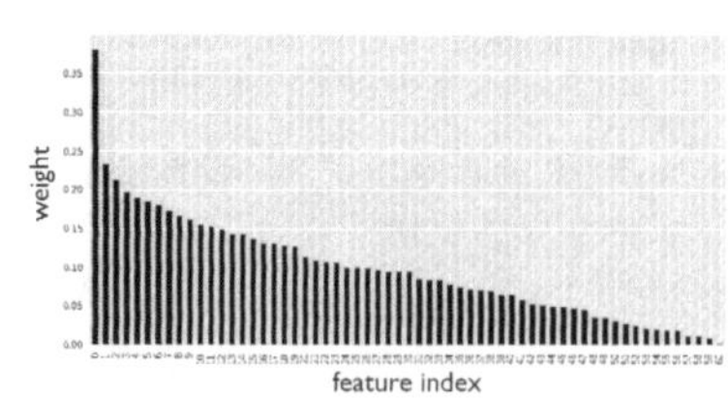

(c) For SVM with linear kernel

Fig. 5: Features with top ten largest weights of the linear classification models. The ranked feature importances are also plotted for all features remaining after applying RFECV.

of RFECV, the linear classifiers perform very similar to each other. The feature selection procedure also improves the performance of each classifier considerably.

In Figure 5, we show the top ten most important features for both regularization schemes. Feature names from the TSFRESH package are used (a full description of all extracted features can be found in the documentation of the package). A positive weight here means that a higher value for the corresponding feature indicates that the device belongs to the stable class. A negative weight means the opposite. The value of the learned weights is also plotted for all features that remain in the classification model. For L1 logistic regression, only 22 features are retained in the final model. For L2 regularization, 71 features remain. For the SVM, 65 features remain. As can be seen from the logistic regression models, a L1 regularization term typically leads to a solution that is more sparse in the number of features [1]. As a result this enhances the interpretability of the final model. We remark that it also gives the best classification performance.

We now focus on two interesting observations concerning the shown features. For all models, the so called Approximate Entropy is the most important feature. This statistic has been developed in order to quantify the amount of regularity and unpredictability in time-series data. It has an important use in the analysis of physiological time-series. Its exact mathematical description can be found in [6]. In this classification task, we try to predict instability in smart TV usage. Hence, it is interesting to observe that a direct measure of unstable behavior emerges as the most discriminative aspect of the time-series with this goal in mind. Another interesting feature to note is the real part of the 28th Fourier coefficient, which appears in all models with a negative weight. Since the length n of the time-series is equal to 336, this corresponds to periodicity on the scale of 12 hours. So if the TV usage pattern shows strong periodicity on the scale of 12 hours, this indicates a higher probability of the device being stable.

5 Conclusion

We have presented an approach to construct a time-series representation of the usage of a smart TV based on its power state logs, visualizing for how many minutes a smart TV has been used per hour throughout the day.

Instability issues in the TVs can be detected using an automated feature extraction procedure of the time-series called TSFRESH. Applying linear classification models using those features leads to predictive models that can be interpreted based on the weights assigned to their features. A feature called the Approximate Entropy is shown to be the most important feature, as it has the highest weight for all classification models. The best classification result is obtained by using L1 logistic regression. It enables the detection of TVs with instability issues with a normalized true positive rate of 0.84 ± 0.10. The normalized true negative rate equals 0.80 ± 0.03.

References

1. Bishop, C.M.: Pattern Recognition and Machine Learning. Springer, Secaucus, NJ, USA (2006)
2. Chandrashekar, G., Sahin, F.: A survey on feature selection methods. Computers & Electrical Engineering **40**(1), 16 – 28 (2014). https://doi.org/10.1016/j.compeleceng.2013.11.024
3. Christ, M., Kempa-Liehr, A.W., Feindt, M.: Distributed and parallel time series feature extraction for industrial big data applications. arXiv preprint **1610.07717** (May 2017)
4. Günther, W.A., Mehrizi, M.H.R., Huysman, M., Feldberg, F.: Debating big data: A literature review on realizing value from big data. The Journal of Strategic Information Systems **26**(3), 191–209 (September 2017). https://doi.org/10.1016/j.jsis.2017.07.003
5. Ng, I.C., Wakenshaw, S.Y.: The internet-of-things: Review and research directions. International Journal of Research in Marketing **34**(1), 3–21 (March 2017). https://doi.org/10.1016/j.ijresmar.2016.11.003
6. Pincus, S.M., Gladstone, I.M., Ehrenkranz, R.A.: A regularity statistic for medical data analysis. Journal of Clinical Monitoring **7**(4), 335–345 (October 1991). https://doi.org/10.1007/BF01619355

WeFreS: Weighted Frequent Subgraph Mining in a Single Large Graph

Nahian Ashraf[1], Riddho Ridwanul Haque[1], Md. Ashraful Islam[1], Chowdhury Farhan Ahmed[1], Carson K. Leung[2][0000-0002-7541-9127] (✉), Jiaxing Jason Mai[2], and Bryan H. Wodi[2]

[1] University of Dhaka, Dhaka, Bangladesh
farhan@du.ac.bd
[2] University of Manitoba, Winnipeg, MB, Canada
kleung@cs.umanitoba.ca

Abstract. Considering edge weights during frequent subgraph mining can help us discover more interesting and useful subgraph patterns when compared to its unweighted counterparts. Although some recent works have proposed weight adaptation in frequent subgraph mining from transactional graph databases, the consideration of edge-weights in mining subgraph patterns from single large graphs is mostly unexplored. However, such graph structures appear frequently, with instances being found in social networks, citation and collaboration graphs, chemical and biological networks, etc. In this paper, we propose *WeFreS*, an efficient algorithm for mining weighted frequent subgraphs in edge-weighted single large graphs. *WeFreS* takes into consideration the weight, or significance of the interactions between different types of entities, and only outputs subgraphs whose weighted support is greater than a given user-defined threshold. The resulting subgraph patterns are both frequent and significant from the application perspective. Moreover, for efficiency, *WeFreS* is also equipped with various pruning techniques and optimizations.

Keywords: Single large graph · Weighted single large graph · Graph mining · Weighted frequent subgraph mining.

1 Introduction

Identifying frequently appearing patterns in large databases is an important domain of data mining [16]. In the modern world, graphs are being increasingly used to model data obtained from various real-life applications [2, 4, 8, 12, 14, 15, 18]. Weighted graphs have even more representational power than unweighted ones, and allow users to specify the relative significance of various edge-relations in the graph. Mining frequent subgraph patterns from weighted graph data can thus enable us to gain useful insights about the features and the nature of the data around us.

Graph mining approaches have traditionally focused on two different setups: (i) transactional graph database (which is viewed as a collection of small graphs) and (ii) single large graph framework (which represents the entire dataset in a single graph). Although several approaches have been proposed for weighted frequent subgraph mining from transactional graph databases [9, 10], there exists a scarcity of efficient approaches addressing the same problem in the context of single large graphs. However, the single large graph representation is inevitable for many fields such as analyzing molecular fragments, image processing, software bug detection, text classification and social network analysis [6, 11]. Thus, considering edge weights during frequent subgraph mining in single large graphs can help us mine important subgraph patterns, which can be used in a variety of different applications [1, 12].

Consider the case of mining patterns of spam dispersion in a social network [7], in which the number of spammers is relatively low. Unweighted graph mining approaches will fail to mine patterns involving spammers and spam dispersion, for not being able to prioritize edge relations that include spammers. A weighted frequent subgraph mining approach, however, would do so if heavier weights were assigned to edges involving spammers. Such an approach could thus lead us to finding frequent patterns of spam dispersion across a community.

Recent literature involving single large graphs use *minimum image-based index* (*MNI*) [3] as the frequency support of a subgraph in a given large graph. Using the MNI measure, weighted support of a subgraph is defined as the product of the average of its edge weights and its MNI value.

In the current paper, we propose an algorithm that takes an edge-weighted single large graph as input and outputs all subgraphs whose weighted support satisfies a given user-defined threshold. Here, we consider graphs, where edge-weights are defined as a function of the labels of the nodes adjacent to an edge. This is a non-trivial task due to the absence of the Apriori property in weighted frequent subgraph mining. Traditional weighted pattern mining approaches [20] avoid extending a pattern if its support multiplied by *MaxW* (highest weight value among all items) is less than the given threshold. Theoretically, extending the current subgraph with infinite edges can make the average weight at most *MaxW*. However, this is generally a rather high over-estimation, which leads to unacceptably high runtimes—especially when working on graphs having highly varying edge-weights.

Further challenges are caused by the computational difficulty of determining the exact value of the MNI. To avoid this costly operation, a *constraint satisfaction problem* (*CSP*) *model* has been applied to determine if the MNI of a subgraph is at least a given threshold (instead of determining its exact value) [5, 17]. During the mining process, the user defines a weighted support threshold value (instead of explicitly defining the required MNI). Our proposed algorithm, ***We****ighted* ***Fre****quent* ***S****ubgraph Miner* (*WeFreS*), efficiently overcomes these challenges by introducing the *MaxPosW* measure, which is a tight upper bound of the highest weight value a subgraph can attain after being extended by one or more remaining edges from the given large graph. We also introduce a redesigned CSP model for the frequency evaluation of a subgraph in an edge-weighted framework. *Key contributions* of this paper include the following:

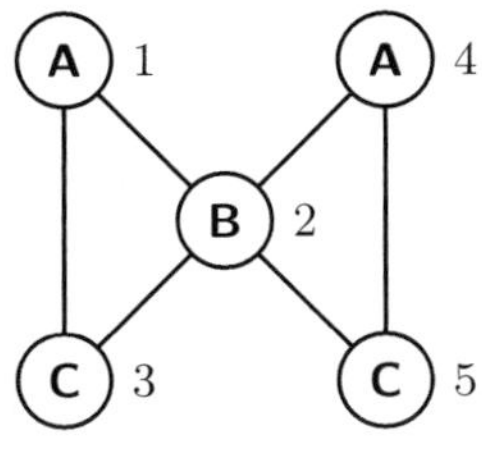

Fig. 1. An input graph G

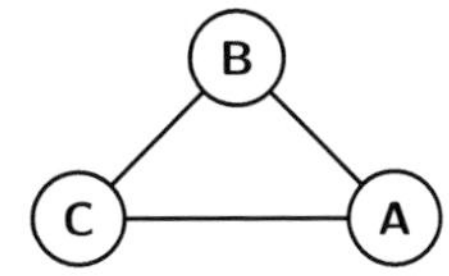

Fig. 2. A sample subgraph S

- Introduction of an efficient method to counter the absence of the *Apriori* property during weighted frequent subgraph mining.
- Proposal of an efficient technique for determining $MaxPosW$ (i.e., maximum possible weight a subgraph can attain after being extended by one or more edges from the large graph).
- Reformulation of the *CSP* model so that it can fit in a weighted framework.
- Development of *WeFreS*, a weighted frequent subgraph mining algorithm that works on edge-weighted single large graphs.
- Demonstration of the efficiency of *WeFreS* in comparison with existing approaches and baseline algorithms using results obtained from experiments on several real-world datasets.

The remainder of this paper is organized as follows. The next section gives the formal problem definition and an overview of some related works. Section 3 presents our proposed method and relevant proofs. Evaluation results and conclusions are given in Sections 4 and 5, respectively.

2 Preliminary Concepts and Related Works

Definition 1. *For a* **weighted single large graph** *described by a five tuple* (V, E, L, l, w), *(i)* V *and* E *are sets of vertices and edges, respectively, such that all* $e \equiv (u, v) \in E$ *where* $u, v \in V$ *and* e *connects nodes* u *and* v; *(ii)* L *is a set of node labels; (iii)* $l{:}V \rightarrow L$ *is a function that maps each node to a certain label; and (iv) the weight of each* $e \in E$ *is defined by the function* $w{:}(LXL) \rightarrow R$ *as* $w(l(u), l(v))$.

Definition 2. *For any subgraph* S *with vertex set* V_S, *let* $f(v)$ *denote the number of distinct nodes in an input graph* G *with a node* $v \in V_S$ *that can be mapped to in order to form at least one valid isomorphism. The* **minimum image-based (MNI) index** *of a subgraph* S *is* $\forall v \in V_S, \min(f(v))$.

For example, subgraph S in Fig. 2 has two isomorphisms in graph G in Fig. 1: (i) {1-2-3} and (ii) {4-2-5}. Here, nodes A and C in S can be mapped to two distinct nodes each to form valid isomorphisms, but node B can be mapped only to node 2 in G. Consequently, the MNI support of S in G is $\min(2, 1, 2) = 1$.

While alternative metrics exist for determining the frequency support of a subgraph in a single large graph, we use the MNI index as the support metric due to (i) the relative computational ease of determining its value and (ii) the mined subgraphs are supersets of those mined by other metrics. MNI is used as the support metric in several recent literature as well [5, 17].

Definition 3. *The* **weight $W(S)$ of a subgraph S** *is the average of the weights of the edges in it. The weighted support $WS(S)$ of S is the product of $W(S)$ and its MNI support $MNI(S)$, i.e., $WS(S) = W(S) \times MNI(S)$.*

For example, in Fig. 2, if the weights of edges connecting labels (A-B), (B-C) and (C-A) in S are 5, 10 and 15 respectively, then $W(S) = \frac{5+10+15}{3} = 10$ and $WS(S) = W(S) \times MNI(S) = 10 \times 1 = 10$. Weighted support is suitable for finding interesting patterns because it takes into account both the MNI support and weight (instead of only the MNI value).

Definition 4. *Given a weighted single large graph G and a threshold τ as input, the* **weighted frequent subgraph mining** *problem is defined as finding all subgraphs S such that $WS(S) \geq \tau$.*

In the context of relevant literature, gSpan [19] mines frequent subgraphs from transactional graph databases. Concepts introduced in gSpan regarding the canonical ordering of edges and subgraphs have been adopted in previous single large graph mining approaches [5, 17] and are used in *WeFreS* to avoid duplicate subgraph generation. GraMi [5] is a state-of-the-art approach for mining frequent subgraphs from single large graphs, with a CSP model to determine if the MNI of a subgraph satisfies a given threshold. GraMi does not take edge-weights into consideration, and thus risks mining subgraph patterns which are frequent but ultimately insignificant. It also misses out on mining subgraph patterns that are relatively less frequent, but nevertheless interesting due to higher weight values.

ReSuM [17] takes edge-weights into consideration and can mine weighted frequent subgraphs when the weights are within the interval [0,1]. ReSuM uses GraMi to identify all frequent subgraphs, and then filters out subgraphs from the output whose weighted support do not satisfy the given threshold. Since the weight of each subgraph is imposed to be within [0, 1], the weighted support is bounded by the MNI support, thus ensuring a complete search. Experiments in Section 4 show this approach to be inefficient compared to *WeFreS*. Furthermore, imposing weights to be within [0, 1] limits the representational power of the graph. As exemplified by the case of spam dispersion in Section 1, many applications require the weighted support of certain patterns to be scaled up from their MNI support, and that is not possible if edge-weights are restricted to being less than 1.

3 Our Proposed WeFreS Algorithm

Mining weighted single large graphs imposes several challenges. First, how do we determine if there is a possibility of an extension of a given subgraph to be weighted frequent? Even though the MNI index of a subgraph maintains the *Apriori* property, the weight of the extensions of a subgraph may exceed its own weight. This paper introduces a novel approach for determining the **Max**imum **Pos**sible **W**eight (i.e., *MaxPosW*-measure) whether a subgraph can attain after being extended by one or more edges. Once the *MaxPosW* for a subgraph S is determined, we define $reqExt = \lceil \tau / MaxPosW \rceil$ as the minimum MNI value that S must have in order for an extension of S to be weighted frequent. Let (i) $W(S)$ the weight of the weighted frequent subgraph S, we define $reqFreq = \lceil \tau / W \rceil$ as the minimum required MNI value.

We begin extending subgraphs after deleting nodes and edges having 'infertile' labels from the large graph. Thus, the steps that are needed to be defined to fully express the mining process are as follows:

- Defining a method to determine *MaxPosW* for a subgraph S.
- Defining a method to determine if the MNI support of a subgraph S is at least *reqExt*.
- Defining a method to determine if the MNI support of a subgraph S is at least *reqFreq*.
- Defining a method to determine if a node or an edge is *infertile*.

Detailed descriptions of all these methods along with necessary mathematical proofs and illustrations are provided in the remainder of this section.

3.1 Calculation of MaxPosW

WeFreS works by (i) initiating a subgraph for each undeleted edge in the input graph and (ii) evaluating its weighted support to determine if it is weighted frequent itself and if it is extendable. Each extendable graph is then recursively extended by adding a single-edge to it, to form all canonical 1-edge extensions of the current subgraph, whose weighted supports are subsequently evaluated. Thus, the entire search space of *WeFreS* can be viewed as a collection of *DFS code trees*, each node of which represents a subgraph whose weighted support was evaluated. *WeFreS* functions by executing a depth first traversal of the tree.

During this traversal, each time we extend a subgraph with an edge, the weight calculations are effected. If there are $|G|$ edges in the entire graph and $|g|$ edges in the subgraph g, we can extend subgraph g by at most $rem(g) = |G| - |g|$ edges. The maximum possible weight an existing subgraph can attain after being extended by exactly i-edges is equal to the weight attained after being extended by the i-edges with the highest edge weights in $rem(g)$ and can be calculated as:

$$h_i(g) = \frac{cur\_sum(g) + sum_i(g)}{|g| + i} \tag{1}$$

where (i) cur_sum gives the summation of edge weights of g and (ii) sum_i returns weight summation of remaining i highest weighted edges in $rem(g)$. *MaxPosW(g)* can be calculated by taking the maximum of all $h_i(g)$ measures:

$$MaxPosW(g) = \max\{h_i(g) : 1 \leq i \leq rem(g)\} \tag{2}$$

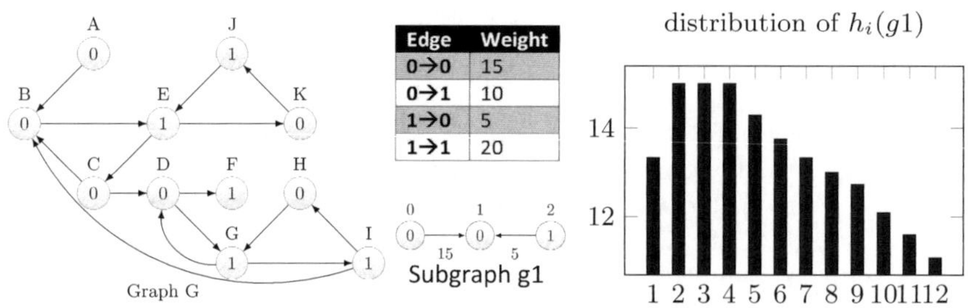

Fig. 3. A sample single large graph G, a subgraph $g1$ of G, and its h_i distribution

We can conclude from the definition of $MaxPosW$ that for any extension of the current subgraph to be frequent, the product of $MaxPosW$ and MNI of the current subgraph must be at least the weighted support threshold τ, i.e., $MaxPosW \times MNI \geq \tau$. So, for a subgraph g, the minimum required MNI for being frequent (i.e., *reqFreq*) and the minimum required MNI for being extendable (i.e., *reqExt*) can be determined by the following:

$$reqFreq(g) = \lceil \tau / weight(g) \rceil \tag{3}$$

$$reqExt(g) = \lceil \tau / MaxPosW(g) \rceil \tag{4}$$

For example, in the single-large graph of Fig. 3, where edge-weights are defined in the given table, weight of subgraph $g1$ is $\frac{15+5}{2} = 10$. It contains one edge connecting the label pair $(0, 0)$, and another connecting the label pair $(1, 0)$. Thus, the list of remaining edges contains two $(1, 1)$-edges of weight 20 each, two 15-weighted $(0, 0)$-edges, five 10-weighted $(0, 1)$-edges, and four 5-weighted $(1, 0)$-edges. As such, the maximum possible weight after extending by one edge, $h_1(g1) = \frac{15+5+20}{2+1} = 13.33$. The other values of $h_i(g1)$ are plotted in Fig. 3. Observed from the bar chart, the maximum weight attainable by $g1$ after extension is $maxPosW(g1) = 15$. If the threshold is 30 and the weight of the subgraph is 10, then the subgraph must have a MNI value of at least 3 to be weighted frequent. Again, since $MaxPosW$=15, the subgraph will be extendable if it has a MNI value of at least 2. Now, the valid isomorphisms of $g1$ are (C, D, G), (A, B, I) and (C, B, I). Thus, each node of the subgraph can be mapped with two distinct nodes of the main graph to form valid isomorphisms, and thus the MNI of the subgraph is 2. Hence, although $g1$ is not weighted frequent, it is extendable.

Theorem 1. *Maximum possible weight a subgraph can attain after being extended by i edges, denoted as* (h_i)*, follows a unimodal distribution.*

Proof. We first prove the following statement is sufficient for unimodality:

$$\forall i \in 1 \leq i \leq rem, h_i \geq h_{i+1} \implies h_{i+1} \geq h_{i+2} \tag{5}$$

Let i be the least value, for which $h_i \geq h_{i+1}$. Thus, $\forall 1 \leq j < i, h_j < h_{j+1}$. This indicates that the portion of the distribution before the decreasing part starts shall be increasing. Now, we prove that, if the aforementioned statement is true, the rest of the distribution shall stay non-increasing once the non-increasing part appears.

Induction base: For $k = i + 1$, as $h_i \geq h_{i+1} \implies h_{i+1} \geq h_{i+2}$ and $h_i \geq h_{i+1}$ are true, $h_{i+1} \geq h_{i+2}$ is true by modus ponens. This implies that the non-increasing part continues at least upto $i + 2$.

Induction step: Suppose the non-increasing portion continues upto k, i.e., $h_i \geq h_{i+1} \implies h_{i+1} \geq h_{i+2} \implies \ldots \implies h_{k-1} \geq h_k$. Again, $(h_{k-1} \geq h_k \implies h_k \geq h_{k+1}) \wedge (h_{k-1} \geq h_k) \implies (h_k \geq h_{k+1})$. Thus, if the non-increasing part extends upto k, it shall extend upto $k + 1$ as well. By principle of mathematical induction, we can conclude that, if the statement in Eq. (5) is proved, it stays non-increasing once the non-increasing part of the distribution of h_i starts. In simple terms, if statement in Eq. (5) is true, we can say that upto a certain value of i, h_i increases and stays non-increasing afterwards.

Now, we prove the statement in Eq. (5), given that $w_i \geq w_{i+1} \geq w_{i+2}$, h_i can be calculated using Eq. (1). Here, w_k denotes the weight of the k-th edge, when the edges are sorted in decreasing order of edge weights. From Eq. (1), $h_i = \frac{cur\_sum+sum_i}{k+i} = \frac{(cur\_sum+sum_i)(k+i+1)}{(k+i)(k+i+1)} = \frac{(cur\_sum+sum_i)(k+i)+(cur\_sum+sum_i)}{(k+i)(k+i+1)} = \frac{cur\_sum+sum_i}{k+i+1} + \frac{cur\_sum+sum_i}{(k+i)(k+i+1)} = \frac{cur\_sum+sum_i+\frac{cur\_sum+sum_i}{k+i}}{k+i+1}$.

$$\therefore h_i = \frac{cur\_sum + sum_i + h_i}{k + i + 1} \tag{6}$$

Eq. (1) also implies that maximum possible weight after extending the subgraph in consideration by $(i+1)$-edges can at most be $h_{i+1} = \frac{cur\_sum+sum_{i+1}}{k+(i+1)} = \frac{cur\_sum+sum_i+w_{i+1}}{k+i+1}$. As $h_i \geq h_{i+1}$, using Eq. (6), we have $\frac{cur\_sum+sum_i+h_i}{k+i+1} \geq \frac{cur\_sum+sum_i+w_{i+1}}{k+i+1} \implies h_i \geq w_{i+1}$. Then, $h_{i+1} = \frac{cur\_sum+sum_i+w_{i+1}}{k+i+1} = \frac{\frac{(cur\_sum+sum_i)}{k+i}(k+i)+w_{i+1}}{k+i+1} = \frac{h_i(k+i)+w_{i+1}}{k+i+1}$. As $h_i \geq w_{i+1}$, we have $h_{i+1} \geq \frac{w_{i+1}(k+i)+w_{i+1}}{k+i+1} = \frac{w_{i+1}(k+i+1)}{k+i+1}$. Therefore, $h_{i+1} \geq w_{i+1}$. Again, from Eq. (6) and using relations, $h_{i+1} \geq w_{i+1}$ and $w_{i+1} \geq w_{i+2}$, we get $h_{i+1} = \frac{cur\_sum+sum_{i+1}+h_{i+1}}{k+(i+1)+1} \geq \frac{cur\_sum+sum_{i+1}+w_{i+1}}{k+i+2}$. Thus, $h_{i+1} \geq \frac{cur\_sum+sum_{i+1}+w_{i+2}}{k+i+2}$ because $sum_{i+1}+w_{i+2} = sum_{i+2}$, $\frac{cur\_sum+sum_{i+1}+w_{i+2}}{k+i+2} = \frac{cur\_sum+sum_{i+2}}{k+i+2}$ Therefore, using Eq. (1), it immediately follows that $\frac{cur\_sum+sum_{i+2}}{k+i+2} = h_{i+2}$ and $h_{i+1} \geq h_{i+2}$, which completes proving Eq. (5). Thus, distribution of h_i is unimodal. □

We proved Theorem 1 that distribution of highest possible weight on remaining edges (h_i) is unimodal. The classical technique of ternary search can be used to find the maximum of a unimodal function in $O(\log_2(rem))$—instead of naively applying a linear search that works in $O(rem)$—where rem is the number of remaining edges for a current subgraph. Thus, we take advantage of the unimodal property and efficiently calculate $MaxPosW$ using ternary search.

To calculate sum_i in Eq. (1) efficiently, we need to maintain a sorted list of remaining edges. While recursively searching for larger subgraphs, we add an edge to the current subgraph and remove that edge from the sorted list and do the opposite during backtracking. Thus, we need a data structure capable of supporting fast insertion, deletion and answering queries regarding the sum of the first i values in a list. Using a *segment tree*, all these operations can be achieved in logarithmic time. To reduce the size of the segment tree, we group edges with equal weights together, and keep count of how many edges map to each distinct weight. Each node of the segment tree shall contain the sum of the weights and the number of 'unremoved' edges present in the interval it represents. Thus, the value of sum_i in Eq. (1) can be determined in $O(\log_2(D))$ where D is the number of distinct edge weights. Thus, *MaxPosW* calculation is achieved in $O(\log_2(rem) \times \log_2(D))$ time, making it feasible to calculate it in large graphs.

3.2 Our Proposed CSP Model

As described previously, for each subgraph in the search space, *WeFreS* determines if the *MNI* of the subgraph is at least equal to *reqFreq* and *reqExt*. Let $max\tau$=max(*reqFreq*, *reqExt*) and $\min\tau$=min(*reqFreq*, *reqExt*). In effect, instead of taking the time-consuming route of determining the exact MNI of a subgraph, it suffices to determine if the MNI is at least equal to $max\tau$, and failing that, if it satisfies $min\tau$.

The problem of determining a lower bound of the MNI of a subgraph can be modelled as a *constraint satisfaction problem* (*CSP*). The subgraph pattern itself represents the constraint graph, with its nodes representing the variables and its edges and labels symbolizing the constraints. The values in the domain of each node in a subgraph are initially all nodes in the input graph having the same labels as it. A valid solution to the CSP is a valid subgraph isomorphism and must satisfy the following constraints.

1. No two different nodes in the subgraph can be assigned to the same node in the large graph.
2. The label of each node in the subgraph must match the label of the node in the large graph it is assigned to.
3. For each edge (u_1, u_2) in the subgraph, if v_1 is the large graph node mapped to u_1 and v_2 is mapped to u_2, there must exist an edge (v_1, v_2) in the large graph.

Initially, we seek to find if the MNI of the subgraph satisfies $\max\tau$. Thus, we iterate over each variable, and try to find $\max\tau$ values in its domain from which a valid subgraph isomorphism can be found. If for any variable, such $\max\tau$ values do not exist, the searched MNI value is changed to $\min\tau$. Thus, for the current variable, and every variable onwards, we seek to find $\min\tau$ values leading to valid isomorphisms. Again, if we can ascertain that $\min\tau$ values do not exist for a certain variable, then neither $max\tau$ nor $min\tau$ shall be satisfied. The MNI_LOWER_BOUND procedure terminates immediately and returns 0. To keep track of the required MNI value to be satisfied, we propose using a *statusFlag*. Initially, the status flag is set to 2, indicating the value in question is max_T. When searching for min_T, the *statusFlag* is updated to 1. After iterating through all the variables for *statusFlag* values 2 and 1, max_T and min_T are returned respectively. The procedure is described in Algorithm 1.

Algorithm 1 MNI_LOWER_BOUND

Input Subgraph S, weighted graph G, min MNI req. min_T, & a max MNI req. max_T
Output Lower bound of the MNI of S in G

```
statusFlag ← 2
if (min size of domain for nodes in S) <maxT then
    statusFlag ← 1
if (min size of domain for nodes in S) <minT then
    return 0
for each node v ∈ S do
    satisfiedValues ← 0
    for each value x ∈ domain(v) do
        if a valid isomorphism is found by assigning x to v then
            satisfiedValues ← satisfiedValues +1
        else
            if statusFlag=2 & (satisfiedValues+(#remaining values)) <maxT then
                statusFlag ← 1
            if statusFlag=1 & (satisfiedValues+(#remaining values)) <minT then
                return 0
if statusFlag = 1 then
    return minT
return maxT
```

If the number of nodes in the subgraph is V_S, the number of nodes in the large graph is V_G, the probabilities of the MNI of a subgraph satisfying max_T and min_T are p_1 and p_2 respectively and the probability of an assignment of a value to a variable leading to a valid subgraph isomorphism is p, the complexity of Algorithm 1 (for the MNI lower bound) is $O(V_S \cdot (p_1(\frac{max_T}{p}) + (1-p_1)\frac{min_T}{p}) \cdot V_G^{V_S-1})$. However, various pruning and optimization measures defined in existing literature for unweighted single large graph mining are preserved here, making the actual runtime much shorter in practice than what is suggested by the time complexity. Use of the *statusFlag* allows for parallel checking for satisfaction of *reqFreq* and *reqExt*, further increasing the efficiency of the model.

3.3 Subgraph Extension

As discussed earlier, *WeFreS* functions through a depth first traversal of some DFS code trees. The traversal occurs according to the recursive procedure outlined in Algorithm 2 (for subgraph extension). Before starting the extension process, *WeFreS* takes some pre-pruning measures to reduce the search space.

WeFreS defines a node label or a label pair as 'infertile' when it is mathematically impossible for any subgraph with that node label or the label pair to be weighted frequent and they are deleted from the node label and label pair list before starting the extension process. The mechanism for detection of infertility of a label pair is similar to determining if a subgraph containing a single edge with that label pair should be extended or not. Node labels not belonging to any 'fertile' label pair are deleted. The remaining labels are then sorted in decreasing order of the sum of the weights of the edges adjacent to nodes of each label, since such labels are more likely to output a higher number of weighted frequent subgraphs. Also, edge relations containing these labels are hence removed earlier, thus reducing the number of edges with high weight values earlier, and this in turn helps reduce the maximum possible weight estimation for subsequent subgraphs. Afterwards, the recursive SUBGRAPH_EXTENSION procedure shown in Algorithm 2 is called after initiating a single-edge subgraph with each of the remaining distinct edges. This function returns a list of weighted frequent subgraphs derived after extending the subgraph S.

Algorithm 2 SUBGRAPH_EXTENSION

Input A subgraph S, a weighted graph G, the minimum weighted threshold τ
Output All subgraphs of G extending from S w/ product of avg weight & MNI $\geq \tau$

if DFSCode(S) $\neq$ min(DFSCode(S)) **then**
    return
reqFreq $\leftarrow \lceil \tau /$current weight of subgraph$\rceil$
reqExt $\leftarrow \lceil \tau / maxPosW(S) \rceil$
$min\tau \leftarrow \min(reqFreq, reqExt)$
$max\tau \leftarrow \max(reqFreq, reqExt)$
mniLowerBound $\leftarrow$ MNI_LOWER_BOUND($S, G, min\tau, max\tau$)
result $\leftarrow \emptyset$
if *mniLowerBound* $\geq reqFreq$ **then**
    result $\leftarrow S$
if *mniLowerBound* $\geq reqExt$ **then**
    for each edge $e \in$ *Edges* and node u of S **do**
        if e can be used to extend u **then**
            Let *ext* be the extension of S with e
            Decrement the count of e in *SegmentTree*
            result $\leftarrow$ *result* $\cup$ SUBGRAPH_EXTENSION(ext, G, τ)
            Increment the count of e in *SegmentTree*
return *result*

The procedure initially checks if the subgraph in question is lexicographically minimal. The concepts of minimum DFS code and lexicographical ordering of subgraphs are introduced in gSpan and are used here to counter duplicate subgraph generation. Afterwards, the values of *reqFreq* and *reqExt* are determined from the current weight and *maxPosW* of S respectively. If *reqFreq* is satisfied, S is added to the list of weighted frequent subgraphs. If *reqExt* is satisfied, S is

Table 1. Datasets

Dataset	#nodes	#edges	#labels	Directed	Distribution	MinW	MaxW	Normalized
MiCo	100k	108,029	29	No	negExp (λ=1.0)	25.75	70.0	No
Amazon	163k	296k	1,856	Yes	normal (μ=10, σ=1)	0.00	1.0	Yes
					negExp (λ=1)			
FreeAssoc	10,617	72,176	10	Yes	normal (μ=25, σ=1)	22.99	27.5	No

recursively extended, making necessary updates on the list of remaining edges, which is maintained using a *segment tree*.

With the time complexity involved with the determination of *maxPosW* being negligible in comparison, the time complexity of *WeFreS* is proportional to the product of the search space and the time complexity of determining the lower bound of the MNI of each subgraph. With the search space being $(2^{V_G})^2$ in the worst case, the worst case complexity of the algorithm is bounded by $O((2^{V_G})^2 \cdot V_S \cdot (p_1(\frac{\tau_1}{p}) + (1-p_1)\frac{\tau_2}{p}) \cdot V_G^{V_S-1})$ where τ_1 and τ_2 are maximums of all values of maxτ and minτ encountered, respectively, in the search space. However, the *maxPosW* pruning technique makes the search space much smaller for reasonable thresholds, making *WeFreS* feasible for use in real life applications, as demonstrated by experimental analysis presented in Section 4.

4 Evaluation Results

Experiments were conducted on the following three real-world graph datasets to evaluate the performance of our proposed approach in comparison with other existing approaches and baseline algorithms w.r.t. runtime and memory usage:

1. MiCo, a co-authorship and collaboration graph representing data from academic.research.microsoft.com;
2. Amazon [13], a co-purchase network consisting of electronic items found in the Amazon website; and
3. FreeAssoc [14], a dataset representing a word association network based on the English language.

Since none of these datasets had pre-specified edge-weights, we generated the weights using normal and exponential distributions. To test the performance of *WeFreS* in graphs containing high values of edge-weights, both the MiCo and FreeAssoc datasets were assigned weights using exponential and normal distributions respectively. For comparison with ReSuM [17], which requires edge-weights to be within the range [0, 1], the Amazon dataset was assigned normalized edge weights using both statistical distributions. Finally, to show that *WeFreS* can perform sufficiently well even in unweighted graphs, we compare *WeFreS* to GraMi [5] by assigning weight equal to 1 in all edges of all three datasets. Table 1 shows the quantitative specifications of each dataset.

All experiments were conducted on a device with 8GB RAM, an intel core i5 7th gen processor, with 2500 MHz clock speed and an Ubuntu 17.10 operating system. All approaches were implemented in Java by modifying a public

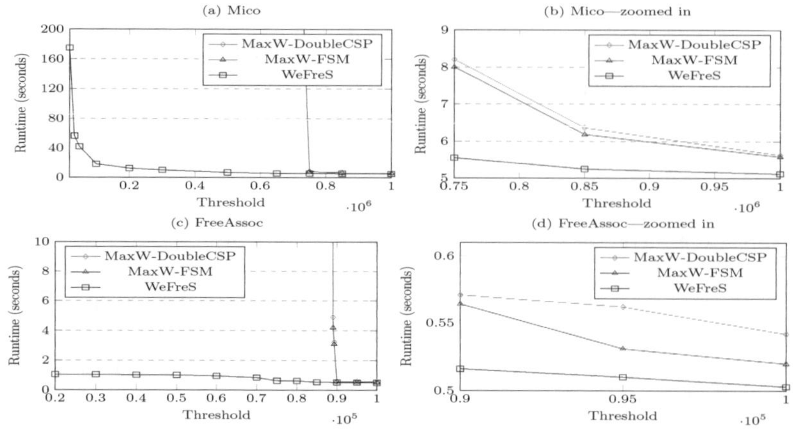

Fig. 4. Runtime comparisons with baseline algorithms

Table 2. Memory usage comparisons

Dataset	Threshold	Memory Usage (MaxW-FSM) (MB)	Memory Usage (WeFreS) (MB)
Mico	850,000	914.97	899.54
	650,000	1,111	907.36
	300,000	–	998.80
FreeAssoc	89,000	200.73	118.23
	88,500	5,231	118.23
	15,650	–	2153

implementation of GraMi [5]. Since there is no existing approach for mining weighted frequent subgraphs from single large graphs where edge-weights can have any numeric value, we defined two baseline algorithms for comparison: (i) *MaxW-DoubleCSP* (which applies the CSP model used in GraMi and issues two successive calls to determine if the MNI of a given subgraph satisfies *reqFreq* and *reqExt*) and (ii) *MaxW-FSM* (which applies the CSP model described in Section 3.2 and thus issues a single CSP call only). Both approaches differ from *WeFreS* in that, instead of using *MaxPosW* to determine the value of *reqExt*, they use the *MaxW* measure (which is applied in traditional weighted pattern mining approaches [20]). The value of *MaxW* is equal to the highest edge-weight present in the input graph.

Being a much tighter upper bound than *MaxW*, the *MaxPosW* estimate helps prune out many subgraphs and their extensions from the DFS code tree that is traversed, which were otherwise visited by algorithms adopting the *MaxW* measure. Thus, *WeFreS* has less search space than *MaxW-FSM* and *MaxW-DoubleCSP*. Furthermore, the reduced pruning tendency of these baseline algorithms mean that they traverse further down the DFS code tree, meaning that they need to evaluate the MNI of subgraphs containing a higher number of nodes, thus requiring longer runtime and more memory. Notably, the segment tree used in *WeFreS* introduces very little memory overhead, which is compen-

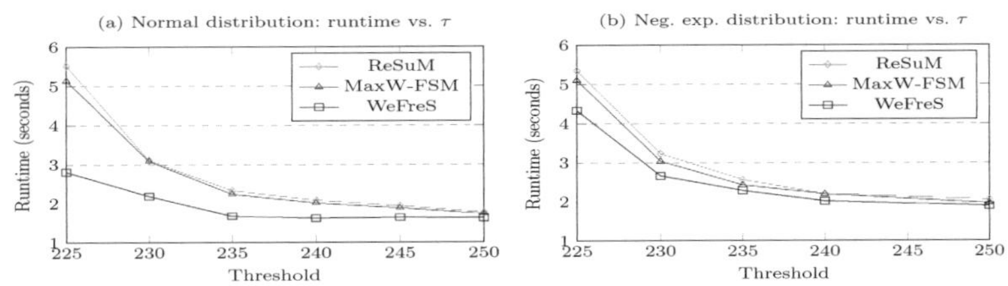

Fig. 5. Runtime comparison with *ReSuM* in the *Amazon* dataset

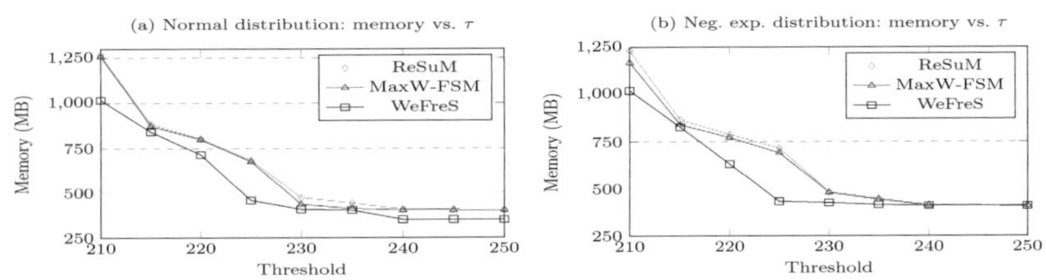

Fig. 6. Memory usage comparison with *ReSuM* in the *Amazon* dataset

sated by the benefits of reduced search space as shown in Fig. 4 and Table 2. For low threshold values, the baseline algorithms failed to produce results even after being run for hours, with such entries being marked X in Table 2.

Comparisons with *ReSuM* are done in the *Amazon* dataset, using both normal and exponential distributions for weight assignments. With $MaxW = 1$, *MaxW-DoubleCSP* behaves identical to *ReSuM* (while mining for subgraphs with high weighted support) in that it first finds frequent subgraphs and then filters out the weighted infrequent ones. Figures 5 and 6 show that *WeFreS* outperforms *ReSuM* in terms of runtime and memory.

Although designed for use in weighted graphs, Fig. 7 shows the runtimes of *WeFreS* are similar to that of *GraMi* in unweighted graph datasets. The additional pre-pruning measure of deleting node labels that are not part of any fertile label pair causes *WeFreS* to be more memory efficient. See Fig. 8.

5 Conclusions

In this paper, we explored an innovative direction of considering edge-weights in mining subgraph patterns from single large graphs. Our novel algorithm—namely, *weighted frequent subgraph miner* (*WeFreS*)—considers both the weight and significance of the interactions between different types of entities and only outputs weighted frequent subgraphs. Experimental results show the feasibility of using *WeFreS* in large graphs (where edge weights can have any real values) and its excellent performance over an existing state-of-the-art approaches (which require edge-weights to have values within the range of [0, 1]). Moreover, *WeFreS* is also feasible for use in unweighted frameworks, making it a truly general solution to the problem of frequent subgraph mining from single large graphs. The

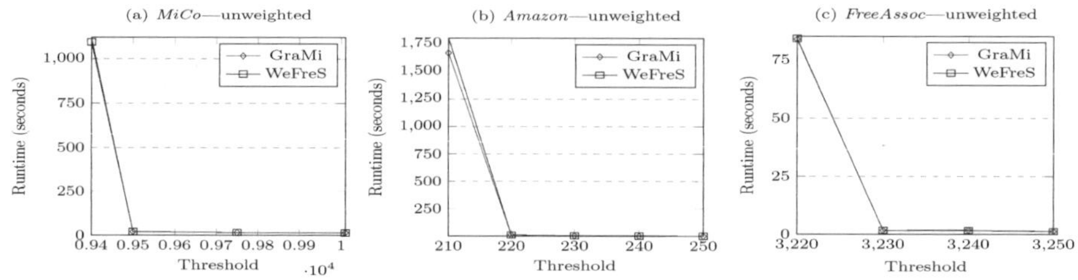

Fig. 7. Runtime comparison with *GraMi* in unweighted datasets

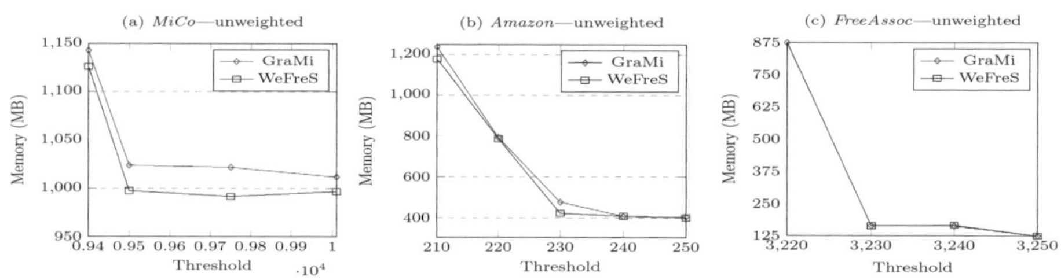

Fig. 8. Memory usage comparison with *GraMi* in unweighted datasets

subgraphs mined by *WeFreS* are both frequent and significant, and can be used in a variety of applications. In addition, we also introduced novel approaches for determining *MaxPosW* and proposed the constraint satisfaction problem (CSP) model. As ongoing and future work, we are extending our WeFreS algorithm, optimizing our determination of *MaxPosW*, and enhancing our CSP model.

Acknowledgements

This project is partially supported by NSERC (Canada) and University of Manitoba.

References

1. Ata, S.K., Fang, Y., Wu, M., Li, X., Xiao, X.: Disease gene classification with metagraph representations. Methods 131, 83–92 (2017)
2. Braun, P., Cuzzocrea, A., Leung, C.K., Pazdor, A.G.M., Tran, K.: Knowledge discovery from social graph data. Procedia Computer Science 96, 682–691 (2016)
3. Bringmann, B., Nijssen, S.: What is frequent in a single graph? In: PAKDD 2008. LNCS (LNAI), vol. 5012, pp. 858–863 (2008)

4. El Bazzi, M.S., Mammass, D., Zaki, T., Ennaji, A.: A graph-based ranking model for automatic keyphrases extraction from arabic documents. In: ICDM 2017. LNCS (LNAI), vol. 10357, pp. 313–322 (2017)
5. Elseidy, M., Abdelhamid, E., Skiadopoulos, S., Kalnis, P.: GraMi: frequent subgraph and pattern mining in a single large graph. PVLDB 7(7), 517–528 (2014)
6. Fan, C., Hao, H., Leung, C.K., Sun, L.Y., Tran, J.: Social network mining for recommendation of friends based on music interests. In: IEEE/ACM ASONAM 2018, pp. 833–840 (2018)
7. Fakhraei, S., Foulds, J., Shashanka, M., Getoor, L.: Collective spammer detection in evolving multi-relational social networks. In: ACM KDD 2015, pp. 1769–1778 (2015)
8. Hoi, C.H.S., Leung, C.K., Tran, K., Cuzzocrea, A., Bochicchio, M., Simonetti, M.: Supporting social information discovery from big uncertain social key-value data via graph-like metaphors. In: ICCC 2018. LNCS (LNISA), vol. 10971, pp. 102–116 (2018)
9. Islam, M.A., Ahmed, C.F., Leung, C.K., Hoi, C.S.H.: WFSM-MaxPWS: an efficient approach for mining weighted frequent subgraphs from edge-weighted graph databases. In: PAKDD 2018, Part III. LNCS (LNAI), vol. 10939, pp. 664–676 (2018)
10. Jiang, C., Coenen, F., Zito, M.: Frequent sub-graph mining on edge weighted graphs. In: DaWaK 2010. LNCS, vol. 6263, pp. 77–88 (2010)
11. Leung, C.K., Middleton, R., Pazdor, A.G.M., Won, Y.: Mining 'following' patterns from big but sparsely distributed social network data. In: IEEE/ACM ASONAM 2018, pp. 916–919 (2018)
12. Liakos, P., Papakonstantinopoulou, K.: On the impact of social cost in opinion dynamics. In: ICWSM 2016, pp. 631–634 (2016)
13. McAuley, J., Targett, C., Shi, Q., Van Den Hengel, A.: Image-based recommendations on styles and substitutes. In: ACM SIGIR 2015, pp. 43–52 (2015)
14. Nelson, D.L., McEvoy, C.L., Schreiber, T.A.: The University of South Florida free association, rhyme, and word fragment norms. Behavior Research Methods, Instruments, & Computers 36(3), 402–407 (2004)
15. Perner, P.: Mining frequent subgraph pattern over a collection of attributed-graphs and construction of a relation hierarchy for result reporting. In: ICDM 2017. LNCS (LNAI), vol. 10357, pp. 323–344 (2017)
16. Phan, H., Le, B.: A novel parallel algorithm for frequent itemsets mining in large transactional databases. In: ICDM 2018. LNCS (LNAI), vol. 10933, pp. 272–287 (2018)
17. Preti, G., Lissandrini, M., Mottin, D., Velegrakis, Y.: Beyond frequencies: graph pattern mining in multi-weighted graphs. In: EDBT 2018, pp. 169–180 (2018)
18. Wang, Y., Cai, Y.: Message passing on factor graph: a novel approach for orphan drug physician targeting. In: ICDM 2017. LNCS (LNAI), vol. 10357, pp. 137–150 (2017)
19. Yan, X., Han, J.: gSpan: graph-based substructure pattern mining. In: IEEE ICDM 2003, pp. 721–724 (2002)
20. Yun, U., Leggett, J.J.: WFIM: weighted frequent itemset mining with a weight range and a minimum weight. In: SIAM SDM 2005, pp. 636–640 (2005)

Predicting e-commerce customer conversion from minimal temporal patterns on symbolized clickstream trajectories

Jacopo Tagliabue[1†], Lucas Lacasa[2], Ciro Greco[1], Mattia Pavoni[1] and Andrea Polonioli[1]

[1] Tooso Labs, San Francisco CA, USA
[2] Queen Mary University, London, United Kingdom
† Corresponding author.
jacopo.tagliabue@tooso.ai

Abstract. Knowing if a user is a "buyer" vs "window shopper" solely based on clickstream data is of crucial importance for e-commerce platforms seeking to implement real-time accurate NBA ("next best action") policies. However, due to the low frequency of conversion events and the noisiness of browsing data, classifying user sessions is very challenging. In this paper, we address the clickstream classification problem in the eCommerce industry and present three major contributions to the burgeoning field of A.I.-for-retail: first, we collected, normalized and prepared a novel dataset of live shopping sessions from a major European e-commerce website; second, we use the dataset to test in a controlled environment strong baselines and SOTA models from the literature; finally, we propose a new discriminative neural model that outperforms neural architectures recently proposed by [1] at Rakuten labs.

Keywords: Clickstream prediction, intent detection, time-series classification, deep neural network.

1 Introduction

The extraordinary growth of online distribution channels [2] has had a significant impact on the retail industry [3] [4]. However, a problem for digital retailers is that the vast majority of sessions are from users with weak buying intention ("window shoppers"). Being able to turn window shoppers into converting customers has thus become a key priority for clicks and mortar stores and solely digital players [5]. In turn, next-best-action marketing and personalization have recently become increasingly popular in an effort to increase conversion rates [6].

In *this* paper, we present the ongoing research that Tooso Labs is conducting on real-time intent detection, by marrying Artificial Intelligence and deep domain knowledge over proprietary eCommerce data. The paper is organized as follows: in Section 2 we define the intent detection problem; in Section 3 we detail our methodology and describe all the models in our study. In Section 4 we present results and a preliminary analysis before concluding, in Section 5, with some final remarks.

2 Problem Statement and Dataset

2.1 Problem Statement

The clickstream challenge is to predict if users on a website are likely/unlikely to buy *within* the session based solely on behavioral evidence (e.g. page view, search activity, etc.); as such it is usually framed as a *classification* problem, where the goal is to classify a session as BUY ("buy-session") or NOBUY ("no-buy-session"). To simplify the exploration of new methods and align with other literature baselines, we start with a version of the problem where the session is entirely available to the classifier, instead of data points being streamed in one at a time (mimicking real-time data streaming on browsing activities).

Formally, a session s is a series of browsing events e_1, e_2, $\ldots e_n$ with timestamps t_1, t_2, $\ldots t_n$ by a user u, where the gap between any two times t is at most 30 minutes [7]; events belong to different *categories*, such that each $e \in \{C \mid$ "view", "click", "detail", "add-to-cart", "remove- from-cart", "buy"$\}$. A session s is classified as BUY ("buy-session") if and only if there is at least one event e in s such that $C_e =$ "buy", NOBUY ("no-buy-session") otherwise; to avoid trivializing the prediction problem, we cut sessions with "buy" events at the timestamp before the event.

2.2 The Tooso Retail Clickstream Dataset

Our "Tooso retail clickstream dataset" (TRCD) contains data from real user sessions on an e-commerce website from a major (>1B year turnover) retail group in Europe. All events in the dataset are sampled from the period from 06/29/2018 to 07/18/2018.

2.3 The symbolized clickstream dataset

We "symbolize" user sessions, so that, for each e in s, the only information we retrieve is the event type. This simplifies the implementation of new algorithms, allows to readily make comparisons with SOTA models in the literature and make the findings imme-diately applicable to a wide range of use cases (in which detailed meta-data about events may be missing). After cleaning the raw datasets (excluding sessions shorter than 10 events and longer than 200 to avoid suspect sessions into the analysis), the final corpus consists of 7,176 BUY sessions and 123,396 NOBUY sessions.

3 Methodology

In what follows, we describe all the models and related implementation details.

3.1 Literature comparisons

3.1.1 Markov chains

We reproduce the methodology of the influential [8], which borrows from the long-standing idea that browsing activities are properly modelled as Markov processes [9] [10]. In particular, two separate Markov chains are trained for BUY/NOBUY sequences. At prediction time, for any session *s*, we predict the class associated with the highest probability, i.e. $s \in$ BUY iff P(BUY|*s*) > P(NOBUY|*s*), $s \in$ NOBUY otherwise. We run several experiments to pick the best degree for the final chains and found that chains of order 5 provide the most reliable classification accuracy (in line with [1]).

3.1.2 LSTM language model

A recent paper [1] reported improvements over the MC approach in [8] using LSTMs [1]. While the authors frame the problem as a three-fold classification (*purchase*, *abandon* or *browsing-only*), they used the same idea of "mixture models" as in [8] just replacing MCs with probabilities from a neural network model (token probabilities are read off intermediate softmax layers in each LSTM model). We built two LSTMs (BUY, NOBUY) with as many input units as there are input classes and the same number of output units. We used Cross Entropy as our loss function and trained the network using Adam. In line with [1], we considered architectures with 1 hidden layer and 4 different values for the number of hidden units (10, 20, 40, 80); we also explored different values for the learning rate (0.01, 0.001) and for the batch size (10, 20, 50). We trained each model with early stopping on the accuracy on the validation set, with a patience of 10 and a maximum number of epochs of 50. At prediction time, each sequence is passed through both LSTMs and the probability of every state in the sequence is retrieved from the softmax layer. Classification happens in the same way as in the MC model.

3.2 Novel contributions

3.2.1 Seq2Label

We implemented a discriminative classifier as an alternative way to conceptualize the clickstream problem. This architecture consisted of one LSTM layer of dimensionality (input units x hidden units) and one fully connected layer with dimensionality (hidden units x 1), whose output was transformed using the sigmoid activation function before computing the loss. Two pooling strategies were explored, changing the information that is used to classify sequences: taking the output of the LSTM at the last time step (ignoring padding indices) and taking the average LSTM output over the entire sequence (again ignoring padding indices). The pooled output of the LSTM was then passed through the fully connected layer and transformed using the sigmoid activation function, which was then taken as the prediction given the sequence. Binary Cross Entropy Loss is used to quantify the error and back-propagate it (Adam was again the chosen optimizer). We tested the same hyper-parameter settings as in the LSTM language model and trained each model with early stopping, considering accuracy on the validation set as the target variable with a patience of 10.

3.2.2 Visibility Graphs

Leveraging the symbolic nature of the clickstream dataset, we explore a completely different prediction method by feeding *k*-grams to visibility graphs [11] [12]. The key intuition of this method is that you can induce a graph from a timeseries by linking events (as "nodes") that can "see" each other in the series, as shown in the figure below (see [12] for a formal introduction):

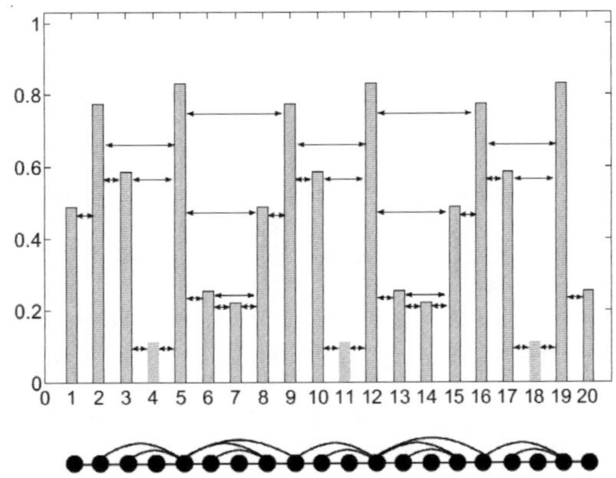

Fig. 1. Sample time series of 20 data and its associated horizontal visibility graph.

After transforming each symbolized session into the corresponding visibility graph, graph patterns are run through PCA to avoid overfitting and the resulting features are fed into a standard SVM classifier.

4 Results and Analysis

After deciding on the best parameter choices for our models, we tested them on the test split of the corpus (since LSTMs depend on random initialization, we trained 10 different instances of the same model). In the following table we report average accuracy scores on the test set and provide the standard deviation over 10 runs in parentheses when necessary.

Table 1. Average accuracy scores

Model	Accuracy
Markov Chain	0.882
LSTM - Language Model	0.909 (± 0.004)
Visibility Graphs	0.868 (± 0.48)
LSTM - S2L ('avg' pooling)	0.927 (± 0.003)
LSTM - S2L ('last')	**0.932 (± 0.002)**

5 Conclusion

We presented preliminary but encouraging results in the clickstream prediction challenge for online retail. Using our novel dataset of live shopping sessions from a major European e-commerce website, we have proposed i) a new discriminative neural model that outperforms SOTA architectures proposed by [1]; ii) a physics-based approach, through visibility graphs, that can be thought as a very strong baseline for timeseries problems, being formally well understood, easy to implement and fast and cheap to compute even on large datasets. In the spirit of reproducibility, the authors plan to re-lease the full dataset and benchmarking code under a research-friendly license.

References

1. Toth, A., Tan, L., Di Fabbrizio, G. and Datta, A., 2017. Predicting shopping behavior with mixture of RNNs. In ACM SIGIR Forum. ACM.
2. Statista. 2019. E-commerce share of total retail revenue in the United States as of February 2019, by product category. Accessed: 2019-04-22.
3. Colombi, C., Kim, P. and Wyatt, N., 2018. Fashion retailing “tech-gagement”: engagement fueled by new technology. Research Journal of Textile and Apparel, 22(4), pp.390-406.
4. Ogonowski, P. 2019. 15 ecommerce conversion rate statistics. Retrieved from: https://www.growcode.com/blog/ecommerce- conversion-rate
5. Roman, E. 2017. Webrooming vs. Showrooming: Are You Engaging Both Types of Shoppers. Retrieved from https://www.huffpost.com/entry/webrooming-vs-showrooming.
6. Deloitte, 2017. The Deloitte Consumer Review. Retrieved from: https://www2.deloitte.com/content/dam/Deloitte/uk/Documents/consu mer-business/deloitte-uk-consumer-review-mass- personalisation.pdf.
7. Clifton, B., 2012. Advanced web metrics with Google Analytics. John Wiley & Sons.
8. Bertsimas, D.J., Mersereau, A.J. and Patel, N.R., 2003, May. Dynamic classification of online customers. In Proceedings of the 2003 SIAM International Conference on Data Mining (pp. 107-118). Society for Industrial and Applied Mathematics.
9. Anderson, C.R., Domingos, P. and Weld, D.S., 2002, July. Relational Markov models and their application to adaptive web navigation. In Proceedings of the eighth ACM SIGKDD international conference on Knowledge discovery and data mining (pp. 143-152). ACM.
10. Deshpande, M. and Karypis, G., 2004. Selective Markov models for predicting Web page accesses. ACM transactions on internet technology (TOIT), 4(2), pp.163-184.
11. Lacasa, L., Luque, B., Ballesteros, F., Luque, J. and Nuno, J.C., 2008. From time series to complex networks: The visibility graph. Proceedings of the National Academy of Sciences, 105(13), pp.4972-4975.
12. Jacovacci, J, L. Lacasa, 2016. Sequential visibility graph motifs, Physical Review E 93, 042309.

Functions and Architecture for Automatic Predictive Targeting and Modelling Real-time On-line Behavior

Petra Perner

Institute of Computer Vision and Applied Computer Sciences, IBaI
PF 30 11 38, 04251 Leipzig
pperner@ibai-institut.de

Abstract. To detect fast changes in customer behavior or to react in as focused a manner as possible, predictive modeling must be done in good quality to get effective predictions of customer behavior and it has to be done fast to be relevant under business aspects. Modeling speed is of great importance in industry as time is a crucial factor. This necessity requires a different technical set up for model development to fulfill both needs: quality and development speed. Today most companies like to develop their models individually with the help of specialists. But for a lot of companies, this way takes too long; even though the models are excellent, the time to develop them sometimes kills the advantages of a better prediction. This article describes the general structure and ideas how to implement industry-focused model production that will help to react quickly to changing behavior. We will discuss the key success factors and the pitfalls of this assembly line model product.

1 Marketing in the Web 2.0

Customer profiles are really valuable if they contain more information than just customers' past behavior, but also include present reactions and give reliable predictions about their future conduct.

A company's existing customer data may, for example, provide information about purchase and payment history, address, age, gender, etc. For all customers that can be identified this data is stored and used for targeting purposes. Even if there is a technical solution enabling you to identify customers who are already known when they visit your website, you never know all the people visiting your site. But there are plenty of reasons to learn more about them and to target them as well and to do it in the same personalized way as you do with those you can identify. But the only information available is what you can filter out of the log file.

So you know which and how many pages they have seen and for how long, where they came from and much more.

To use this information each individually brings obvious advantages: With the knowledge of the typical click patterns of customers reacting similarly and the knowledge of the positioning and placement of advertising for a product which appeals to most customers you will create a big benefit. With information such as entry and exit page, or click behavior, the structuring of web sites can be continually improved and their representation can be optimized on the web. Knowledge of the origin, points to the channels, which should best be addressed by the specific target groups.

All this information put together gives a multifaceted view of customers and target groups. To measure success, in order to recognize and to identify trends, changes and new needs of the target groups early, and seize enterprise opportunities, consider off- and online market study as well as on the analysis of the volume of data existing in the enterprise reporting, data mining and market observations. On-line measures of interested parties use the clicking advice or page impressions consulted as yardsticks [2].

But nothing changed in the last years as rapidly as the use of the Internet. 10 years ago Web 1.0 offered static websites, Web 1.5 offered dynamic websites and since 2005 more users expect interactive Websites (Web 2.0). The World Wide Web develops itself constantly in large steps and Web 3.0 will start soon.

The Internet medium penetrates the market with its various application possibilities and offers world-wide access - across all society and ethnical layers. Currently 79.9% of the Germans are already on the Web. [8]

Ever more humans use the Internet ever more extensively (for search, E-Mail, forums, Blogs, Podcasting, on-line one of plays…) - briefly: The Internet is a fast, global, highly competitive marketplace. Above all, the Web is used increasingly by many customers and enterprises as a starting point for the search for services and products.

The expenditure for on-line marketing today already takes more than 19,2% [13] of the total expenditure for advertising. This will continue to rise in all industries, because this market place opens various marketing possibilities - and demands completely new marketing strategies. Medium-spreading, target-group-specific, relevantly - today must be tailored advertising best personally to each customer. For it is necessary to improve customer loyalty, facilitate the acquisition of new customers and improve the response or the conversion rate - all at very low cost advertising [3].

The current challenges facing new methodologies and technologies are, for example, the analysis of log files [14], information on the origin of the visitor, what browser he uses, which and how many pages he has viewed. The advantages are obvious: the person who knows the typical click behavior of their customers can determine with this knowledge, the positioning and placement of advertising for a product that appeals to its customers the most. With information such as exit and entry side, the structuring of web sites can be continuously improved and the representation can be optimized on the web [4].

Of exceptional value for strategic planning are reliable predictions about future developments in the behavior and needs of customers. The development of predictive behavioral targeting ensures that such predictions are placed on a statistically validated foundation.

2 Predictive Behavioral Targeting

For a company to receive exciting customer profiles, improve the relevance of its online offerings and optimize its long term online marketing ROI, it would not only need information about the historical and current habits of its customers, but also about their future conduct [5], [10], [11]. So it is important to discover patterns in customer behavior, for this we need to identify a specific user. This makes the predictive behavioral targeting.

Methods such as descriptive statistics, click-stream analysis [6], discriminant analysis, regression methods [3], decision trees, neural networks, case-based reasoning (CBR) [12], cluster analysis [1] and time series analysis are used.

Based on analysis of user profiles and user structures (such as age, lifestyle, peer group affiliations, browsing behavior) predictive models are created for future behavior [13]. For example, the decision on where to place banners which users should be shown, is based on the sites he visited or on the basis of what he's doing on these sites.

Previously contextual advertising based on the content of a website, identified content which is best suited for a display. The predictive behavioral targeting based on the users actual and past behavior, the right person for a quote with the ability to identify user profiles, which opens the way for predictive behavioral targeting relevant advertising.

Predictive targeting makes a lot and that information gain immensely in value when they are in the right place as quickly as possible in the right form ready. Fully automatic Predictive Targeting and modelling real-time of on-line behavior create for it the conditions.

3 Fully automatic Predictive Targeting and modelling real-time on-line behavior

Using the necessary algorithms for analysis in real time opens up the new fully automated predictive targeting, individual and lasting forms of communication and offers a head start by modeling the real-time online behavior.

This means an evolution step comparably from the handicraft to the production - inclusive reductions at the complexity. The classical way to build complex forecast models by hand, is in the role of "Master Workshop". But even a large staff of analysts (craftsmen) can not cope with the huge amounts of data and the high number of models-this needs a fully automated "assembly line" for prediction models.

3.1 Function

The core of the fully automatic predictive targeting system is the construction of prediction models. It includes all functionality to build with a team of analysts complex forecast models by hand ("Master Workshop") but also in a second module ("assembly line") it builds very fast fully automated simple, click-based predictive models, automatically backs up its quality and makes it available for use.

In the "assembly line" all models are calculated, which is a relatively simple task in the field of predictions (predictive modeling), for example, only the models whose target variable is a dichotomous structure (click vs. not clicked, purchased vs. not. bought, visits vs. not visited, etc.)[9]. These prediction models cover, for example, a large portion of the orders for banners and optimization behavior targeting. Special analysis such as cluster analysis, are performed by the analysis team in the "Master Workshop".

It is decided by an administrative process whether a forecast model goes in the workshop or in the assembly line to be manufactured. Each model receives a clear ID and is archived. The substantial elements the assembly line contains are shown in Figure 1.

Modules of the Automatic Targeting System

- **Control**
  - Administration
  - Model Management
  - Management of the Variables
- **Learning of the Model**
  - Selection of the Target Variable =1 and Selection of the Target Variable=0
  - Model specific random sampling to obtain a data set
  - Supply of a Learning Data Set and aTest Data Set
  - Learning the Model
  - Evaluation of the Model
  - Quality Assurance Monitor
  - Release process
  - Handing over process
- **Model examination**
  - Model specific random sampling to obtain a data set
  - Model examination
  - Quality Assurance Monitor
  - Confirmation process
- **Model Archive**
- **Variable processing and Supply**

Fig. 1. The Elements of an Assembly Line

3.2 Architecture

The areas of "Master Workshop" (working range of the analysis team) and "assembly line" (automatic targeting) are in the existing architecture of a company included in a way that the environment and its benefits can be used as far as possible. This includes especially all tasks around data preparations.

In general: All the developed models will be passed as a code / script and archived in an archive, including its metadata and also about their use. The application of models based on the scripts is the final step of the calculation of variables at the end of a session or a slot. For each active model the prediction is calculated as relevant forecast value per unique client (UC) and is stored in a separate variable and made available to the Target Builder.

In the Target Builder (an instrument for targeted delivery of content), these predictive capabilities of profiles are used to provide target audiences for online campaigns and make them ready to be marked. So every user with fitting profile is addressed.

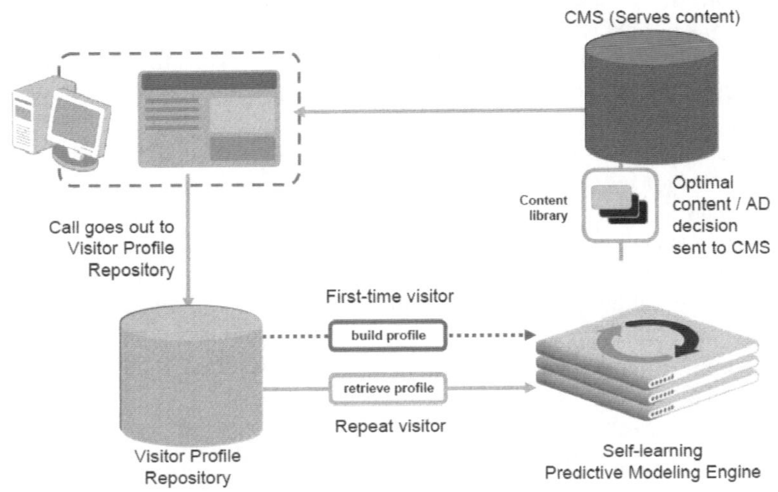

Fig. 2. Automatic Predictive Targeting

3.3 Data flows and database

The bases for all analyses are the behavior data of the UC on the respective websites. Ideally the behavior data can be enriched by information from questioning or login data. One can differentiate between standard/general behavior and/or interest-conditioned information These profile and behavior data per UC are computed relative to different time windows. Both are formed from large numbers of variables. The variables should reflect different views on the UC.

In the context of the modelling in the assembly line, only an examined subset of variables is used, in order to grant stability, robustness and performance essential for automation. That can be seen somehow as the standard dataset. The size and content of it is the outcome of experience and domain knowledge obtainable from the analyses team. Using the Pareto principle the dataset should contain roughly 20 % of all potential data to be the basis of 80% of all easy prediction problems. To ensure that data preparation fits the time constraints of the Assembly line, it is important to use optimization techniques that help to deliver the data as fast as possible. After the structure of standard dataset is defined and adjusted, it will be created fully automatically by the systems.

As in other industrial processes it is important to identify and separate different process steps, such as data handling and calculations so that they can be standardized and optimized to deliver an outcome of reliable quality and with a more or less small standard error. About the data preparation including all necessary (automatically done) transformations, it lead us to the fact we should choose robust methods that will help to generate data that fits most (modeling) situations but might not be the optimal one for every single case as you would get, when you do the analytics by hand through an expert in your company. Where you try to optimize the modeling result by doing a constant looping out of data preparation, analytics and measurement, especially under time constraints, this looping has to be at a minimum.

An essential part of the daily profile building step is data preparation. It is needed both for the modeling / verification as well as for the application of existing scores. All of has to be done in a time-critical area.

So that modeling or deployment can take place in the current session, it is indispensable that the session data can be accessed at any time in the session.

To train and validate a model, very fast sampling is mandatory. Please keep in mind that the relation between those who act (target=1) and those who do not act (target=0) is very unbalanced. It is very likely that you have just 500 UC acting and 5 million UC not acting. As part of the modeling issue, it makes a big difference in calculation time whether you have to calculate slightly more than 5 million records or just a couple of hundred. So if you start to build an assembly line it is required to work out and test a sampling strategy that best suits your individual situation.

3.4 Modelling Aspects

Similar to the data preparation, the assembly line needs for its modeling engine a data mining algorithm that will deliver good and stable models without any interaction with an expert. The algorithm should be fast and the time needed for the deployment of models should be as small as possible, especially if it is planned to use the assembly line for nearly real time forecasting. If it is under business reason not so important to be real time, for example it is enough if you use the data of the last finished session as the newest one to be included in the forecasting, or as a base forecast that is shaped by the content click on or searched for, then the time for modeling and deployment might not be so time critical. Based on many tests simulating the situation like an assembly line, out of all the algorithms, the family of decision trees wins most, and delivers fast very good results.

The fully automated quality control is the next step in the process to deal with; the task here is to define the small border between not "quite as good" and "good enough under business reason". If your expectations for the modelling quality are too high you will end up with lots of models transferred back from assembly line to workshop to be redone by the experts, so you will lose time and it will cost you more money to produce the models. If your quality is too low you will lose business, e.g. lower click rates.

In quality control we are looking after new (freshly developed) models as well as after models that have been in duty for a while, so the chosen quality control process and it measurements must be able to do a constant quality control on all active models to notice in time when a model needs refreshment.

3.5 Challenges and critical success factors

The complexity of the process of fully automated predictive targeting and modeling of real-time online conduct presents some statistical challenges: During sampling the minimum reasonable number of events = 1 (e.g. clicks), stratification, sampling routines has to be fixed sensitively. Forecasting methods are judged in terms of prediction quality, stability, development, etc. Performance, durability, run-time behavior, parameterization, and automation of error detection must be considered in the selection of quality assurance methods.

Similarly, critical success factors should not be ignored: Are uncontrollable optimization steps / algorithms influencing the ad server that originally predicted massive click behavior? Are tags are missing in the banner? Are there so few clicks that it takes too long to get a critical mass for modeling?

4 Results

Fully automatic targeting and predictive modeling of real-time online behavior are at the very beginning of their development and are valuable tools provided critical success factors and requirements are carefully observed in the implementation and the environment. All being well we can obtain fully automated predictive targeting even based literally on the last click in real time, and these predictions can be flexible and up to date. This allows rapid response to changes and trends in the rapidly changing online marketplace.

References

1. Alberto Messina et all: A generalised cross-modal clustering method applied to multimedia news semantic indexing and retrieval, Juan Quemada et all (Ed.), Proceedings of the 18th International Conference on World Wide Web, WWW 2009, Madrid, 2009
2. Alice Klever: Behavioural Targeting: An Online Analysis for Efficient Media Planning?, Diplomica, 2009
3. Andrea Ahlemeyer-Stubbe: Behavioral Targeting: Which Method produces the most Robust Prediction? A Confrontation between Decisions Trees, Neural Networks and Regressions, Petra Perner (Ed.): Advances in Data Mining. 9th Industrial Conference, ICDM 2008, Ibai Publishing, 2009
4. Andrea Ahlemeyer-Stubbe: Predictive Targeting: Buzzword or Reality - The potential of Automatic Behavioral Targeted Advertising in Online Marketing, Petra Perner (Ed.), Advances in Data Mining. 9th Industrial Conference, ICDM 2008, Ibai Publishing, 2009

5. David S.Evans:, The Online Advertising Industry: Economics, Evolution, and Privacy, The Journal of Economic Perspectives, Volume 23, Number 3, Summer 2009 , pp. 37-60(24), 2009
6. Deepak Agarwal et all: Spatio-temporal models for estimating click-through rate, Juan Quemada et all (Ed.), Proceedings of the 18th International Conference on World Wide Web, WWW 2009, Madrid, 2009
7. Foster J. Provost et all: Data acquisition and cost-effective predictive modeling: targeting offers for electronic commerce, Maria L. Gini et all (Ed)., Proceedings of the 9th International Conference on Electronic Commerce: The Wireless World of Electronic Commerce, 2007, Minneapolis, 2007
8. Internet World Stats 2011, http://www.internetworldstats.com/stats4.htm, 25.September 2011
9. Joseph Reisinger, Marius Pasca: Bootstrapped extraction of class attributes. Juan Quemada et al (Ed.), Proceedings of the 18th International Conference on World Wide Web, WWW 2009, Madrid, 2009
10. Jun Yan, et al: How much can behavioral targeting help online advertising?, Juan Quemada et all (Ed.), Proceedings of the 18th International Conference on World Wide Web, WWW 2009, Madrid, 2009
11. OVK Online-Report 2011/01, Online-Vermarkterkreis(OVK) im Bundesverband Digitale Wirtschaft (BVDW) e.V., (Hrsg), Düsseldorf, 2011
12. P. Perner, Case-based reasoning and the statistical challenges, Journal Quality and Reliability Engineering International Volume 24 Issue 6 (October 2008), p 705-720.
13. Petra Perner, G. Fiss: Intelligent E-marketing with Web Mining, Personalization, and User-Adpated Interfaces, Petra Perner (Ed.), Advances in Data Mining, Applications in E-Commerce, Medicine, and Knowledge Management [Industrial Conference on Data Mining, Leipzig, Germany, June 2002]. Lecture Notes in Computer Science, Springer 2002
14. M. Reichle, P. Perner, K.-D. Althoff, Data Preparation of Web Log Files for Marketing Aspects Analyses, In: Petra Perner (Ed.): Advances in Data Mining, Applications in Medicine, Web Mining, Marketing, Image and Signal Mining, lncs 4065, Springer 2006,p. 131-145.

Cluster-Based Relative Outlier Under-Sampling Technique

Atif Hassan, Rohini Banerjee, Pabitra Mitra and Pralay Mitra

Department of Computer Science and Engineering, Indian Institute of Technology, Kharagpur - 721302, INDIA
atif.hassan@iitkgp.ac.in, rbanerjee@connect.ust.hk, pabitra@cse.iitkgp.ac.in, pralay@cse.iitkgp.ac.in

Abstract. Machine learning algorithms work optimally when the training dataset is balanced, that is, when the number of samples per class is comparatively the same. However, real-life datasets are usually severely imbalanced. To reduce the skewness, under-sampling techniques are used. Unfortunately, they may delete majority samples that carry valuable information. To improve the approach above, we propose two novel cluster-based relative outlier under-sampling techniques (CROUST and ICROUST), which selectively removes majority class samples to minimize the information loss while maximizing the model efficiency. An empirical comparison of results between CROUST, ICROUST and multiple well-known techniques on various real-world data prove that our proposed methods are an improvement of other state of the art results.

Keywords: Data sampling; clustering; data skewness

1 Introduction

Advancement in science and technology has resulted in a surge of raw data which can be utilized for research in data analytics and data science. However, most real-world data are found to be imbalanced, that is, the majority class is much higher than the minority class. Medical diagnosis of rare diseases [1, 2], spam detection [3], electricity pilferage [4], software quality detection [5] and fraud detection [6] are few examples of imbalanced datasets. As traditional machine learning algorithms are designed to improve accuracy by reducing the error whereas ignoring the class distribution of the dataset, training on such datasets result in poor performance of classifiers and other supervised learning techniques.

Elkan [7], Zadrozny and Elkan [8], and Ling and Sheng [9] proposed eminent works focused on the effects of class sensitive learning on imbalanced datasets. Kubat and Matwin [10] presented a one-sided selection of majority samples to address the problems of imbalanced data. By classifying the majority class into noise, borderline, redundant and safe samples, they isolated the important majority class information by eradicating noise and borderline events. Nevertheless, these methods still suffered from the problem of removing noisy samples from minority class, although keeping the dataset balanced.

Re-sampling using under-sampling techniques have been known to perform more optimally than their over-sampling counterparts. Zhang and Mani [11] proposed four innovative under-sampling approaches based on the distance between the majority and minority samples of a dataset. "NearMiss-I" selected those majority samples whose average distance to three nearest minority samples was the least. Complimentary to "NearMiss-I" "NearMiss-II" chose those majority samples whose average distance to three farthest minority samples was the least. Yen and Lee [12] suggested five cluster-based under-sampling approaches primarily based on Zhang and Mani's "NearMiss" and "Most Distant" techniques. Individually, their under-sampling based clustering (SBC) approach is taken up in this paper as one of the state of the art techniques. The Cluster-Based Undersampling (CBU) technique proposed by B. Das et al. [13] tries to solve the class imbalance problem by clustering the training dataset into k clusters and then discarding majority instances in overlap regions.

Outlier detection and outlier removal have remained a critical research area for improving clustering algorithms. Most statistical functions are highly sensitive to outliers. Escalante [14] compared six approaches of outlier detection while inserting artificial noise and bias on datasets. The paper concluded the kernel-based novelty detection method to be the best performer. Gan and Ng [15] incorporated an additional cluster into the usual K-means algorithm which would hold all the outliers. R.A. Sowah et.al. [16] proposed the removal of repeated outliers and noisy instances using clustering during the process of undersampling (CUST) while Liu et al. [17] proposed a cluster with outlier removal (COR) algorithm based on the relationship between outliers and clusters.

To increase the performance of under-sampling while retaining relevant information, we propose a technique based on outlier detection with K-means clustering and K-nearest neighbor. Our adaptive method removes those majority samples which are furthest away from the centroid of its cluster; and those majority samples which are in proximity to the closest M majority samples, while also being nearest to the closest minority centroid. Classifiers when trained on the two resultant datasets achieve better prediction accuracy than traditional state-of-the-art under-sampling techniques over various metric evaluation scores (Precision, Recall, ROC AUC, Macro F1-measure and G-mean).

2 Method

The Cluster based Relative Outlier Under-Sampling Technique (CROUST) proposes a unique way of removing majority samples via analysis of cluster outliers. This helps in improving under-sampling accuracy by minimizing the extent of information loss. In this section, we discuss two novel methods: CROUST and iterative CROUST (i.e., ICROUST).

2.1 The Vanilla CROUST Approach

Let us assume that our imbalanced dataset consists of S_{MA} majority samples and S_{MI} minority samples, where $S_{MA} \gg S_{MI}$. The total number of majority data points that is targeted to be deleted for balancing the dataset is given by the following equation:

$$MA_{rem} = S_{MA} - \left[\frac{m}{1-m} * S_{MI}\right] \quad (1)$$

where m lies between $[50\% \ to \ 100\%)$and depicts the percentage of majority class samples in the final, processed dataset.

To figure out which particular majority samples need to be picked and removed, we divide our entire dataset into k clusters. If S_{MA}^{i} depicts the total number of majority samples present in the ith cluster, and $S_{MA_j}^{i}$ represents the jth majority sample in the ith cluster, then the outlier detection analysis of $S_{MA_j}^{i}$ is given by the Euclidean distance between that point and the centroid of the ith cluster, C_i.

Once the distances between every majority point $S_{MA_j}^{i}$ and C_i is calculated, the complete set of these distances is given by:

$$D_i = \{a \mid a = dist(X, Y) \ \ \forall \ X \ \in S_{MA}^{i}, \ Y = C_i\} \quad (2)$$

where $dist(X, Y) = (\sum_{i=1}^{d} |X_i - Y_i|^p)^{1/p}$ is the generic distance between any two points X and Y. In our experiments have used $p = 2$ which is the Euclidean distance.

After dividing the imbalanced dataset into k clusters, CROUST determines the D_i set for each such cluster. All the above sets are then concatenated to give rise to the following global set (equation 3):

$$D_{global} = \{a \mid a = D_i \ \forall \ i \ \in k\} \quad (3)$$

The D_{global} set comprises of the distances of each majority class sample with the centroid of its respective cluster. The values of D_{global} set are then transferred to a list where they are arranged in descending order. The first MA_{rem} samples are deleted from the list, retaining the remaining majority data points. The concept behind the basic CROUST model is that the majority points which are the furthest from the centroid of a particular class are most likely to be outliers and redundant data. However, not all outliers can be considered to be irrelevant. To assimilate this concept into the algorithm, we chose the MA_{rem} furthest points from the global list of all clusters combined, and then eradicated the necessary number of samples. This action helped in information preservation whilst improving the accuracy of the dataset.

2.2 The Iterative CROUST Approach (ICROUST)

Our second proposed technique is an extensive modification of the K-nearest neighbor (KNN) algorithm while also retaining the crux of the CROUST approach. Here, the method is iterative, thus giving it the name ICROUST. Unlike the basic CROUST approach, this method only segregates the minority class samples into k clusters.

If MA_j refers to the jth majority data point and C_i^{MI} refers to the centroid of the ith minority cluster, the algorithm follows the rudimentary summation concept of two distances: the minimum distance (d_1) between MA_j and the nearest C_i^{MI} (equation 4); and the average distance (d_2) of MA_j with M nearest neighbour majority points, where the nth nearest neighbour is denoted as MN_n (equation 5).

$$d_1 = min\left(dist(MA_j, C_i^{MI})\right), \forall i \in k \quad (4)$$

$$d_2 = \frac{1}{M}\sum dist(MA_j, MN_n)\ , n \in [1, M]; n \neq j \quad (5)$$

Unlike the vanilla CROUST approach, ICROUST identifies a majority point as an outlier after gaining information about both inter and intra-class neighborhood.

ICROUST adds d_1 and d_2 for each jth majority sample, MA_j, and then creates a list to arrange these values in ascending order. The data point corresponding to the least value of the summation of d_1 and d_2 is then selected and deleted. The entire process is then repeated anew for MA_{rem} number of points.

This single point majority-outlier eradication method shuffles the cluster concentration and hence the skewness of the dataset after each iteration. Iterative deletion of $\boldsymbol{MA_{rem}}$ points provides much stable results when compared to collective deletion of the first $\boldsymbol{MA_{rem}}$ points. This is because the clusters and the requisite majority-minority distances keep changing after a particular point is removed. The information captured through this skewness shift provides insight to the importance of a specific majority outlier data point.

2.3 Graphical Representation of the Approach

Fig. 1 depicts a model-wise comparison of the majority and minority data clustering for a synthetic dataset. The image distinctly shows the classifier's approach to eradicate the majority sample data. As expected, the All KNN model creates a clear separation between the majority and minority data points. NearMiss-II eliminates all the majority points which are far from the centroid of the majority cluster, creating a clean but extremely concise boundary space for the majority samples. Since SBC is primarily based on random under-sampling, its feature space resembles the original imbalanced feature space. The proposed vanilla CROUST model uniquely creates small, clear clusters of data points while spanning over the entire area of the feature space. The ICROUST clustering shows least information loss from the majority of data samples. While retaining the exact structure of the original imbalanced data, the ICROUST feature space is a much sparser version of it. This is because ICROUST considers both the intra and inter distances of majority-minority data points before deleting a particular majority sample. Its iterative deletion technique also aids in a reshuffling of the feature space points before the next sample is removed. This helps in reducing those majority points which have other similar majority samples nearby, i.e., if G majority points have similar information structure, at least one of those G points are retained.

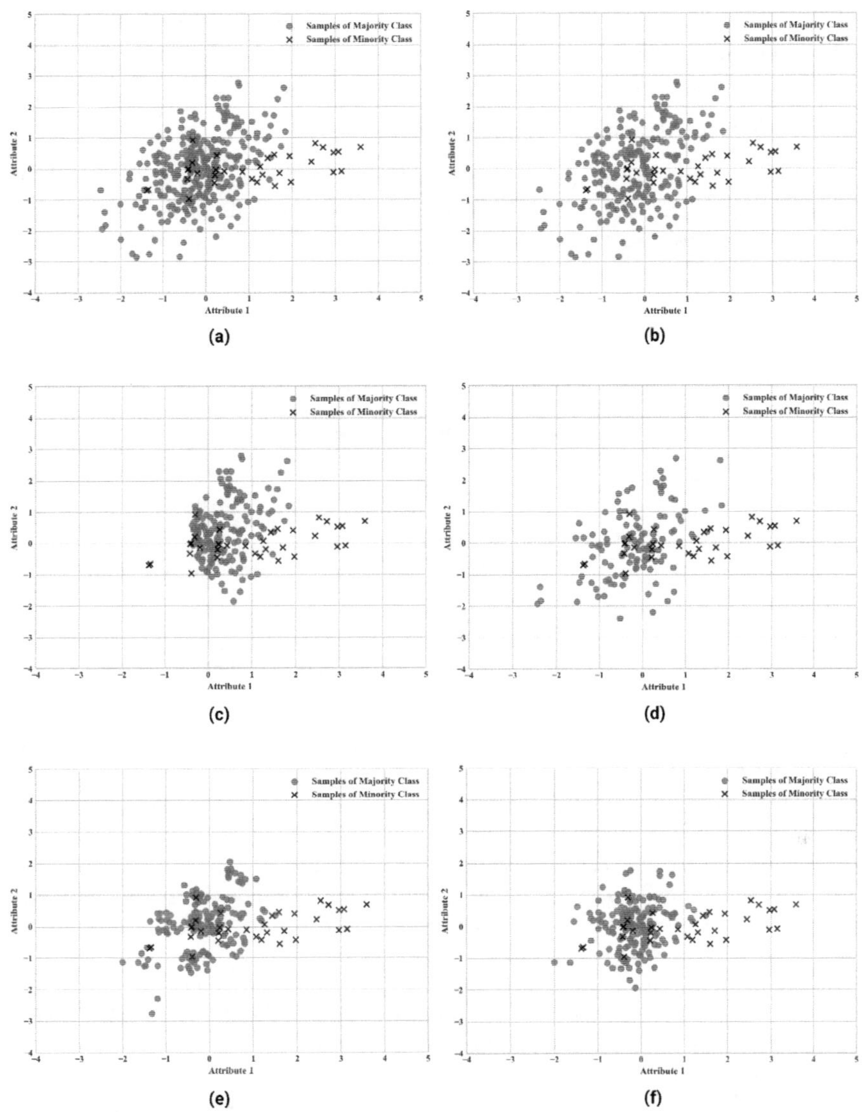

Fig. 1. Graphical representation of the majority and minority class distribution for a two-attribute play dataset: (a) Original dataset (b) All KNN (c) NearMiss-II (d) SBC approach (e) CROUST approach (f) ICROUST.

3 Experiments

This section focuses on the evaluation and results analyses of our proposed under-sampling method on multiple real-world imbalanced datasets. A brief overview of each dataset and the evaluation criterions are provided along with result comparisons with another state of the art techniques.

3.1 Dataset Review and Experimental Method

Six real-world datasets from the publicly available KEEL repository [18] are utilized to test the performance of the two proposed novel methods against three well-accepted procedures. To test the robustness of our method, the datasets have been chosen such that the imbalance ratio ranges from low to high. Table 1 provides a concise description of the imbalanced datasets. The number of attributes and samples the datasets contain and their data imbalance ratio is also mentioned.

Table 1. Descriptions of KEEL repository datasets

Dataset name	No. of samples	No. of attributes	Data imbalance ratio
Ecoli3	336	7	8.6
Glass6	214	9	6.38
Segment0	2308	19	6.02
Vehicle0	846	18	3.25
Yeast3	1484	8	8.1
Abalone	2338	8	39.31

In the experiments conducted, we have used linear SVM [19–21] as the classifier. Our approaches are juxtaposed with an all KNN model, a NearMiss-II model and an SBC model [12]. The basic random under-sampling technique has not been exhibited separately as the SBC model itself is an improved version of it [12]. Also, in our experiments we found that SBC outperformed both CUST and CBU so we have not shown their results in the comparison table. The approaches involved in this research focuses on the various processes required to alter the inter and intra-class Euclidean distance between the majority and minority class points. Hence, the distance-based classifier of linear SVM is identified to be the most suitable one.

In this paper, we have used 10-Fold cross-validation for training and testing our models. In each fold, the data is broken down into train and test sets: the algorithm is run on the training set, and the test set is kept untouched.

3.2 Performance Metrics

The quality and reliability of a classifier are often determined by its performance in a test environment based on a metric evaluation result. Accuracy, the universal performance assessment criteria, is known to be unsuitable while providing results for class imbalanced datasets [22]. This paper focuses on five performance metrics, namely: Precision, Recall, Macro F-measure, ROC AUC, and Geometric Mean (G-Mean).

A confusion matrix is generally used to coherently summarize the performance of a classifier on a test data with known true output values. For a binary classifier, the confusion matrix can hold one of four values: correctly predicted positive values, True Positive (TP); correctly predicted negative values, True Negative (TN); wrongly predicted negative values, False Positive (FP); and wrongly predicted positive values, False Negative (FN).

For imbalanced datasets, precision and recall have a quid pro-quo relationship. It is not possible to sustain one without diminishing the other. Thus, F-measure, which gauges the trade-off between precision and recall, is identified to be a more superior evaluation metric. G-mean maximizes the accuracy of the true positive rate and true negative rate with a sufficient trade-off in between, while AUC [23] generates a single value for the receiver operating characteristics (ROC) without considering misclassification costs and prior probabilities. Overall, F- measure, G-mean and AUC are considered to be more precise metric evaluation techniques for imbalanced data classifiers than precision and recall.

3.3 Results and Discussions

This section examines the results obtained from the experiments conducted on six KEEL datasets. For every dataset, the metric evaluation outputs are obtained for multiple majorities to minority ratios and the best results for each method are displayed. This is because the end user may not always require the majority to minority samples to be in a simple 1:1 ratio. Thus, the performance of a model cannot be purely based on its yield when the dataset is completely balanced. While comparing the potential of multiple approaches, there should be at least one such majority-minority ratio position where the model outperforms all other classifiers. Based on the averaged 10-Fold cross-validation score, Table 2 depicts the best performing under-sampling technique and the majority-minority ratio at which it is achieved for macro F1-measure, AUC, G-mean, precision and recall. It is clearly noted that both CROUST and ICROUST dominate over All KNN, NearMiss-II and SBC models. Figures 2 to 4 depict the average AUC, G-mean and F1-measure for different majority to minority class ratios.

Table 2. Comparison of model performance for various performance metrics over six datasets

Dataset	Algorithm	Macro F1-score	AUC (ROC)	G-Mean
Abalone	All KNN	68.66	65.15	54.89
	NearMiss-II	33.53	58.99	55.66
	SBC	63.34	59.16	38.17
	CROUST	55.04	85.56	84.61
	ICROUST	69.27	82.62	82.42
Ecoli3	All KNN	76.58	84.97	84.18
	NearMiss-II	75.61	76.77	75.07
	SBC	77.75	79.12	75.28
	CROUST	78.1	88.16	87.93
	ICROUST	80.73	85.7	85.32
Glass6	All KNN	90.83	88.82	90.58
	NearMiss-II	90.56	87.93	90.36
	SBC	91.18	89.64	90.88
	CROUST	92.83	90.4	92.68
	ICROUST	93.18	92.15	92.68
Segment	All KNN	99.24	99.14	99.14
	NearMiss-II	96.84	98.54	98.54
	SBC	99.35	99.16	99.16
	CROUST	97.22	98.41	98.4
	ICROUST	99.46	99.36	99.35
Vehicle0	All KNN	94.85	97.04	97.02
	NearMiss-II	94.89	96.31	96.29
	SBC	95.18	96.13	96.11
	CROUST	95.54	97.27	97.26
	ICROUST	95.26	95.82	96.4
Yeast3	All KNN	82.13	86.46	86.06
	NearMiss-II	80.91	86.83	86.72
	SBC	81.57	79.56	77.54
	CROUST	80.45	89.83	89.63
	ICROUST	82.8	88.64	88.59

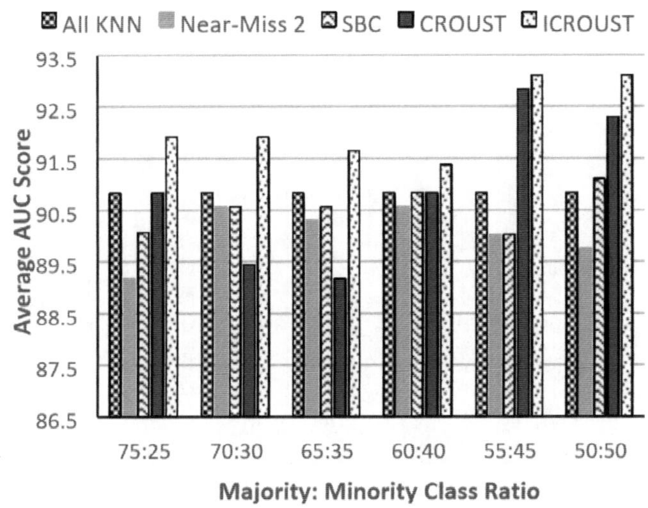

Fig. 2. Average AUC score for the different majority to minority class ratios for the Glass6 dataset

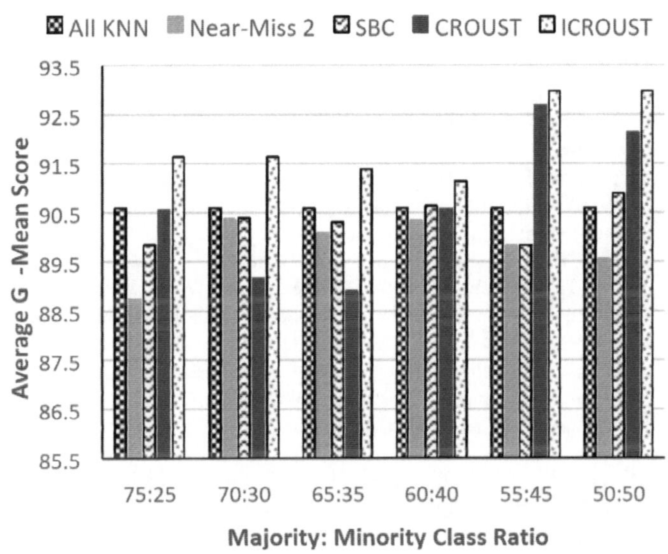

Fig. 3. Average G-mean score for the different majority to minority class ratios for the Glass6 dataset

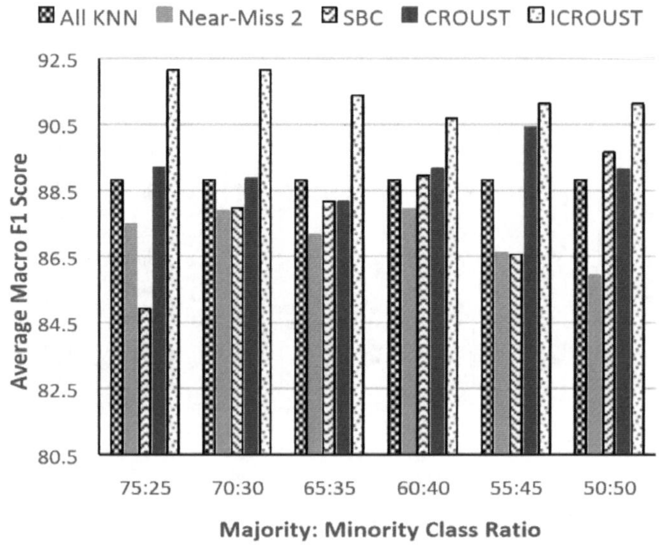

Fig. 4. Average macro F1 measure for the different majority to minority class ratios for the Glass6 dataset

Even though we have given a comprehensive comparison of the performance of our algorithm over others, we also need to make sure that the prediction of a model is improved by applying our method prior than when our method is not applied. To show this, we chose to use a significance test. If the p-value is under 5%, we can reject the null hypothesis which is, our method does not improve performance and the better results are simply by chance. As we did not make any assumptions on the data distribution of the six datasets, the significance of our approach is captured by the non-parametric Wilcoxon signed rank test. The results were obtained by running the test on non-CROUST applied and CROUST applied macro F1-measure of the ten folds for each dataset. Table 3 summarizes the p-values attained by the Wilcoxon test. It is to be noted that the experiment was performed by using both the default and fine-tuned parameters. We wanted to demonstrate that it is not necessary that the default parameters will always work. Thus, for some datasets, the p-value was not < 5% as each dataset has different class distributions. By fine-tuning of the parameters, i.e., trying out different majority to minority ratios and also changing the number of clusters improved the results. We found that a good starting value for the number of clusters is the total number of samples in your data divided by the number of minority samples. The performance of a model is drastically affected by the majority and minority class ratios and even though both CROUST and iCROUST reduce the loss of important information, one needs to find the ratio which works best for the given data. The default ratio which we use is 70:30

Table 3. Results of the p-value from the Wilcoxon Signed Rank Test using the macro F1-measure obtained during 10-Fold cross-validation

Datasets	Default P Value	Tuned P Value
Ecoli3	0.4×10^{-1}	0.2×10^{-3}
Glass6	0.2×10^{-1}	0.1×10^{-4}
Segment0	0.1×10^{0}	0.3×10^{-3}
Vehicle0	0.8×10^{-1}	0.25×10^{-3}
Yeast3	0.1×10^{-1}	0.13×10^{-4}
Abalone	0.1×10^{0}	0.37×10^{-3}

3.4 Benchmark on Credit Card Fraud Detection

Finally, we benchmarked our proposed technique on the Kaggle dataset (https://www.kaggle.com/mlg-ulb/creditcardfraud) which housed credit card fraud detection data. The dataset is highly imbalanced data and is thus a prefect suit for application of our technique. We divided the dataset randomly into 80% train and 20% test. We trained the LinearSVC classifier in six different ways including no sampling, cost sensitive LinearSVC, NearMiss-II, SBC, CROUST and ICROUST. Table 4 indicates that our proposed CROUST outperform all other techniques.

Table 4. Benchmarking on Kaggle dataset

Method	Accuracy
Simple LinearSVC	33.17%
Cost-sensitive LinearSVC	11.54%
NearMiss-II	12.12%
SBC	28.27%
CROUST	45.75%
iCROUST	35.70%

4 Conclusion

Due to its high frequency and delicate complexity, learning from imbalanced datasets has gained importance in recent years. Various classification techniques are being proposed to find the optimum accuracy and least misclassification rate for minority data points. Our recommended novel CROUST and ICROUST approaches intertwine outlier detection with the under-sampling methodology. While CROUST simply removes majority samples based on its distance to the centroid of a cluster, ICROUST iteratively eliminates those majority samples which are a certain distance away from both the closest minority centroid and the nearest M neighbouring majority samples. The ICROUST process allows reshuffling of data points and captures majority sample information after each iteration. Via this process, we have minimized the loss of intricate details from majority samples whilst maximizing the prediction accuracy of the classifier. Trained with a linear SVM algorithm and tested on 6 real world KEEL datasets, CROUST and ICROUST have proven to outperform All KNN, NearMiss-II and SBC techniques. ICROUST's consideration for the data distribution of both the minority and majority samples allows it to eliminate majority samples while retaining information from the entire feature space. Experimental results of various evaluation metrics (precision, recall, F-measure, AUC and G-mean) indisputably side with our proposed algorithms. It is to be noted that considering the computational expensiveness of ICROUST for high dimensional datasets, interesting research on time complexity minimization can be carried out in the future.

References

1. Parvin, H., Minaei-Bidgoli, B., Alizadeh, H.: Iranian cancer patient detection using a new method for learning at imbalanced datasets. In: International Conference on Intelligent Data Engineering and Automated Learning. pp. 299–306. Springer (2011).
2. Yoon, K., Kwek, S.: A data reduction approach for resolving the imbalanced data issue in functional genomics. Neural Comput. Appl. 16, 295–306 (2007).
3. Sasaki, M., Shinnou, H.: Spam detection using text clustering. In: null. pp. 316–319. IEEE (2005).
4. Di Martino, M., Decia, F., Molinelli, J., Fernández, A.: Improving Electric Fraud Detection using Class Imbalance Strategies. In: ICPRAM (2). pp. 135–141 (2012).
5. Khoshgoftaar, T.M., Seliya, N.: Comparative assessment of software quality classification techniques: An empirical case study. Empir. Softw. Eng. 9, 229–257 (2004).
6. Phua, C., Alahakoon, D., Lee, V.: Minority report in fraud detection: classification of skewed data. Acm sigkdd Explor. Newsl. 6, 50–59 (2004).
7. Elkan, C.: The foundations of cost-sensitive learning. In: International joint conference on artificial intelligence. pp. 973–978. Lawrence Erlbaum Associates Ltd (2001).
8. Zadrozny, B., Elkan, C.: Learning and making decisions when costs and probabilities are both unknown. In: Proceedings of the seventh ACM SIGKDD international conference on Knowledge discovery and data mining. pp. 204–213. ACM (2001).
9. Zhou, Z.-H.: Cost-sensitive learning. In: International Conference on Modeling Decisions for Artificial Intelligence. pp. 17–18. Springer (2011).
10. Kubat, M., Matwin, S.: Addressing the curse of imbalanced training sets: one-sided selection. In: Icml. pp. 179–186. Nashville, USA (1997).
11. Mani, I., Zhang, I.: kNN approach to unbalanced data distributions: a case study involving information extraction. In: Proceedings of workshop on learning from imbalanced datasets (2003).

12. Yen, S.-J., Lee, Y.-S.: Cluster-based under-sampling approaches for imbalanced data distributions. Expert Syst. Appl. 36, 5718–5727 (2009).
13. Das, B., Krishnan, N.C., Cook, D.J.: Handling imbalanced and overlapping classes in smart environments prompting dataset. In: Data mining for service. pp. 199–219. Springer (2014).
14. Escalante, H.J.: A comparison of outlier detection algorithms for machine learning. In: Proceedings of the International Conference on Communications in Computing. pp. 228–237 (2005).
15. Gan, G., Ng, M.K.-P.: k-means clustering with outlier removal. Pattern Recognit. Lett. 90, 8–14 (2017).
16. Sowah, R.A., Agebure, M.A., Mills, G.A., Koumadi, K.M., Fiawoo, S.Y.: New Cluster Undersampling Technique for Class Imbalance Learning. Int. J. Mach. Learn. Comput. 6, 205 (2016).
17. Liu, H., Li, J., Wu, Y., Fu, Y.: Clustering with Outlier Removal. arXiv Prepr. arXiv1801.01899. (2018).
18. Alcalá-Fdez, J., Fernández, A., Luengo, J., Derrac, J., García, S., Sánchez, L., Herrera, F.: Keel data-mining software tool: data set repository, integration of algorithms and experimental analysis framework. J. Mult. Log. Soft Comput. 17, (2011).
19. Akbani, R., Kwek, S., Japkowicz, N.: Applying support vector machines to imbalanced datasets. In: European conference on machine learning. pp. 39–50. Springer (2004).
20. Durgesh, K.S., Lekha, B.: Data classification using support vector machine. J. Theor. Appl. Inf. Technol. 12, 1–7 (2010).
21. Boser, B.E., Guyon, I.M., Vapnik, V.N.: A training algorithm for optimal margin classifiers. In: Proceedings of the fifth annual workshop on Computational learning theory. pp. 144–152. ACM (1992).
22. Hoens, T.R., Chawla, N. V: Imbalanced datasets: from sampling to classifiers. Imbalanced Learn. Found. Algorithms, Appl. Wiley. (2013).
23. Menzies, T., Greenwald, J., Frank, A.: Data mining static code attributes to learn defect predictors. IEEE Trans. Softw. Eng. 2–13 (2007).

Weather Impacts on Wine, A BiMax examination of Napa Cabernet in 2011 and 2012 Vintage

Bernard Chen[1*], David Jones[1], Mustafa Tunc[1], Kristen Chipolla[1] and Jorge Beltran[1]

[1] University of Central Arkansas, Conway, AR, USA
bchen@uca.edu

Abstract. This Wineinformatics research paper attempts to leverage previous research that created the Computational Wine Wheel, a data mining tool that distills the key attributes present in human-language-format wine expert reviews into computational data. Utilizing this tool, we attempt to discover the effects of different years' weather on the flavor qualities of wines. It does this by utilizing a Bi-Max Bi-Clustering algorithm on these distilled reviews, with controls for region, winery, reviewer, and grape. Dominate attributes in 2011 and 2012 vintage for Napa Cabernet are extracted and compared to understand the difference between bad and good Napa Cabernet Sauvignon vintages. To the best of our knowledge, this is the first paper using computational algorithms to discover the effects of weather on wine.

Keywords: Bi-Max Bi-Clustering; Wineinformatics; Computational Wine Wheel; Napa Valley; Cabernet Sauvignon

1 Introduction

The intricate process of winemaking has been altered and perfected over the years by top competing wine companies and producers. Each step in this process is imperative for the quality of a wine, and can be affected by numerous factors. It all starts with grapes on the vine: and it's important that these are properly ripe. The grapes as they are harvested contain the potential of the wine; Bad wine can result from good grapes, however not vice versa. Grapes can either be hand-picked or machine harvested. The harvest date of the grapes is one of the most important factors in wine making. Picking early will produce wines with higher acidity, lower alcohol and perhaps more green flavors and aromas while picking the wines later will yield wines with lower acidity, higher alcohol (or sweetness) and slight presence of tannin. Techniques used in the process can also generate different attributes and overall quality of wines. Some of these practices include but are not limited to cold soaking, skin contact, hot and cold fermentation, and oak aging vs steel aging. In addition to picking the grapes at the perfect harvest and utilizing technique, weather can also severely determine the quality of the wine.

Every vintage is different. Local temperature is the most important climatic aspect and the type of wine usually depends on the location [2]. While many harvest areas tend to be near bodies of water, some continental climates are also suitable for wine production. Largely because of this climatic variable, the length of the growing season varies in different regions. This begs the question "What is good wine harvesting weather?". The influences of fog exposure, wind exposure, rainfall and humidity can determine the label of the harvest year. Grapes thrive in hot, dry weather, which helps develop high sugar content in the fruits. Greg Scheinfeld, founder of Uproot Wines in Napa Valley said a vintage relies on two major elements rain and temperature. Experts say a good harvest starts with a slow spring with light rains especially during flowering, which would provide plump and ample berries. Summer during a good vintage is dry and has a mild heat index. July is usually considered a perfect month because of the lack of rain and the constant sunshine. This provides the grapes with an uninterrupted ripening. However, a bad vintage consists of a prolonged winter. The effects of the cold weather would produce destroyed budding leaves, flowers, and vines. Summer during a bad vintage is too hot and for long periods of time, and causes the grape vines to stop metabolizing and the fruit to dry up. Though there are very distinct factors in what makes a good vintage year and contrariwise, the weather factors do not provide a definite outcome. This means that possibly good wine can emerge from what is considered a bad vintage. Data Science is used to further study the weather effects on wine.

Data Science is the study that incorporates varying techniques and theories from distinct fields, such as Data Mining, Scientific Methods, Math and Statistics, Visualization, natural language processing, and the Domain Knowledge, to discover useful information from domain-related data [1]. Currently, almost all existing data mining research about wine is focused on the physicochemical laboratory tests [10-13]. This focus is because of the dataset availability. However, based on Figure 1, sensory analysis is much more interesting to wine consumers and distributors because they describe aesthetics, pleasure, complexity, color, appearance, odor, aroma, bouquet, tartness, and the interactions with the senses of these characteristics of the wine [12]. Using Data science on the study of professional wine reviews is referred to as Wineinformatics. To better examine wines, wine reviewers from professional wine magazines, such as Wine Spectator, Wine Advocate, Wine Enthusiast, and Decanter, use human language to describe them, and data science has since converted that language into data to be analyzed [7].

This paper attempts to analyze weather effects on red wine by examining the attributes of Napa Valley reds in 2012, a "textbook" harvest year, and contrarily 2011 by analyzing wine reviews through the Computational Wine Wheel [6]. The BiMax bi-clustering is then applied to discover representative attributes of the specific year. Finally, the comparison of representative attributes for each year is studied to conclude what is the important wine attributes appeared in excellent vintage. To the best of our knowledge, this is the first paper using computational algorithms to discover the effects of weather on wine.

2 Experimental Methods

2.1 Selecting a data set

In order to isolate the weather effects from any effects of any other input variable of the winemaking process it is important to choose a data set that minimizes or eliminates other factors. To this end this study focused on one particular region: Napa California, one particular type of wine: Cabernet Sauvignon, one wine review site: Wine Spectator, and then further focused in only wines that were produced in the focused weather years: 2011 and 2012. According to Wine Spectator, the 2012 vintage of Cabernet Sauvignon in Napa California scored 96 with the description of "Record-sized crop with many stars amid a solid vintage across the board; tannic"; while 2011 vintage of Cabernet Sauvignon in Napa California scored merely 86 with the description of "Rare rainy harvest proved it can happen; few sunny spots, variable quality" [14].

Wine Spectator had over 400 Napa Valley red wines reviewed from 2011 wines, and over 600 reviewed for the good weather year, 2012. When these lists of reviewed wines were cross compared there were 296 matched wines. These 592 wines were used as our data set. As these wines were all exactly the same wines, from the same wineries, reviewed by the same reviewers, and so on, with the only difference being the bad weather of 2011 and the good weather of 2012 they were perfect for trying to determine the weather effect on wine.

To give a clear example of how the data set was generated from these reviews, let's look at the review for a single wine and then also look at that what that wine looks like as the review gets turned into data to be worked with. As shown in the example, the review has been boiled down into a series of attributes that will be signaled as on, or 1's in our data set for this wine, with all missing attributes filled in as a 0. In this way we create a large binary data set ready for analysis.

Wine: Colgin Syrah Napa Valley IX Estate 2011

Review: Offers beautifully rich dark berry fruit definition, with pure boysenberry, blackberry and blueberry flavors framed by cedary oak and spicy, floral scents. The flavors are big, yet this is elegant and graceful on the palate and long on the finish. Drink now through 2028. 200 cases made.

Attributes:
BERRY|BLACKBERRY|BLUEBERRY|BOYSENBERRY|FRUIT|FLORAL|SPICE|
FINISH|BEAUTY|BIG|DARK|DEFINED|ELEGANT|FLAVORS|GRACE|LONG|PU
RE|RICH|CEDAR|OAK

2.2 Methodology

This paper builds heavily off the Wineinformatics tool known as the Computational Wine Wheel 2.0 [6]. This tool was used on the wine reviews to give the wine qualities of each wine for statistical analysis and data mining.

Because these were the exact same wines from year to year we first did statistical comparison between the wine years, without any deeper analysis. Looking at some simple counts of attributes and z-score representations of attributes across the wines reveals that prior to any data mining techniques the two years present some basic differences. 8 attributes are shown to have very statistically significant differences in their representations. These attributes are: HERBS, DRY, TANNINS_LOW, DENSE, FINISH, WELL_STRUCTURED, BLACKBERRY, and OAK.

Bi-clustering [8], also known as block or two-mode clustering, is a data analysis technique that finds and groups like items in a data set. It does this by manipulating the rows and columns to create blocks, or clusters, of similar values across different items in a repeated and recursive way. Figure 1 gives a simple example for the bi-clustering input data and output result. For this data set, a list of wines with binary markings on the presence of each attribute, Bi-Max bi-clustering was utilized [9]. This type of clustering arranges and rearranges the rows, which are wines, and the columns, which are qualities of the wines, to find clusters where every wine in the cluster has every attribute in the cluster.

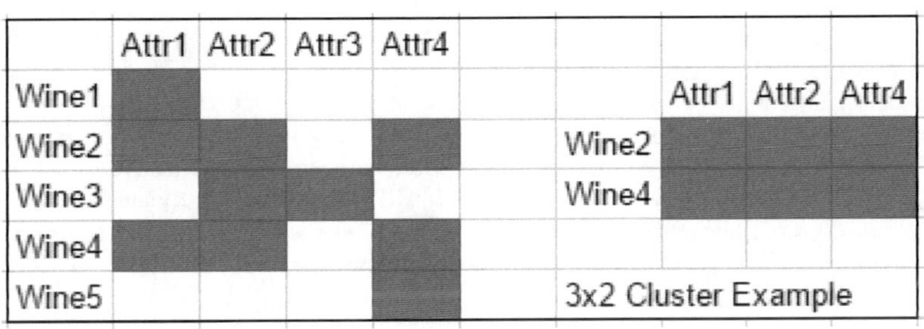

Fig 1. A simple example of bi-clustering input data and output result

We performed BiMax Clustering [9] on all of the 592 wines attributes, with two added binary attributes signifying if a wine belonged to 2011 or 2012. With the goal being our analysis focusing on the weather effects, we focused on clusters that contained numerous wines. If weather is the cause of the clustering, it should be something that appears in a wide amount of wines as they all faced that weather. To this end our minimum threshold for a cluster was set at 3 attributes and 10 wines.

3 Results

After this clustering was complete we further filtered out any clusters that did not have a year attribute. Because the year attribute signifies weather, they are the only relevant clusters for our study. At the conclusion of this extensive filtering to focus in on the effects particular to weather we still end up with a robust amount of clusters to analyze, 32498 from 2011 and 39631 from 2012.

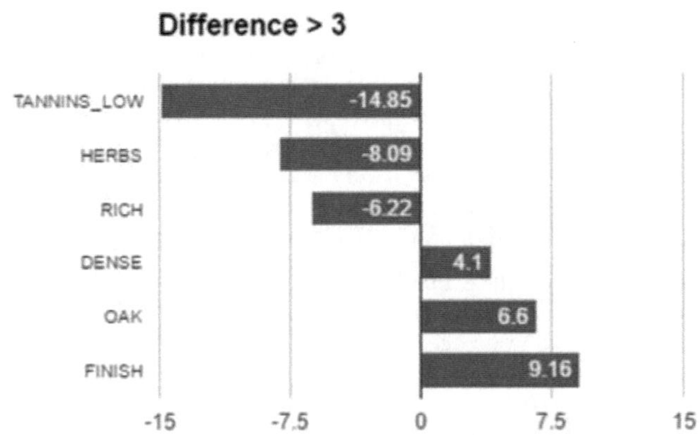

Fig 2. Dominate attributes appeared in 2011 and 2012.

To analyze these clusters we then performed a count of each attribute present in each cluster, which allowed us to find what percentage of clusters from either year contained any given attribute. We then compared these numbers as a strict difference, as well as ratio differences. These differences (showed in figure 2) showed many drastic changes from 2011 to 2012 that form the basis for our conclusions that weather does have a significant impact on the final taste of a wine. 2012 vintage, which is considered as textbook vintage, demonstrates much more attributes in "dense", "oak" and "finish". All those three attributes are considered as the characteristics of the cabernet sauvignon. These three important attributes are less observed in the vintage 2011, indicates vintage 2011 demonstrate more in "low tannins", "Herbs" and "Rich". However, cabernet sauvignon is a full body wine; "low tannins" should not be appeared in the description which gives a perfect explanation of why 2011 is considered as a less ideal vintage. More detailed analysis in each vintage is given in the following subsections.

3.1 Effects seen in bad weather, 2011

When comparing the flat difference of attributes seen in 2011 clusters versus 2012 clusters, 3 attributes are seen in a substantial way. RICH, HERBS, and TANNINS_LOW were represented in a huge number of clusters; with RICH and HERB being in over 11% of all 2011 clusters, and TANNINS_LOW being in over 31%. The tannins being lower in this batch of wines may be a particular item causing the weather of 2011 to be considered bad. This is because Napa Valley red wines are Cabernet Sauvignon red wines, which are known to have a profile involving medium to high tannins. Failing to achieve this may be a considerable reason why the types of weather seen in 2011 are not loved by the wineries in the region. [4]

Analyzing the changes seen in 2011 on a ratio basis, and defining a significant difference as being greater than 50% more represented, reveals 12 more significantly different attributes, while confirming that the 3 from the strict difference comparison, for a total of 15 attributes that are considerably impacted by weather. These observations are described in table 1 and figure 3. Of these 14 TANNINS_LOW actually is the smallest percent difference, at a considerable 91%, despite being the largest real difference. The impact quickly rises to numerous factors being 200-430% more represented in the 2011 wines, and finally spikes on the last three qualities: RED, BALANCE, and FRESH, reaching into the thousands of percent more represented.

TABLE 1. 2011 ATTRIBUTES SEEN MORE

Attribute	*% More*
FRESH	2800
BALANCE	1900
RED	775
FOCUSED	429
BLACK LICORICE	404
TIGHT	400
RIPE	347
SPICE	300
CHERRY	267
HERBS	243
PERSIST	200
MOCHA	133
RICH	109
TANNINS_LOW	91
GREAT	53

TABLE 2. 2012 ATTRIBUTES SEEN MORE

Attribute	*% More*
PENCIL LEAD	2800
COMPLEX	800
ESPRESSO	800
LICORICE	686
PURE	600
BLACK CHERRY	600
DUSTY	454
OAK	346
CRUSHED ROCK	335
SAVORY	333
STYLE	250
FIRM	216
DENSE	203
TOAST	200
SUPPLE	150
SAGE	100
SMOKE	100
TEXTURE	100
FINISH	53

3.2 Effects seen in good weather, 2012

Once again looking at the flat difference, 3 qualities are shown to be in significantly more 2012 wines than 2011. These qualities are DENSE, OAK, and FINISH. Of these qualities, one can again be identified as an important factor when considering

Cabernet Sauvignon wines, and that is the presence of OAK. Typically these wines incorporate the OAK during fermentation or in the barrel aging process [5]. In particular, American Cabernet Sauvignon is especially known for stronger OAK flavors, when compared to French wines. The good weather of 2012 allowing for the OAK flavor to come through may be a considerable part of the definition of it being a good year. These observations are described in table 2 and figure 4.

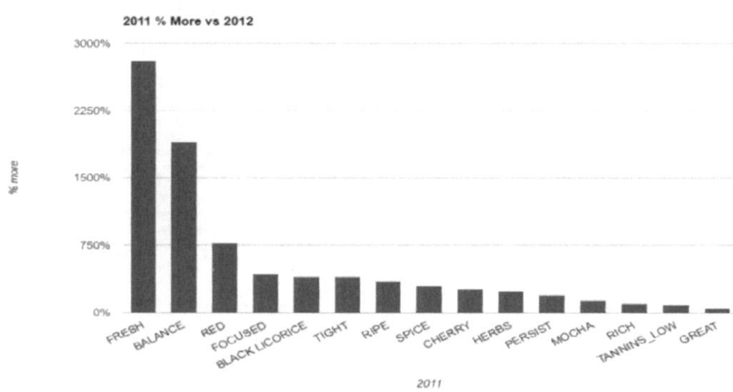

Fig 3. Ratio differences in representation of attributes in 2011 clusters when compared to 2012 clusters where difference is > 50%

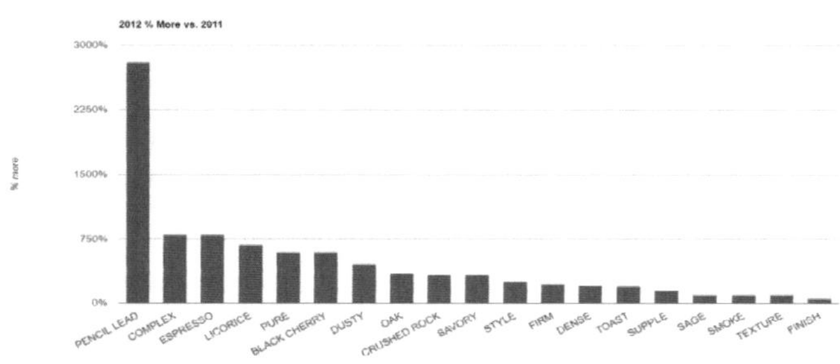

Fig. 4 Ratio differences in representation of attributes in 2012 clusters when compared to 2011 clusters where difference is > 50%

Once again comparing the ratios of attributes more represented in 2012 and focusing on those qualities that are seen at a 50% greater rate or more reveals a set of attributes that can be regarded as the weather impact. For 2012 this includes 19 total attributes, 16 new ones and the 3 from the flat difference comparison. We see a similar sort of distribution to the differences in the 2011 comparison, with many qualities in a similar sort of variable difference, and then a final spiking into the thousands of percent difference.

4 Conclusion and Future Works

Through this very surface level data mining and analysis we've shown that there is some basis or merit to the general idea that there are good and bad years for wine weather. While this will not come as news to wineries around the world, it does give a more objective value to that knowledge. The sorts of weather seen in 2011 are not conducive to bringing out the sorts of flavors wine enthusiasts expect in a good Cabernet Sauvignon wine. In particular the 2011 wine was lacking in tannins and the flavors that oak brings to wine. These are only the bare surface level conclusions that data mining can bring to the world of wine in regards to weather, and hopefully open a door into deeper analysis in the pursuit of ever more delicious wines. To the best of our knowledge, this is the first paper using computational algorithms to discover the effects of weather on wine.

Our paper offers a framework into which much deeper data mining efforts can follow. While it does provide compelling evidence that weather matters, it does not narrow down exactly what about the weather matters, and in what respects. For instance it may be relative humidity levels that cause OAK flavors to come out more, or sunshine might be the important factor driving tannins. In order to get at questions like that this sort of study would need to be done for a much larger number of years, and also various weather attributes would need to be added in a binary fashion to each wine. This would be a good future analysis.

References

1. Chen, B., Rhodes, C., Crawford, A., & Hambuchen, L. (2014, December). Wineinformatics: Applying Data Mining on Wine Sensory Reviews Processed by the Computational Wine Wheel. In Data Mining Workshop (ICDMW), 2014 IEEE International Conference on (pp. 142-149). IEEE.
2. Wine Spectator Magazine http://www.winespectator.com/ (accessed March 2017)
3. Chemical analysis of grapes and wine: techniques and concepts. Campbelltown, Australia: Patrick Iland wine promotions, 2004.
4. Wine Folly Blog: Guide to Cabernet Sauvignon Red Wine www.winefolly.com/review/guide-to-cabernet-sauvignon-red-wine (accessed April 2017)
5. Wikipedia: Cabernet Sauvignon https://en.wikipedia.org/wiki/Cabernet_Sauvignon (accessed April 2017)
6. Chen, Bernard, Christopher Rhodes, Alexander Yu, and Valentin Velchev. "The Computational Wine Wheel 2.0 and the TriMax Triclustering in Wineinformatics." In Industrial Conference on Data Mining, pp. 223-238. Springer International Publishing, 2016.
7. Chen, Bernard, Valentin Velchev, Bryce Nicholson, Joey Garrison, Moani Iwamura, and Ryan Battisto. "Wineinformatics: Uncork Napa's Cabernet Sauvignon by Association Rule Based Classification." In Machine Learning and Applications (ICMLA), 2015 IEEE 14th International Conference on, pp. 565-569. IEEE, 2015.
8. Prelić, Amela, Stefan Bleuler, Philip Zimmermann, Anja Wille, Peter Bühlmann, Wilhelm Gruissem, Lars Hennig, Lothar Thiele, and Eckart Zitzler. "A systematic comparison and evaluation of biclustering methods for gene expression data." Bioinformatics 22, no. 9 (2006): 1122-1129.

9. Prelić, A., Bleuler, S., Zimmermann, P., Wille, A., Bühlmann, P., Gruissem, W & Zitzler, E. (2006). A systematic comparison and evaluation of biclustering methods for gene expression data. Bioinformatics, 22(9), 1122-1129.
10. Cortez, Paulo, António Cerdeira, Fernando Almeida, Telmo Matos, and José Reis. "Modeling wine preferences by data mining from physicochemical properties." Decision Support Systems 47, no. 4 (2009): 547-553.
11. Capece, Angela, Rossana Romaniello, Gabriella Siesto, Rocchina Pietrafesa, Carmela Massari, Cinzia Poeta, and Patrizia Romano. "Selection of indigenous Saccharomyces cerevisiae strains for Nero d'Avola wine and evaluation of selected starter implantation in pilot fermentation." International journal of food microbiology 144, no. 1 (2010): 187-192.
12. Edelmann, Andrea, Josef Diewok, Kurt Christian Schuster, and Bernhard Lendl. "Rapid method for the discrimination of red wine cultivars based on mid-infrared spectroscopy of phenolic wine extracts." Journal of Agricultural and Food Chemistry 49, no. 3 (2001): 1139-1145.
13. Yeo, Michelle, Tristan Fletcher, and John Shawe-Taylor. "Machine Learning in Fine Wine Price Prediction." Journal of Wine Economics 10, no. 2 (2015): 151-172.
14. https://www.winespectator.com/vintagecharts/search/id/15 (accessed June 2018)

Context Aware Image Annotation in Active Learning

Yingcheng Sun and Kenneth Loparo

Case Western Reserve University, Cleveland, OH 44106, USA
{yxs489,kal4}@case.edu

Abstract. Image annotation for active learning is labor-intensive. Various automatic and semi-automatic labeling methods are proposed to save the labeling cost, but a reduction in the number of labeled instances does not guarantee a reduction in cost because the queries that are most valuable to the learner may be the most difficult or ambiguous cases, and therefore the most expensive for an oracle to label accurately. In this paper, we try to solve this problem by using image metadata to offer the oracle more clues about the image during annotation process. We propose a Context Aware Image Annotation Framework (CAIAF) that uses image metadata as similarity metric to cluster images into groups for annotation. We also present useful metadata information as context for each image on the annotation interface. Experiments show that it reduces that annotation cost with CAIAF compared to the conventional framework, while maintaining a high classification performance.

Keywords: Images Annotation, Context Information, Metadata, Active Learning

1 Introduction

Digital photos are now part of our everyday life due to the popularization of digital cameras, smartphones, surveillance systems, and other image capture devices [1, 2]. The number of photos and pictures taken per day increases every year. In semantic image classification or Content-Based Image Retrieval (CBIR) tasks such as face recognition and automatic pilot, a large amount of labeled data is necessary in the form of a training set, and it will entail significant manual effort. Hence, developing a strategy to minimize human annotation effort in a multi-label problem is of paramount practical importance. Though various automatic or semi-automatic annotation techniques are proposed [3, 4], the results are still not satisfactory and convincing enough [5], so manual annotation is inevitable at the present stage.

Active learning algorithms iteratively query only the most informative instances to label have gained popularity to reduce human annotation effort. When exposed to large quantities of unlabeled data, such algorithms automatically select the promising and exemplar instances to be labeled manually. This tremendously reduces the annotation effort and also endows the model with greater generalization capability as it gets trained on the salient examples from the underlying data population [6]. In most applications, batch mode active learning, where a set of items is picked all at once to be labeled and then used to re-train the classifier, is most feasible because it does not require the model to be re-trained after each individual selection and makes most efficient use of human labor for annotation [7].

Most previous work focuses on developing the strategies of selecting samples, but the way of querying labels from the annotators are seldom discussed. Burr et al. [8] proposed that minimizing the number of queries does not guarantee the reduction of the whole annotation cost because the queries that are most valuable to the learner may be the most difficult or ambiguous cases, and therefore the most expensive for an oracle to label accurately. Figure 1 shows such an example of image annotation of the Statue of Liberty.

Fig. 1. Left: the original Statue of Liberty in New York City. Right: the replica in Las Vegas.

Given such two images in monument recognition [9] or landmark classification [10] task, it is very hard to annotate them correctly if the oracle does not know there is a replica of Statue of Liberty in Las Vegas, since the photos in Figure 1 depict almost the same visual objects. Even with some background knowledge, it still takes time for the oracle to tell them apart because of the uncertainty. However, the image metadata such as the geographical location can help the oracle to annotate them fast and accurate enough in this case.

In traditional active learning frameworks with batch mode, a group of images are picked up and shown to annotators without any specific order. Sometimes the class label of images switch frequently during annotation process, which might increase the annotation time and error rate. Like the example shown in Figure 2, the left image might be wrong annotated on its own without any context because it might be a flower petal, but it could also be a piece of fruit or possibly an octopus tentacle which is very ambiguous. However, in the context of a neighborhood of images (the right column) with similar metadata like taken time, author or user tags, it is clearer that the left one shows a flower. The context of additional unannotated images disambiguates the visual classification task [11].

To address the above issues, we proposed a Context Aware Image Annotation Framework (CAIAF) [34]. In this paper, we will discuss more details about using image metadata as context information to organize images during annotation process.

Most images on the web carry metadata; the idea of using it to improve visual classification is not new. Prior work takes advantage of user tags for image classification and retrieval [12, 13], uses GPS data [14, 15] to improve image classification, and utilizes timestamps [16] to both improve recognition and study topical evolution over time. The motivation behind much of this work is the notion that images with similar metadata tend to depict similar scenes.

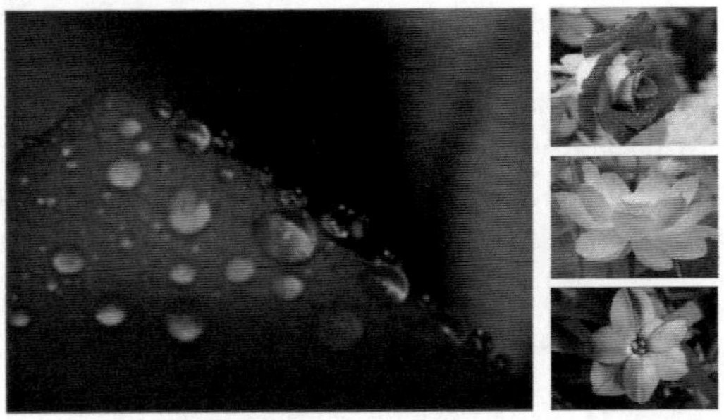

Fig. 2. Left: a flower petal. Right: neighbors of the left one in terms of metadata.

In CAIAF, similar images display together in each batch after clustering by the assigned metadata, and useful metadata information of the image to be labeled is also presented on the annotation interface. By doing these, annotators will have more clues about each image during the annotation process and thus reduce the annotation cost and improves the performance. Experiments show that CAIAF saves the annotation time and also leads to a better annotation performance.

The rest of this paper is organized as follows. In Section 2, we present related work. In Section 3, we propose the CAIAF and explain the metadata used in this framework. In Section 4, we introduce the dataset, comparison methods and evaluation metrics, as well as the experimental results. We conclude our work in Section 5.

2 Related Work

2.1 Improve Image Classification by Exploiting Metadata

Most images on the web carry metadata that can be very useful to improve image visual classification. One class of image metadata where this notion is particularly relevant is social-network metadata, which can be harvested for images embedded in social networks such as Flickr. In [12] the authors study the relationship between tags and manual annotations, with the goal of recovering annotations using a combination of tags and image content. The problem of recommending tags was studied in [17], where possible tags were obtained from similar images and similar users. The same problem was studied in [18], who exploit the relationships between tags to suggest future tags based on existing ones. Friendship information between users was studied for tag recommendation in [19], and in [20] for the case of Facebook. McAuley and Leskovec [21] pioneered the study of multilabel image annotation using metadata, and demonstrated impressive results using only metadata and no visual features. Justin et al. [11] exploits social-network metadata to improve image annotation.

Another commonly used source of metadata comes directly from the camera, in the form of Exif and GPS data [10, 22, 23]. Such metadata can be used to determine whether two photos were taken by the same person, or from the same location, which provides an informative signal and context for certain image categories. Kevin et al. [24] use the GPS coordinates as location context to improve image classification. Matthew et al. [25] integrates Exif metadata like exposure time, flash use and subject distance to tackle the "indoor-outdoor" image classification problem.

These researches discuss different methods to build a better image classification model. Our work differs from them because we focus on the annotator (oracle) side, and tries to reduce the annotation cost by using image metadata.

2.2 Reduce Image Annotation Cost in Active Learning

Machine learning methods such as active learning, distant learning and reinforcement learning are widely used in classification tasks [35- 39]. Most previous work in active learning has assumed a fixed cost for acquiring each label, i.e., all queries are equally expensive for the oracle. Burr et al. [8] prove that the cost is not fixed, and they make an empirical study of annotation costs in four real-world text and image domains. They predicted the annotation cost in the text domain but failed in the image domain. Burr et al. later [26] propose an annotation paradigm DUALIST that solicits and learns from labels on both features and instances. It is fast enough to support real-time interactive speeds in text field. Qiang et.al [27] explored the possible factors are associated with the cost of time in clinical text annotation. Stefan et al. [28] discussed the "difficulty" of tweet that affects labeling performance of annotators. However, the problem of how to reduce the image annotation cost has not been studied.

Some researchers try to reduce the human annotation effort in active learning by using the current learned model to assist in the labeling of query instances in structured-output tasks like parsing [29] or named entity recognition [30]. Haertel, et al. [31] proposed a parallel active learning method which can eliminate the wait time with minimal staleness. Thiago et al. [32] introduce a ranked batch-mode active learning framework to reduce the manual labeling delays. However, these methods do not actually represent or reason about costs. Instead, they attempt to reduce the number of annotation actions required for a query. Our research tries to solve this problem from another perspective that uses metadata to give annotators more context, and then to reduce the annotation cost and improve the performance.

3 Context Aware Image Annotation Framework

Traditional active learning frameworks query the oracle one instance per time to label, even in batch mode, because the selected images are usually shown in an order of their informative vale or just randomly. It will not help the annotation too much if the oracle knows the previous labeled and following unlabeled images. However, we design a Context Aware Image Annotation Framework (CAIAF) by using the image metadata, and try to give annotators more clues in the annotation activity. In CAIAF, each batch of images are clustered by the similarity of their metadata and displayed in groups. Fig. 3 shows the process.

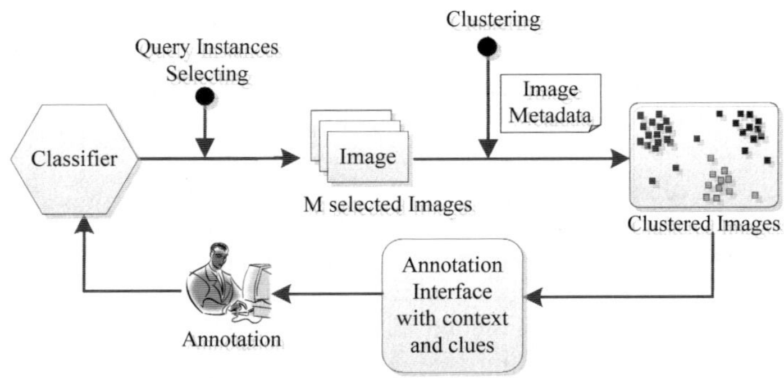

Fig. 3. The framework of labeling images with metadata as context information

First, M images are selected from corpus by query instances selecting algorithm with batch mode. Next, the selected images are clustered by the similarity of metadata. In this paper, we use K-means as the clustering method. Next, the clustered images will be shown to the annotator by groups. Each image is displayed with its metadata information. This process iterates until the threshold is met. In order to support a context description relevant for annotating photos, we have defined four context dimensions: location, time, user tags, and camera tags.

Location With the widespread availability of cellphones and cameras that have GPS capabilities, it is common for images being uploaded to the Internet today to have GPS coordinates associated with them. With this geographical information in hand, it is much easier to correctly deduce the label of geo-related images, like the example of Statue of Liberty shown in Figure 1. Images will be clustered by their geodesic distance if the location is set as the context clue. The real location like "New York City" transferred from coordinates will also be shown on the annotation interface.

Time The creation time (and date) of the photo is another dimension that can be used to organize the images. It allows the association of an instant (date and time) with a photo, and also of the different time interpretations and attributes listed above (e.g., night, Monday, July). Thus, the temporal concept can be used to cluster photographs by events such as sunrise and sunset. Images will be grouped by closeness of their timestamps if the time is set as the context clue. The time will also be shown on the annotation interface.

User Tags One class of image metadata where this notion is particularly relevant is social-network metadata, which can be harvested for images embedded in social networks such as Flickr. These metadata, such as user-generated tags are applied to images by people as a means to communicate with other people; as such, they can be highly informative as to the semantic contents of images. We compute the distance between images using word embedding since it can capture the semantic similarity between texts [40, 41, 42]. Images will be clustered by their similarity if the "user tags" is set as the context. The original user- generated tags location will display the annotation interface.

Camera Tags Exif metadata recorded by the camera provides cues independent of the scene content that can be exploited to improve image annotation. The Exif metadata standard for JPEG images includes a number of tags related to picture taking conditions, including FlashUsed, FocalLength, ExposureTime, Aperture, FNumber, ShutterSpeed, and Subject Distance. It is clear that some of these cues can help discriminate between certain scene types (e.g., long subject distances occur primarily on landscape photos); the scene classification problem at hand determines which cues help the most. We do not use the camera tag metadata as context in our paper because it is not a distinguishable feature for our dataset, but it has been proved that the scene brightness, subject distance and flash are salient in the problem of "indoor-outdoor" classification problem [25].

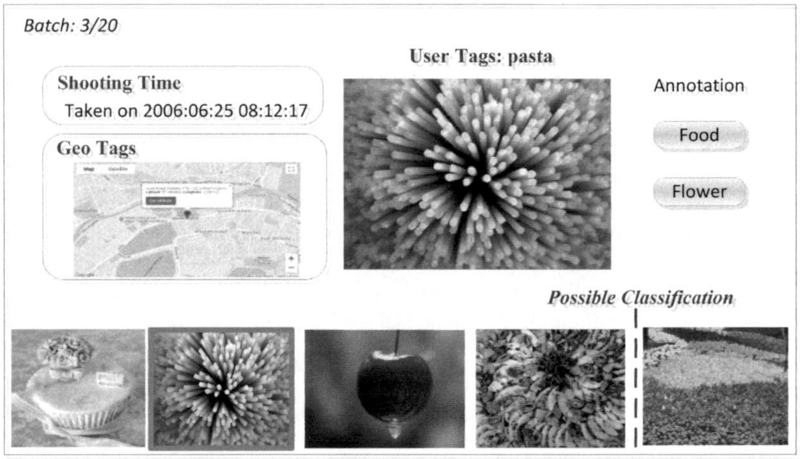

Fig. 4. A screenshot of the annotation interface developed based on CAIAF

A simple annotation interface is developed based on the proposed framework CAIAF. A screenshot of it is shown in Figure 4. In this interface, a batch of images are all presented to the oracle. In our experiment, we set the batch size as five, so there are five images listed in a row. The oracle needs to label them one by one, and choose the class of the current image with the button on the right corner. After clicking any of the class buttons, the next image will be chosen and shown on the upper part. In Figure 4, the "food or flower" image classification is being queried for annotation. The left column lists the temporal and geographical information of the current image being labeled. The "user tags" are listed the top of the image that can help to understand the content of the image. Besides these clues, the row of images is also clustered by the metadata, and partitioned by a dashed red line. With all these information as context, it is easier for the oracle to annotate the image fast and accurate. The number of batch of images that have been annotated and the total number of batches are shown on the left corner. The annotation time of each batch of images is logged.

4 Experiment And Analysis

4.1 Dataset

In this paper, we use the NUS-WIDE dataset [43] for our experiments. This dataset is created by NUS's Lab for Media Search and has been widely used for image labeling and retrieval. It consists of 269,648 images collected from Flickr with plentiful metadata, each manually annotated for the presence or absence of 81 labels. To make it easier for the annotation experiment, we picked 8 categories from them and make four pairs of comparison sets: bird and cat, flower and food, lake and ocean, town and temple and use five types of metadata information: image description, data and time, geographical coordinates, headline, and keywords as shown in Fig. 5. We discard images which metadata is not complete or unavailable. Following [44] we also discard images that labels are absent. We randomly picked 100 images from the left ones for each category, and 800 in total.

<**Image Description**> Yup, that's Bill Cosby.
<**Date and Time**> 2007:12:20 11:50:15
<**Geo**> (40.810001, -73.959982)
<**Headline**> Cool Cos
<**Keywords**> 2007, december, bill cosby, celebrity, bokeh, portrait, man, sunglasses, fuji, s5 pro, 85mm f/1.4D, actor, columbia university, teachers college, flash, sb-800, strobist

Fig. 5. Selected pieces of metadata information and the raw image

We developed a conventional image annotation interface without any metadata clues as the comparison. Image is queried one by one in that interface. We call it "plain interface" in this paper.

4.2 Experiment

We use a python active learning module[1] offered by Google for the image annotation experiment. We set the batch size as 5, and choose "Informative and diverse" as the active learning method and "Linear SVM" as the classification model. We choose the "image description" and "keywords" as the main metadata clues for the "bird and cat" and "town and temple" annotation, "data and time" for the "flower and food" annotation and "geographical coordinates" for the "lake and ocean" annotation.

[1] https://github.com/google/active-learning

Two volunteers in my Lab as annotators are involved in the image annotation experiment. Since one will be familiar with the images labeled by himself before, each of the annotators should label an image either with the plain interface or with our proposed CAIAF. In our experiment, each annotator labels two pairs with plain interface, and the other two pairs with CAIAF. We count their time used for labeling each batch of images as the annotation cost, and Figure 6 shows the results.

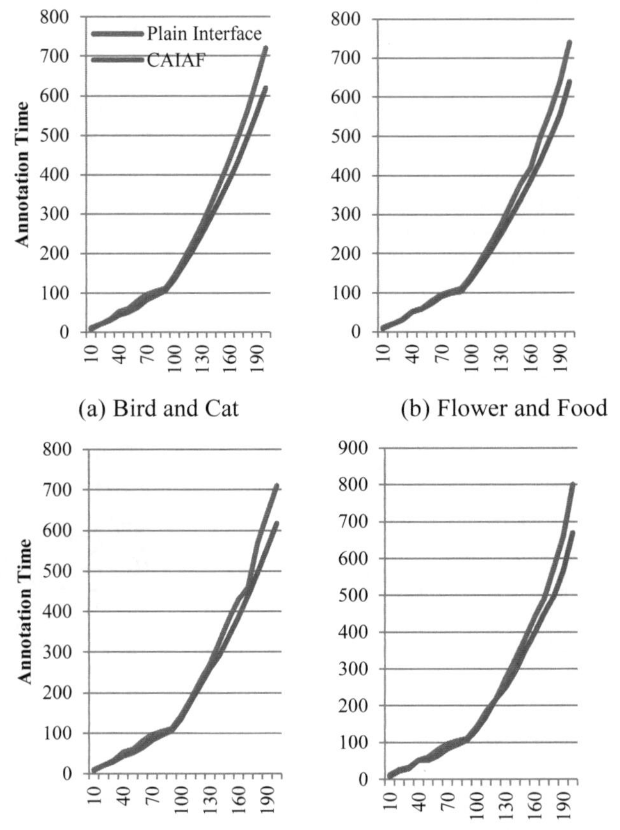

(a) Bird and Cat (b) Flower and Food

(c) Lake and Ocean (d) Town and Temple

Fig. 6. The comparison of CAIAF and conventional image annotation framework with plain interface without metadata clues and context in terms of cumulative annotation time.

From the result we can see that for all the four pairs of images, it takes less time for the annotation with CAIAF than plain framework as the annotation goes on. Images with useful context information yield to better annotation performance than plain interface without any context clues. The annotation of "Town and Temple" takes more time on average than the other three pairs, but it still uses less time with CAIAF than one with conventional active learning framework. Also, images labeled by CAIAF have less or at least equal errors than the plain one. Table 1 shows the final classification result. We can see that the F1 score of classification with CAIAF is equal to the plain one for the first pair, but a little bit higher for the other three pairs.

Table 1. F1 score of classification result (%)

	Learning with plain interface	Learning with CAIAF	Improvement
Bird and Cat	61.6%	61.6%	0%
Flower and Food	63.7%	63.9%	0.3%
Lake and Ocean	61.4%	62.3%	1.4%
Town and Temple	58.3%	59.7%	0%

5 Conclusions and Future Work

Given a large pool of unlabeled images, active learning provides a way to iteratively select the most informative unlabeled images to label. In practice, batch mode active learning, where a set of items is picked all at once to be labeled and then used to retrain the classifier, is most feasible because it does not require the model to be retrained after each individual selection and makes most efficient use of human labor for annotation.

In this paper, we explored the possibility of reducing the annotation cost while maintaining the active learning performance. The experiment shows that our proposed context aware image annotation framework with plentiful metadata clues takes less time for the oracle to label images than the plain one without any metadata information as context. Also, the classification performance of active learning with CAIAF is equal or better than the plain one. In the future, we will explore the combination of multiple dimensions of context information and make more efficient annotation method such as semi-automatic or automatic annotation framework. We are also interested in the possibility of reducing annotation cost in other domains such as text or emails.

Acknowledgment

This work was supported by the Ohio Department of Higher Education, the Ohio Federal Research Network and the Wright State Applied Research Corporation under award WSARC-16-00530 (C4ISR: Human-Centered Big Data).

References

1. De Figueirêdo HF, Lacerda Y, de Paiva A, Casanova M, de Souza BC.: PhotoGeo: a photo digital library with spatial-temporal support and self-annotation. Multimed Tools Appl 59, pp. 279–305 (2012)

2. Ionescu B, Radu A-L,Menéndez M, Müller H, Popescu A, Loni B.: Div400: a social image retrieval result diversification dataset. In: Proceedings of the 5th ACM Multimedia Systems Conference, pp. 29–34. ACM, New York, NY, USA (2014)
3. Viana, W., Bringel Filho, J., Gensel, J., Oliver, M.V. and Martin, H.,: PhotoMap–Automatic Spatiotemporal Annotation for Mobile Photos. In: International Symposium on Web and Wireless Geographical Information Systems, pp. 187-201. Springer, Berlin, Heidelberg (2007)
4. Firmino, A.A., de Souza Baptista, C., de Figueirêdo, H.F., Pereira, E.T. and Amorim, B.D.S.P.,: Automatic and semi-automatic annotation of people in photography using shared events. Multimedia Tools and Applications, 1-35 (2018)
5. De Andrade, D.O.S., Maia, L.F., de Figueirêdo, H.F., Viana, W., Trinta, F. and de Souza Baptista, C.,: Photo annotation: a survey. Multimedia Tools and Applications, 77(1), 423-457 (2018)
6. Druck, G., Settles, B. and McCallum, A.,: Active learning by labeling features. In: Proceedings of the 2009 Conference on Empirical Methods in Natural Language Processing: Volume 1-Volume 1, pp. 81-90. Association for Computational Linguistics (2009)
7. Ravi, S. and Larochelle, H.,: Meta-learning for batch mode active learning. In: Proceedings of 6th International Conference on Learning Representations (ICLR 2018) workshop (2018)
8. Settles, B., Craven, M. and Friedland, L.,: Active learning with real annotation costs. In: Proceedings of the NIPS workshop on cost-sensitive learning, pp. 1-10 (2008)
9. Amato, G., Falchi, F. and Gennaro, C.,: Fast image classification for monument recognition. Journal on Computing and Cultural Heritage (JOCCH), 8(4), p.18 (2015)
10. Li, Y., Crandall, D.J. and Huttenlocher, D.P.,: Landmark classification in large-scale image collections. In: 2009 IEEE 12th international conference on computer vision, pp. 1957-1964. IEEE (2009)
11. Johnson, J., Ballan, L. and Fei-Fei, L.,: Love thy neighbors: Image annotation by exploiting image metadata. In: Proceedings of the IEEE international conference on computer vision, pp. 4624-4632 (2015)
12. Guillaumin, M., Verbeek, J. and Schmid, C.,: Multimodal semi-supervised learning for image classification. In 2010 IEEE Computer society conference on computer vision and pattern recognition, pp. 902-909. IEEE (2010)
13. Hwang, S.J. and Grauman, K.,: Learning the relative importance of objects from tagged images for retrieval and cross-modal search. International journal of computer vision, 100(2), pp.134-153 (2012)
14. Hays, J. and Efros, A.A.,: IM2GPS: estimating geographic information from a single image. In 2008 IEEE conference on computer vision and pattern recognition, pp. 1-8. IEEE (2008)
15. Roshan Zamir, A., Ardeshir, S. and Shah, M.,: Gps-tag refinement using random walks with an adaptive damping factor. In: Proceedings of the IEEE Conference on Computer Vision and Pattern Recognition, pp. 4280-4287 (2014)
16. Kim, G., Xing, E.P. and Torralba, A.,: Modeling and analysis of dynamic behaviors of web image collections. In European Conference on Computer Vision, pp. 85-98. Springer, Berlin, Heidelberg (2010)
17. Lindstaedt, S., Pammer, V., Mörzinger, R., Kern, R., Mülner, H. and Wagner, C.,: Recommending tags for pictures based on text, visual content and user context. In 2008 Third International Conference on Internet and Web Applications and Services, pp. 506-511. IEEE (2008)

18. Sigurbjörnsson, B. and Van Zwol, R.,: Flickr tag recommendation based on collective knowledge. In: Proceedings of the 17th international conference on World Wide Web, pp. 327-336. ACM (2008)
19. Sawant, N., Datta, R., Li, J. and Wang, J.Z.,: Quest for relevant tags using local interaction networks and visual content. In: Proceedings of the international conference on Multimedia information retrieval, pp. 231-240. ACM (2010)
20. Stone, Z., Zickler, T. and Darrell, T.,: Autotagging facebook: Social network context improves photo annotation. In 2008 IEEE computer society conference on computer vision and pattern recognition workshops, pp. 1-8. IEEE (2008)
21. McAuley, J. and Leskovec, J.,: Image labeling on a network: using social-network metadata for image classification. In European conference on computer vision, pp. 828-841. Springer, Berlin, Heidelberg (2012)
22. Luo, J., Boutell, M. and Brown, C.,: Pictures are not taken in a vacuum-an overview of exploiting context for semantic scene content understanding. IEEE Signal Processing Magazine, 23(2), pp.101-114 (2006)
23. Kalogerakis, E., Vesselova, O., Hays, J., Efros, A.A. and Hertzmann, A.,: Image sequence geolocation with human travel priors. In 2009 IEEE 12th international conference on computer vision, pp. 253-260. IEEE (2009)
24. Tang, K., Paluri, M., Fei-Fei, L., Fergus, R. and Bourdev, L.,: Improving image classification with location context. In: Proceedings of the IEEE international conference on computer vision, pp. 1008-1016 (2015)
25. Boutell, M. and Luo, J.,: Photo classification by integrating image content and camera metadata. In: Proceedings of the 17th International Conference on Pattern Recognition, ICPR 2004. Vol. 4, pp. 901-904. IEEE (2004)
26. Settles, B.,: Closing the loop: Fast, interactive semi-supervised annotation with queries on features and instances. In: Proceedings of the conference on empirical methods in natural language processing, pp. 1467-1478. Association for Computational Linguistics (2011)
27. Wei, Q., Franklin, A., Cohen, T. and Xu, H.,: Clinical text annotation–what factors are associated with the cost of time?. In AMIA Annual Symposium Proceedings, Vol. 2018, p. 1552. American Medical Informatics Association (2018)
28. Räbiger, S., Saygın, Y. and Spiliopoulou, M.,: How does tweet difficulty affect labeling performance of annotators?. arXiv preprint arXiv:1808.00388 (2018)
29. Baldridge, J. and Osborne, M.,: Active learning and the total cost of annotation. In Proceedings of the 2004 Conference on Empirical Methods in Natural Language Processing pp. 9-16 (2004)
30. Culotta, A. and McCallum, A.,: Reducing labeling effort for structured prediction tasks. In AAAI, Vol. 5, pp. 746-751 (2005)
31. Haertel, R., Felt, P., Ringger, E. and Seppi, K.,: Parallel active learning: eliminating wait time with minimal staleness. In: Proceedings of the NAACL HLT 2010 Workshop on Active Learning for Natural Language Processing, pp. 33-41. Association for Computational Linguistics (2010)
32. Cardoso, T.N., Silva, R.M., Canuto, S., Moro, M.M. and Gonçalves, M.A.,: Ranked batch-mode active learning. Information Sciences, 379, pp.313-337 (2017)
33. Sun, Y., Li, Q.: The research situation and prospect analysis of meta-search engines. In: 2nd International Conference on Uncertainty Reasoning and Knowledge Engineering, pp. 224-229. IEEE, Jalarta, Indonesia (2012).
34. Sun, Y., Loparo, K.: Context Aware Image Annotation in Active Learning with Batch Mode. In: 43rd Annual Computer Software and Applications Conference (COMPSAC), vol. 1, pp. 952-953. IEEE (2019).

35. Li, Q., Zou, Y., Sun, Y.: Ontology based user personalization mechanism in meta search engine. In: 2nd International Conference on Uncertainty Reasoning and Knowledge Engineering, pp. 230-234. IEEE, Jalarta, Indonesia (2012).
36. Li, Q., Sun, Y., Xue, B.: Complex query recognition based on dynamic learning mechanism. Journal of Computational Information Systems 8(20), 8333-8340 (2012).
37. Li, Q., Zou, Y., Sun, Y.: User Personalization Mechanism in Agent-based Meta Search Engine. Journal of Computational Information Systems 8(20), 1-8 (2012).
38. Li, Q., Sun, Y.: An agent based intelligent meta search engine. In: International Conference on Web Information Systems and Mining, pp. 572-579. Springer, Berlin, Heidelberg (2012).
39. Sun, Y., Loparo, K.: Learning - based Adaptation Framework for Elastic Software Systems. In: Proceedings of 31st International Conference on Software Engineering & Knowledge Engineering, pp. 281-286. IEEE, Lisbon, Portugal (2019).
40. Sun, Y., Loparo, K.: A Clicked-URL Feature for Transactional Query Identification. In 2019 IEEE 43rd Annual Computer Software and Applications Conference (COMPSAC), vol. 1, pp. 950-951. IEEE (2019).
41. Sun, Y., Loparo, K.: Topic Shift Detection in Online Discussions using Structural Context. In 2019 IEEE 43rd Annual Computer Software and Applications Conference (COMPSAC) , vol. 1, pp. 948-949. IEEE (2019).
42. Sun, Y., Loparo, K.: Information Extraction from Free Text in Clinical Trials with Knowledge-Based Distant Supervision. In: IEEE 43rd Annual Computer Software and Applications Conference (COMPSAC), vol. 1, pp. 954-955. IEEE (2019).
43. Chua, T.S., Tang, J., Hong, R., Li, H., Luo, Z. and Zheng, Y.,: NUS-WIDE: a real-world web image database from National University of Singapore. In Proceedings of the ACM international conference on image and video retrieval, p. 48. ACM (2009)
44. Gong, Y., Jia, Y., Leung, T., Toshev, A. and Ioffe, S.,: Deep convolutional ranking for multilabel image annotation. arXiv preprint arXiv:1312.4894 (2013)

Risk and Error Matrix Charts

H.K. Koesmarno

Data Science and Engineering, ATO, Canberra, Australia
hari.koesmarno@ato.gov.au

Abstract. Measuring classifier performance is important in machine learning. Risk charts and error matrix charts have been developed for this purpose. The strengths and weaknesses of using these charts are outlined. Challenges with using these charts are discussed including how base rates and using prevalence data for building models and incidence data for evaluating models affect model performance. A number of solutions for overcoming these challenges are covered

Keywords: Error Matrix, Confusion Table, Cumulative Gain Chart, Risk Chart

1 Introduction

1.1 Measuring classifier performance

The performance of binary classifier will be illustrated using risk chart [10] and error matrix charts [4,6] for two types of target variables, i.e. binary and continuous variables. The binary variable, for example, distinguishes risk cases from non-risk cases, while the continuous variable represents the magnitude of the risk. For example, risk to revenue with tax collections has dollar amount while risk of rain has the magnitude of precipitation in either inches or millimetres. In some applications the magnitude of the risk variable can have "negative or positive" values or "debit or credit" in accounting term. When developing a supervised learning model, the priority is frequently aimed at the ranked order of the magnitude of the risk, e.g. revenue. Hence the modelling process should take into consideration both the classification of the risk and the magnitude of the risk.

In order to measure and visualise the performance of the classifiers using both the binary and continuous target variables, a revised risk chart and error matrix chart are proposed in this paper. An example of risk chart is given in Fig. 1, while an example of error matrix chart is given in Fig. 3. There are a number of reasons for using these charts. Firstly they are useful for evaluating the effects of the weighted classification problem [8]. Some classification problems can be weighted based on the importance of the cases. For example, with a tax avoidance and evasion detection model, some cases are likely to provide greater revenue than the others and hence are given greater weight. In some cases, there will be not much difference in terms of their strike rates, but there can be significant differences in their risk to revenue. The risk to revenue is particularly useful if only a portion of the population will be actioned for recovering the revenue because of limited audit and investigatory resources.

Both Risk charts and Error Matrix charts are sensitive to classifiers performance when compared to receiver operating curve (ROC) charts [2]. One challenge with measuring the performance of classifiers is class imbalance. Recent use of risk charts and error matrix charts indicate that they are very sensitive to class imbalance when compared with ROC. However, ROC charts cannot be used to evaluate the magnitude of the risk where risk chart and error matrix charts can.

Risk charts and error matrix charts are ideal for (i) measuring classifier performance including risk which is a measure of the size of the risk gain or loss associated with target variable of each observation; (ii) comparing classifier performance prior and post intervention (iii) further improving risk charts and error matrix charts for measuring classifier performance.

1.2 Base-rate variation with prevalence and incidence data

If a sample of size n is drawn for a binary classification problem, then the numbers of sample instances, n_0 and n_1 are respectively in class 0 and 1, $n_0 + n_1 = n$. The base rate is the ratio of n_1 and n, $\alpha = n_1 / n$. When the base rate is not 0.5, then there is class imbalance. One of the challenges with assessing classifier performance is on sample selection bias. This refers to differences in the proportion of cases selected for prevalence data when compared to incidence data. Prevalence data is used for model building, while the incidence data contains the cases which were actioned. Selection bias can distort the assessment of the classifier using several known methods such as misclassification rate and cumulative gain chart. Base rates can affect how well a classifier performs with identifying positive and negative cases. If the base rate is low then the classifier will have a low strike rate although the misclassification rate is high. If the base rate is high, then the classifier will have a high strike rate although the misclassification rate is low. These will be demonstrated in section 2 and 3.

The base rate of the prevalence dataset and incidence dataset can be very different and these will cause issues in obtaining accurate measures of comparative model performance. Unlike ROC charts, which are not affected by base-rates, risk charts and error matrix charts can be misinterpreted when the base-rate changes from the data used to develop a model compared to the data employed to evaluate the performance of a model. These changes can arise because:

1. Each modeller has a tendency to use different base-rate from prevalence for sampling prior model building unless each modeller uses class imbalance data. Having understood the characteristics of risk charts and error matrix charts, it is likely that the modeller who used smallest base-rate in his/her sample, will produce smaller error or bigger AUC, although their model performances are the same.
2. Once the model has been built, new data is used to obtain risk score for independent evaluation. Cases being selected for intervention are generally those which are high risk with those that are either low risk or no risk being excluded from consideration when it comes to evaluation of model perfor-

mance. This distorts the results obtained using risk charts and error matrix charts.

Hence, the incidence data for evaluating model performance needs to be corrected for this bias. Solutions for doing this are proposed in Section 4 of this paper.

1.3 Objectives

These include (i) to illustrate the development and the usage of risk charts and error matrix charts for measuring model performance, (ii) to show how the performance of models are affected by the samples used to develop the models compared to the samples used to evaluate the models and (iii) to outline solutions that can be employed to improve the evaluation of models.

2 Risk charts

Detailed description of risk chart can be found in [10]. This chart involves plotting two variables, i.e. target variable (being 1 or 0) and risk variable (see Fig. 1). An example is where the data set has two class target variable, e.g. adjusted or not adjusted cases when it comes to revenue collection; and the risk variable, e.g. the magnitude of the adjustment if made to recovery of revenue. The adjustment value is a measure of the size of the risk associated with each observation. Cases which have no adjustment following an intervention will of course have no risk associated with them (i.e. Adjustment). Cases that do have an adjustment will have a risk associated with them, and for convenience the value of the adjustment is viewed as the magnitude of the risk.

Gain is a measure of the effectiveness of a classification model calculated as the percentage of correct predictions obtained with the model, versus the percentage of correct predictions obtained without a model. It shows the percentage of positive predictions that the model gains with each slice of the population. A higher overall gain indicates better performance. A cumulative gains chart (see Fig. 1) helps visualize the benefit of using a predictive model. It also allows the effectiveness of different predictive models to be compared. The information from the cumulative gains chart can be applied to determine which portion of the overall population is to be targeted.
The advantages of using these charts include to:

i. Investigate why models improve when error increases due to the changes on base-rate of prevalence and incidence data
ii. Understand the characteristics, strength and weaknesses of the tools for measuring classifier performance.
iii. Identify the methods to be used for comparing performance prior and post modelling, especially when the base-rate changes

An example of a risk chart in shown in Fig. 1(a). If the lowest scores (i.e. the least risky cases) were removed from the sample, then the results as shown in Fig. 1(b) could be obtained. Hence, the area under curve for the risk chart cannot be used for measuring the model accuracy unless further factors are taken onto consideration. A more realistic measure for visualising the risk chart is proposed as in Fig. 2: this shows upper and lower limits of maximum area under curve for the risk chart.

There are three curves in the risk chart in Fig. 1(a). The first is the strike rate for each risk scored population, with the score going from high to low (i.e. left to right). The second shows the cumulative revenue based on the risk scores. The third is the cumulative cases based on the risk scores. Fig. 1(a) is the performance of a classifier for prevalence data. It is assumed that the performance of this model is reliable and when new data is scored, it still produces same performance. As noted previously, in practice only the high risk cases are usually selected for targeting to minimize costs. Hence, by reducing the potential true negative cases (as incidence data), the area under risk curves reduces (see Fig. 1(b)). In fact the performances are the same, but the area is relative to the upper and lower limit (trapezoidal shape) of the risk charts, which are also consistently dependent on the base-rate. Hence, the proposed standardisation of the AUC measures is proposed.

In Fig. 2, class imbalance is illustrated and how it affects the risk chart. The slope of the dashed line shows the percentage of positive cases. The higher the percentage, the more the gradient of the line decreases. If it was 100 percent positive cases, the line would be a diagonal going from bottom left to top right of the chart. The line would be vertical if there were very small or no positive cases. Fig. 2 can be used for evaluating the risk. The x-axis is the case load which can be sorted either (1) high-to-low positive scores from 1 to 0 or (2) low-to-high for negative scores from -1 to 0. The curves will be reversed if the caseload was sorted from (i) low-to-high positive scores from 0 to 1 or (ii) high-to-low negative scores from 0 to -1.

In order to improve the usage and utilise the risk chart for model comparison, the risk chart illustrated in [9] need to be revised. The two main characteristics are used to revise risk charts, i.e. establishing risk chart limit and standardising AUC, i.e. (1) introducing risk chart limit. Let's defined λ = caseload or percentile of population sorted by its ranked scores, $0 \leq \lambda \leq 1$; $\lambda_i = \sum_{i=1}^{N} \frac{1}{N}$. Let's also define Θ = The cumulative gain or risk, $0 \leq \Theta \leq 1$,

(a) For r_i is binary (1 or 0) then the following formula applies:

$\Theta(\lambda_i) = \frac{1}{n}\sum_{i=1}^{N} r_i$ where I = 1,…., N and n = count of r_i when r_i =1.

(b) For quantifying the magnitude of r_i , m(r_i) continuous variable is used:

$\Theta(\lambda_i) = \frac{1}{M}\sum_{i=1}^{N} m(r_i)$ where I = 1,…., N and M = $\sum_{i=1}^{N} m(r_i)$

Let's define α is the base rate, α = n/N; where n = count of (r_i) when r_i= 1 and N = count of (r_i) when r_i= 1 or r_i= 0 (N = total number of instances).

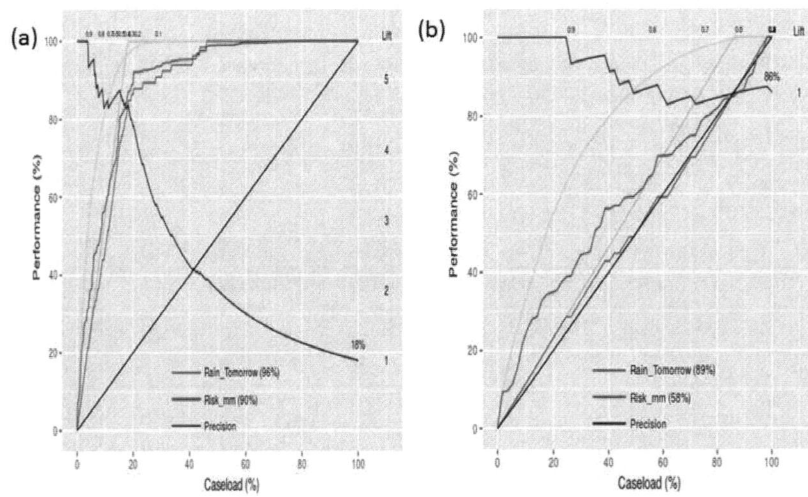

Fig. 1. Risk charts of classifier model performance prior (a) and after selecting score ≥ 0.5 (b)

The risk chart limit consists of

(a) upper boundary of the instances which are ranked from highest to the lowest.

(b) lower boundary of the instances which are ranked from lowest to the highest.

In order to obtain consistent measure of AUC for risk chart, the standardised AUC is proposed as : AUC – min(AUC)/[max(AUC) – min(AUC)], this will give the range of standardised AUC between 0 and 1. In classification, the risk chart limit of the binary target variable has the following upper boundaries are:

.

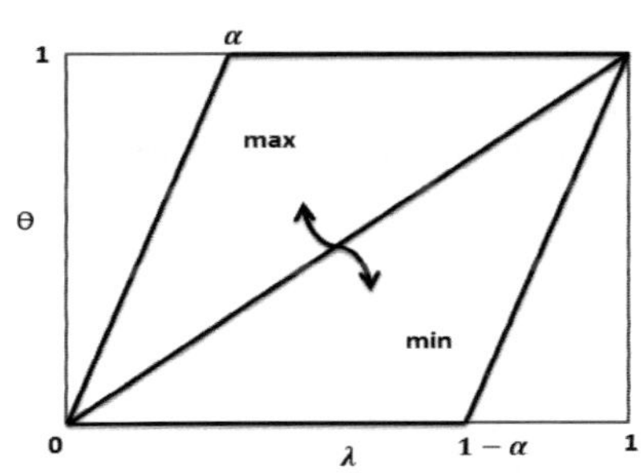

Fig. 2. Upper and Lower limit of Maximum Area Under Curve of Risk Chart where α is the base rate of binary classification

(a) $\Theta = \frac{\lambda}{\alpha}$ for $\lambda < \alpha$

(b) $\Theta = 1$ for $\lambda \geq \alpha$

And lower boundaries are:

(a) $\Theta = 0$ for $\lambda < 1-\alpha$

(b) $\Theta = \frac{\lambda}{\alpha} + \left(1 - \frac{1}{\alpha}\right)$ for $\lambda \geq 1-\alpha$

The performance measure of classifier with binary target variable can be simply expressed as the standardized AUC :

$$\Omega = \frac{(AUC - \frac{\alpha}{2})}{1-\alpha} = \frac{2\,AUC - \alpha}{2(1-\alpha)} \tag{1}$$

It must satisfy $0 \leq \Omega \leq 1$ (2)

Where Θ = performance, λ = Caseload, Ω = Standardised AUC (Area Under Curve). There are two properties can be derived from equation (1) and (2):

$2\text{ AUC} - \alpha > 0$, so $\alpha < 2\text{ AUC}$ (3)

$2(1-\alpha) > 0$, so $\alpha < 1$ (4)

The performance measure of classifier with binary target variable for balance class distribution can be derived by substituting $\alpha = 0.5$ in equation (1), to give: $\Omega = 2AUC - 0.5$. and for random performance where the original AUC is the lower triangle. The standardized AUC can be obtained by substituting AUC=0.5 to equation (1), to give $\Omega = 0.5$. Hence, both AUC and Ω are symmetrical at the diagonal: $\Omega = AUC = 0.5$. The performance measure of classifier with binary target variable for class Imbalance, in particular applying to rare case problems:

As $\alpha \to 0$, the equation (1) gives $\Omega \approx AUC$

As $\alpha \to 1$, the performance becomes less reliable, as it is not satisfy the condition in equation (1). Whenever possible, it is suggested to consider the conversion of α and scores by using $(1-\alpha)$ and (1-scores) if the condition in equation (2) and (3) cannot be achieved.

3 Risk and error matrix charts

A confusion matrix [7] or also known as an error matrix contains information about actual and predicted classifications provided by a classification model. Performance of such models is commonly evaluated using the data in the matrix. The construction of the error matrix chart is based on the generation of proportion score function (PSF) [5] which was developed from [4]. The algorithm for generating a PSF is in Algorithm 1.

Error matrix chart is, as indicated previously, illustrated in Fig. 3. It is called by this name because of the characteristics of the charts in which the area can be represented as an error matrix. The vertical dash lines which illustrates the cut-off points and the horizontal curve line which represent as PSF. They are used to divide these charts onto four regions of the upper right hand of the chart containing the false positives (FP) and the lower right hand of the chart containing the true positives (TP). The upper left hand of the charts contains the false negatives (FN), the lower left hand of the chart contains the true negatives (TN). The error matrix can be represented as:

$$\begin{bmatrix} FN & FP \\ TN & TP \end{bmatrix}$$

Let's consider introducing low, medium and high risk by the low risk vertical line and the high risk vertical line.

Algorithm 1 : Generation of PSF

```
Input(score, predictedClass, trueClass, numberBin)
rankedScore ← rank(score, by numberBin)
For i = 1 to numberBin
  sortedRS[i] ← get(rankedScore,i)
  binSize[i] ← count(sortedRS[i])
  correct[i] ← count(sortedRS[i], if predClass = trueClass)
  psf[i] ← correct[i]/binSize[i]
  lambda[i] ← i/numberBin;
End;
plot(psf,lambda)
```

Let's consider the y-axis Θ, and the x-axis λ. The four quadrant which formed by proportion score function, $\Theta(\lambda)$ and the cut-off point c, in the Fig. 3, represent the error matrix, hence it is called as error matrix chart, where:

$$TP = (1-\lambda) - \int_c^1 \Theta(\lambda)\, d\lambda \tag{5}$$

$$FP = \int_c^1 \Theta(\lambda)\, d\lambda \tag{6}$$

$$FN = \int_0^c \Theta(\lambda)\, d\lambda \tag{7}$$

$$TN = \lambda - \int_0^c \Theta(\lambda)\, d\lambda \tag{8}$$

Hence other characteristics such NPV and PPV can be derived:

$$NPV = 1 - \frac{1}{\lambda}\int_0^c \Theta(\lambda)\, d\lambda \tag{9}$$

$$PPV = 1 - \frac{1}{1-\lambda}\int_c^1 \Theta(\lambda)\, d\lambda \tag{10}$$

In order to obtain error matrix decomposition, low, medium and high risk lines were introduced in Fig. 3 and the error matrix decomposition was obtained. The objective of the error matrix decomposition is to enable local classifier performance analysis of for example either high, medium or low risk cases.

Error Matrix charts enables the examination of classification hits and errors. It provides different measures than AUC in ROC or revised risk chart. Some of the measures produced in the error matrix chart and its composition can be useful in certain applications. An example is where the predictive model was intended to identify rare cases of serious non-compliance. If the targeting was based on the overall model performance, then it means the intention is to maximise the strike rate of the non-risk (compliant) cases as they are the majority in the population. In error matrix charts, the matrix can be decomposed into areas of interest and the region of various components in the error matrix charts can be compared to select which model's performance is relevant to identifying rare cases of non-compliance.

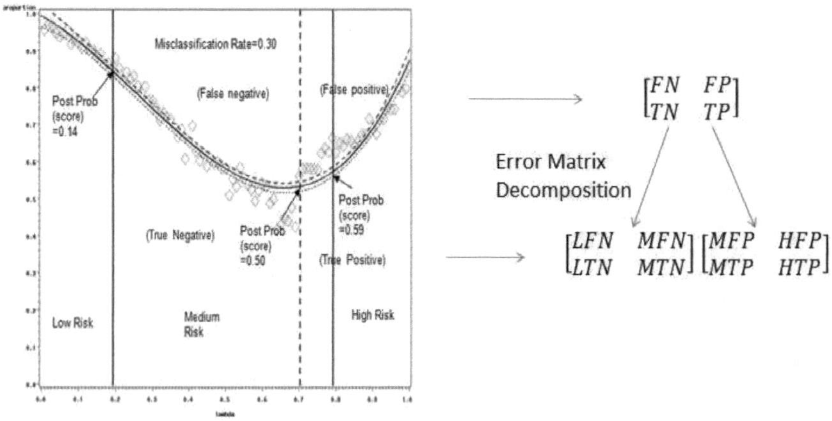

Fig. 3. Error Matrix charts with low and high risk cut-off points and their matrix representation.

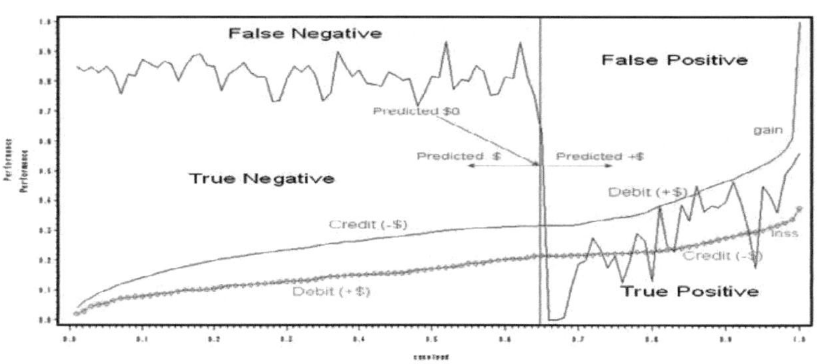

Fig. 4. Error Matrix with gain and loss risk for describing two stage model.

There are many binary classification models which are required to measure 'gain' and 'loss' associated to the classifications. Gain risk variable is the magnitude of the risks when the prediction is correct and has positive impact or value, while loss risk variable is the magnitude of the risk when the prediction is incorrect and has negative impact or value. When an instance is predicted positive, the actual can be either (a) positive, then it has gain risk variable and (b) negative, then it has loss risk variable. Similarly when the instance is predicted negative, the actual can be either (a) positive, then it has loss risk variable and (b) negative, then it has gain risk variable.

A detection model can be used to illustrate the gain and loss risk in revenue. Each outcome of the detection would produce positive or negative revenue. This problem can also be considered as two-stage modelling [3]. The first stage is to predict if a case will result positive or negative outcome. The second stage is to predict the revenue gain for both positive and negative outcomes. PSF has been used to demonstrate the first stage, i.e. the measure for false positive, true positive, false negative and false negative as in Fig. 4. In order to provide a more comprehensive view of the classifier performance, the 'gain' and 'loss' chart should be part of the PSF. The 'gain' and 'loss' chart is also demonstrated in Fig. 4.

Another example of misleading or biased results is where the sample of prevalence and the sample of incidence cases are different:

i. Let's consider sample with 41 is true negative, 5 false positive, 3 false negative, 5 true positive.
ii. In order to minimise the intervention cost, the true negative cases being reduced, by reducing the true non-risk cases from 41 to 5, it saves 35/58 = 35.185% resources.
iii. The representation of error matrix are changing as shown below:

$$\begin{bmatrix} 3 & 5 \\ 41 & 5 \end{bmatrix} \rightarrow \begin{bmatrix} 3 & 5 \\ 5 & 5 \end{bmatrix}$$

The initial misclassification error which is e = 0.14814815 becomes $e =$ 0.444444.

The approach to deal with these issues will be discussed on next section.

4 Performance of models using prevalence and incidence data

When comparing classifier performance of prevalence and incidence data are required, it is important to make sure the results are comparable. There are several issues when the sampling used for model building and/or sampling of model evaluation are not randomly drawn. These issues are illustrated next.

4.1 Reasons

Comparisons of classifier performance utilising prevalence and incidence data is necessary for several reasons:

i. **Improving model deployment**. Constructing the risk and error matrix charts using the incidence data are required for analysing the effects of changing the threshold/cut-off points and case-load selection for model deployment.
ii. **Monitoring model performance**. One question that often needs resolution is "Has there been any concept drift with model performance where for example it strays from detecting fraud?" If there is concept drift and the model performance is not at an acceptable level, then the model should be rebuilt.
iii. **Business reporting and analysis evaluation**. Model/classifier performance using incidence data is frequently requested for business performance analysis and reporting.

4.2 Prevalence and incidence sampling

In order to achieve the objectives for comparing model performance using prevalence and incidence data, the sampling selected for both types of data needs to be from the same distribution. For example, if the prevalence sampling is drawn from accidental sampling (see below), then the incidence sampling should be the same as used in prevalence sampling. The focus of this paper is on measuring classifier performance where the base-rate of prevalence and incidence data is significantly different. This issue is generally due to the method of sampling used to build the model (prevalence) and the sampling used to analyse the modelling outcome (incidence) are frequently different in practice. In order to compare the performance of prevalence and incidence data, the sampling used for building the model should be the same as that used for model evaluation. Generally a model can be constructed using:

i. **Accidental sampling.** This is the most applicable solution for many data mining applications especially for detecting fraud. The known cases of fraud are usually rare in terms of their occurrence and can be expensive to obtain. Hence the need to maximise the data set used for training purposes. The sample used will often be what is readily available and convenient. This is known as grab, convenience or opportunity sampling. It involves the sample being drawn from that part of the population which is close at hand. The model developer using such a sample cannot scientifically make generalizations about the total population from this sample because it would not be representative. This type of sampling can be useful for initial model building.

ii. **Non-Accidental sampling** The most common forms of non-accidental samplings are random sampling, systematic sampling, stratified sampling, cluster sampling and probability-proportional-to-size sampling. While these are the preferred methods for building models, they can have the disadvantages that the positive cases included in these samples may not be readily apparent to those who develop models. That is, those who have this responsibility may not identify all the true positive cases. This is another way of saying some true positive cases remain invisible in the selected sample. If the non-accidental sample contains a limited number of positive cases, this can undermine model performance.

As has been emphasized incidence data usually has cases that have high risk scores and have been actioned. Therefore, the outcomes with these cases are known. Hence, this accidental sample is very different from the sample used to develop the model.

Here the distribution of incidence data has significantly changed from the distribution of prevalence data. There are three possible methods for dealing this challenge. They are:

i. ***Oversampling*** – where all the cells/clusters/strata and scoring percentiles have at least 'minimum' required number of subjecrs, while several others have more data than what is required. The "correction sampling incidence data" proposed in this paper can be utilised and this should provide a reliable correction sampling.
ii. ***Under Sampling*** – There are two scenarios: (i) One or more of the cells/strata/cluster have less data than what are required by the threshold of the sampling. The correction sampling incidence data can be employed, however, the result may generally be less reliable than the one with over-sampling. (ii) One or more of the cells/strata/cluster have no samples or missing data. Here the accuracy of the corrected sampling for these entries depends on the accuracy of the assumptions applied about the distribution they were drawn.
iii. ***Same sampling*** – This sampling usually occurs when the prevalence and incidence data are drawn using the same methods.

There are two possible methods with same sampling to select the incidence data for model evaluation: (i) Non-Accidental Sampling such as random sampling can be used for measuring classifier performance; (b) Accidental sampling. This is not recommended for model evaluation as it will cause errors

If prevalence data is drawn using accidental sampling and is used for building the model, then there is a need to reconstruct the incidence data prior measuring model performance. This can be called 'corrected sampling incidence data". The reconstruction or correction of the incidence data can be done by "substitution sampling". Substitution sampling is a sampling algorithm used to reconstruct the prevalence data using the incidence data. The main characteristics of substitution sampling is "drawing a random sample" from prevalence data, then substituting each instance using incidence data. The substitution of the prevalence instances which are the same strata or cluster or cell as the incidence data is being substituted. The sample size of prevalence data is not the same as incidence data in practice. There are three possible scenarios of sampling being over, under or the same size with the 'random sample' drawn from prevalence data. If the data in each strata or cluster or cell are either over or under sampling, then bootstrap or jackknife method [9] can be utilised for substituting instances in each strata or cluster or cell, until all instance from "substitution sampling" comes from incidence data. The main advantage with substitution sampling is how it captures key population characteristics in prevalence data, the sample collected for model building and the data drawn from 'accidental sampling'. This method of sampling produces characteristics in the sample that are proportional to the prevalence data. The detail is provided in next section.

4.3 Corrected Sampling Incidence Data

Substitution sampling is a method of sampling that involves the substitution and division of a population into smaller groups known as strata or cluster or cell. The strata and cluster are formed based on members' shared attributes or characteristics. A random sample from each stratum or cluster is taken in a number proportional to the stratum's or cluster's size when compared to the population. These subsets of the strata or clusters are then pooled to form a random sample. Fig. 5 illustrates the description of "substitution sampling" when the sample has only two strata or cluster. The bigger data set (LHS) indicates the sample drawn from prevalence data, while the smaller data set (RHS) is the sample belongs to incidence data.

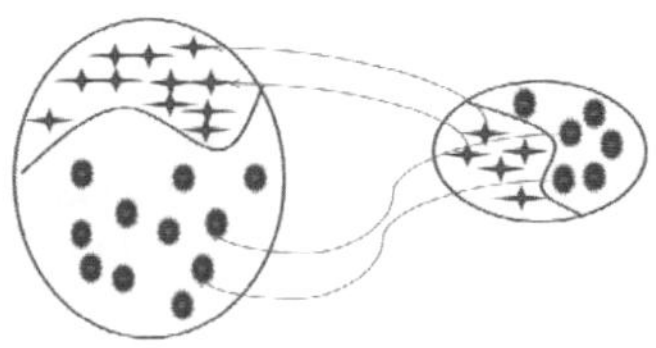

Fig. 5. Substitution sampling, the bogger data set (LHS) indicates the sample drawn from prevalence data, while the smaller one (RHS) is the sample belongs to incidence data.

There are two substitution sampling strategies which are described below.

Mixed Resampling procedure. Let's define the prevalence stratified data is $x_1, x_2, \dots, x_n$, where x_n is the number of cell size at n[th] cell. The incidence stratified data is is $y_1, y_2, \dots, y_n$, where y_n is the number of cell size at n[th] cell. The stratified sampling need to be carried out and the incidence data should be added by a number of sample in order to match with some proportion of prevalence data which can be formulated as:

$$y_i + \Delta_i = \alpha x_i \quad (11)$$

In order to minimise the increase of the overall sample size:

$$\text{Minimise } \sum_{i=1}^{n} \Delta_i \quad (12)$$

$\sum_{i=1}^{n} \Delta_i \geq 0$ for increasing the overall sample size. (13)

Equation (11) can be expressed as: $\Delta_i = \alpha x_i - y_i$ (14)

Substituting (14) onto expression (13) and (12)

$$\text{Minimise } \sum_{i=1}^{n} \alpha x_i - y_i \text{ and } \sum_{i=1}^{n} \alpha x_i - y_i \geq 0. \quad (15)$$

Let us minimise $f(a) = a \sum_{i=1}^{n} x_i - \sum_{i=1}^{n} y_i \; and \; f(a) \geq 0$

Hence $a = \frac{\sum_{i=1}^{n} y_i}{\sum_{i=1}^{n} x_i}$ and $\Delta_i = \left(\frac{\sum_{i=1}^{n} y_i}{\sum_{i=1}^{n} x_i}\right) x_i - y_i$ (16)

There are 3 possibilities of cell sampling required:

If $y_i < x_i$ then use y_i plus additional re-sampling Δ_i with replacement from y_i
If $y_i = x_i$ then use y_i
If $y_i > x_i$, then use sampling without replacement from y_i

Over Re-sampling procedure. For over re-sampling procedure applied, the following condition applies: $\forall i : \Delta_i \geq 0$ then we need to introduce β adjustment, so that all sample are not being reduced, but being increased. We need to substitute Δ_i with $(\beta + \delta_i)$ where $\forall i : \Delta_i \geq 0$, substituting this to equation 11 in order to get

$$y_i + (\beta + \delta_i) = \alpha x_i \tag{17}$$

Equation (17) is used the same way as in expression (12) to (15) in order to obtain

$$a = \frac{(\sum_{i=1}^{n} y_i) + \beta}{\sum_{i=1}^{n} x_i} \tag{18}$$

and substituting α onto equation (17) to give:

$$\delta_i = \left(\frac{(\sum_{i=1}^{n} y_i) + \beta}{\sum_{i=1}^{n} x_i}\right) x_i - y_i - \beta \tag{19}$$

Substituting equation (18) to $\Delta_i = (\beta + \delta_i)$ gives:

$$\Delta_i = \left(\frac{(\sum_{i=1}^{n} y_i) + \beta}{\sum_{i=1}^{n} x_i}\right) x_i - y_i \tag{20}$$

Hence, we need to minimise Δ with the following constraint:

$$\forall i : \Delta(\beta) = \Delta_i \geq 0 \tag{21}$$

The search the value of β is required in order to
minimise Δ_i *and* $\Delta_i \geq 0$ for I = 1, …, n
where n is the number of stratified cells as in Algorithm 2.

Algorithm 2: Corrected Sampling

```
β ← abs (Σ_{i=1}^{n} f(Δ_i)); where f(Δ_i) = Δ_i if Δ_i < 0 and f(Δ_i) = 0 if Δ_i ≥ 0
g0 = 0; β0 = 0; Θ = 0; r = (1+sqrt(5))/2; converge = false;
Evaluate: Δ(β); if Δ(β) < 0 then g = 0; else g = 1;
While convergence eq false then
  Ω = (1-r) * (β-β0);
  if g eq 1 then β01 = β0 + Ω; β11 = β − Ω;
        Evaluate: Δ(β01); if : Δ(β01) < 0 then g01 = 0; else g01 = 1;
        Evaluate: Δ(β11); if : Δ(β11) < 0 then g11 = 0; else g11 = 1;
        if g01 eq 1 and g11 eq 1 then
            Diff = β01 – β0; β = β01; g=g01;
        If g01 eq 0 and g11 eq 1 then
            Diff = β11 – β01; β0 = β01; β = β11;g0=g01;g=g11;
        If g01 eq 0 and g11 eq 0 then
            Diff = β – β11; β0 = β11;g0=g11;
        If diff < 3 then converge = true
     else β0 = β; β = β + Ω + Θ; Θ = Ω;
          Evaluate: Δ(β); if : Δ(β) < 0 then g = 0; else g = 1;
     EndWhile;
  β = round(β); Δ = Δ(β)
While Δ < 0
  β = β +1; Δ = Δ(β)
endWhile;
Output(β)
```

The white wine data from UCI data repository [1] was used for the experiment using mixed resampling procedure and over resampling procedure. The data was clustered into seven clusters. One of the clusters consists of only one instance and was removed. The random sample of 200 instances was selected as incident data, while the remaining 4697 instance was selected as prevalence data. The results of experimentation using the methods illustrated above for optimized mixture sample is shown in Table 1 while optimized over sampling is shown in Table 2.

Table 1. Optimised mixture sampling of incidence data

	Prevalence		Incidence		Adjusted Incidence Sample		
Cluster	n_0	%	n	%	Δ	Δ_1	(n+Δ)/n
1	675	14.3678	26	13.0	2.7356	3	1.10522
2	1227	26.1175	56	28.0	-3.7650	-4	0.93277
3	101	2.1499	5	2.5	-0.7003	-1	0.85994
4	1309	27.8629	66	33.0	-10.2742	-10	0.84433
5	948	20.1788	35	17.5	5.3576	5	1.15307
6	437	9.3018	12	6.0	6.6037	7	1.55031

Table 2. Optimised over sampling of incidence data

	Prevalence		Incidence		Adjusted Incidence Sample			
Cluster	n_o	%	n	%	Δ	Δ_1	(n+Δ)/n	%
1	675	14.3678	26	13.0	7.9080	8	1.30416	17.0
2	1227	26.1175	56	28.0	5.6373	6	1.10067	31.0
3	101	2.1499	5	2.5	0.0736	0	1.01473	2.5
4	1309	27.8629	66	33.0	-0.2435	0	0.99631	33.0
5	948	20.1788	35	17.5	12.6220	13	1.36063	24.0
6	437	9.3018	12	6.0	9.9523	10	1.82936	11.0

5 Conclusion and Future Directions

Error Matrix charts enables the visualisation of classification errors and their composition. It provides different measures from AUC in ROC or AUC in Revised risk chart. The measures from error matrix chart and its composition can be very useful for many applications especially class imbalance and rare-cases where the overall measure such as the AUC in ROC may not be a useful. Both risk chart and error matrix charts are very sensitive to base-rates which usually occur when class-imbalance data are used for modelling. Two approaches have been suggested for comparing classifier performance with risk and error matrix charts as both approaches provides different types of measures of model performance.

When evaluating model performance of prior and post interventions, it is important to make sure the same sampling strategy is applied to both prevalence and incidentence datasets, otherwise it can bias the measure of model performance. Although the sampling of incidence data can be corrected with the algorithm proposed in this paper; the severe under-sampling of incidence data still cannot be solved with any resampling methods. This is due to mainly the sample size being too small or alternatively due to data being missing in each cell. Future research of the proposed methods need to be directed towards understanding further the properties and characteristics of risk charts, error matrix charts and their comparative performances with respect to sampling for prevalence and incidence data.

Acknowledgement

The author is very grateful to Graham Williams for implementing some of the proposed earlier risk chart revision to Rattle and Warwick Graco for assistance editing this paper. No real ATO data was used in the paper due to privacy, legal and security requirements.

References

1. Cortez, P, Cerdeira, A., Almeida, F., Matos, T. and Reis, J.: Modeling wine preferences by data mining from physicochemical properties. In Decision Support Systems, Elsevier, 47(4):547-553. ISSN: 0167-9236. (2009)
2. Fawcett, T.: An introduction to ROC analysis. Pattern Recognition Letters, 27, 861-874. (2006)
3. Heckman, J. J.: "The Common Structure of Statistical Models of Truncation Sample Selection and Limited Dependent Variables and a Simple Estimator for Such Models", *Annals of Economic and Social Measurement,* 5/4, (1976)
4. Koesmarno, H.K.: Class-size percentile transformation for reconstructing a distribution function. Journal of Applied Statistics, 23 (4): 423-434. (1996)
5. Koesmarno, H.K.: Measuring classifier performance with PSF. Paper presented at ATO Analytics Community of Practice (2010).
6. Koesmarno, H.K.: Risk and Error Matrix Charts. Paper presented at Whole of Government Data Analytics Centre of Excellence, Research Week 20 November 2014.
7. Kohavi, R., Provost, F: Glossary of terms, Machine Learning, Vol. 30, No. 2/3, pp. 271-274 (1998)
8. Polo, J. L., Berzal, F., & Cubero, J. C.: Taking class importance into account. In *Hybrid Information Technology, 2006. ICHIT'06. International Conference on* (Vol. 1, pp. 1-6). IEEE (2006)
9. Shao, J. and Tu, D. The Jackknife and Bootstrap. Springer-Verlag, Inc. (1995)
10. Williams, G.J.: Data mining with Rattle and R: The Art of Excavating Data for Knowledge Discovery. Springer (2011)

Rapidly Determining the Starting Sample Size in Progressive Sampling: Mean Convergence is Sufficient

Amr ElRafey[1] and Janusz Wojtusiak[1]

[1] George Mason University
4400 University Dr, Fairfax, VA 22030, USA
aelrafey@gmu.edu

Abstract. Progressive Sampling (PS) techniques are a widely used class of sampling methods which start with an initial sample and incrementally add data points to this initial sample up to the point beyond which model accuracy no longer significantly improves. An important and ongoing area of research in PS has to do with determining the initial sample size to be used and the two main techniques found in the literature for doing so are to use meta-learning to predict the shape of the entire learning curve or to use information based measures to assess the quality of the starting sample. In the following paper we propose a simple mean convergence based approach which does not require scanning the entire data set. Our experiments on real data sets indicate that our proposed method is capable of determining an appropriate starting sample size in significantly less time.

Keywords: Progressive Sampling, Sampling, Learning Curve, Divergence, Meta-learning.

1 Introduction

Over the past decade or so, sampling techniques have received a growing interest in the data mining / machine learning community, primarily due to the rapid growth in the size of data sets [1]. It is worth noting here, that there is a distinction between the classical notion of sampling in statistics and the notion of sampling in the data mining context. In statistics, the primary goal of sampling is usually to estimate population parameters such as the mean, variance and so on, whereas in data mining applications, the primary goal of sampling is to reduce the size of the data set without losing any important patterns in the data. More specifically, in the context of data mining, given a data set $D = (x_i\ ,\ y_i)\ for\ i = 1,2,\ ,\ ,\ ,\ ,\ ,\ N$ where x_i represents the independent variables and y_i represents the dependent variable, and given a learning algorithm f with performance $Per(f)$, we wish to select a sample $S_{Optimal}$ from D such that

1. $Per\ (f(S_{Optimal})) \simeq Per\ (f(D))$
2. $|S_{Optimal}\ | \leq |S_i\ |\ \forall\ i, where\ Per(f(Si)) \simeq Per(f(D))$

where |.| refers to the cardinality of the sample. That is, we wish to find the smallest possible sample where the performance of f on the sample is approximately the same as the performance of f on the entire data set. Furthermore, we would also like to have a method $M_{Optimal}\ (D)$ for finding $S_{Optimal}$ such that

3. $T\ (M_{Optimal}\ (D)) \leq T\ (M_j\ (D))\ \forall\ j, where\ M_j\ (D) = S_{Optimal}$

where $T(.)$ refers to the computational time of a method. Specifically, we would like to have a procedure for finding $S_{Optimal}$ which requires less computational time than all other procedures.

The three main categories of sampling techniques found in the data mining literature are Random Sampling [2], Active Learning [3] and Progressive Sampling [4]. Generally speaking, random sampling methods operate by selecting an arbitrary sample of predetermined size N from the data and in so doing, they attempt to satisfy the complexity constraint outlined above without paying much attention to the first 2 requirements. Active learning techniques attempt to find the most informative observations to include in a sample of predefined size N and as such they ignore the requirement of finding the smallest possible sample and they ignore the complexity constraint.

Progressive sampling methods apply a learner f to an initial sample and then grow this initial sample up to the point beyond which there are no further improvements in $Per(f)$. As such, they appear to be the only class of sampling methods which attempt to satisfy both requirements 1 and 2 above. However, the process of applying the learning algorithm f to the progressive samples can be computationally expensive and ideally, we would want to start the PS algorithm with an initial sample $S_{Initial} \simeq S_{Optimal}$. That is, we would want the difference between our initial sample and the optimal sample to be as small as possible.

There are in the literature two main methods for determining an optimal size of $S_{Initial}$. The first of these methods involves using meta-learning to predict the shape of the learning curve usually based on the first few iterations of PS [5]. The problem with this method, is that in-order to improve the prediction, a greater number of iterations are needed. The second method is the one proposed by Gu et al. which uses information divergence to compare the progressive samples to the entire data set [6]. This method requires scanning the entire data set to generate descriptive statistics in-order to carry out the comparisons with progressive samples and as such may be infeasible with extremely large data sets.

We propose here a simple and somewhat obvious technique for determining an appropriate $S_{Initial}$. Instead of comparing the progressive samples to the entire data set we compare the means of each of the k features of each sample S_i to the means of the

k features of the sample immediately preceding it S_{i-1} and terminate the procedure once the difference between the successive means has converged. Our experiments with publicly available data sets indicate that our proposed technique achieves a significant reduction in the time required to determine the size of the initial sample.

This paper is structured as follows, firstly we provide an overview the PS algorithm along with detailed explanations of both the information divergence technique and the meta-learning techniques found in the literature. We then outline our proposed technique followed by results on real data. We conclude this paper with a summary of our findings and a conclusion.

2 Background and Related Work

2.1 Progressive Sampling

The central theme of PS is the learning curve, depicted in Fig. 1) below. Essentially, this curve expresses an expectation that, for any data set D and any classifier f, as the sample size grows, so too will the performance $Per(f)$ of f trained on this sample. This improvement in performance however, slows down and eventually plateaus once the sample exceeds a certain size. As such the standard PS algorithm usually follows the following steps

Algorithm 1: Standard Progressive Sampling

1. *Select an initial sample $S_{Initial}$ (usually the first n observations in a given data set)*
2. *Train a classifier on this initial sample ($S_{Initial}$) and calculate an initial performance $Per_{Initial}$ ($f(S_{Initial})$) (usually the performance of f will be classifier accuracy on a test data set)*
3. *Add n data points to $S_{Initial}$ and calculate $Per_{Initial+n}$ ($f(S_{Initial+n})$)*
4. *Test for convergence in performance*
5. *While convergence not detected*
   Repeat steps 3 and 4
6. *Return $S_{Optimal}$*

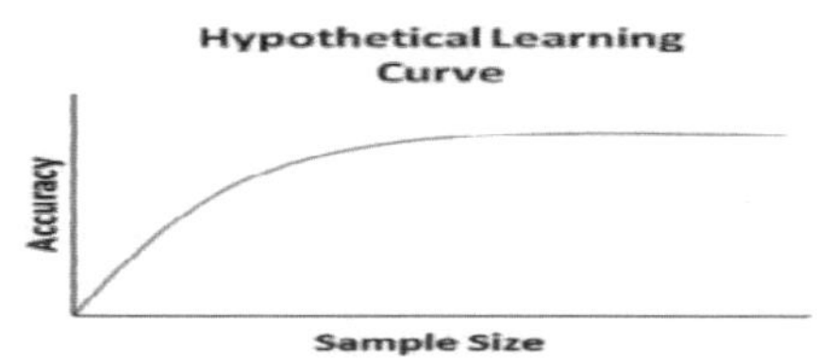

Fig. 1. A hypothetical learning curve

Notwithstanding the apparent simplicity of this technique, it nonetheless attempts to satisfy the first 2 sampling requirements outlined in the introduction by only adding new points at each iteration if convergence has not yet been detected.

A number of methods have been proposed in the literature for adding data points to successive samples (step 3), including arithmetic sampling [1], geometric sampling [1] and progressive batch mode uncertainty sampling [7]. Furthermore, a number of methods have been proposed for testing for convergence (step 4) including linear regression with local sampling [8] and adaptive sampling using Chebyshev bounds [9]. All of these refinements have been attempts at ensuring that the algorithm satisfies the first 2 sampling requirements we set out in the introduction.

The focus of this paper is step 1 in the algorithm above, namely, the selection of an initial sample $S_{Initial}$. To clarify the importance of this step, let us consider a hypothetical example in which we have a data set with N = 20,000,000 observations and let us suppose that $S_{Optimal} \simeq$ 10,000,000. Suppose further that we begin with $S_{Initial}$ = 200,000 and we decide to add 200,000 data points at each iteration of the PS algorithm (that is, we have decided to simply add 1% of the data at each iteration). Finally, suppose that our classifier has complexity $O(n3)$. In this example, a simple calculation reveals that the time required to execute the PS algorithm and determine $S_{Optimal}$ is actually greater than the time required to run the classifier on the entire data set. We have also completely ignored the time required to determine the classifier performance on each of the samples, which would have required a substantial amount of time. If, as is often the case, our performance measure is the area under the curve (AUC) statistic, then the complexity of calculating AUC is $O(n \log(n))$ [13] and depending on the size of the validation set, this could have required a significant amount of time.

The hypothetical example above serves to demonstrate the difficulties of generating a learning curve for a specific classifier on large data sets. In many situations, it may simply be infeasible to execute the PS algorithm given the size of the data set. Alternatively, we may be tempted to add a very large number of observations at each iteration of PS in order to reduce the time required to find $S_{Optimal}$. To clarify, we had chosen to add on 1% of the data set at each iteration in the example above, but we could have chosen to add on, for example, 5% or we could have used a geometric progression, whereby the number of points being added at each iteration grows geometrically. These solutions may save us some time, but they run of the risk of overshooting $S_{Optimal}$ resulting in a final sample which may be much larger than necessary. As such, it is necessary to have some method of rapidly determining an appropriate starting sample $S_{Initial}$.

2.2 Methods for Finding $S_{Initial}$

Meta Learning Techniques

The first and more recently developed group of methods found in the literature for determining OSS involve using the n first iterations of PS to predict the shape of the learning curve [10]. These techniques were proposed as a way to determine the total sample size required $s_{Optimal}$ and not just the initial sample size $S_{Initial}$ furthermore they were proposed as a method to allow for rapid comparison of different learning algorithms on large data sets [10]. The main idea here is to fit a nonlinear inverse-law power model of the form

$$Acc\big(f(S_i)\big) = \alpha + \beta N_{S_i}^{-\gamma} \quad (1)$$

where $Acc\big(f(S_i)\big)$ represents the accuracy of the classifier on the sample S_i and the parameters α, β and γ represent the minimum accuracy achievable on the data set D, the scale and the learning rate respectively. One major drawback of this technique is that, generally speaking, in order to better predict the shape of the learning curve a large number of iterations of PS are needed. To tackle this issue, Figueroa et al. [5] proposed a weighted version of the model above, whereby the sample sizes were used as weights in the non-linear regression model. However, and notwithstanding the improvements in predictive accuracy, their technique still required a relatively large number of data points in-order to predict the learning curve with satisfactory accuracy.

Information Based Technique

In their paper titled Efficiently determining the starting sample size for progressive sampling [6] authors Gu et al. argue that larger samples will resemble the entire data set more so than the smaller samples. To measure resemblance, the authors make use of Kullback's information measure [11], which is usually referred to as divergence. Divergence is a statistical concept used to express the level of difficulty of discriminating between two competing hypothesis H_1 and H_2 regarding the underlying distribution of a random variable X. To clarify, suppose that we sample a single observation x from variable X and suppose further that there are 2 possible underlying probability density functions which may have generated x , $f_1(x)$, $f_2(x)$ representing our two competing hypothesis H_1 and H_2. The information divergence of this observation x is given by

$$J(1,2) = \int \big(f_1(x) - f_2(x)\big) \log \frac{f_1(x)}{f_2(x)} \quad (2)$$

where J (1,2) above quantifies the difficulty of discriminating between H_1 and H_2. In the event that the random variable X is multinomial with c categories, the 2 competing hypothesis would be that X belongs to population 1 p_{1_j} or X belongs to population 2 p_{2_j} where $j = 1,2, \dots, c$. In this case, information divergence is given by

$$J(1,2) = \sum_{j=1}^{c} \left(p_{1_j} - p_{2_j}\right) \log \frac{p_{1_j}}{p_{2_j}} \quad (3)$$

The definitions above naturally extend to data sets with k multinomial features. Given a data set D and a sample S the information divergence between D and S for each feature k with c categories is given by

$$J(D,S) = \sum_{j=1}^{c} \left(p_{D_j} - p_{S_j}\right) \log \frac{p_{D_j}}{p_{S_j}} \quad (4)$$

and the averaged information divergence between D and S for all features k is then

$$J(D,S) = \sum_{i=1}^{k} J_k(D,S) \quad (5)$$

Finally, the authors define a measure of sample quality Q which is given by

$$Q(S) = \exp(-J(D,S)) \quad (6)$$

The above measure of sample quality is applied to data sets with continuous features k by calculating the histograms of each the continuous features and then treating each bin as a categorical value. Gu et al. then outlined an algorithm for finding $S_{Initial}$ which essentially involved calculating descriptive statistics for the entire data set D then calculating sample quality S_i for each of the successive samples until convergence of the quality measures is detected.

The authors tested out their proposed algorithm on four publicly available data sets and their results indicated that in some cases the initial sample returned by their method was almost equal to, that is, the sample size returned was the size at which PS detected convergence. However, according to the results presented in their paper, the time required to find , was in many cases, only a marginal improvement on the time required for PS to converge without $S_{Initial}$ and this is not surprising given the number of computations required by their algorithm.

3 Proposed Technique

As explained earlier, Gu et al.'s technique requires calculating descriptive statistics of the entire data set and in cases where the data set is extremely large, this may be computationally expensive. We propose here a technique which does not rely on the distribution of the entire data set D but instead on the means of the successive samples S_i,S_(i+1),.....,D. We appeal to the law of large numbers [12] which states that for independent and identically distributed variables $X_1, X_2, \ldots$, with $E(X_1) = E(X_2) = \cdots \ldots, = u$, the sample average of n such variables $\overline{X_n} = \frac{1}{n}(X_1 + X_2 + \cdots \ldots, X_n)$ converges almost surely to the expected value u. In the context of a hypothetical data set D with K features, for each feature, we know a priori that the strong law of large numbers holds and implies that

$$\overline{X_{n_k}} \overset{a.s}{-} u_k \quad as\, n \to \infty \tag{7}$$

meaning that the averages of the successive samples converge almost surely to the average of the entire data set. Furthermore, a necessary and sufficient condition of almost sure convergence is that

$$P(|\overline{X_{n_k}} - \overline{X_{n-1_k}}| > \varepsilon) \to 0 \quad as\, n \to \infty \tag{8}$$

suggesting the terms of the sequence $\overline{X_{n_k}}, \overline{X_{n+1_k}}, \ldots$, grow arbitrarily closer to one another. This implies that that it would be sufficient to simply compare the averages of the successive samples to each other instead of comparing them to the entire data set, in-order to ascertain whether mean convergence has occurred or not. We therefore propose the following method for determining an appropriate size for $S_{Initial}$. For each sample S_i, we calculate the mean of each of the k features and then calculate

$$C_{S_i} = \sum_{j=1}^{k} \frac{|\overline{X_{i_j}} - \overline{X_{i-1_j}}|}{\overline{X_{i-1_j}}} \tag{9}$$

representing the sum of the absolute percentage differences in the means for each of the k features from the preceding sample S_{i-1}. The reason why we propose using absolute percentage differences as opposed to absolute differences is due to the fact that some features will have values that are substantially larger than others and therefore, using percentage differences allows us to overcome this issue. As such, our proposed technique involves producing a mean difference curve as demonstrated in Fig. 2 below and testing for convergence to determine the size of S_i.

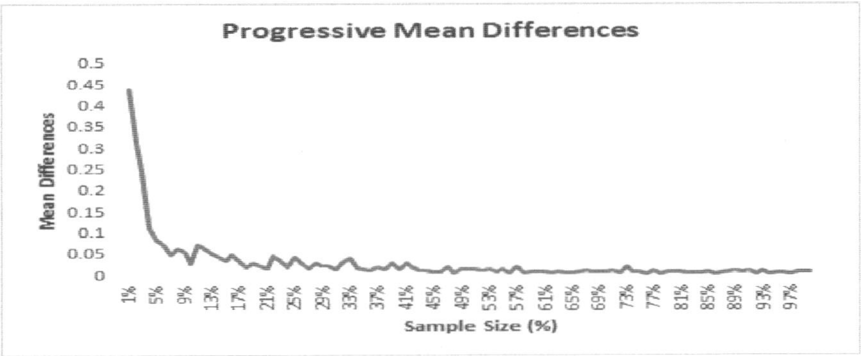

Fig. 2. Plot of successive $C_{S_i}'s$ on a real data set.

4 Results on Real Data

We tested out our proposed technique on 7 publicly available datasets available on the UCI and Kaggle repositories (Credit Card Fraud Detection [14] , Rain In Australia [15], Diabetes for 130 US-hospitals [16] , Poker Hand [17] , Covertype [17] , Census Income KDD [17] and Dota2 Games Results [17]). For each data set, we started with a sample of 1%, calculated the means for this sample then proceeded to iteratively add an additional 1% and calculate the new means along with C_{S_i} from expression (9) above. Once we had reached a sample of 10%, we started to test for convergence. Specifically, at each iteration, we ran an ordinary least squares regression of the last 10 $C_{S_i}'s$ on the numbers {1: 10} and recorded the confidence intervals of the regression coefficient. If the confidence interval crossed 0, then convergence had been achieved and we reported the size of this sample as $S_{Initial}$ along with the time required to reach convergence.

We further tried the information divergence measure proposed by Gu et al. For each data set, we firstly calculated the statistics of the entire set and then starting with a sample of 1% we calculated the quality of the sample Q_{S_i} from expression (6) above and then iteratively added 1% of the data to the sample and calculated an updated quality measure. Once we reached a sample of 10%, we started testing for convergence in exactly the same way we did for our mean convergence technique. We again recorded the sample size at which convergence was achieved along with the time required to execute this technique on the data.

Finally, for each data set we used standard PS to determine. Starting again with 1% of the data, we applied a classification algorithm to this sample and then recorded it's AUC statistic for predicting a testing data set if the outcome variable was binary or classification accuracy if the outcome variable had more than 2 categories. We then proceeded to add an additional 1% to this data and reapplying the classifier. Convergence was tested for in the exactly the same way as was done for the previous 2 properties exhibited by these materials are dictated by the concentration, type and arrangement of atoms in the material. A novel and more efficient algorithm to study and analyze the arrangement of atoms in a given alloy is proposed in this study. Analysis of these microstructures in the materials can aid material scientists in identifying potential vulnerabilities in existing materials, and developing better new materials.

Alloys are traditionally developed by mixing small quantities of metals or other elements in a primary metal lattice. The primary element is called the solvent, and the other elements form the solutes in the solid state solution. The arrangement of atoms in these materials under different conditions can significantly alter the physical and functional properties of the material. Extreme temperature and pressure conditions can cause clustering tendencies in the solute atoms in some materials leading to a non homogeneous distribution which can affect their mechanical properties. The change in the distribution of Nickel atoms in the alloy used in nuclear reactor systems after prolonged use, may lead to catastrophic failures [2]. Compositional analyses for material samples are currently being conducted by using a technique called Atom Probe Tomography (APT). An Atom Probe is an instrument that probes through the surface of an element by removing layers of atoms from the specimen through successive evaporation[3]. Computational methods are then used to build a three dimensional reconstruction of the sample prior to its evaporation, providing atomic scale information on the structure of a sample and the composition of atoms in those structures. The instrument is equipped with a software system to study frequency distributions of different elements in the sample. The frequency distribution analysis is conducted by a technique called voxelization[5]. The material is divided into cubic blocks or voxels with equal atoms or volume, and these voxels or bins are used to create the histogram plots. A new shape invariant binning algorithm, the Uniform Partitioning Algorithm is proposed in this paper. This algorithm partitions the data into bins based on atomic distances instead of shape or volume restrictions, hence it is better at detecting spatial correlations. Synthetic datasets with known heterogeneous and homogeneous distributions were created to validate the distributions detected by the binning algorithm. Existence of solute clusters, which are regions in the material with a significantly higher number of solute atoms than the number in a similar region in a homogeneous solution, leads to heterogeneities in the material. Two novel methods to create realistic solute clusters in the synthetic alloy dataset are also presented. These techniques simulate the formation of solute clusters in the material.

Bin size and the method of constructing the bins are crucial factors that affect the obtained frequency distributions. We compare the proposed algorithm with the voxelization and spherical (nearest-neighbor) binning techniques on different types of distributions and varying bin sizes, and show that it is more efficient and scalable than the other two techniques.

Existing statistical tools used for analyzing materials are introduced in the next section. The Uniform Partitioning Algorithm is presented in the Methodology section along with the the creation of synthetic homogeneous and heterogeneous methods. We also randomly assigned one of 3 classifiers, Logistic Regression (LR), C5.0 decision trees or Random Forests classifier (RF) to each data set.

As such, for each of the data sets we used, we reported the execution time and the size of the $S_{Initial}$ returned by each technique along with the size of $S_{Optimal}$ using PS. Our results are presented in Table 1. below and they clearly indicate that not only is our proposed technique significantly faster, but that the initial samples returned by it are closer to $S_{Optimal}$ than the information based technique.

To begin with, the execution time of our proposed technique averaged 8.42 seconds per data set whereas the information based technique averaged 59.8 seconds per data set, a result which is barely surprising considering the simplicity of our proposed method. More interestingly however, our technique produced an $S_{Initial}$ which deviated from the PS $S_{Optimal}$ by only 4% per data set. On the other hand, the information divergence technique produced an $S_{Initial}$ which, on average deviated by 9% per data set from the PS $S_{Optimal}$.

5 Conclusion

In the previous sections, we have demonstrated how the use of an exceedingly simple mean convergence technique can be used to rapidly and effectively determine the size of an appropriate initial sample for progressive sampling. Our proposed method does not require scanning the entire data set, nor does it require performing any kind of complex calculations on the successive samples. One objection to our proposed method is that it neglects many of the statistical properties of each of the k features of the data such as the variance, kurtosis and correlation with other features and focuses solely on the mean of each feature. However, what we are trying to achieve is to rapidly find an appropriate starting sample which we can train a classifier on and obtain results which are not far from those which would be obtained using $S_{Optimal}$. As demonstrated experimentally, our proposed method is capable of achieving this. Furthermore, and while it is true that the information divergence measure proposed by Gu et al. is more statistically sound, it may, in many cases, be unnecessary. This is due to that fact that a number of features may not actually add much predictive power to our classifier and yet the information divergence technique would expend a considerable amount of time in calculating detailed statistics for those features and would converge much later than necessary as we suspect may have been happening in our experiments above. We therefore conclude that the technique we propose here, while being crude, will in many cases be sufficient.

Table 1. Results on real data sets.

Data Set / Number of Independent Variables / Classifier	$S_{Initial}$ **returned using Mean Convergence Technique**	$S_{Initial}$ **returned using Information measure**	$S_{Optimal}$ **returned using Progressive Sampling**
Credit Card Fraud Detection / 29 / Logistic Regression	11% (5 secs)	11% (87 secs)	11%
Rain In Australia / 22 /Logistic Regression	21% (2 secs)	13% (15 secs)	33%
Diabetes – USA 130 Hospitals / 44 / Logistic Regression	26% (4 secs)	33% (24 secs)	19%
Poker Hand / 10 / C50	28% (13 secs)	25% (53 secs)	30%
Covertype / 54 / C50	16% (22 secs)	23% (142 secs)	16%
Census – Income / 41 / C50	19% (9 secs)	26% (82)	22%
Dota2 Games Results / 117 / Random Forests	11% (4 secs)	26% (16 secs)	12%

References

1. ElRafey, Amr, and Janusz Wojtusiak. "Recent advances in scaling-down sampling methods in machine learning." *Wiley Interdisciplinary Reviews: Computational Statistics* 9, no. 6 (2017): e1414
2. L. Huan and H. Motoda, "Instance selection and construction for data mining," Springer Science & Business Media, vol. 608, 2013.
3. B. Settles, 2012, "Active learning," Synth Lect Artif Intell Mach Learn, vol. 6, no. 1, pp. 1–114.
4. C. Meek, B. Theisson, and D. Heckerrnan, "The learning-curve sampling method applied to model- based clustering," The Journal of Machine Learning Research, 2002.

5. Figueroa, Rosa L., Qing Zeng-Treitler, Sasikiran Kandula, and Long H. Ngo. "Predicting sample size required for classification performance." *BMC medical informatics and decision making* 12, no. 1 (2012): 8.
6. Gu, Baohua, Bing Liu, Feifang Hu, and Huan Liu. "Efficiently determining the starting sample size for progressive sampling." In *European Conference on Machine Learning*, pp. 192-202. Springer, Berlin, Heidelberg, 2001.
7. ElRafey, Amr, and Janusz Wojtusiak. "A Hybrid Active Learning and Progressive Sampling Algorithm." *International Journal of Machine Learning and Computing* 8, no. 5 (2018).
8. P. Foster, D. Jensen, and T. Oates. "Efficient progressive sampling," in Proc. the Fifth ACM SIGKDD International Conference on Knowledge Discovery and Data Mining, ACM, 1999, pp. 23-32.
9. Satyanarayana, Ashwin. "Intelligent sampling for big data using bootstrap sampling and chebyshev inequality." In *Electrical and Computer Engineering (CCECE), 2014 IEEE 27th Canadian Conference on*, pp. 1-6. IEEE, 2014.
10. Mukherjee, Sayan, Pablo Tamayo, Simon Rogers, Ryan Rifkin, Anna Engle, Colin Campbell, Todd R. Golub, and Jill P. Mesirov. "Estimating dataset size requirements for classifying DNA microarray data." *Journal of computational biology* 10, no. 2 (2003): 119-142.
11. Kullback, Solomon. *Information theory and statistics*. Courier Corporation, 1997.
12. Loeve, M. "Probability theory–Graduate texts in mathematics." (1978).
13. Calders, Toon, and Szymon Jaroszewicz. "Efficient AUC optimization for classification." In *European Conference on Principles of Data Mining and Knowledge Discovery*, pp. 42-53. Springer, Berlin, Heidelberg, 2007.
14. Andrea Dal Pozzolo, Olivier Caelen, Reid A. Johnson and Gianluca Bontempi. Calibrating Probability with Undersampling for Unbalanced Classification. In Symposium on Computational Intelligence and Data Mining (CIDM), IEEE, 2015
15. http://www.bom.gov.au/clmate/dwo/ and http://www.bom.gov.au/climate/data.
16. Beata Strack, Jonathan P. DeShazo, Chris Gennings, Juan L. Olmo, Sebastian Ventura, Krzysztof J. Cios, and John N. Clore, "Impact of HbA1c Measurement on Hospital Readmission Rates: Analysis of 70,000 Clinical Database Patient Records," BioMed Research International, vol. 2014, Article ID 781670, 11 pages, 2014.
17. Dua, D. and Karra Taniskidou, E. (2017). UCI Machine Learning Repository [http://archive.ics.uci.edu/ml]. Irvine, CA: University of California, School of Information and Computer Science.

Series of Optimized Predictive Models for Forecast of Global Waste Water Treatment Plant Performance

Bharat B. Gulyani[1]and Arshia Fathima[2]

[1]Department of Chemical Engineering, BITS Pilani Dubai Campus, Dubai 345055, UAE.
gulyani@dubai.bits-pilani.ac.in
[2]Independent Researcher, Riyadh, KSA (Alumna BITS Pilani Dubai Campus).
f2009053@dubai.bits-pilani.ac.in

Abstract. The process control of wastewater treatment plants using data analytics can improve the process efficiency and economics. Machine-learning models such as Neural Network models (ANN) were developed for WWTP process control. Ensemble models such as bagging and rotation forest have shown to be more stable than base classifier alone (like ANN) with lower tendency for overfitting. However, these models have not been used widely to predict wastewater treatment plant performance. This paper highlights a series of predictive models to provide forecasts on global plant performance. The predictive models will be a mixture of data mining models including bagging, ANN or SVM. The prediction of global plant performance employs the combination of individual unit performance forecasts. Thereby the global model will be providing a feedback control model based on current input quality parameters and estimated performances.

Keywords: Ensemble model, Wastewater treatment, Plant performance prediction, Process control.

1 Introduction

Water treatment plants are now becoming an integral part of the economy in order to meet the growing water demands and develop cities sustainably. The main objectives of research on water treatment plants includes boosting the efficiency in a sustainable manner and lowering the costs for the plant. A control system based on artificial intelligence will be able to adapting to variable influent quality, thereby lowering of operating costs for WWTP with consistent effluent standards. The benefits of using AI based control system were shown by a study that implemented a fuzzy neural control to predict aeration performance in an Aerated Submerged Biofilm Wastewater Treatment Process. The savings on operating costs after implementing the AI controller was found to be 33%. The controller was reliable and was easy to integrate into the global control system [1] thereby increasing process control efficiency.

Many AI models have been developed that either predict process variables such as dissolved oxygen, COD (chemical oxygen demand), BOD (biological oxygen demand), SS (suspended solids) [2], effluent quality [3–5]. AI based controls have been used to run processes such as coagulation [6], dissolved oxygen control [7–9] or nutrient control for biological treatment process [10]. However, there have been few such models that have predicted performance of the plant [11, 12] or process efficiency [13] and thereby integrated it for overall plant process control.

The development of artificial intelligence systems for water treatment control has been evolving from predicting variables or effluent quality to controlling a process via adaptive sensors. Online and real-time analysis of water treatment process conditions including biological treatment processes is possible due to instrumentation advances and "soft sensors" based on easy-to-measure process/secondary variables. The "soft sensors" are mathematical models that offer inexpensive ways to predict variables and monitor processes/instruments. The soft sensors can be based on either first principles or be data-driven. The most popular modelling methods were multivariate statistical methods based on PLS and ANN including FFNN (Feed-Forward Neural Networks) and Fuzzy ANN. Some other models used for prediction of the process variables include SOM (Self Organizing Maps), ANFIS (Adaptive Neuro Fuzzy Inference System) and hybrid models such as PCA-FFN, Fuzzy PLS or NN-PLS. These methods were applied on various processes such as ASP (Activated Sludge Process), MBR (Membrane Bioreactors) etc., and often were found to predict the output variables with good accuracy even at pilot scale plants. The soft sensors also showed good capacity to monitor WWTPs and enabled process control through early fault detection and large process changes/disturbances [2].

Implementation of soft sensor control system in real WWTP face some challenges including unfamiliarity of engineers with AI models, risk of overfitting, data interpretability and noisy data [2]. Ensemble methods solve these challenges as highlighted in this paper. The work focusses on performance modelling based on influent and effluent BOD as municipal wastewater plants aim to decrease effluent BOD levels before discharge [2]. The paper also highlights development of a series of prediction models built to use predicted data from its predecessors as inputs. The objective of these models is to predict performance on local (unit operation) level and use these predictions as inputs for global level model in an attempt to automate the process control of the entire plant.

2 Materials and Methods

2.1 Dataset Pre-processing

The dataset from UCI Repository [14]contained data attributes obtained via daily measurement using sensors for the primary and secondary settlers in the plant during the years 1990-91. The dataset had 38 attributes in addition to the date of measurement. For our purpose, an attribute called "number of days in operation" was introduced by converting the dates with the earliest date considered as Day 1 (i.e. 1 Jan

1990 as Day 1). This was done to model the performance with respect to time (in days) to account for measurements that were missing in the time series. The dataset had 527 instances and with elimination of data rows with missing values resulted in 380 instances (72% of the dataset). The list of attributes includes pH, conductivity, Biochemical Oxygen Demand (BOD), suspended solids (SS), sediments, volatile suspended solids, local performance of the settlers based on input BOD and the global performance of the plant based on the input BOD.

As the BOD measurements in the dataset were found using sensors, these attributes were used for the model development. In actual implementation, these parameters can also be predicted/modelled based on other water quality measurements [2].This predicted BOD data will be used as inputs in the subsequent prediction models. Other pre-processing such as sample selection to discard outliers or data reconciliation (fixing errors) [2] was not performed as the dataset had only 380 instances in comparison to the large data generated from an actual WWTP.

2.2 Model Performance Measures

The performance measures used in the present study were mostly based on minimizing residuals and are detailed below:

1. Root Mean Squared Error (RMSE): It is calculated by the following formula:

$$RMSE = \sqrt{\sum_{i=1}^{N} \frac{(p_i - a_i)^2}{N}} \tag{1}$$

where p_i is the predicted value for the ith instance, a_i is the actual value for the ith instance and N is the total number of instances in the given dataset. The smaller the RMSE, the better the performance of the model[15]. The RMSE tends to have a bias towards larger events[16], so other performance measures need to be evaluated for model selection. RMSE values less than half the standard deviation of measured data can be considered low[17].

2. Mean Absolute Error (MAE): This is the average of the absolute values of the difference between the predicted and actual values. It reduces the bias towards large events unlike RMSE. The equation for MAE [16] is:

$$MAE = \frac{1}{N} \sum_{i=1}^{N} |p_i - a_i| \tag{2}$$

where p_i is the predicted value for the ith instance, a_i is the actual value for the ith instance and N is the total number of instances in the given data set. MAE values less than half the standard deviation of measured data can be considered low [17].

3. Relative Absolute Error (RAE): It is the relative equivalent of MAE [15] and is given by:

$$RAE = \frac{\sum_{i=1}^{N} |p_i - a_i|}{\sum_{i=1}^{N} |a_i - \bar{a}|} \tag{3}$$

where p_i is the predicted value for the ith instance, a_i is the actual value for the ith instance $\bar{a}$is the mean of the actual values and N is the total number of instances in the given data set.

4. Correlation Coefficient (R): It measures the degree of linear relation between two variables. A correlation coefficient of 0 implies no correlation between variables while a value of 1 implies perfect correlation. The correlation coefficient between actual and predicted variables enables us to get the accuracy of the prediction model[15]. Hence it is also known as prediction efficiency [17]. This measure is calculated by [15]:

$$R = \frac{S_{pa}}{\sqrt{S_p S_a}} \tag{4}$$

where$\bar{a}$ and $\bar{p}$ are the averages respectively, and

$$S_{pa} = \frac{\sum_{i=1}^{N} (p_i - \bar{p})(a_i - \bar{a})}{(N-1)}$$

$$S_p = \frac{\sum_{i=1}^{N} (p_i - \bar{p})^2}{N-1}$$

$$S_a = \frac{\sum_{i=1}^{N} (a_i - \bar{a})^2}{N-1}$$

5. Nash – Sutcliffe Efficiency (NSE): The NSE is a normalized statistic that gives the comparison between residual variance and measured data variance. With an optimal value of 1 for model that fits data perfectly, NSE also gives a mathematical value for the scatterplot for observed vs predicted data line that fits the 1:1 line. For NSE values ≤ 0, the mean observed value will be a better predictor that the given model predictions. The formula to compute NSE[17] is:

$$NSE = 1 - \left[\frac{\sum_{i=1}^{N} \left(Y_i^{obs} - Y_i^{pred}\right)^2}{\sum_{i=1}^{N} \left(Y_i^{obs} - Y^{mean}\right)^2}\right] \tag{5}$$

whereN is the total number of observations; Y_i^{obs} is the i[th] observation, Y_i^{pred} is the i[th]predicted value and Y^{mean} is the mean of observed data for the attribute being forecasted.

6. RSR:The RMSE – Standard Deviation Ratio or RSR, is a model evaluation statistic to standardize RMSE using observations' standard deviation. An optimal value of 0 indicates a perfect model. The RSR is calculated by[17]:

$$RSR = \frac{RMSE}{STDev_{obs}} = \frac{\sqrt{\sum_{i=1}^{N}\left(Y_i^{obs} - Y_i^{pred}\right)^2}}{\sqrt{\sum_{i=1}^{N}\left(Y_i^{obs} - Y^{mean}\right)^2}} \quad (6)$$

3 Results and Discussion

The data mining models were developed using the open source software Waikato Environment for Knowledge Analysis (Weka) [18]. Here, 10-fold cross validation was used for model development. Acceptable results were obtained without parameter tuning and default model parameters defined in Weka were used. The only parameter changed was for kernel type in SVM. The kernel was changed from polykernel (default) to normalized polykernel as it was found to enhance performance in all models except for global model performance. Individual prediction models were built from these data mining algorithms to predict the primary and secondary settler performance and the global plant performance. The details on the attributes used for input and output are given in the appendixes. The results obtained for the above mentioned models are discussed below.

In continuation of our previous work, dimensionality reduction was attempted to reduce the number of attributes used as inputs and simplify the model development. The variable selection is crucial as it affects the model output. Most commonly used techniques include filtering, wrapping and embedded methods. Filters and wrappers select variables by evaluating and ranking them on their significance. Due to complexity of criteria search schemes employed for feature selection when there are large number of inputs, feature extraction is used to reduce the dimensionality by producing small combinations of original variables. These methods include Principal Component Analysis (PCA) and Partial Least Squares (PLS). Further information on application of such techniques can be found in the reference [2].

Feature selection was applied using in-built Weka algorithms including "WrapperSubsetEval" (selection based on cross-validation) and "CfsSubsetEval" (selection based on low intercorrelation and high correlation with output). However, the models built after feature selection had low R^2 (<0.5) and high values for other error statistics as compared to models without feature selection. Dimensionality reduction using feature extraction, in particular Principal Component Analysis (PCA), was also tested to improve model performance. In contrast, models with PCA extracted attributes had lower performance compared to the models without PCA extracted attributes possibly due to loss of correlated data after feature selection. Therefore, for the model development, the input attributes were manually selected based on their correlation with the output attribute and limited to local variables for the specific unit operation. The results for the models developed for individual units are discussed below.

3.1 Model Selection for Primary Settler Performance Forecast

The primary settler performance based on BOD (attribute # 30) was modelled using 8 local attributes as follows:

1. Input pH (attribute #10)
2. Input BOD (attribute #11)
3. Input SS (attribute #12)
4. Input VSS (attribute #13)
5. Input sediments (attribute #14)
6. Input conductivity (attribute #15)
7. Input BOD to secondary settler (attribute #17) equal to output BOD from primary settler
8. Number of days in operation

It was observed that by including the input flow to the plant (attribute # 1), the model performance improves slightly (RMSE reduces by 0.3) but not significantly. Therefore, by including flow as an input attribute, we can have a good process control without affecting model performance. Similarly, excluding the suspended solids and sediments attributes only improves model performance for ANN but has no significant effect for other models. Overall, bagging with ANN as base learner gives the best prediction performance as shown in Table 1. The ensemble bagging improved the ANN model by reducing error by 50% as depicted in Figure 1.

A simple model built with linear regression had $R^2 = 0.94$ with RMSE = 4.92 and RAE =29.4%. The linear regression in WEKA, by default, uses Akaike criterion for attribute selection (M5 and Greedy method) and eliminates collinear attributes. The models obtained using both attribute selection methods were same and the equation from the linear regression was derived by equation (7):

$$PerformancePrimarySettlerBO(\#30)=1.97*InputpH(\#10)+0.24*InputBOD(\#11)+0.004*InputSS(\#12)-0.446*InputBOD(\#17)+25.98 \quad (7)$$

In comparison to the other models, this model did not have acceptable error and bagging did not improve the model performance.

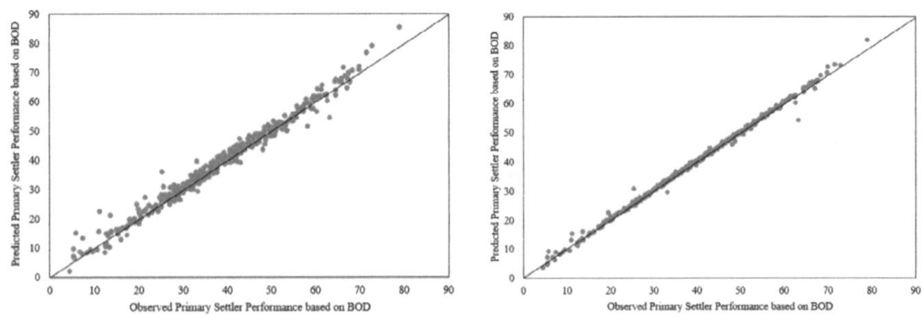

Fig. 1. Scatterplot for predicted vs observed primary settler performance based on BOD for models – ANN (left)and Bagging with ANN (right)

Table 1. Model Comparison for Prediction of Primary Settler Performance based on Input BOD (attribute # 30)

Model	R	MAE	RMSE	RSR	NSE	RAE(%)
ANN	0.99	1.52	2.14	0.14	0.98	12.72
SVM (normalized polykernel)	0.98	1.89	2.87	0.19	0.96	15.74
SVM (polykernel)	0.94	3.31	5.11	0.34	0.88	27.64
Bagging with ANN (10 iterations)	0.99	0.45	0.87	0.06	0.99	3.76
Bagging with SVM (10 iterations)	0.98	1.90	2.90	0.19	0.96	15.88
Additive Regression (ANN)	0.99	0.90	1.40	0.09	0.99	7.51
Additive Regression (SVM)	0.99	1.56	2.45	0.16	0.97	12.89

3.2 Model Selection for Secondary Settler Performance Forecast

The secondary settler performance based on BOD (attribute # 33) was modelled using 8 local attributes as follows:

1. Input pH (attribute #16)
2. Input BOD (attribute #17)
3. Input SS (attribute #19)
4. Input VSS (attribute #20)
5. Input sediments (attribute #21)
6. Input conductivity (attribute #22)
7. Output BOD (attribute #24)
8. Number of days in operation

It was observed that by including the input flow to the plant (attribute # 1), the model performance decreases slightly (RMSE increases by 0.01) but not significantly. Similarly, excluding the suspended solids and sediments attributes reduces model performance (increases the error by 3%). By incorporating these parameters, process control of secondary settler as well as previous unit operations can also be enhanced. Overall, bagging with ANN as base learner gives stable prediction performance as shown in Table 2 and Figure 2 as it improves the ANN model by reducing error by 50%.

A simple model built with linear regression had $R^2 = 0.92$ with RMSE = 2.9 and RAE =32.8%. Using the default parameter setting, the models obtained was by equation (8):

$$PerformanceSecondarySettlerBOD\,(\#33) = 0.13 * InputBOD(\#17) - 0.81 * InputSediments(\#21) - 0.7 * OutputBOD(\#24) + 80.04 \quad (8)$$

Similar to the linear regression model for primary settler, this model also did not have acceptable error and bagging did not improve the model performance.

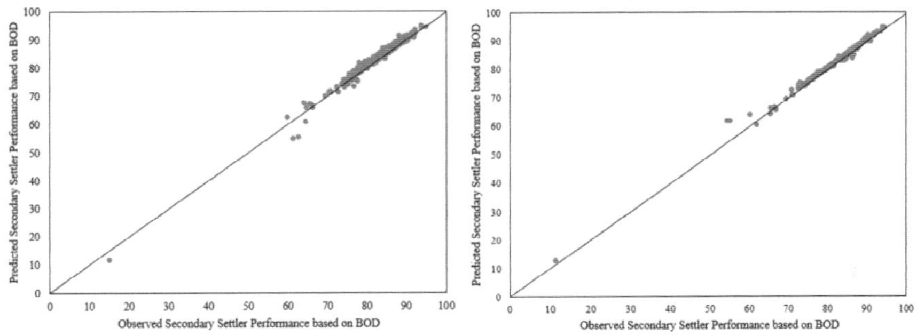

Fig. 2. Scatterplot for predicted vs observed secondary settler performance based on BOD for models - ANN (left) and Bagging with ANN (right)

Table 2. Model Comparison for Prediction of Secondary Settler Performance based on Input BOD (attribute # 33)

Model	R	MAE	RMSE	RSR	NSE	RAE(%)
ANN	0.99	0.58	0.98	0.14	0.98	12.81
SVM (normalized polykernel)	0.93	0.76	2.79	0.40	0.84	16.74
SVM (polykernel)	0.92	1.24	2.84	0.41	0.83	27.23
Bagging with ANN (10 iterations)	0.99	0.28	0.66	0.10	0.99	6.16
Bagging with SVM (10 iterations)	0.93	0.73	2.84	0.41	0.83	15.99
Additive Regression (ANN)	0.99	0.48	0.87	0.13	0.98	10.42
Additive Regression (SVM)	0.95	0.66	2.40	0.35	0.88	14.52

3.3 Model Selection for Global Plant Performance Forecast

The global performance based on BOD (attribute # 35) was modelled using 3 global attributes and 2 local performance attributes as follows:

1. Input flow to plant (attribute #1)
2. Input BOD to the plant (attribute #4)
3. Output BOD (attribute #24)
4. Performance of Primary Settler based on input BOD (attribute #30)
5. Performance of Secondary Settler based on input BOD (attribute #33)
6. Number of days in operation

Models were first built using all available global plant attributes including input conductivity, pH, SS, VSS, BOD, and sediments to the plant. However, as most of these variables are dependent on settler's variables as well, these global attributes were replaced by the local performance attributes (attributes #30 and 33). The models built using local performance attributes had the same or better level of performance than the models built on global plant attributes.

It was observed that by excluding the input flow to the plant (attribute # 1), the model performance decreases slightly but not significantly. However, excluding the suspended solids and sediments attributes reduces model performance significantly (increases the error to 56%). Besides, bagging with ANN that gave the best prediction results, additive regression (AR) with ANN also gave similar results. It was also observed that for global performance data, the polynomial kernel for SVM outperformed normalized kernel as shown in Table 3.

Table 3. Model Comparison for Global Performance Prediction based on Input BOD (attribute# 35)

Model	R	MAE	RMSE	RSR	NSE	RAE(%)
ANN	0.99	0.48	0.89	0.16	0.97	14.81
SVM (normalized polykernel)	0.80	0.69	3.37	0.62	0.62	21.25
SVM (polykernel)	0.96	0.86	1.61	0.30	0.91	26.74
Bagging with ANN (10 iterations)	0.99	0.28	0.86	0.16	0.97	8.70
Bagging with SVM (10 iterations)	0.79	0.62	3.43	0.63	0.60	19.34
Additive Regression (ANN)	0.99	0.35	0.74	0.14	0.98	10.79
Additive Regression (SVM)	0.96	0.85	1.64	0.61	0.63	26.47

The linear regression model for global performance prediction had a R^2 value of 0.96 with MAE =0.96 and RAE = 29.7% which was comparable to the SVM model performance as given in Table 3.

In order to build a series of prediction models for process control automation, the local performance attributes (attributes #30 and 33) from original dataset were replaced with predictions from models built for primary and secondary settlers. The predictions were chosen from the top 3 performing models namely Bagging with ANN, Additive Regression with ANN and ANN. The results indicated that there is no significant change between the models built using original data or predicted data as observed from Tables 3 -4 and figure 3. This confirms that by replacing certain attributes with accurate forecasts based on easily measured inputs, the automation of process control system for a wastewater treatment plant is possible.

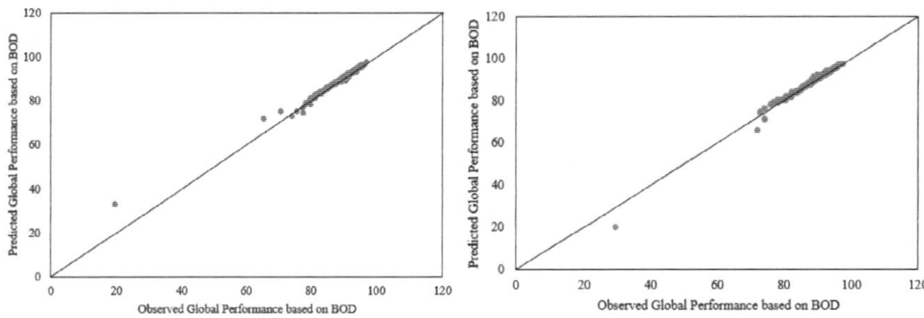

Fig. 3. Scatterplot for predicted vs observed global performance based on BOD for models - Bagging with ANN using original data set (left) and Bagging with ANN using predicted local performance inputs (attributes #30 and 33) (right)

A mix of model predictions used as input data for local performance attributes was also tested. For example, for attribute # 30 – predictions from bagging with ANN was taken and for attribute #33 – predictions from Additive Regression with ANN was taken. The model performance based on the mixed model prediction data was similar to the ones found in Table 4 with no significant difference in their error statistics as well.

Table 4. Model Comparison for Global Performance Prediction based on Input BOD (attribute# 35) using Predicted Local Performance Attributes as inputs

Prediction Model for attributes 30& 33	Model for global performance	R	MAE	RMSE	RSR	NSE	RAE(%)
ANN	ANN	0.99	0.47	0.84	0.15	0.98	14.66
	SVM (polykernel)	0.96	0.87	1.67	0.31	0.91	26.91
	Bagging with ANN (10 iterations)	0.99	0.27	0.72	0.13	0.98	8.34
	Bagging with SVM (10 iterations)	0.96	0.86	1.67	0.31	0.91	26.74
	Additive Regression (ANN)	0.99	0.38	0.74	0.14	0.98	11.79
	Additive Regression (SVM)	0.96	0.86	1.68	0.31	0.90	26.54
Bagging with ANN	ANN	0.99	0.48	0.87	0.16	0.97	14.73

Prediction Model for attributes 30& 33	Model for global performance	R	MAE	RMSE	RSR	NSE	RAE(%)
	SVM (polykernel)	0.96	0.86	1.65	0.30	0.91	26.71
	Bagging with ANN (10 iterations)	0.99	0.28	0.81	0.15	0.98	8.65
	Bagging with SVM (10 iterations)	0.96	0.86	1.65	0.30	0.91	26.65
	Additive Regression (ANN)	0.99	0.38	0.74	0.13	0.98	11.92
	Additive Regression (SVM)	0.96	0.85	1.66	0.31	0.91	26.43
Additive Regression with ANN	ANN	0.99	0.46	0.84	0.15	0.98	14.36
	SVM (polykernel)	0.96	0.86	1.65	0.30	0.91	26.62
	Bagging with ANN (10 iterations)	0.99	0.27	0.74	0.14	0.98	8.41
	Bagging with SVM (10 iterations)	0.96	0.86	1.66	0.30	0.91	26.70
	Additive Regression (ANN)	0.99	0.37	0.73	0.13	0.98	11.39
	Additive Regression (SVM)	0.96	0.85	1.68	0.31	0.91	26.42

4 Conclusion

In this paper, attempts were made to build a series of prediction models to enable total automation of a wastewater treatment plant. From various models tested, it was observed that ensembles always gave a higher performance compared to the base learners (ANN and SVM) tested. The series of prediction models built using ensembles highlighted that predicted attributes can be used as model inputs to subsequent models with minimal loss of accuracy or efficiency. This study paves the way for incorporating prediction models for water quality parameters that require complex measurement techniques and devices as inputs in the overall process control system. In this way, implementation of automated WWTP is possible, thereby improving efficiency and reducing costs.

Acknowledgments

We would like to thank UCI Repository for making the data set available as open source. This research did not receive any specific grant from funding agencies in the public, commercial, or not-for-profit sectors.

References

1. Mingzhi, H., Jinquan, W., Yongwen, M., Yan, W., Weijiang, L., Xiaofei, S.: Control rules of aeration in a submerged biofilm wastewater treatment process using fuzzy neural networks. Expert Systems with Applications. 36, 10428–10437 (2009).https://doi.org/10.1016/j.eswa.2009.01.035

2. Haimi, H., Mulas, M., Corona, F., Vahala, R.: Data-derived soft-sensors for biological wastewater treatment plants: An overview. Environmental Modelling & Software. 47, 88–107 (2013).https://doi.org/10.1016/j.envsoft.2013.05.009
3. Pai, T.Y., Wan, T.J., Hsu, S.T., Chang, T.C., Tsai, Y.P., Lin, C.Y., Su, H.C., Yu, L.F.: Using fuzzy inference system to improve neural network for predicting hospital wastewater treatment plant effluent. Computers & Chemical Engineering. 33, 1272–1278 (2009).https://doi.org/10.1016/j.compchemeng.2009.02.004
4. Pai, T.Y., Yang, P.Y., Wang, S.C., Lo, M.H., Chiang, C.F., Kuo, J.L., Chu, H.H., Su, H.C., Yu, L.F., Hu, H.C., Chang, Y.H.: Predicting effluent from the wastewater treatment plant of industrial park based on fuzzy network and influent quality. Applied Mathematical Modelling. 35, 3674–3684 (2011).https://doi.org/10.1016/j.apm.2011.01.019
5. Wan, J., Huang, M., Ma, Y., Guo, W., Wang, Y., Zhang, H., Li, W., Sun, X.: Prediction of effluent quality of a paper mill wastewater treatment using an adaptive network-based fuzzy inference system. Applied Soft Computing. 11, 3238–3246 (2011).https://doi.org/10.1016/j.asoc.2010.12.026
6. Wu, G.-D., Lo, S.-L.: Predicting real-time coagulant dosage in water treatment by artificial neural networks and adaptive network-based fuzzy inference system. Engineering Applications of Artificial Intelligence. 21, 1189–1195 (2008).https://doi.org/10.1016/j.engappai.2008.03.015
7. Belchior, C.A.C., Araújo, R.A.M., Landeck, J.A.C.: Dissolved oxygen control of the activated sludge wastewater treatment process using stable adaptive fuzzy control. Computers & Chemical Engineering. 37, 152–162 (2012).https://doi.org/10.1016/j.compchemeng.2011.09.011
8. Han, H.-G., Qiao, J.-F., Chen, Q.-L.: Model predictive control of dissolved oxygen concentration based on a self-organizing RBF neural network. Control Engineering Practice. 20, 465–476 (2012).https://doi.org/10.1016/j.conengprac.2012.01.001
9. Ruan, J., Zhang, C., Li, Y., Li, P., Yang, Z., Chen, X., Huang, M., Zhang, T.: Improving the efficiency of dissolved oxygen control using an on-line control system based on a genetic algorithm evolving FWNN software sensor. Journal of Environmental Management. 187, 550–559 (2017).https://doi.org/10.1016/j.jenvman.2016.10.056
10. Huang, M., Ma, Y., Wan, J., Chen, X.: A sensor-software based on a genetic algorithm-based neural fuzzy system for modeling and simulating a wastewater treatment process. Applied Soft Computing. 27, 1–10 (2015).https://doi.org/10.1016/j.asoc.2014.10.034
11. Hamed, M.M., Khalafallah, M.G., Hassanien, E.A.: Prediction of wastewater treatment plant performance using artificial neural networks. Environmental Modelling & Software. 19, 919–928 (2004).https://doi.org/10.1016/j.envsoft.2003.10.005
12. Nasr, M.S., Moustafa, M.A.E., Seif, H.A.E., El Kobrosy, G.: Application of Artificial Neural Network (ANN) for the prediction of EL-AGAMY wastewater treatment plant performance-EGYPT. Alexandria Engineering Journal. 51, 37–43 (2012).https://doi.org/10.1016/j.aej.2012.07.005
13. Bieroza, M., Baker, A., Bridgeman, J.: New data mining and calibration approaches to the assessment of water treatment efficiency. Advances in Engineering Software. 44, 126–135 (2012).https://doi.org/10.1016/j.advengsoft.2011.05.031
14. Dheeru, D., Karra Taniskidou, E.: UCI Machine Learning Repository. University of California, Irvine, School of Information and Computer Sciences (2017).

15. Witten, I.H., Frank, E.: Data Mining: Practical Machine Learning Tools and Techniques, Second Edition (Morgan Kaufmann Series in Data Management Systems). Morgan Kaufmann Publishers Inc., San Francisco, CA, USA (2005).
16. Bennett, N.D., Croke, B.F.W., Guariso, G., Guillaume, J.H.A., Hamilton, S.H., Jakeman, A.J., Marsili-Libelli, S., Newham, L.T.H., Norton, J.P., Perrin, C., Pierce, S.A., Robson, B., Seppelt, R., Voinov, A.A., Fath, B.D., Andreassian, V.: Characterising performance of environmental models. Environmental Modelling & Software. 40, 1–20 (2013).https://doi.org/10.1016/j.envsoft.2012.09.011
17. D. N. Moriasi, J. G. Arnold, M. W. Van Liew, R. L. Bingner, R. D. Harmel, T. L. Veith: Model Evaluation Guidelines for Systematic Quantification of Accuracy in Watershed Simulations. Transactions of the ASABE. 50, 885–900 (2007).https://doi.org/10.13031/2013.23153
18. Hall, M., Frank, E., Holmes, G., Pfahringer, B., Reutemann, P., Witten, I.H.: The WEKA Data Mining Software: An Update. SIGKDD Explor. Newsl. 11, 10–18 (2009).https://doi.org/10.1145/1656274.1656278

Compositional Analysis for Metallic Systems: Sampling Methods *

Harsha Gwalani[1][0000-0002-9202-6405], Martin O'Neill II[1], Armin R. Mikler[1], Talukder Alam[1] and Rajarshi Banerjee[1]

University of North Texas
harshagwalani@my.unt.edu

Abstract. Metallic systems are used in the construction of transportation, electrical, medical, agricultural and other industrial equipment. Alloys are metallic systems created by combining metals with other metals or elements. Combination of metals reduces the cost of the material without the loss of important properties. Alloys usually consist of a primary metal called the base or solvent with secondary constituents or solutes. The arrangement of atoms of different types within the material plays a key role in defining the physical and electrical properties of the material. In-depth study of microstructures in materials is crucial for understanding the properties exhibited by them and engineering new materials with desirable properties. Atom Probe Tomography is a technique used to analyze material samples by creating three-dimensional reconstructions of atoms in the sample. Material samples consist of millions or billions of atoms, therefore compositional analysis at the atomic scale is not trivial. A novel algorithm, Uniform Partitioning Algorithm (UPA) for sampling atoms to study the atomic distribution in a material is presented in this paper. The algorithm is shown to be more efficient in capturing spatial correlations and neighborhood properties between atoms in the material than the existing voxelization and spherical binning techniques. These comparisons are performed on synthetic datasets with known distributions for validation. In order to create datasets with heterogeneous distributions, two new approaches that simulate clustering tendencies between atoms of same type are also presented.

Keywords: Binning Algorithms · Frequency Distributions · Compositional Analysis · Big Data

1 Introduction

Metallic systems or alloys can be defined as materials created by combining metals with other metals or elements. These materials have many applications in everyday life. For example, steel is used for construction of roads, railways, buildings; Aluminum based alloys are used for manufacturing automobiles, utensils; and Titanium based alloys are a major component in medical equipment. The

* Supported by organization University of North Texas.

datasets. The performance of UPA and other binning algorithms with respect to bin size and distributions is evaluated in the Experiments and Results section. We summarize the results and discuss future applications in the Conclusion section.

2 Background and Related Work

Counting statistics are an efficient means to assess the distribution of elements in an inter-metallic system. Frequency distribution analyses are performed on the given crystal structure to study important attributes like density, concentration, and clustering or anti-clustering tendencies. These compositional analyses are usually performed by partitioning the 3D data into bins, such that the size of each bin is constant. The size constraint is usually defined in two ways:

1. Volume: The geometrical space occupied by each bin is almost equal. The atomic density of a single element in each bin is calculated as the ratio of the number of atoms of that type in a bin, and the volume of the bin.
2. Count: The number of atoms in each bin is constant. The concentration of an element in the bin is defined as the ratio of the number of atoms of that type in a bin and the total number of atoms in the bin.

Voxelization is the simplest and most commonly used method to create these bins [5][6][1]. The data is divided into discrete cubic or cuboid blocks. These blocks act as the bins for the compositional analyses. These grid based counting techniques are often preferred because of their ease of application even on large datasets. Analyses of neighborhood of each atom in the material however, result in more detailed frequency distribution statistics. Stephenson et al present the construction of spherical bins around each atom for the compositional analysis in [7]. Each bin represents the k-Nearest Neighborhood (kNN) of an atom. These methods, while more accurate are computationally infeasible and not scalable for larger datasets. About 20-25% of total atoms are not detected by the Atom Probe used for this study because of the evaporation process. Furthermore, the reconstructed atomic positions do not align perfectly with the lattice sites defined by the crystal structure due to energy related atomic movements and re-constructional artifacts[5]. Therefore, even if the crystal structure of the material is cubic, the atomic positions in the resulting dataset may not form cubes. This makes overlaying a 3-dimensional grid on the atomic dataset obtained from Atom Probe Tomography challenging without performing additional operations on the data[4]. Furthermore, voxelization restricts the sample size and the shape of bins due to the inherent forced gridding. The proposed binning algorithm employs a distance based partitioning technique that is not restricted by any shape. Hence, it is better at detecting spatial correlations in the data.

Binomial distributions are directly compared with the experimental frequency distribution to study the deviation from a random distribution. This deviation is usually quantified by applying the χ^2 measure [5] [6]. The comparison with the binomial distribution is based on the assumption that the solution contains

a single phase with the solute atoms mixed randomly with the solvent atoms throughout the solution with an average concentration value. However, regions with randomly mixed solute atoms, but with varying mean concentrations, can coexist in the solution. The Square Wave Model [9] is used to approximate the frequency distributions of such alloy solutions. The frequency distribution of the solute atom in this model is defined as the sum of two displaced binomial distribution for a dataset with two coexisting phases.
The size of the bin in terms of volume or count plays a critical role in characterizing the arrangement of atoms. Slight deviations from randomness may remain undetected if the bin size is too large due to positional errors[5]. Smaller bin sizes, on the other hand, can lead to statistical errors [11]. Most of the bins in such a scenario may be irrelevant if the solute concentrations are extremely low in the alloy system. We present a sensitivity analysis for the Uniform Partitioning Algorithm, and the two existing binning algorithms with respect to varying bin sizes and distributions. This analysis is used to determine the lowest resolution (largest bin size) at which the algorithms successfully detect heterogeneities in the dataset.

3 Methodology

3.1 Uniform Partitioning Algorithm (UPA)

The Uniform Partitioning Algorithm (UPA) can be used to divide a region into k contiguous sub regions such that all sub-regions have approximately equal weights. This weight can be any attribute of the data. It was originally developed to partition two-dimensional spatial data to solve challenging resource allocation problems[10]. This algorithm can be applied in a three dimensional context to partition the atomic dataset into k parts, such that each part has an equal number of atoms. These parts can then be used as the bins. UPA is a recursive algorithm that divides the input lattice of size N into two parts such that each part contains $\frac{Nk}{2}$ and $N(\frac{k}{2}+(k \bmod 2))$ atoms respectively, where k is the desired number of bins for that lattice segment. The algorithm is called recursively on the two parts with updated k and N values until k is equal to 1. The atoms in the input lattice are assigned to one of the two parts represented by the two farthest points in the input lattice at each stage. The farthest two points in the lattice are identified by calculating the bounding cuboid of the structure. The material structure can be of any shape. An atom may not necessarily exist at the eight corners of the bounding cuboid. The locations of these 8 corners are updated to the locations of their closest atoms. The four body diagonals corresponding to these 8 corners represent the longest distances in the lattice. The atoms connecting the longest of these four body diagonals are the two farthest points in the lattice. Figure 1a shows these atoms (encircled in red) for an example lattice. The function $farthestAtomsInTheLattice(L)$ in Algorithm 1 (Line 7) returns these two points. The input lattice is now partitioned by assigning atoms to the two parts based on distance in a round robin fashion (Lines 15-21 in Algorithm 1), such that one part has $N\frac{k}{2}$ atoms while the other

Algorithm 1: Uniform Partitioning Binning Algorithm

```
UPA()
Input  : Input Lattice : L = {A_1, A_2 ... A_N}, Number of parts: k, Part List: P
/* P is an empty list initially                                        */
Output: P = {P_1, P_2 ... P_k}
if k == 1 then
    /* Termination Condition for the recursion                         */
    P.append(L) return
N = size(L)
k1 = k/2
k2 = (k/2 + k%2)
[point1, point2] = farthestAtomsInTheLattice(L)
L_1 = [], L_2 = []
LP1 = sortByDistanceFromPoint(point1, L)
/* sort atoms in the input lattice by their distance from point1 in
   increasing order                                                    */
LP2 = sortByDistanceFromPoint(point2, L)
i = 0, j = 0
while i < N(k1/k) do
    atom_1 = LP1.pop()
    atom_2 = LP2.pop()
    while atom_1 not in L_2 do
        atom_1 = LP1.pop()
    L_1.append(atom_1)
    i = i + 1
    while atom_2 not in L_1 do
        atom_2 = LP2.pop()
    L_2.append(atom_2)
    j = j + 1
while j < N(k2/k) do
    atom_2 = LP2.pop()
    while atom_2 not in L_1 do
        atom_2 = LP2.pop()
    L_2.append(atom_2)
    j = j + 1
return UPA(L_1, k_1, P)
return UPA(L_2, k_2, P)
```

part has $N(\frac{k}{2} + (k \bmod 2))$ atoms as illustrated in Figure 1*b*. The function is executed recursively on these two resulting lattices with $k = \frac{k}{2}$ and $k = \frac{k}{2} + (k \bmod 2)$ respectively (Lines 29-30 in Algorithm 1). This can be seen in Figure 1*c*, the process is repeated for one of the two lattices obtained in part *b*). The result of partitioning the initial dataset into four bins is demonstrated in part *d*.

The time complexity of the algorithm can be computed as the sum of the complexity of three steps in the function.
Assuming $k = 2^m$ for some $m \in I_+$, size of the lattice in iteration i is $N/(2^i)$ and lattice of size $N/(2^i)$ is processed 2^i times.
Farthest Points Calculation is linear for the size of the input lattice, $S_1 = \Sigma_{i=0}^{m} 2^i(N/2^i)$, Sorting by distance from the two points is $O(nlogn)$ for an n sized lattice, $S_2 = 2(\Sigma_{i=0}^{m} 2^i(N/2^i)log(N/2^i)$, and assignment to corresponding lattice is again linear, $S_3 = \Sigma_{i=0}^{m} 2^i(N/2^i)$. Therefore, $S = S_1 + S_2 + S_3 = O(NlogN)$ for $k << N$, and $S = S_1 + S_2 + S_3 = O(Nlog^2N)$ for $k \approx N$.

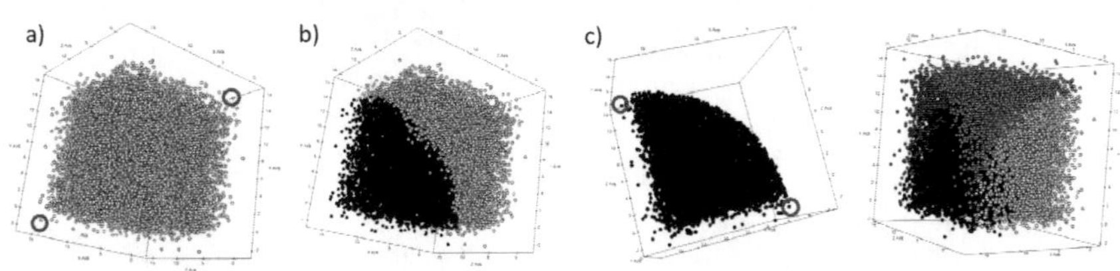

Fig. 1. UPA Binning Example: The red circles represent the farthest atoms in the input lattice.

3.2 Data Generation and Collection

The Uniform Partitioning Algorithm is evaluated based on its ability to detect significant variations in the distribution of solutes in the lattice. These results can be validated using datasets with known concentrations and distributions. Hence, performance of each binning algorithm was analyzed using synthetic datasets. Additionally, data collection using an Atom Probe is an expensive and time consuming process, thus it is not feasible for testing algorithms. Furthermore, the APT data is both incomplete due to low detector efficiency and noisy due to artifacts introduced by the reconstruction and detection process. The creation of synthetic datasets that simulate alloy systems involves two steps, lattice creation and atom distribution.

Lattice Creation: The first step of creating a synthetic dataset is to simulate a lattice. Metallic systems usually occur as cubic crystal structures. There are three types of cubic lattices, Simple Cubic (SC), Body Centered Cubic(BCC) and Face Centered Cubic(FCC). Figure 2 shows the unit cells for a simple cubic lattice, a BCC lattice and an FCC lattice. For this research, Face Centered Cubic lattices was created by repeating the corresponding unit cell in the x, y, z direction.

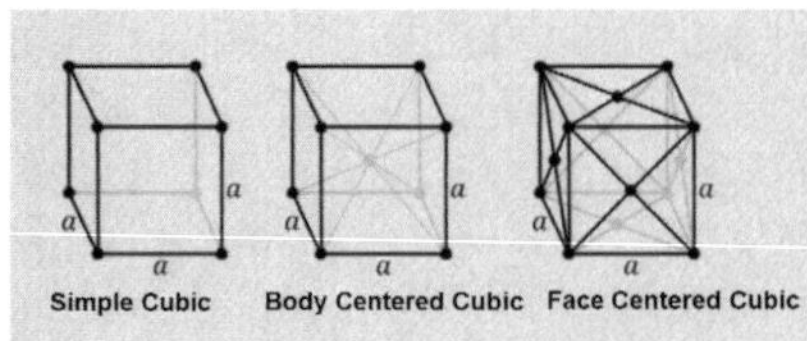

Fig. 2. Unit Cells: Simple Cubic, Body Centered Cubic and Face Centered Cubic[14]

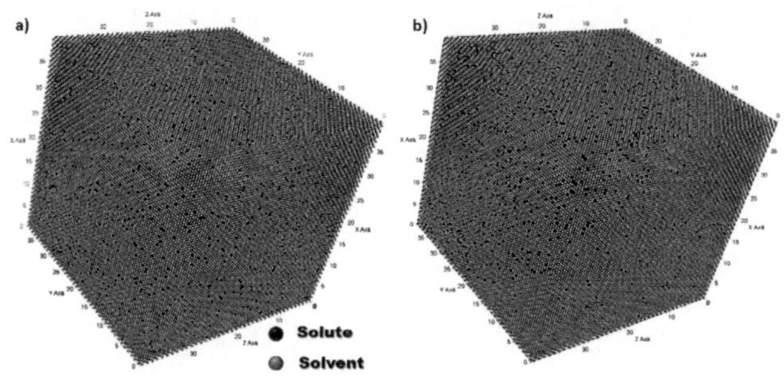

Fig. 3. Homogeneous Distributions : a) Random/Uniform Distribution b) Multi-Phase Distribution with 2 phases.

Distribution of atoms: Once the positions of the lattice sites are known, different atoms in the synthetic material need to be assigned to these lattice positions. These atoms are assigned in proportion to the average concentration for each element. We assume the alloy has two different elements A and B with concentrations $c_A = 0.04$ and $c_B = 0.96$ in this study. These values are arbitrarily chosen as examples, the methodology can be used to simulate and analyze any composition. Atoms are distributed across the lattice either homogeneously or heterogeneously. These distributions along with their variants are discussed in detail below.

Homogeneous Distributions

1. Random/Uniform Distribution: This distribution simulates a binomial distribution, the probability of an atom of a specific type to be located at any lattice site is equal to the concentration of that element in the system. Such datasets can be created by generating random numbers between 0 an 1 for each lattice site, and comparing those with the concentrations. Figure $3a$ shows an example of a conventional alloy dataset with 256,000 atoms, $c_A = 0.04$ and $c_B = 0.96$ homogeneously distributed across the lattice.
2. Multi-Phase Distribution: As discussed earlier, the arrangement of solutes and solvents is dependent on temperature and pressure conditions. Certain alloy solutions can form multiple phases in the the lattice where each phase denotes a region with homogeneously distributed solute and solvent atoms with different concentrations. Figure $3b$ shows an example of an alloy dataset

with 256,000 atoms with two phases, half of the lattice (bottom left) has higher average concentration of the solute atom A, $c_A = 0.07$ and the other half has lower concentration of the solute $c_A = 0.01$. The mean concentration of the solute in the material is still $c_A = 0.04$. This dataset was created by dividing the lattice into two equal parts along the longest body diagonal and randomly distributing atoms within these parts with corresponding concentrations. This process can be used to create more than two phases if necessary.

Heterogeneous Distributions

The probability that a solute atom, an atom of type A will have at least one solute atom as its direct neighbor in a homogeneous solution can be calculated as $p(AA) = (1-(1-c_A)^n)$, where n is the number of direct neighbors for the crystal structure. $FCC(n) = 12$, $BCC(n) = 8$ and $SC(n) = 6$. If the concentration of solute atoms is significantly higher in a region in the lattice, this group of solute atoms is defined as a cluster, if it also satisfies additional constraints like the volume and number of atoms. Clustering tendencies can be increased in synthetic datasets by increasing the probability of solute-solute (AA) neighborhood i.e, if $p(sim) >> p(AA)$, the dataset will have segregation tendencies. We created and experimented with four types of heterogeneous distributions with varying degrees of segregation tendencies.

1. Fixed Clusters: In order to test the ability of the algorithm to detect non uniformity within the dataset, clusters were placed at known locations in the dataset. The clusters were created by selecting a cube of side $= s/4$, where s is the side of the entire lattice. The concentration of solute atoms was increased to 0.16 within these cubes. Four such cubes were created at the corners of the lattice, as can be seen in Figure 4*a*. The remaining solute atoms are distributed randomly within the lattice.
2. Cluster Introduction: Instead of creating artificial zones with higher concentrations of solute atoms with known locations, the objective is to organically create clusters. In this distribution, randomly distributed solute atoms were swapped with the solvent atoms such that the likelihood of solute-solute neighborhood is much higher than $p(AA)$. For the simulated FCC dataset, $p(AA) \approx 0.39$ and $p(sim) = 0.85$. For a fixed number of iterations, a solute atom is randomly selected, and a random number ($p_c = [0-1]$) is compared with $p(sim)$. If $p_c < p(sim)$, this solute atom is swapped with a solvent atom that has at least one solute neighbor. The algorithm is loosely based on the methodology presented in [6]. If $p_c > p(sim)$, anti clustering tendencies are not introduced in our simulation unlike in the one described in [6]. Figure 4*b* shows an example of the solute distribution in such a dataset. The distribution obtained after ensuring that solute atoms have solute neighbors, while deviating from a homogeneous distribution does not result in wider or denser clusters.
3. Hierarchical Clustering: The mth coordination number of an atom is defined as the number of nearest neighbors for an atom at the mth level in the lattice. In a perfect FCC lattice, m^{th} nearest neighbors of an atom are located at

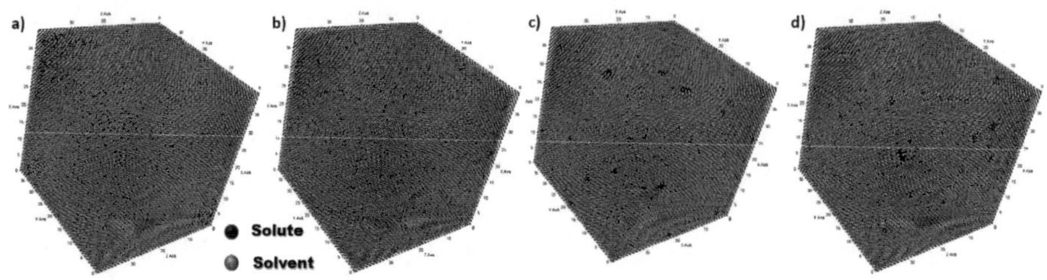

Fig. 4. Heterogeneous Distributions : a)Fixed Clusters b)Cluster Introduction c)Hierarchical Clusters d)Incremental Clusters

a distance of $a\sqrt{m/2}$ from the atom, where a is the side of the unit cell in the lattice. In order to create wider clusters, the likelihood of solute-solute m^{th} neighborhood was increased to $p(sim)$, starting from $m = 1$ to a predefined maximum ($maxLevel$). Solute-solute neighborhood at the kth level for a solute atom signifies that the atom has at least one solute atom within $a\sqrt{m/2}$ for all $m = 1$ to k. For example, in Figure 5a part i), the solute atom at site 1 satisfies the second level solute-solute neighborhood condition, but fails the third level condition. To ensure m^{th} solute-solute neighborhood for a solute atom that satisfies k^{th} condition for $k < m$, a solvent atom that has solute neighbors at least until m levels is selected. The solvent atom at site 2 in Figure 5a part ii) is an example of such an atom for $m = 3$. Finally, the solute atom and its kth solute neighborhood is swapped with the selected matrix element and its kth solvent neighborhood, as shown in Figure 5a part iii). Figure 4c shows a dataset with hierarchical clustering with $maxLevel = 4$.

4. Incremental Clustering: The cluster introduction simulation ensures that each solute atom is more likely to have at least one solute atom as a direct neighbor. This condition can be extended to ensure that each solute atom is more likely to have at least k solute atoms as direct neighbors to create denser clusters. k cannot be greater than the first coordination number. This process is repeated iteratively starting from $k = 1$ through $k = maxNeighbors$. In Figure 5b, the solute atom at site 1 does not have two direct neighbors. This solute atom along with its one direct solute neighbor are swapped with the solvent atom and one of its direct solvent neighbors. Figure 4d shows a dataset with incremental clustering with $maxNeighbors = 4$.

3.3 Compositional Analysis

If all atoms are homogeneously distributed in an alloy, then the probability of selecting i solute atoms (type: A) in an n_b sized sample is equal to $p(i) = \binom{n_b}{i}((c_A)^i(1 - c_A)^{n_b - i})$. If the total number of bins or samples is n, then the number of bins expected to have i solute atoms is equal to $e(i) = np(i)$. The deviation of any distribution from a homogeneous distribution can be studied

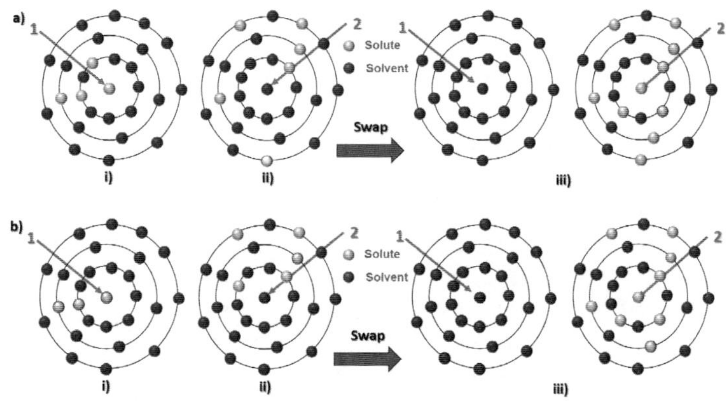

Fig. 5. a)Hierarchical Clustering Example b)Incremental Clustering Example. The levels are for illustration purposes only and do not reflect the accurate coordination number.

by using the χ^2-statistic for the number of bins with i solute atoms for $i = 0$ to n_b. $\chi^2 = \Sigma_{i=0}^{n_b}(e(i) - f(i))^2/e(i)$, where $f(i)$ is the observed number of bins with i solute atoms. The p-value for this comparison can be calculated by using the obtained χ^2 statistic value and n_b degrees of freedom. Smaller values of $e(i)$ tend to bias the χ^2 statistic value. Therefore, it is a common practice to sum up $e(j) + e(j+1) \ldots e(n_b)$, if $e(j)$ is considerably small ($e(j) < 5$), and adjust the degrees of freedom as j instead of n_b. As it is known, the χ^2 statistic increases with increasing sample size or the number of bins (n) for these experiments[6], Pearson's coefficient, μ is used to normalize the effect of large n where $\mu = \sqrt{\chi^2/(n + \chi^2)}$.

For a multi-phase homogeneous distribution, if the dataset contains two phases with different mean solute concentrations, the distribution is modeled as a sum of two displaced binomial distributions. In the square wave model, the number of bins expected to have i solute atoms is given by:

$$e_{sq}(i) = n\binom{n_b}{i}(\alpha((c_{1A})^i(1 - c_{1A})^{n_b - i}) + (1 - \alpha)((c_{2A})^i(1 - c_{2A})^{n_b - i})) \text{ where,}$$

c_{1A} is the concentration of A in the first phase and c_{2A} is the concentration of A in the second phase. Since α is the proportion of the total atoms in the first phase, $1 - \alpha$ is the proportion of atoms in the second phase. The values α and c_{1A} were estimated by using a maximum log likelihood function [12]. Once α and c_{1A} are estimated, c_{2A} can be calculated using c_{1A}, α and c_A. There is a caveat in comparing the expected distribution of this kind with observed counts. It is an inherent assumption in the expected distribution that no bin will overlap between the two phases i solute atoms are either selected from one phase or the other. This assumption might be violated by any binning technique, hence, more sophisticated models may be required to estimate the expected distribution.

4 Experiments and Results

Voxelization, spherical binning and UPA binning were used to detect the heterogeneities in the different synthetic datasets. Creating spherical bins for every atom in the dataset with 256,000 atoms is computationally infeasible, hence sampling was used to create spherical bins. In spherical binning, an atom can be assigned to multiple bins resulting in overlapping bins. Further, due to the sampling, it is not guaranteed that all atoms are assigned to a bin. In voxelization and UPA binning, every atom is assigned to a unique bin. For a given bin size n_b, the expected total number of bins is $k = \lfloor N/n_b \rfloor$, where N is the total number of atoms, and the value of n_b is adjusted accordingly, $n_b = N/k$. The input lattice is a cube, therefore, in order to create k cubic voxels with equal atoms, $k^{1/3}$ must be an integer. The effective bin size in case of voxelization is therefore equal to a perfect cube integer less than or equal to $\lfloor N/n_b \rfloor$. To achieve almost complete coverage for spherical binning, $3k$ atoms are selected to create $3k$ bins instead of k bins. Figure 6 shows the spherical bins(a), voxels(b) and UPA bins(c) for a dataset with $256,000$ atoms; the bin size was set to 1500; change in color denotes change in bin in the figure. As discussed earlier, both Pearson's coefficient and the p-value with respect to the χ^2-statistic were used to quantify the deviation of the observed distribution from the expected binomial curve. The distribution is said to be heterogeneous if p-value < 0.05 and μ is close to 1. In case of the phased distribution, the square wave model was used to estimate the expected distribution. The model was able to estimate the solute concentrations in the two phases and the proportion of one phase over another accurately.

4.1 Sensitivity to Bin Size

Figure 7 shows the degree of homogeneity detected by the different binning algorithms for the two homogeneous datasets described in the previous section. It can be seen that $\mu << 1$ for the completely random distribution for all types of binnings, specially for UPA because it provides complete coverage and more detailed neighborhood information. The increase in μ in spherical binning for the phase distribution can be explained by increased overlap between the two phases in the bins. In case of a mid range μ value or a low but not significantly lower p-value, the bins in question can be further inspected by material scientists.

Figure 8 shows the degree of heterogeneity detected by the different binning algorithms for the four heterogeneous datasets. Clustering tendencies introduced by increasing the probability of solute-solute neighborhood are detected by the binning algorithms only for smaller bin sizes. Increase in μ at lower bin sizes is indicative of segregation tendencies. The clustering tendencies are much more obvious for the incremental and hierarchical clustering datasets. The value of the Pearson's coefficient, μ is equal to one for all binning techniques for bin size

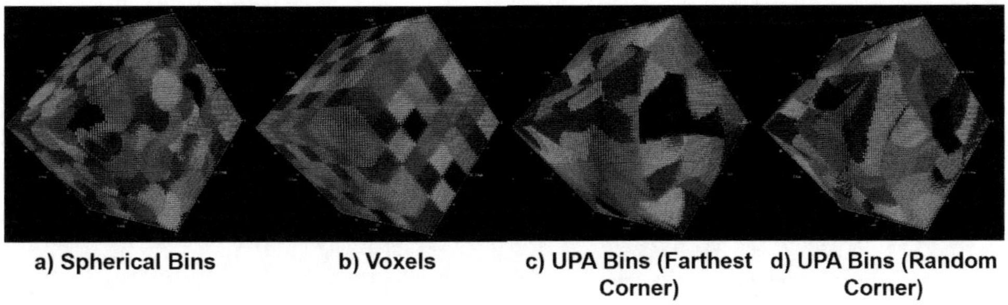

Fig. 6. a)Spherical Bins, number of bins = 512 b)Voxels, number of bins = 216 c)UPA: Farthest Corner, number of bins = 171 d)UPA: Random Corner, number of bins = 171. Change in color denotes change in bin.

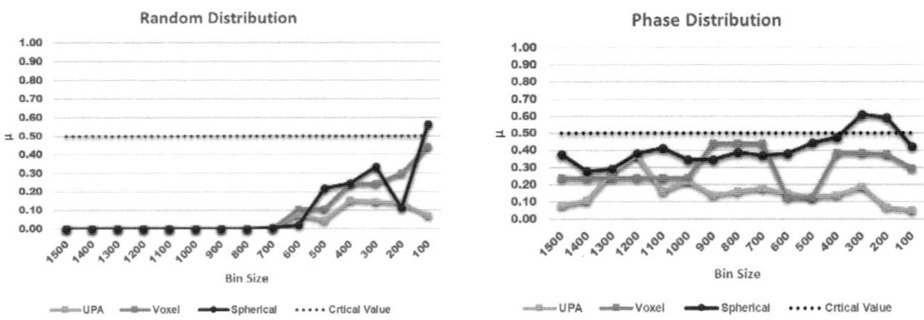

Fig. 7. Pearson's coefficient vs Bin Size: Homogeneous Distributions

less than 1000. The effective bin size for voxelization is about 1180 even for bin sizes greater than 1200. Hence, it appears that voxels catch the clusters even in larger bins for incremental clusters but, this is caused by the effective bin size being smaller than the expected bin size. The fixed clusters are detected only if the bin size is smaller than 800. An iterative bin size analysis can aid materials scientists in discovering the lowest resolution at which heterogeneities occur, hence in quantifying the degree of clustering.

4.2 Random UPA

The Uniform Partitioning Algorithm can be further enhanced as a sampling tool to capture the neighborhood relations even more completely by partitioning along two random atoms instead of the farthest two atoms at every recursive step. The bins resulting from partitioning using such a scheme are shown in Figure 6*d*. This process can be repeated t times to collect kt samples that are truly shape invariant and include all the atoms. The results obtained from this binning scheme are shown in Figure 9. It can be seen that this binning technique is able to detect heterogeneities at the lowest possible resolution (largest bin size). The results for the phase distribution ($\mu > 0.5$) for most bin sizes are not representative of the actual distribution due to the overlapping phases in bins,

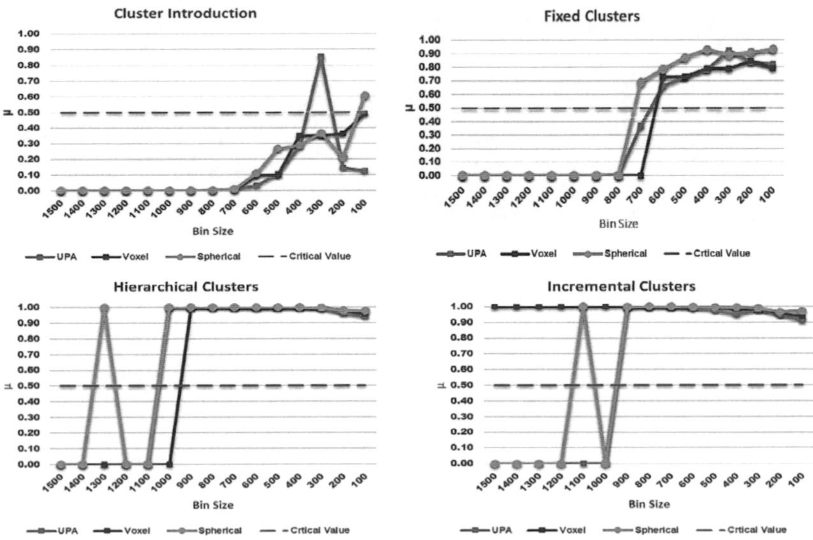

Fig. 8. Pearson's coefficient vs Bin Size: Heterogeneous Distributions

This effect is more pronounced for larger bin sizes. As depicted in Figure 10, the experimental distribution is close to the expected distribution, except for the concentrations in between the two peaks as the model does not account for these bins.

5 Conclusion

The $O(NlogN)$ Uniform Partitioning Algorithm proposed in this study is completely parallelizable and can detect spatial correlations and heterogeneities in distributions more efficiently than existing techniques. The distributable nature of this algorithm makes it a perfect candidate for use with large datasets containing billions of atoms. Additionally, this approach can be used to study the composition of High Entropy Alloys (HEAs). HEAs are metallic systems developed using a new technique of mixing metals, where five or more metals are mixed in almost equal proportions. These materials are characterized by increased randomness in the micro-structure due to no clear solvent/solute elements and are assumed to have a homogeneous random mixing of atoms. The expected homogeneous mixing of the elements is yet to be verified at the nano-scale[13]. The proposed algorithm can be repeated for each element as a solute for detecting atomic affinities.

Two novel approaches to simulate clustering tendencies in alloys were also discussed. These methods can be used to validate other distribution analysis techniques or cluster discovery algorithms. A broader application of the Uniform Partitioning Algorithm is the ability to physically locate the clusters in the dis-

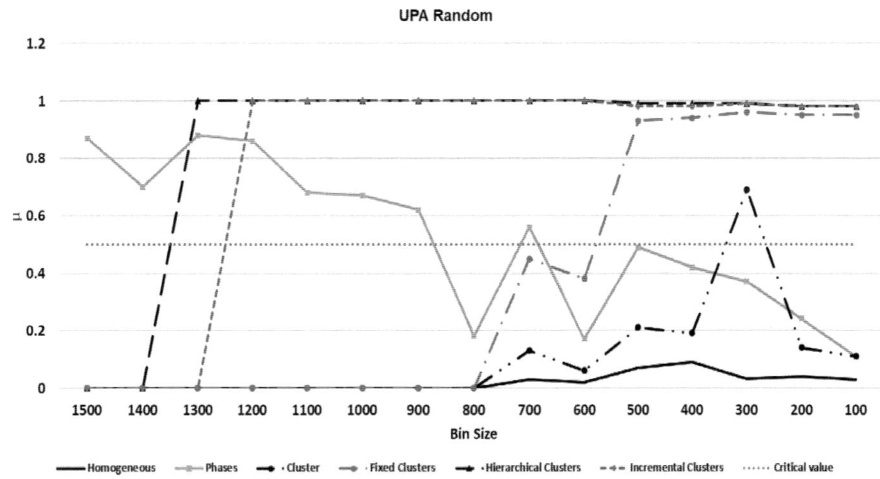

Fig. 9. Pearson's coefficient vs Bin Size: Random UPA

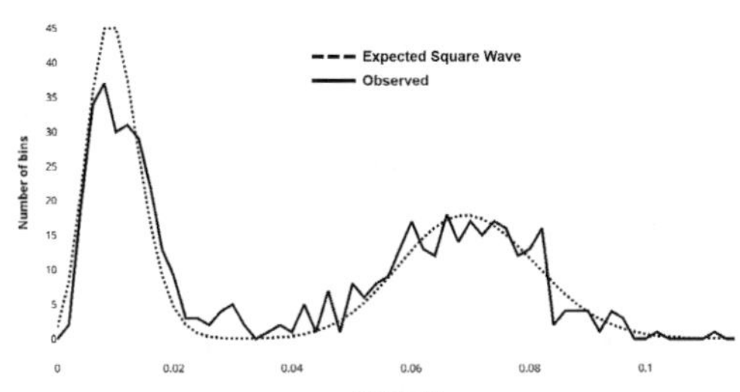

Fig. 10. Expected vs Observed Frequency Distribution for Multi Phase Distribution: UPA Random (Bin Size = 1500, 10 runs)

tribution. If the compositional analysis detects segregation tendencies, then the Uniform Partitioning Algorithm can be used to partition a dataset containing only the solute atoms. Higher density bins (number of solute atoms by volume) can be studied further to isolate clusters in the dataset.

References

1. Michael K. Miller, *Atom probe tomography :analysis at the atomic level*, 1 ed., Springer US, 2000.
2. B. Gwalani, T. Alam, C. Miller, T. Rojhirunsakool, Y.S. Kim, S.S. Kim, M.J. Kaufman, Yang Ren, and R. Banerjee, *Experimental investigation of the ordering pathway in a ni-33at. cr alloy*, Acta Materialia 115 (2016), 372 – 384.
3. Cameca Science and Metreology Solutions, *Introduction to apt*, 2018.

4. Olof C. Hellman, John Blatz du Rivage, and David N. Seidman, *Efficient sampling for three-dimensional atom probe microscopy data*, Ultramicroscopy 95 (2003), 199 – 205, IFES 2001.
5. Julie M. Cairney Simon P. Ringer Baptiste Gault, Michael P. Moody, *Atom probe microscopy, springer series in materials science*, Chapter 8, 2 ed., Springer-Verlag New York, 2012.
6. Michael P. Moody, Leigh T. Stephenson, Anna V. Ceguerra, and Simon P. Ringer, *Quantitative binomial distribution analyses of nanoscale like-solute atom clustering and segregation in atom probe tomography data*, Microscopy Research and Technique 71, no. 7, 542–550.
7. Leigh T. Stephenson, Anna V. Ceguerra, Tong Li, Tanaporn Rojhirunsakool, Soumya Nag, Rajarshi Banerjee, Julie M. Cairney, and Simon P. Ringer, *Point-by-point compositional analysis for atom probe tomography*, MethodsX 1 (2014), 12 – 18.
8. T GODFREY, M HETHERINGTON, J SASSEN, and G SMITH, *The characterization of spinodal structures in duplex cf3 steels*, JOURNAL DE PHYSIQUE 49 (1988), no. C-6, 421–426.
9. J. S. Langer, M. Bar-on, and Harold D. Miller, *New computational method in the theory of spinodal decomposition*, Phys. Rev. A 11 (1975), 1417–1429.
10. Tiwari C. Jimenez T, Mikler AR, *A novel space partitioning algorithm to improve current practices in facility placement*, IEEE Trans Syst Man Cybern Syst 42 (2012), no. 5, 11941205.
11. Olof C. Hellman, Justin A. Vandenbroucke, Jörg Rüsing, Dieter Isheim, and David N. Seidman, *Analysis of three-dimensional atom-probe data by the proximity histogram*, Microscopy and Microanalysis 6 (2000), no. 5, 437–444 (English (US)).
12. P. Auger, A. Menand, D. Blavette. *STATISTICAL ANALYSIS OF ATOM-PROBE DATA (II) : THEORETICAL FREQUENCY DISTRIBUTIONS FOR PERIODIC FLUCTUATIONS AND SOME APPLICATIONS.* Journal de Physique Colloques, 1988, 49 (C6), pp.C6-439-C6-4440
13. Y.F. Ye, Q. Wang, J. Lu, C.T. Liu, and Y. Yang, *High-entropy alloy: challenges and prospects*, Materials Today 19 (2016), no. 6, 349 – 362.
14. Wikipedia: Cubic crystal system, May 15, 2019, https://en.wikipedia.org/wiki/Cubiccrystalsystem

Scalable Cloud-based ETL for Self-serving Analytics

Eftim Zdravevski[1], Cas Apanowicz[2], Krzysztof Stencel[3], and Dominik Ślęzak[4]

[1] Faculty of Computer Science and Engineering
Ss. Cyril and Methodius University, Skopje, Macedonia
eftim.zdravevski@finki.ukim.mk
[2] CogniTrek, Toronto, Canada
cas.apanowicz@cognitrek.com
[3] Faculty of Mathematics, Informatics and Mechanics
University of Warsaw, Warsaw, Poland
stencel@mimuw.edu.pl
[4] QED Software, Warsaw, Poland
dominik.slezak@qed.pl

Abstract. Nowadays, companies must inevitably analyze the available data and extract meaningful knowledge. As an essential prerequisite, Extract-Transform-Load (ETL) requires significant effort, especially for Big Data. The existing solutions fail to formalize, integrate and evaluate the ETL process for Big Data in a scalable and cost-effective way. In this paper, we introduce a cloud-based architecture for data fusion and aggregation from a variety of sources. We identify three scenarios that generalize data aggregation during ETL. They are particularly valuable in the context of machine learning, as they facilitate feature engineering even in complex cases when the data from an extended time period has to be processed. In our experiments, we investigate user logs collected with Kinesis streams on Amazon AWS Hadoop clusters and demonstrate the scalability of our solution. The considered datasets range from 30 GB to 2.5 TB. The results were deployed in the domains, such as churn prediction, fraud detection, service outage prediction, and more generally – decision support and recommendation systems.

Keywords: Data warehouses, Data streams, ETL, Business analytics

1 Introduction

Ubiquitous smart devices, sensors and social media result in sheer data volumes, while consumers became accustomed to personalized services that are available instantaneously. Delivering targeted information shapes the success of many companies, health providers and governmental institutions. In the past, they could decide which data to store by making compromises between available resources and capabilities to manage the data. In the era of Big Data, companies experience growing pressure to store and analyze the whole data that is being collected just to stay competitive in the data-driven marketplace.

Several steps are needed to make the data available in a usable format: identification of all relationships and business context, data collection and ETL, which usually is time-consuming in terms of both development and execution. Once the data is processed and loaded into a data warehouse (DWH), it needs to be fully ready for reporting, visualization, analytics and decision support. Even though all building blocks for efficient ETL and Big Data analytics are present on the market, there is no comprehensive cloud-based architecture offering an integrated, scalable and cost-effective solution. Most approaches are either for specific purposes or only provide general definitions [1, 2].

In this article, we propose an architecture that first addresses the integration of high-velocity data by using scalable streaming technologies and Lambda functions. Then, it performs ETL using a combination of traditional tools for processing dimensional data, and Spark – for processing high-volume transactional data. We discuss detailed steps for performing three generic ETL scenarios covering a variety of real applications, ranging from traditional Business Intelligence (BI), to feature engineering in machine learning, such as churn prediction and fraud detection. In such applications, events like "the time that passed from the last occurrence of event X", "the time since the user's last login", "last use of a service", or "last bought product" could be valuable features.

Most importantly, the whole process is integrated from end-to-end and evaluated in a production environment on real high-velocity Big Data, something that lacks in most related approaches. The three scenarios were evaluated with different workloads ranging from 30 GB to 2.5 TB using the proposed architecture on Hadoop clusters deployed on Amazon AWS. The evaluation of each step of the three ETL scenarios showed that the cluster size could be optimized so it can process the required data volume within the expected time.

2 Related Work

Traditional BI relies on ETL tools for data import into DWH servers [3]. For reasonably sized data volumes there are ETL tools that have been successfully used in organizations throughout the years, such as Informatica, IBM Infosphere Datastage, Ab Intio, Microsoft SQL Server Integration Services (SSIS), Oracle Data Integrator, Talend, Pentaho Data Integration Platform (PDI), etc. Recently, ETL tools started to evolve into Enterprise Application Integration (EAI) systems that now perform much more functionalities than just ETL. Traditional ETL and ELT (Extract-Load-Transform) tools are reviewed in [4], with a focus on description of their terminology and capabilities, but without a discussion on how to tackle Big Data challenges. Scalable loading of data in NoSQL tables is one such challenge, which could be addressed by proper row key designs (i.e., their clustered index), as elaborated in [5].

The authors of [6] propose the BigDimETL approach, which aims to conserve the multidimensional DWH structure while integrating Big Data. However, the work is only theoretical, with no experimental evaluation.

Quite often, a user prefers a "quick and dirty" approximation over a correct answer that takes much longer to compute. Online aggregation in [7] was proposed to address this issue, as the batch-oriented nature of traditional MapReduce implementations makes these techniques hard to apply.

The idea of in-database analytics is pursued by the MADlib open source library [8]. It provides an evolving suite of SQL-based algorithms for machine learning, data mining and statistics that run at scale within a database engine, with no need for the data import/export to other tools.

GraphLab [9] expresses asynchronous, dynamic, graph-parallel computation while ensuring data consistency and achieving a high performance degree in the shared-memory setting, which is not originally supported by MapReduce and Spark. Our approach also recognizes that data consistency is essential, but achieves it differently, by relying on consistent dimensional tables. Consistent DWHs allow using data mining and machine learning libraries directly within the database system. Alternatively, consistent data in DWH could be used with more traditional visualization, reporting and BI services.

Another distributed parallel architecture for Big Data ETL is proposed in [10], but its limitation is that ETL should be completed before the data is aggregated. It is alleviated with our solution by performing aggregation during the ETL process. An approach that proposes a set of rules to map star schemas into NoSQL logical models with a pre-computed aggregate lattice is described in [11]. Similar to our case, the aggregate metrics need to be defined up front so that ETL can calculate them. The CloudETL system presented in [12] exploits MapReduce and Hive for distributed data processing, focusing on slowly changing dimensions. Our approach goes beyond it by using Spark for faster processing and Lambda functions for handling high-velocity data.

GENUS system [13] deals with data veracity by cleansing and tagging, similarly to our idea of standardization by templates. However, a drawback of this approach is poor evaluation, especially concerning high volume, versatility and velocity of the data. From the veracity perspective, the authors consider just one simple example. Moreover, the document store used is XML, without any scalability considerations. A real-time data ETL framework was presented in [14] to process historical/incoming data separately. Dynamic mirror replication technology was proposed to avoid the contention between OLAP queries and OLTP updates. A kind of drawback is that the evaluation of this methodology was conducted on a static dataset of only 16 GB.

Reference architecture for Big Data systems and classification implementation technologies and products/services, which is based on analysis of published implementation architectures of Big Data use cases, is provided in [15]. It aimed to facilitate architecture design and selection of technologies or commercial solutions when constructing Big Data systems. Their recommendations are considered in the design of the proposed system. From the perspective of the aforementioned areas of deployment of the proposed architecture, we also compared our work with other approaches referring to Big Data analysis in combination with data mining and machine learning, such as [16].

3 Architecture

The proposed system is shown in Figure 1. In organizations, commonly there are traditional data sources, such as relational database systems and structured/semi-structured data from internal or third-party data providers, that generate reasonably-sized data. This kind of data can be processed with traditional data integration tools. In our experiments, Pentaho Data Integration Platform (PDI) was utilized for such ETL tasks, which process the incoming low-volume data and store it in DWH (marked with light gray arrows in Figure 1).

We chose PDI because it enables users to ingest, blend, cleanse and prepare diverse data from any source. Its visual tools eliminate coding and complexity of creating data pipelines. It offers the data agnostic connectivity spanning from flat files to Hadoop, powerful orchestration and scheduling capabilities (including notifications and alerts), agile views for data modeling/visualization on the fly during the data preparation process, support for Hadoop distributions, Spark, NoSQL data stores and analytic databases, etc.

On the other hand, if there are data producers that generate Big Data with high volume, velocity or versatility, then the classical approach for ETL is not suitable. Big Data streams can be efficiently collected and processed by Distributed Streaming Platforms (DSP), which are scalable, replicated and fault-tolerant (e.g., Apache Kafka, Amazon Kinesis, etc.).

By defining a retention policy, DSPs can be configured to retain the data on the queue for a specific time after it was published, regardless if it was consumed or not. For example, for Amazon Kinesis the maximum data retention period is one week. DSPs allow the same data stream to be consumed by multiple consumers independently and simultaneously, each of them working at their own pace. Accessing the data on a DSP queue can be performed by either push or pull mechanisms. The pull mechanism is innate for Amazon Kinesis and Apache Kafka, so each consumer has and manages its read pointer.

Our solution allows consumption of DSP queues by the three most common types of consumers: Push Lambda functions (stream-based model), as well as Storage and Analytics Stream Pullers. The first two types are redundant alternatives for permanent raw data storage on different Object Storage containers, such as Amazon S3 or Windows Azure Blob Storage (WABS). Each of them is reliable with guaranteed Service Level Agreement (SLA). Using both of them can simplify deployment procedures and further improve the system's reliability. If the data format changes drastically or sources vary, consumers can be updated without any downtime or risk of data loss. Having both alternatives also provides integration convenience with the existing infrastructure.

Once the data is permanently stored on S3 or WABS in a raw format, we employ another Lambda function, which triggers after new files are deposited in a particular location. This function can cleanse the data (e.g., extract plain text from HTML files) and ingest it to Full-text search indexing services, such as Elasticsearch or Solr, which would subsequently provide free-text search functionality [17]. To some extent, this results with robustness to data veracity and complements the analytical capabilities of DWHs.

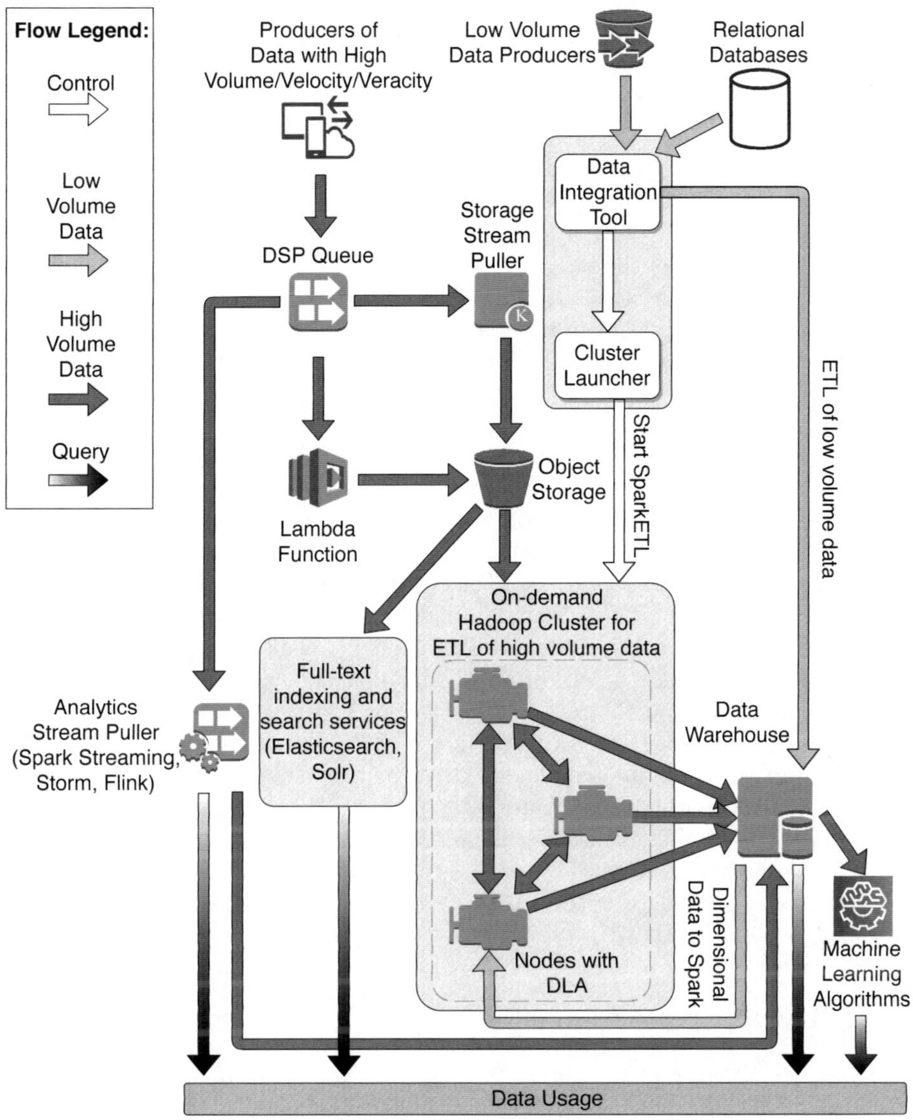

Fig. 1: Architecture of scalable cloud-based Big Data Warehouse.

Analytics Stream Pullers (e.g., Apache Spark Streaming, Apache Storm or Apache Flink) are a different kind of consumers that process data streams to provide near real-time insights and analytics. Our architecture complements this by employing on-demand Spark clusters for implementing more sophisticated algorithms for ETL and feature engineering. They can analyze changing trends over extended time periods (e.g., week-by-week or month-by-month comparisons of various metrics) or find the time since some particular event happened. Such metrics are not computable with Analytics Stream Pullers.

To facilitate on-demand starting of Spark clusters, on the machine that hosts Data Integration Tool (DIT) there is a Cluster Launcher module. It can be invoked manually or based on a predefined schedule by DIT. Cluster Launcher can start an Amazon EMR or Azure HDInsight cluster with configurable size and can run a particular Spark job. After the Spark cluster is started, it downloads the source code from a release branch of a code repository and automatically starts it. Code development and management adhere to the adopted organization's strategy (e.g., GitFlow), which defines rules and best practices for conflict resolution, peer-review, merging to staging and production branches, etc. Each Spark cluster during its lifetime executes only a specific ETL job. If the organization requires multiple ETL processes of unrelated data, then multiple Spark jobs can be defined and for each of them a separate workflow is managed (i.e., separate code repositories, execution schedules, target DWHs).

Next, the so-called Distributed Load Agent (DLA) is executed on all cluster nodes to process distinct portions of HDFS data generated by Spark. After DLA work is complete, the data is available in DWH for various BI tools and data mining or machine learning methods. Traditionally, data ingestion is a massive burden on database servers and often is a bottleneck. After Extract-Transform steps are completed and the primary/foreign keys are set, the load needs to be performed. The idea of DLA comes from the principles of edge computing, and it is partly inspired by the technology described in [18]. The goal is to offload most of the work to remote machines away from DWH. These edge nodes would compress the data and prepare an output, which could be simply copied to the database end. Thus, the overall impact on the database server would be minimal. In the proposed architecture, the whole on-demand cluster is considered as being on the edge from the DWH perspective (see Figure 1).

4 ETL Data-flow Scenarios

Let us describe three ETL data-flow scenarios commonly needed in organizations. These scenarios relate to the significant data portion to be stored in DWH, i.e., fact tables. The volume of dimensional data is considerably smaller. Thus, it usually does not require processing based on Big Data technologies; rather traditional ETL tools are sufficient. The proposed architecture assumes that traditional ETL tools already process dimensional data and that one only needs to handle the data to be stored in fact tables. The steps for implementing the ETL process of the three scenarios are shown in Figure 2.

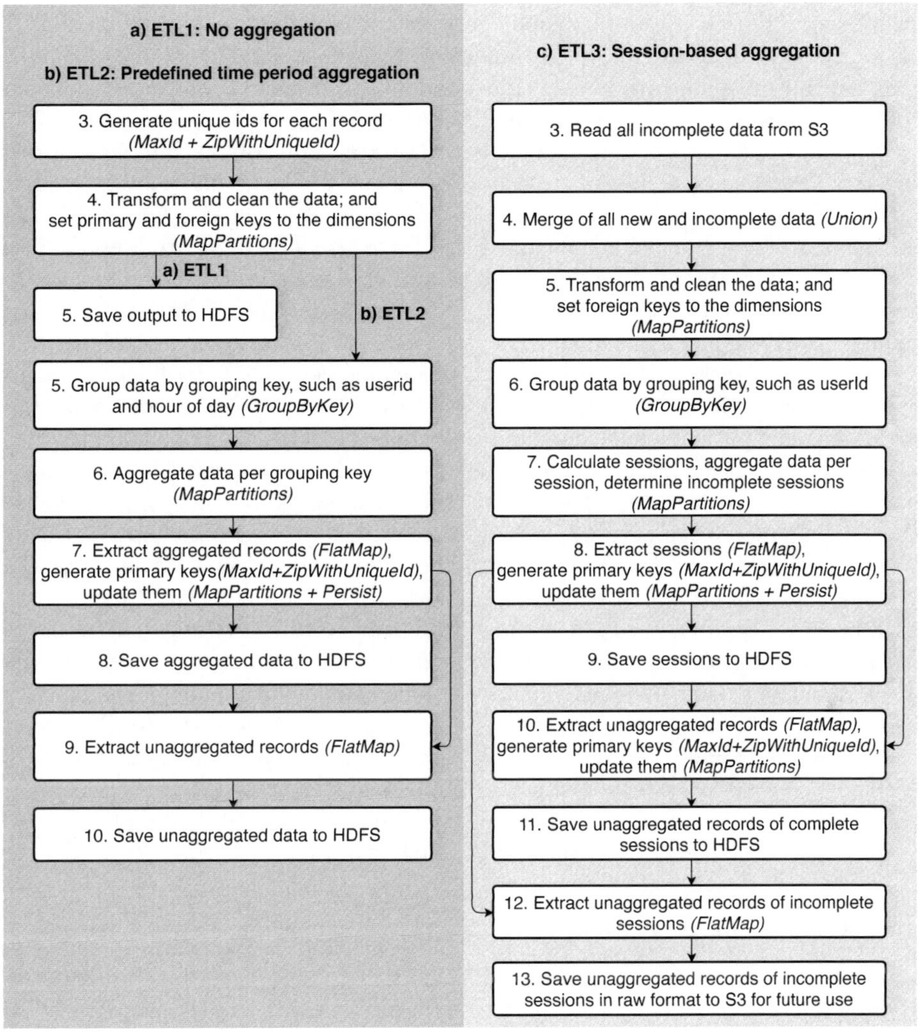

Fig. 2: Extract/Transform steps in Spark for completing the three ETL scenarios

Business (i.e., natural) keys denote unique record identifiers that could have some business meaning, but most importantly, they are managed by operational data stores (ODS). In DWH, a surrogate key is a necessary generalization of the ODS business key and is one of the essential elements of DWH design. Every join between dimension tables and fact tables in a DWH environment is based on surrogate keys, not business keys. It is up to the data extraction logic to systematically look up and replace every incoming business key with a DWH surrogate key each time either a dimension record or a fact record is brought into DWH. Surrogate keys provide independence from ODS business keys, which could be subject to deletion, updating or recycling.

Populating foreign keys in fact tables in a traditional way with joins between the fact and dimension tables would be inefficient for large datasets because it requires shuffling and redistributing the data across the cluster nodes. On the other hand, if the dimensions' business and surrogate keys are distributed across nodes in advance, populating foreign surrogate keys is a simple dictionary lookup operation based on business keys with $O(1)$ complexity. This method does not require reshuffling and adheres to the data locality principle.

Figure 2 shows the data flow for all proposed scenarios. The first two steps are common, so they are omitted. Each scenario is described in details in the following subsections. After the cluster is started per a defined schedule, Spark first loads business and surrogate keys of all processed dimensions. Also, the maximum values of surrogate keys for each table are calculated in step 1, because they define the starting values of new surrogate keys to be generated during a subsequent run of the ETL process. Then, Spark distributes them with the Broadcast operation to each node. For non-existing business keys, new surrogate keys are generated as a sequence of increasing integers, starting from the current maximum key for the table. Gaps in the generated sequence of numbers are allowed by design (for computational efficiency). During the surrogate key generation, their density is calculated (defined as the ratio of the total number of surrogate keys and the maximum), which shows how efficiently they are used. If the density is low and the maximum value of surrogate keys increases rapidly, this may be used to recommend a redesign. Step 2 reads all new data from S3 (using Spark operations TextFiles or WholeTextFiles).

4.1 ETL Scenario 1: No Aggregation

The first scenario requires parsing, data type conversion, setting foreign keys (Extract-Transform steps) and loading only into the fact tables of DWH. This scenario is the simplest of the three and does not need any aggregations in the fact tables. It is required for the whole generated data be available at the lowest level of granularity (after performing proper cleansing), including associations with other entities in the system. Some typical use-cases of this workflow refer to the log analysis in resource management, application troubleshooting, marketing insights, regulatory compliance, security, etc. What is common about these use-cases is that the original data needs to be preserved entirely without any level of aggregation so that particular events can be pinpointed. Hence, it is also worth mentioning one more application aspect – regulatory compliance and security. Indeed, maintaining compliance with industry regulations often requires the data to be preserved in a source format to tag certain events.

Step 3 generates unique numeric identifiers for each record with the ZipWithUniqueId transformation. Even though there can be gaps in the generated numbers, it does not require data shuffling, making it very efficient. When the maximum surrogate key value (MaxId) is added to the generated number, a unique surrogate key of each record is obtained. In step 4 the transform phase of ETL is performed, consisting of data transformations, data cleaning, type casting, setting primary surrogate keys (using unique IDs generated in the previous step) and setting foreign keys to the dimensions (by performing lookups in the dictionary already distributed to each node in step 1). This step uses the MapPartitions Spark operation, which guarantees that the transformations will not cause shuffling, thus adhering to the data locality principle. Step 5 stores the output of the transformations to HDFS in text format.

4.2 ETL Scenario 2: Predefined Time Period Aggregation

Scenario 2 refers to a predefined time period aggregation. It is present through aggregating the data for nominal or dynamically quantized column domain (e.g., user, campaign, asset) in conjunction with some predefined time period. Associating the aggregated records with the actual records that comprise them, allows drilling down. For example, if suddenly a spike in the number of daily signups happens, the change can be quickly validated by checking logs to see who signed up and when. Such functionality is not always possible with traditional dashboards, as they do not maintain the data source that is used to calculate the metrics. Another use of aggregated data is for concept drift detection, trend analysis over extended periods, or feature engineering [19].

The corresponding steps are shown in Figure 2, flow b. Steps 1 to 4 are like in scenario 1. The GroupByKey operation handles records with the same grouping key in step 5. Step 6 aggregates records within the same group, thus producing a new record with one or more aggregate values (e.g., count, sum). For each such new record, all records that comprise it are also preserved. Step 7 extracts the aggregated records (with the Map or FlatMap operations), generates primary keys for them with the same method as applied in step 3 and updates the aggregated records to reflect primary keys. It also sets the foreign key to the new record in all records that comprise it. Step 8 stores new records (without the comprising records) on HDFS. Step 9 extracts the comprising records of each new record with the FlatMap operation in one set of the unaggregated records. Then these records are stored to HDFS in step 10.

4.3 ETL Scenario 3: Session-based Aggregation

Aggregation on predefined time periods still does not cover all use-cases. For instance, consider the task of feature engineering. In many applications, e.g., churn prediction and fraud detection, meaningful features may be defined as: "the time that passed from the last occurrence of event X", "the time since the user's last login", "last use of a service", or "last bought product". Similar attributes could be utilized in other data mining applications, such as identifying reasons for service outages or even predicting them. Even though such features are easy to understand, their calculation requires to look in a variable, practically unlimited data periods [20]. On the other hand, in typical streaming scenarios, only the very recent data portions are accessible.

Scenario 3 calculates user sessions, performs aggregation on session level and loads the data in both aggregated and unaggregated formats. We show ETL for this scenario in Figure 2, flow c. Incomplete sessions are defined as those that were still active at the end of the period that is being processed. Records of incomplete sessions are then stored separately so that they could be taken into account in the next run. Step 3 reads the data corresponding to incomplete sessions. Step 4 merges two datasets – new and incomplete data. In step 5, the data is cleansed and transformed, and foreign keys to dimensions are set. In step 6, the records are grouped by a more coarse grouping key, such as the user id. This enables implementation of complex business rules in step 7 for determining user sessions because all recent user records are available sequentially in one logical and physical location. During step 7, full sessions are determined, along with the records that comprise them and some aggregations are performed per session. Step 8 extracts full sessions with the FlatMap operator, generates primary keys for them and updates the records to reflect the generated keys: aggregated to have proper primary keys and comprising records to have proper foreign keys to the corresponding aggregate (session) records. The result of this step is preserved in memory as it will be needed three times in the following steps. Step 9 stores full sessions to HDFS. Using the result from step 8, Step 10 combines the unaggregated records that comprised completed sessions, and generates and sets their primary keys. In step 11, these records are stored to HDFS. Step 12 extracts the unaggregated records of incomplete sessions into one set and then step 13 stores them in the original format (without any data cleansing and transformations) in S3 so they can be used in the next run in step 3.

4.4 Data Load Steps for All Scenarios

After the last step described in each scenario, Data Load steps are executed. First, the data is loaded to DWH, using the proposed distributed data load algorithm that processes one table at a time in a parallel way. Finally, all metadata that was collected during the cluster lifetime (i.e., various metrics such as duration of each step, the number of processed records per table, etc.) is loaded into DWH and then the cluster self-terminates.

5 Experimental Results

Let us present the results of evaluation of three ETL scenarios with the proposed architecture. Table 1 shows information about the considered datasets.

Table 1: Statistics on datasets and generated records in each ETL scenario

	ETL scenario			
	ETL1	ETL2	ETL3	ETL3 (100 days)
Source type	CSV	JSON	JSON	JSON
Source columns	31	17	17	17
Destination aggregated columns	-	86	86	86
Destination unaggregated columns	86	26	26	26
Source S3 objects	550	410K	410K	36M
Source size (GB)	53	30	30	2603
Source records	137M	44M	46M	3987M
Destination unaggregated records	137M	44M	44M	3985M
Destination unaggregated size (GB)	94	28	28	2427
Destination aggregated records	-	2M	1M	108M
Destination aggregated size (GB)	-	2	1	70

The data was provided from a service that collects user logs very frequently, and the processing result was timely and actionable information. All three scenarios were used to populate data marts that we designed for a subscription video-on-demand company that was competing with Netflix in their local market. First, decision support systems leveraged the aggregated data for evaluating investment opportunities and tracking historical performance. ETL scenarios 2/3 were applied for feature engineering to build machine learning systems for: churn prediction, fraud detection (i.e., account sharing against the terms of use), and predicting service outages. Finally, we preprocessed the log data to infer implicit user feedback, in order to build a recommendation system.

The experiments with each of the scenarios were repeated ten times and all presented times represent the average of the repetitions. All scenarios were evaluated on clusters with 5, 10, 15, 20, 30, 40 and 60 nodes so that we could investigate the impact of cluster size on the speedup.

ETL scenario 1 We experimented with the whole data stored in one large text file, as well as 550 smaller text files (see Table 1, column ETL1). The size of the source files did not influence the performance of the system, which is understandable, considering that S3 is a distributed storage system. The performance of each step (Spark duration and DLA duration) depending on cluster size is shown in Figure 3a. Note that Amazon does not bill the booting duration. Similarly, the cost depending on cluster size is shown in Figure 3b. It is evident that the 15-node cluster was the most cost-effective because its chargeable duration is just under one hour. It is also notable that when we used more than 30 nodes, the overall duration did not improve significantly.

ETL scenario 2 Duration of each step and the cost for this case study (Table 1, column ETL2) depending on cluster size is shown in Figures 4a and 4b, respectively. Obviously, the 5-node and 15-node clusters are the cheapest. However, the latter completes the job faster for the same cost.

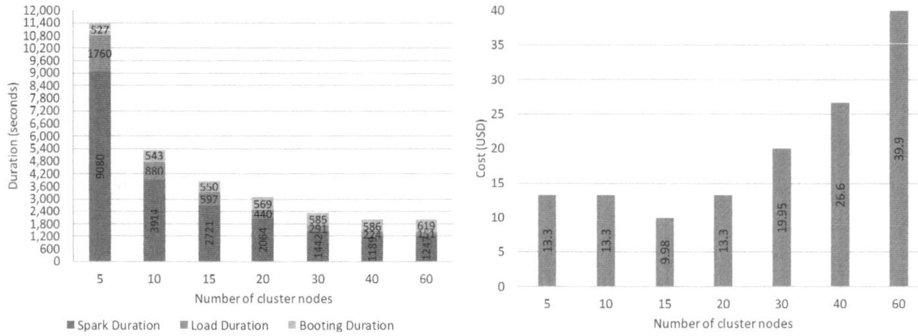

(a) Duration (b) Cost

Fig. 3: Duration of each step (a) / cost (b) for ETL scenario 1 per cluster size

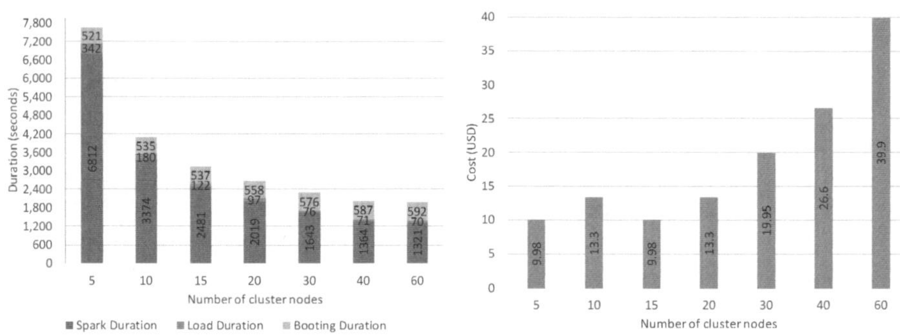

(a) Duration (b) Cost

Fig. 4: Duration of each step (a) / cost (b) for ETL scenario 2 per cluster size

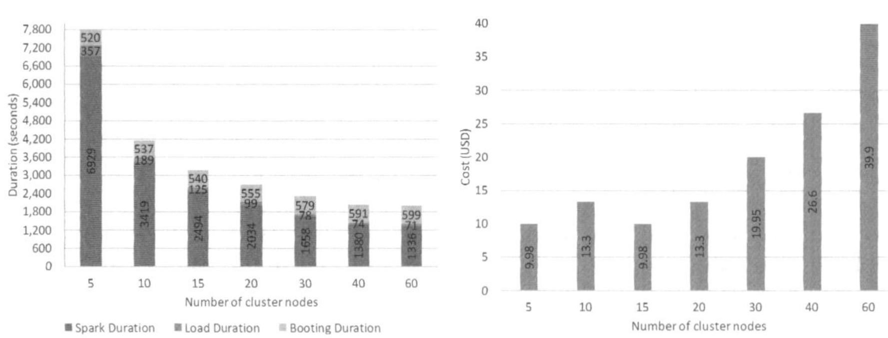

(a) Duration (b) Cost

Fig. 5: Duration of each step (a) / cost (b) for ETL scenario 3 per cluster size

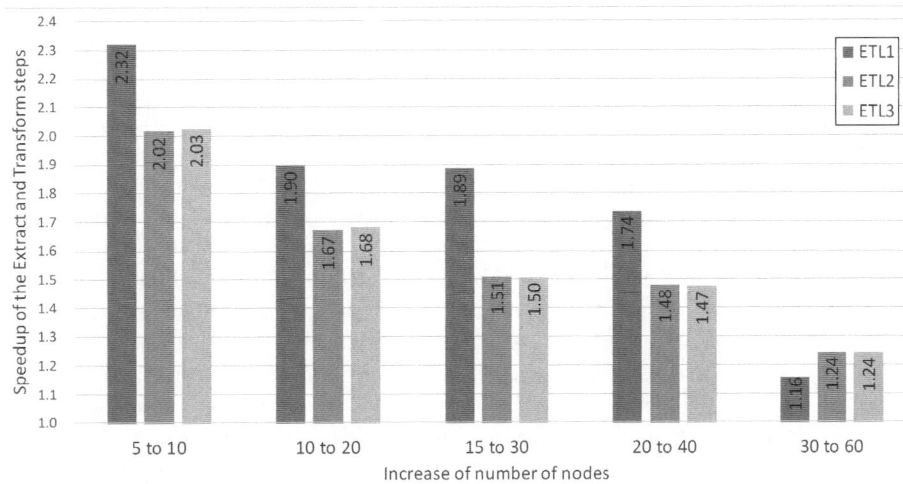

Fig. 6: Speedup of Extract-Transform steps (Spark) of the three ETL scenarios.

ETL scenario 3 The results of the experiments with the third scenario, which performs session-based aggregation, are shown in Figures 5a and 5b. As before, the most cost-effective is the 15-node cluster.

To verify that our architecture is reliable and sustainable, we executed scenario 3 (the most complex one) on a considerably increased workload using the data collected during 100 days (Table 1, column ETL3 (100 days)). We used a 20-node cluster with "r3.2xlarge" instances. Considering that the volume of source data (2.6 TB) exceeds the cluster's storage capacity ($20 \times 160 = 3.2$ TB total hard drive space, of which less than 1 TB is available for HDFS), the Spark and DLA jobs were executed interchangeably one day at a time (i.e., flow c shown in Figure 2 was executed 100 times on the same cluster). Execution in a one-day-at-a-time fashion also enabled the results of the ETL to be available even though the whole process is still in progress. The Spark jobs completed in 174,481 seconds in total, or on average about 1,745 seconds per daily data volume. This is considerably less than when a cluster of same size processes daily data (2,034 seconds, see Figure 5a). We attribute these savings to the overhead of starting a Spark job on a new cluster and to the variance in daily data volumes. DLA completed in 8,514 seconds, an increase which is linearly proportional to the processed data volume. Figure 6 shows the obtained speedup of Extract-Transform steps in Spark when comparing different cluster sizes for the three ETL scenarios, which is based on the results reported in Figures 3a-5a. Obviously, as the number of nodes increases, the speedup decreases.

6 Conclusions

We proposed a cloud-based architecture for efficient ETL of Big Data. Spark performs Extract-Transform phases. Then the results are loaded into a data warehouse using distributed load agents that utilize the processing resources of the cluster slaves (edge nodes), instead of the database server. To that end, ETL employs on-demand Hadoop clusters with a variable size that run for a limited duration on Amazon AWS. By defining and evaluating three ETL scenarios that cover a variety of use cases, we demonstrated the scalability of our solution. Most notable was the non-trivial usage of the proposed scenarios for feature engineering in the considered data mining applications.

Having such run-time facilities, one can think about automatizing ETL's design too. Elemental data analysis (file formats, data types, measure units), data model recovery, dimensional model identification, are activities that at least to some extent can be performed by a computer program. Our initial experiments are promising. We believe that the full ETL effort from the design to a running data warehouse can be limited to days instead of months.

References

1. Apanowicz, C.: Data Warehouse Discovery Framework: The Foundation. In: Proceedings of International Conferences on Database Theory and Application (DTA 2010) and Bio-Science and Bio-Technology (BSBT 2010), Held as Part of Future Generation Information Technology Conference (FGIT 2010). Volume 118 of Communications in Computer and Information Science., Springer (2010) 142–154
2. Apanowicz, C.: Data Warehouse Discovery Framework: The Case Study. In: Proceedings of International Conferences on Database Theory and Application (DTA 2010) and Bio-Science and Bio-Technology (BSBT 2010), Held as Part of Future Generation Information Technology Conference (FGIT 2010). Volume 118 of Communications in Computer and Information Science., Springer (2010) 155–166
3. Chaudhuri, S., Dayal, U., Narasayya, V.: An Overview of Business Intelligence Technology. Communications of the ACM **54**(8) (2011) 88–98
4. Mukherjee, R., Kar, P.: A Comparative Review of Data Warehousing ETL Tools with New Trends and Industry Insight. In: Proceedings of IEEE 7th International Advance Computing Conference (IACC 2017). (2017) 943–948
5. Zdravevski, E., Lameski, P., Kulakov, A.: Row Key Designs of NoSQL Database Tables and Their Impact on Write Performance. In: Proceedings of 24th Euromicro International Conference on Parallel, Distributed, and Network-based Processing (PDP 2016). (2016) 10–17
6. Mallek, H., Ghozzi, F., Teste, O., Gargouri, F.: BigDimETL: ETL for Multidimensional Big Data. In: Proceedings of 16th International Conference on Intelligent Systems Design and Applications (ISDA 2016). Volume 557 of Advances in Intelligent Systems and Computing., Springer (2017) 935–944
7. Condie, T., Conway, N., Alvaro, P., Hellerstein, J.M., Elmeleegy, K., Sears, R.: MapReduce Online. In: Proceedings of 7th USENIX Conference on Networked Systems Design and Implementation (NSDI 2010), USENIX Association (2010) 21–21

8. Hellerstein, J.M., Ré, C., Schoppmann, F., Wang, D.Z., Fratkin, E., Gorajek, A., Ng, K.S., Welton, C., Feng, X., Li, K., Kumar, A.: The MADlib Analytics Library or MAD Skills, the SQL. Proceedings of the VLDB Endowment **5**(12) (2012) 1700–1711
9. Low, Y., Bickson, D., Gonzalez, J., Guestrin, C., Kyrola, A., Hellerstein, J.M.: Distributed GraphLab: A Framework for Machine Learning and Data Mining in the Cloud. Proceedings of the VLDB Endowment **5**(8) (2012) 716–727
10. Boja, C., Pocovnicu, A., Batagan, L.: Distributed Parallel Architecture for "Big Data". Informatica Economica **16**(2) (2012) 116
11. Chevalier, M., El Malki, M., Kopliku, A., Teste, O., Tournier, R.: How Can We Implement a Multidimensional Data Warehouse Using NoSQL? In: Proceedings of 17th International Conference on Enterprise Information Systems (ICEIS 2015). Volume 241 of Lecture Notes in Business Information Processing., Springer (2015) 108–130
12. Liu, X., Thomsen, C., Pedersen, T.B.: CloudETL: Scalable Dimensional ETL for Hive. In: Proceedings of 18th International Database Engineering Applications Symposium (IDEAS 2014), ACM (2014) 195–206
13. Souissi, S., BenAyed, M.: GENUS: An ETL tool treating the Big Data Variety. In: Proceedings of IEEE/ACS 13th International Conference on Computer Systems and Applications (AICCSA 2016). (2016) 1–8
14. Li, X., Mao, Y.: Real-time Data ETL Framework for Big Real-time Data Analysis (ICIA 2015). In: Proceedings of IEEE International Conference on Information and Automation. (2015) 1289–1294
15. Pääkkönen, P., Pakkala, D.: Reference Architecture and Classification of Technologies, Products and Services for Big Data Systems. Big Data Research **2**(4) (2015) 166–186
16. Singh, K., Guntuku, S.C., Thakur, A., Hota, C.: Big Data Analytics Framework for Peer-to-peer Botnet Detection Using Random Forests. Information Sciences **278** (2014) 488–497
17. Bai, J.: Feasibility Analysis of Big Log Data Real Time Search based on Hbase and ElasticSearch. In: Proceedings of 9th International Conference on Natural Computation (ICNC 2013), IEEE (2013) 1166–1170
18. Ślęzak, D., Synak, P., Wojna, A., Wróblewski, J.: Two Database Related Interpretations of Rough Approximations: Data Organization and Query Execution. Fundamenta Informaticae **127**(1-4) (2013) 445–459
19. Zdravevski, E., Lameski, P., Kulakov, A., Gjorgjevikj, D.: Feature Selection and Allocation to Diverse Subsets for Multi-label Learning Problems with Large Datasets. In: Proceedings of Federated Conference on Computer Science and Information Systems (FedCSIS 2014), IEEE (2014) 387–394
20. Ślęzak, D., Grzegorowski, M., Janusz, A., Kozielski, M., Nguyen, S.H., Sikora, M., Stawicki, S., Wróbel, Ł.: A Framework for Learning and Embedding Multi-Sensor Forecasting Models into a Decision Support System: A Case Study of Methane Concentration in Coal Mines. Information Sciences **451-452** (2018) 112–133

An Exploration into the Contexts of Errors and Value Patterns in Data Classification

William Wu

Faculty of Engineering and Information Technology
University of Technology Sydney, Australia
William.Z.Wu@student.uts.edu.au

Abstract. Quoting out of context can be deceiving, likewise, data mining without context can be misleading. Context consideration is important because it provides additional information in terms of background, connection and perspectives, as profoundly illustrated in the parable of "The Blind Men and the Elephant", and this can be a reminder of the need to explore the context of errors.
Errors in data mining and classification are inevitable due to various factors such as sampling and computation restrictions, measurement and assumption limitations, therefore it may be worthwhile exploring and learning from errors from various perspectives and within contexts, rather than simply directing all effort and resources with the intention of eliminating them.
Instead of taking a typical and direct approach to tackle errors head-on by way of theory and algorithm enhancement to reduce errors, this paper discuses a retrospective way which focuses on the examination of errors from the context of value ambiguity between class labels, to explore various aspects of errors and value patterns by transforming a confusion matrix from a classification result table into a matrix of categorical, incremental and correlational context, to emulate a kind of internal context to help identify and understand errors and value patterns in a contextual and introspective way for the benefit of knowledge discovery.

Keywords: Context, value ambiguity, confusion matrix, context construction, contextual analysis

1 Introduction

1.1 Importance of Contexts and Errors

One example to demonstrate the importance of context analysis is the detection of the fraudulent financial data patterns of Enron in data mining research based on publicly available financial data [1]. Enron, an American energy company, declared bankruptcy in December 2001 and its share price dived from $90 in August 2000 to $0.12 in January 2002. Its collapse was due to financial fraud committed by the management team, which resulted in the loss of thousands of jobs and the demise of Arthur Andersen, one of the largest accounting firms in the world at the time [2].

It is widely accepted that the identification of management fraud can be difficult because high-level management authorities can easily overrule internal controls and protocols to falsify reports with a high level of sophistication and collusion. However, by comparing the reported data from a fraudulent firm like Enron with contextual information, such as a "centroid" model from an aggregated and balanced data set of industry-representative firms, together with finer-grained historical data integration and comparison based on quarterly reports in addition to yearly reports, some unusual patterns became more conspicuous in Enron's data within the context of "centroid" values, especially when compared progressively in a quarter-by-quarter way, as shown in Figure 1.

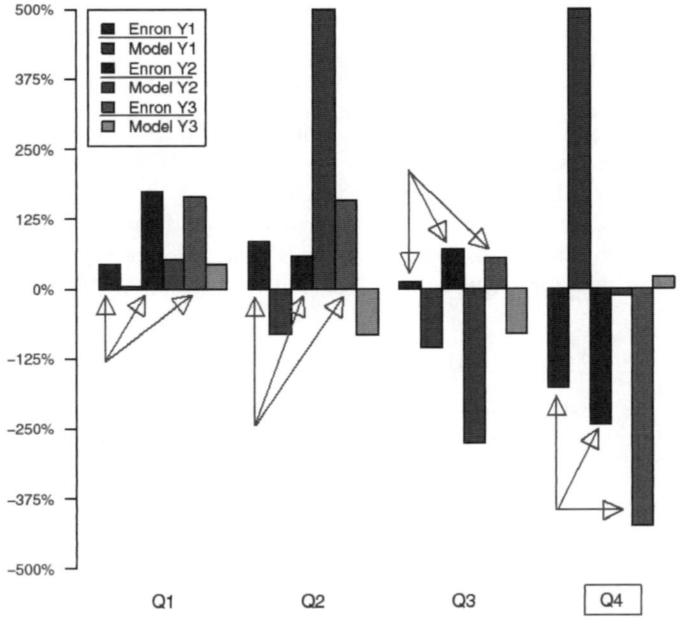

Figure 1 - Quarterly cash flow earnings ratio comparison between Enron and its industry model

This figure shows that Enron's cash flow earnings ratio increased as the fraud progressed in its final three years. While showing increases in the first three non-audited quarters of each year, each fourth quarter turned sharply negative when it was audited as part of the year-end activities and with more special purpose entities to be included or manipulated in the annual balance sheet.

On the other hand, unusual financial data patterns do not necessarily indicate a certain fraud, as shown in Figure 2. While Enron's Year 2000 revenue was showing too good to be true and it indeed committed management fraud, it would be wrong to speculate Texaco and Goldman Sachs were also likely associated with management fraud simply because they were showing similarly and exceptionally good performance but on a smaller scale.

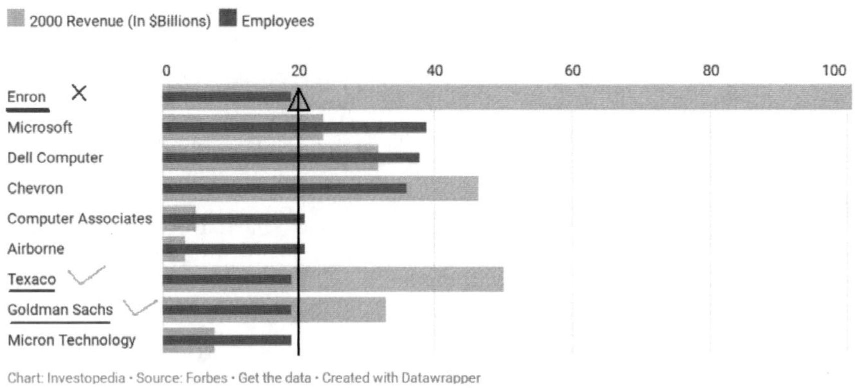

Figure 2 - Enron's Year 2000 Reported Revenue vs. Similarly Sized Companies

Nevertheless, wrong decision and errors are inevitable, so instead of attempting to avoid them or get rid of them at all costs, it may be more sensible to look into the errors closely in order to understand them better, to analyze errors and value patterns from various perspectives, to examine and evaluate errors and value patterns rationally, systematically and contextually; in essence, and within context, to consider errors as a part of the knowledge in order to help develop better preventive and corrective measures.

1.2 Measuring the Ambiguity of Value Ranges as Contexts of Errors

An error can be considered as a kind of discrepancy between one's expectation and their observation and perception, and such discrepancy sometimes may be due to ambiguity. The word ambiguity in this context indicates there may be more than one option available and that the number of options and the exact meaning of each option can be open for interpretation, which can subsequently cause confusion and lead to misjudgment, misclassification and errors in scientific and data mining terms.

In an attempt to explore this idea of treating ambiguity as contexts of error in order to help understand errors in data mining tasks, one way is to study the ambiguous value patterns to examine if ambiguous value patterns may be more error-sensitive and more likely to lead to errors. If such ambiguous and error-sensitive value patterns can be identified in a systematic and effective way, they may become a form of contexts of error which can consequently provide meaningful clues about errors to help improve error preventive and corrective measures and knowledge discovery about the data as a whole. Some specific terms introduced in an error-sensitive pattern evaluation study can be adapted as a part of this context of error exploration when discussing binary classification scenarios [3], as illustrated in Figure 3.

For example, the term *ambiguous value range* which describes a value range in which the attribute values of negative samples in green and positive samples in red coexist, colored in blue; the term *attribute-error counter* describes the number of misclassified samples with their attribute values being within such an *ambiguous value range* of a specific attribute; and the term *error-sensitive attribute* describes an attribute that is considered to be more prone to errors compared to others during a data mining and classification task, and its risk assessment is initially based on counting and ranking the *attribute-error counter* values amongst the involved attributes, and selecting the attribute with the highest count as the most error-sensitive attribute.

Figure 3 – Ambiguity due to overlapped value ranges may constitute contexts of errors

1.3 Transforming Confusion Matrices into Matrices of Contexts

Based on the idea of contexts of errors by value range ambiguity in data classification, its error-sensitive attributes can then be incorporated into a confusion matrix transformation process as the lead attributes when used in constructing a multi-dimensional contextual model, and the application scope of this transformation process can subsequently be expanded from weakly supervised learning to contextual analysis for error and value pattern analysis [4].

A confusion matrix is a simple and effective way to summarize classification results by tallying the category results in a tabular form, which makes result comparison easy between class label categories, especially for the binary classification scenarios used in this study (true negatives and true positives), and also for the error categories (false negatives and false positives) [5], as shown in Figure 4.

Confusion matrices can be easily constructed based on categorized classification results and do not depend on any specific classification algorithm. In fact, standard data mining tools, such as WEKA and R, already include a confusion matrix as a built-in feature of their classifier packages.

Because of these advantages, such a cross-category comparison can be viewed as a form of context for individual category statistics, in conjunction with other performance statistics such as accuracy and sensitivity, to provide some forms of contextual environment as a part of the post-classification analysis, to help explore and evaluate potential relationships between value patterns and classification results within their categorical, incremental and correlational context in a simple, visual and systematic way.

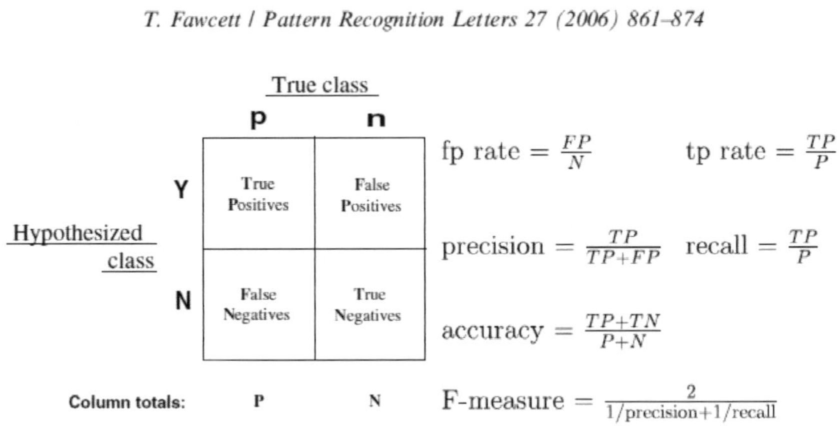

Figure 4 - Fawcett's illustration of a confusion matrix and performance metrics calculation

The rest of this paper is organized as follows. Section 2 reviews some influential work that inspired this study. Section 3 outlines the key steps involved in this contextual analysis. Section 4 summarizes the experiments and results on selected datasets. Section 5 discusses potential problems and issues. Finally, Section 6 concludes this context evaluation for errors and value patterns and outlines a plan for future exploration.

2 Related Work

The primary focus of ambiguous value pattern analysis in the field of data mining and classification has been on algorithm and application development, such as the various enhancements to the k-NN algorithm, the SVM algorithm and neural networks. Their related theories are mostly based on statistics, such as entropy and information theory [6,7], prior and posterior probability [8,9], and uncertainty theories [10,11].

On the other hand, research on context in terms of data mining has mainly focused on external factors, such as domain context in relation to personal and medical history when analyzing diagnostic data, location context in relation to geographical and altitude area, user context in relation to the user and the team conducting the research and their profile and query history [12-14]. These external contexts are defined and utilized to sense and collate, to integrate and reason about the circumstantial and correlated information on *who*, *when*, *where*, *what* and *why* in terms of ontology and in relation to the datasets in order to select and reach optimized decisions.

Several studies have investigated the extraction of finer-grained information from within the data as a form of internal context to help identify useful value patterns in data mining tasks, but the scale and number of these research studies is limited. One recent example is research into management fraud by adding categorical context based on creating industry-representative centroid models, and adding temporal context based on the quarterly breakdown of financial indicators and data, to improve the detection of fraud patterns when examining the publicly available data of large corporations [1,2].

A confusion matrix is a simple and effective way to summarize and compare classification results and has recently been used in attribute selection model development and error detection [15-17], but it is predominately used to highlight the basic numerical variation between result categories at their face values rather than to explore further into the hierarchical differential in value patterns categorized by each matrix cell, to identify and evaluate potentially contextual information represented by such value patterns between categories in an integrated and implicit way.

There has been criticism of the confusion matrix over its inadequacy in dealing with imbalanced class labels and cost sensitive classification issues. For example, in the case of medical diagnostic data classification, if errors such as false negatives are fewer than false positives, the cost can be far more expensive and the associated risk can be far more serious; therefore, more advanced measures for performance results, such as the receiver operating characteristic (ROC) curve and F-score should be considered more favorably [5,18,19]. While agreeing with the criticism, this study takes a pragmatic approach to making use of a confusion matrix because of its simplicity and its capability of accommodating and visualizing more forms of context in a single place.

3 Context Exploration for Error and Value Pattern Analysis

3.1 Post-Classification Analysis and Context Identification

This study of contextual analysis starts as a part of the post-classification analysis process, while the underlying classification platform can be based on any classification algorithm, e.g. decision tree, neural network or naive Bayes, as illustrated in Figure 5.

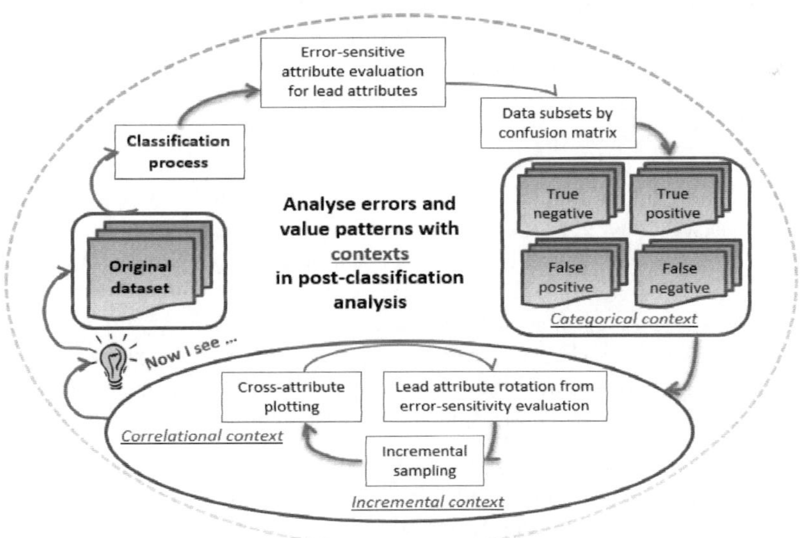

Figure 5 - Post-classification analysis is utilized to construct matrices of contexts

3.2 Evaluate Context of Ambiguity and Error-Sensitive Value Patterns

Key steps in evaluating error-sensitive attributes include:

1. Calculate ambiguous value ranges and attribute-error counter values
   For each involved attribute
     For each correctly classified sample
       find negative samples' min & max value and their mean value;
       find positive samples' min & max value and their mean value;
       compare these values to determine the ambiguous value ranges;
     For each misclassified sample
       if the attribute value is within its attribute's ambiguous value range
         then increase its attribute's attribute-error counter by one;
2. Sort the attribute-error counter values in descending order to highlight the most ambiguous and error-sensitive attributes in the top-ranking positions

This is a kind of reverse-engineering process to evaluate which attribute and which value range is more likely to be associated with errors, and the identified error-sensitive attributes can be highlighted and prioritized to be key lead attributes in constructing matrices of contexts for error and value pattern analysis as the next step.

3.3 Transform a Confusion Matrix into a Matrix of Categorical, Incremental and Correlational Context

Key steps in this transformation process include:

1. Evaluate initial classification result and its confusion matrix
2. Define a list of lead attributes by reviewing/comparing the error-sensitive attributes and the significant attributes returned by gain ratio and info gain evaluator
3. Select a lead attribute and redistribute its data records with standardized values into categorized subsets according to their confusion matrix result categories
4. For each categorized subset sorted by the current lead attribute
   Extract the median record from each decile to simulate ten value growth stages in a vertical way within its categorized cell as incremental context;
   Start from the current lead attribute and for its ten growth stages, connect and plot lines across other attributes accordingly as correlational context;
   Evaluate these incremental and correlational contexts in the form of line and value patterns between matrix categories as categorical context;
5. Select the next lead attribute from the rotation list determined in Step 2 and repeat Steps 3 & 4 to construct more contextual models for further analysis

If significant patterns can be observed between matrix categories for a lead attribute, it can be an indication that some specific characteristics of this lead attribute and value patterns may have a greater influence or association with the underlying result categories, and may provide additional clues for domain experts and researchers to conduct exploration with new focus and more context to understand the patterns and data better.

4 Experiments and Analysis

4.1 Utilization of Existing Classification Models and Results

Experiments are conducted on ten UCI datasets [20], and WEKA's [21] C4.5/J48 decision tree is the classification algorithm used in the experiments with a standard configuration, but other classifiers can also be used. WEKA's gain ratio and information gain evaluators for attribute ranking are also used for comparison in the experiments.

In the experiment with the Pima Indians Diabetes dataset which has eight attributes and 768 records, the initial classification result and confusion matrix are shown in the left-hand column of Table 1. The top-3 ranked error-sensitive attributes by attribute-error counter, together with the top-3 most significant attributes by gain ratio and information gain evaluator are shown in a comparison child-table within the right-hand column of Table 1. Because the top-3 attributes ranked by these three different methods are the same, it can be an indication that the most ambiguous and error-sensitive attributes may also be the most deterministic and significant attributes in this specific dataset.

Table 1 - Classification result for Pima diabetes dataset and options for lead attributes

<table>
<tr>
<td>Correctly Classified 567 at 73.83 %
Incorrectly Classified 201 at 26.17 %

== Confusion Matrix ==
a b <-- classified as
407 93 | a = negative
108 160 | b = positive</td>
<td>
<table>
<tr><td>Attribute-error counter</td><td>Gain ratio</td><td>Info gain</td></tr>
<tr><td>plas (83)</td><td>plas (0.10)</td><td>plas (0.19)</td></tr>
<tr><td>mass (70)</td><td>mass (0.09)</td><td>mass (0.07)</td></tr>
<tr><td>age (31)</td><td>age (0.07)</td><td>age (0.07)</td></tr>
</table>
</td>
</tr>
</table>

4.2 Constructing Contexts for "plas" as the Lead Attribute in the Pima Indians Diabetes Dataset

After normalizing original attribute values to the standardized range of [0, 100], these 768 data records are redistributed into four data subsets according to their confusion matrix result categories - 407 in the true negative subset, 160 in the true positive subset, 108 in the false positive subset and 93 in the false negative subset. The attribute "plas" is selected as the first lead attribute because it is ranked as the most ambiguous and error-sensitive attribute in this experiment. Ten key value growth stages based on sorted deciles, together with values of other attributes from the same ten related instance records, are extracted to prepare for the construction of the incremental and correlational context accordingly, as shown in Table 2.

When positioning the lead attribute in the first column and connecting and plotting the values across other attributes from their corresponding records horizontally, the ups and downs of the line patterns shown in the graphs can represent how these attributes correlate and "work together" with the lead attribute "plas" along its incremental growth path. Some interesting plotting patterns can be observed amongst the four matrix categories as shown in Table 3, and they help visualize this multi-contextual model from a high-level perspective and specific patterns of interests for further analysis.

Table 2 - Establishing categorical and incremental context for “plas” as the lead attribute

“plas” is the lead attribute in this round of incremental sampling by the confusion matrix for the Pima diabetes dataset																			
Decile by plas	**plas**	mass	age	preg	pres	skin	insu	pedi	Class	Decile by plas	**plas**	mass	age	preg	pres	skin	insu	pedi	class
1st - lowest	**37**	40	10	29	49	0	0	8	true negative	1st - lowest	**55**	48	28	0	72	30	0	33	true positive
2nd	**42**	57	3	0	67	31	15	7	true negative	2nd	**64**	48	10	18	59	25	22	20	true positive
3rd	**45**	42	0	6	54	23	11	4	true negative	3rd	**68**	42	35	65	69	35	15	8	true positive
4th	**48**	37	30	18	46	34	14	37	true negative	4th	**72**	69	42	6	67	46	21	11	true positive
5th	**51**	53	8	0	62	0	0	5	true negative	5th	**76**	64	25	47	64	32	25	19	true positive
6th	**53**	30	2	0	56	22	0	7	true negative	6th	**81**	79	7	0	62	57	12	29	true positive
7th	**56**	51	7	6	59	30	21	19	true negative	7th	**84**	52	52	6	72	29	0	35	true positive
8th	**59**	50	10	6	49	23	13	17	true negative	8th	**88**	50	52	18	70	27	18	46	true positive
9th	**63**	59	10	18	72	41	28	27	true negative	9th	**92**	53	33	41	69	33	0	12	true positive
10th - highest	**70**	33	0	0	51	17	25	6	true negative	10th - highest	**97**	52	7	18	57	31	0	7	true positive
Decile by plas	**plas**	mass	age	preg	pres	skin	insu	pedi	class	Decile by plas	**plas**	mass	age	preg	pres	skin	insu	pedi	class
1st - lowest	**48**	50	37	29	61	18	8	39	false positive	1st - lowest	**42**	44	42	71	59	31	0	9	false negative
2nd	**51**	44	18	18	61	0	0	2	false positive	2nd	**50**	55	42	82	64	25	22	14	false negative
3rd	**56**	51	5	35	52	39	0	8	false positive	3rd	**53**	39	13	41	49	24	0	9	false negative
4th	**62**	63	8	12	39	32	20	19	false positive	4th	**56**	70	40	65	69	40	0	36	false negative
5th	**65**	49	7	12	61	26	24	22	false positive	5th	**58**	52	18	6	57	30	11	19	false negative
6th	**70**	40	60	59	66	0	0	58	false positive	6th	**61**	51	20	0	54	30	20	5	false negative
7th	**74**	45	12	29	61	0	0	15	false positive	7th	**63**	41	47	35	64	31	0	21	false negative
8th	**77**	44	30	35	61	32	23	32	false positive	8th	**68**	46	2	24	57	0	0	47	false negative
9th	**81**	41	55	59	69	0	0	4	false positive	9th	**74**	73	10	6	77	41	0	12	false negative
10th - highest	**90**	51	65	41	78	31	0	4	false positive	10th - highest	**89**	52	0	0	49	29	57	42	false negative

Table 3 - Matrix of incremental, correlational and categorical context for "plas" as the lead attribute

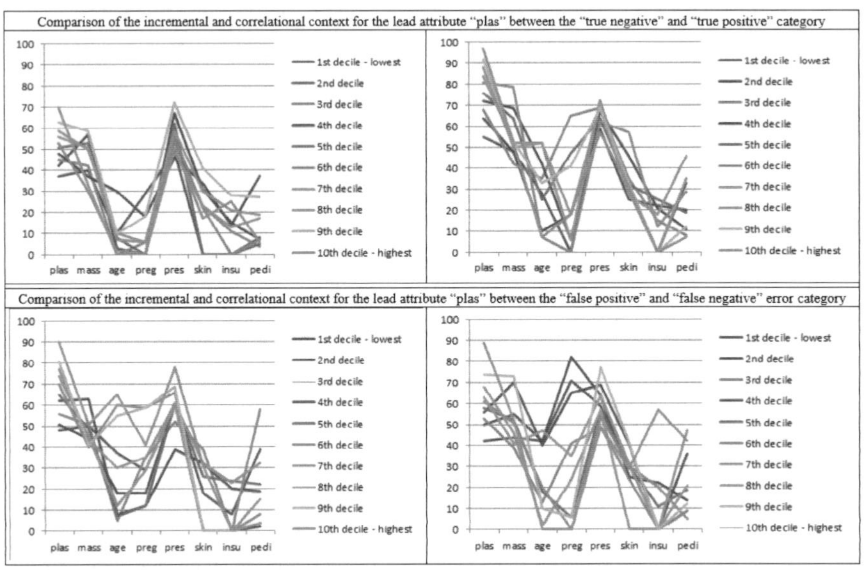

One distinctive pattern is that the majority of the “plas” values in the true negative category are bounded in the middle range between the normalized median value of 37 and 70, and the sample values are distributed rather evenly between these four deciles. As the “plas” value increases, the values of the other attributes vary rather uniformly and most are confined within a narrow value range. In contrast, the “plas” values in the true positive category start from a higher point of 55 and scatter in a wider value range up to 97, and the values of other related attributes, e.g. “mass”, “age” and “pedigree”, also fluctuate in a wider value range with higher starting points. For the two error categories, false positives and false negatives, they share similar bigger value variation patterns with the true positive category.

So, at a glance, the true negative samples show more uniformity than the true positive samples and the categories of error samples, a distinctive pattern which is common for all ten UCI datasets selected for the experiments, a kind of close reflection of what Aristotle stated in his work on Nicomachean Ethics, "it is possible to fail in many ways (for evil belongs to the class of the unlimited ... and good to that of the limited), while to succeed is possible only in one way".

While it is true to argue that this visual evaluation is too simplistic and does not reveal anything substantial, it does illustrate certain contextual differences between result categories and demonstrates one systematic way to construct an indicative contextual model as an overview. It may seem to be a naïve way to construct contexts, but it can be one way to explore within the data themselves to examine errors and value patterns closely and internally, to link and correlate such internal patterns in a more hierarchical and contextual way. It is not about challenging the established views, but rather, it is about encouraging more thoughts by constructing and reviewing patterns from different perspectives and in a systematic, complementary and contextual way.

4.3 Constructing Contexts for Other Lead Attributes in the Pima Diabetes Dataset

When applying this contextual evaluation to other attributes, it may help to create a fuller picture of the overall contexts for the involved attributes in a high-level comparative view, and help prepare the groundwork for a later comparison and consolidation of their individual context evaluation with additional information and area of focus.

Table 4 - Matrix of incremental, correlational and categorical context for "mass" as the lead attribute

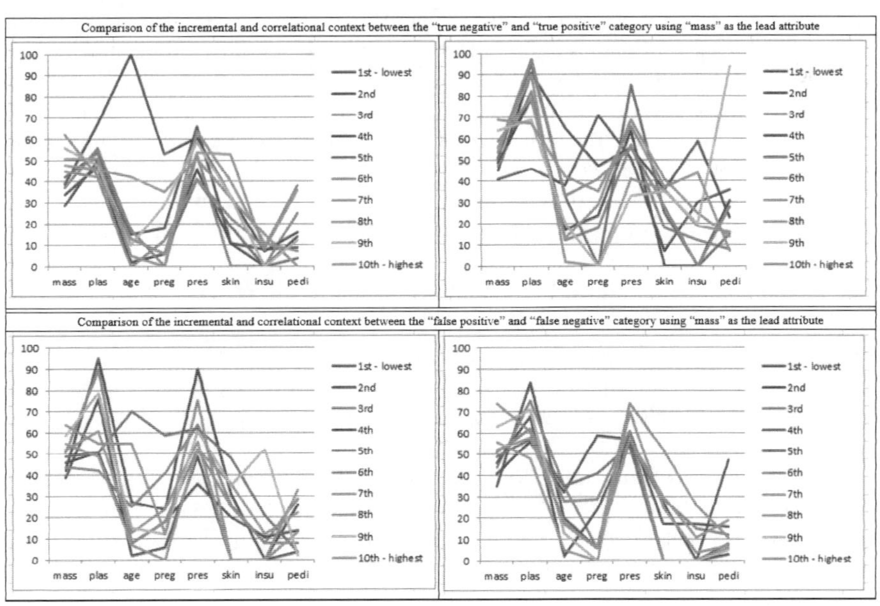

The attribute “mass” is selected as the next lead attribute in this experiment and its incremental and correlational context are first prepared in a confusion matrix structure similar to that shown in Table 2 but with “mass” in the left-hand starting column. After this, lines from the “mass” column are connected and plotted across values of other attributes of the relevant sample records at each key growth stage and in each category cell to illustrate a contextual model for the attribute “mass", as shown in Table 4.

One distinctive pattern for “mass” as the lead attribute is that for most true negative samples, the values of all attributes are within their lower six deciles and have small variation margins along the value growth path of “mass”, and the false negative samples have similar patterns except some “plas” and “pres” values are above the sixth decile. In contrast, the true positive and false positive samples have many values above the sixth decile and have bigger variation margins along the value growth path of “mass”.

On completion of multi-contextual models for selected lead attributes, such contextual analysis on errors and value patterns can be performed between attributes, to provide high-level guidance for further attribute cluster and covariance analysis based on specified patterns identified from the models. For example, when comparing the contextual models between “plas” as the lead attribute in Table 3 and “mass” as the lead attribute in Table 4, the context comparison of true negative samples shows that when “mass” is the lead, it has the incremental range [29~62] and its associated “plas” attribute has the value range [42~67]; and when “plas” is the lead, it has the incremental range [37~70] and its associated “mass” has the value range [33~59], which is a much smaller variation margin compared to the other attributes. This close-coupled pattern can be an indication of a close association between “plas” and “mass”, as proved by the gain ratio and information gain evaluator shown in Table 1.

Context construction and evaluation of the other attributes of this Pima diabetes dataset also present similar patterns, however these results are not included in this paper due to size constraints, but they all indicate that true negative and healthy samples share more consistent and predictable value patterns within their incremental and correlational context. Meanwhile, true positives and errors, meaning the unhealthy and error-prone samples, have more inconsistent and unpredictable value patterns, echoing the results from “plas” as the lead attribute.

This again demonstrates how contextual analysis may become meaningful and useful in connecting and comparing attributes and patterns for a better understanding.

4.4 Context Construction for Other Datasets

Other interesting patterns have been observed in experiments with nine other UCI datasets. One such example is the Page Blocks dataset, its attributes showing in different raking orders between the attribute-error counter, gain ratio and information gain evaluator, as shown in the child table in the right-hand column of Table 5.

To illustrate a different way to construct a matrix of contexts for comparison, the most significant attribute “length” ranked by the gain ratio evaluator has been selected as the lead for context construction as demonstration instead of the most ambiguous and error-sensitive attribute “mean_tr” ranked by attribute-error, as shown in Table 6.

Table 5 - Classification result for the Page Blocks dataset and options for lead attributes

Correctly Classified 5321 at 97.22%
Incorrectly Classified 152 at 2.78%

=== Confusion Matrix ===

```
   a    b   <-- classified as
4844   69 |   a = text
  83  477 |   b = non_text
```

Attribute-error counter	Gain ratio	Info gain
mean_tr (89)	length (0.30)	height (0.24)
p_black (43)	height (0.15)	mean_tr (0.18)
eccen (29)	mean_tr (0.14)	wb_trans (0.15)

Table 6 - Matrix of incremental, correlational and categorical context for "length" as the lead attribute

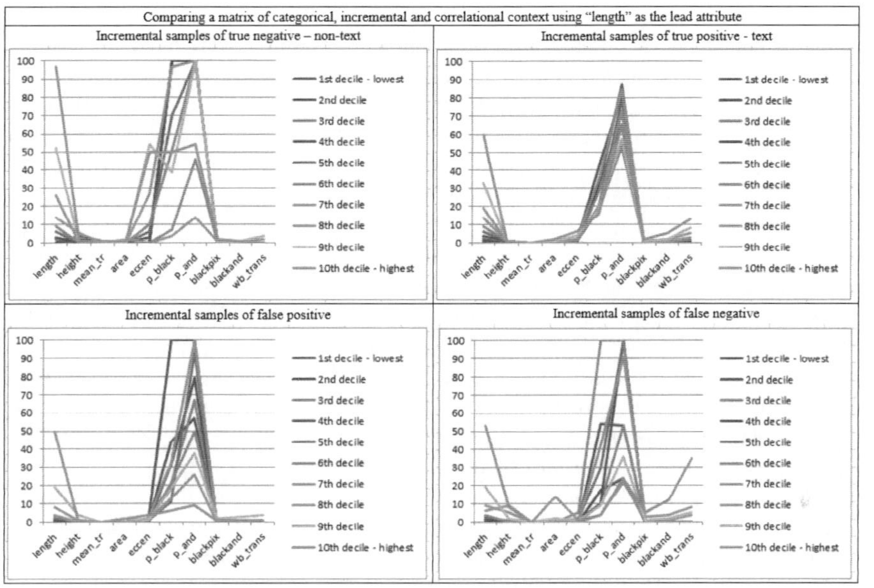

One obvious resulted pattern is the contextual difference between the true positive samples (text) and the other categories. The true positive samples show close-coupled lines between "length" and the other attributes, especially the consistent and narrow value range for the "p_black" (percentage of black pixels within the block) and the "p_and" (percentage of black pixels after the application of the Run Length Smoothing Algorithm) attribute in high deciles, which is a strong hint of black and regular text blocks, which in turn, becomes a sign of correlation between the true positive (text) category and those long and black regular text blocks.

On the other hand, the non-text and error samples show widely fluctuating line patterns, especially the large value margin in attributes "p_black" and "p_and", hinting at a large variation in color pigment and text font-size, therefore they are more likely correlated with colorful and rich format graphics or Hyper Markup text blocks, and these Hyper Markup text blocks can be a source of confusion and misclassification for the classifier to determine if a page block is really in the format of text or not, which is another reflection of what Aristotle stated in his work on Nicomachean Ethics about the many possible ways to fail and only few ways succeed.

Such comparison indicates that inviting field experts with domain knowledge to join the exploration of contexts can be a more productive way to conduct academic research on domain-specific contexts and patterns, and this indication may seem like an echo of the participation of experienced financial auditors in the mentioned management fraud research [1]. Having the right context and interpretation can be more important than making a quick claim, as philosophized in "The Blind Men and the Elephant" parable.

5 Discussion of Potential Issues

Simplicity can sometimes mean naivety and liability. Using an overlapped value range between class labels of an attribute as its ambiguous value range is an example of over-simplification even in a binary classification scenario. Context construction by the coupling of incremental sampling by a lead attribute with cross-attribute plotting under the confusion matrix structure may sound trivial, and its representation of incremental, correlational and categorical context may look inconsequential.

On the other hand, the focus of this study is not about breaking and winning in complexity, it is about exploring ways to identify internal contexts from within the data, and sorting and connecting data elements to gain more understanding about errors and data within context and to start such contextual analysis with simplicity and practicality, the inclusion of ROC curve, F-score and other techniques will be considered next.

A more specific issue concerns the suitability and adequacy of using ten sorted deciles to represent ten value growth stages of a lead attribute. Although this is not a rigid method of data sampling and its value growth representation can be over-optimistic, an initial value path can still be established by using deciles as a basic form of systematic sampling in terms of incremental context in an early stage of a study for an overview.

Another serious issue is the use of the min-max normalization method. Its application and results can be impacted by distorted value conversion and outlier values at both min and max ends, and the use of median records from each decile is one attempt to reduce such an impact.

There is no doubt that there is a long list of other problems and issues in relation to this study. On the other hand, these problems and issues can also become the contexts of further discussion and improvement.

6 Conclusion

This context construction process can be considered as an attempt to outline and construct internal context from within the data and its classification result. The ambiguous and error-sensitive value patterns can be examined as contexts of error at an attribute level, and the matrix of contexts can be analyzed as a multi-dimensional contextual model for class labels and errors from various perspectives, starting with an incremental, correlational and categorical context.

The next development may include the ROC curve and F-score with an enhanced data sampling method as a part of the context and with a dynamic selection capability, so context construction can be localized into problematic value patterns across multiple attributes with more accurate measures for a better understanding of the data and errors.

References

1. Whiting, D.G., Hansen, J.V., McDonald, J.B., Albrecht, C. and Albrecht, W.S. Machine Learning Methods for Detecting Patterns of Management Fraud. Computational Intelligence 28, No. 4, pp.505-527 (2012).
2. Segal, T. Enron Scandal: The Fall of a Wall Street Darling. Retrieved from https://www.investopedia.com/updates/enron-scandal-summary.
3. Wu, W. and Zhang, S. Evaluation of Error-Sensitive Attributes. Pacific-Asia Conference on Knowledge Discovery and Data Mining 2013, International Workshops on Trends and Applications in Knowledge Discovery and Data Mining, pp. 283-294. Springer, Berlin, Heidelberg (2013).
4. Wu, W. Weakly Supervised Learning by a Confusion Matrix of Contexts. Paper accepted for Presentation to Pacific-Asia Conference on Knowledge Discovery and Data Mining 2019, International Workshop on Weakly Supervised Learning: Progress and Future (2019).
5. Fawcett, T. An introduction to ROC analysis. Pattern recognition letters, 27(8), pp.861-874 (2006).
6. Shannon, C.E. A Mathematical Theory of Communication. The Bell System Technical Journal, vol. 27, pp. 379–423 (1948).
7. Quinlan, J.R. C4.5: Programs for Machine Learning. Morgan Kaufmann (1993).
8. Trappenberg, T.P., Back, A.D. and Amari, S.I. A Performance Measure for Classification with Ambiguous Data. BSIS Technical Report (1999).
9. Provost, F. and Fawcett, T. Robust Classification for Imprecise Environments. Machine Learning, 42(3), pp.203-231 (2001).
10. Ligeiro, R. and Mendes, R.V. Detecting and Quantifying Ambiguity: A Neural Network Approach. Soft Computing, 22(8), pp.2695-2703 (2018).
11. Klibanoff, P., Marinacci, M. and Mukerji, S. A Smooth Model of Decision Making under Ambiguity. Econometrica, 73(6), pp.1849-1892 (2005).
12. Singh, S., Vajirkar, P. and Lee, Y. Context-Based Data Mining Using Ontologies. In International Conference on Conceptual Modeling, pp. 405-418. Springer, Berlin, Heidelberg (2003).
13. Salim, F.D., Krishnaswamy, S., Loke, S.W. and Rakotonirainy, A. Context-Aware Ubiquitous Data Mining Based Agent Model for Intersection Safety. In International Conference on Embedded and Ubiquitous Computing, pp. 61-70. Springer, Berlin, Heidelberg. (2005).
14. Xiang, L. Context-Aware Data Mining Methodology for Supply Chain Finance Cooperative Systems. In 2009 Fifth International Conference on Autonomic and Autonomous Systems, pp. 301-306. (2009).
15. Kohavi, R., and Provost, F. On Applied Research in Machine Learning. In Editorial for the Special Issue on Applications of Machine Learning and the Knowledge Discovery Process, Columbia University, New York, volume 30 (1998).
16. Visa, S., Ramsay, B., Ralescu, A.L. and Van der Knaap, E. Confusion Matrix-based Feature Selection. In MAICS, pp. 120-127 (2011).
17. Patel, K., Bancroft, N., Drucker, S.M., Fogarty, J., Ko, A.J. and Landay, J. Gestalt: Integrated Support for Implementation and Analysis in Machine Learning. In Proceedings of the

23nd annual ACM symposium on User interface software and technology, pp. 37-46. ACM (2010).
18. Provost, F.J., Fawcett, T. and Kohavi, R. The Case Against Accuracy Estimation for Comparing Induction Algorithms. In ICML, vol. 98, pp. 445-453 (1998).
19. Sokolova, M., Japkowicz, N. and Szpakowicz, S. Beyond Accuracy, F-score and ROC: A Family of Discriminant Measures for Performance Evaluation. In Australasian Joint Conference on Artificial Intelligence, pp. 1015-1021. Springer, Berlin, Heidelberg. (2006).
20. Bache, K., Lichman, M. UCI Machine Learning Repository [http://archive.ics.uci.edu/ml]. University of California, School of Information and Computer Science, Irvine, CA (2013).
21. Hall, M., Frank, E., Holmes, G., Pfahringer, B., Reutemann, P., and Witten, I. The WEKA Data Mining Software: An Update. SIGKDD Explorations, Volume 11, Issue 1 (2009).

Autors Index

Announcement

World Congress DSA 2020

The Frontiers in Intelligent Data and Signal Analysis
July 12 - 23, 2020, New York, USA

www.worldcongressdsa.com

We are inviting you to our fourth World congress on the Frontiers of Signal and Image Analysis DSA 2020 to New York, Germany.

This congress will feature three events:

- the 16th International Conference on Machine Learning and Data Mining MLDM (www.mldm.de),
- the 20th Industrial Conference on Data Mining ICDM (www.data-mining-forum.de),
- and the 15th International Conference on Mass Data Analysis of Signals and Images in Artificial Intelligence&Pattern Recognition MDA-AI&PR (www.mda-signals.de).

Workshops and Tutorial will also be given.

Come to join us to the most exciting event on Intelligent Data and Signal Analysis.

Sincerely your,
Prof. Dr. Petra Perner

MLDM icdm mda

www.mldm.de www.data-mining-forum.de www.mda-signals.de

Transactions on Mass-Data Analysis of Images and Signals

(ISSN:1868-6451)

The International Journal "Transactions on Mass-Data Analysis of Images and Signals" is a periodical appearing once a year.

The automatic analysis of images and signals in medicine, biotechnology, and chemistry is a challenging and demanding field. Signal-producing procedures by microscopes, spectrometers and other sensors have found their way into wide fields of medicine, biotechnology, economy and environmental analysis. With this arises the problem of the automatic mass analysis of signal information. Signal-interpreting systems which generate automatically the desired target statements from the signals are therefore of compelling necessity. The continuation of mass analyses on the basis of the classical procedures leads to investments of proportions that are not feasible. New procedures and system architectures are therefore required.

Net Price (per issue): EURO 100
Germany (per issue): EURO 107 (incl. 7% VAT)

Submission for the journal should be send to:
info@ibai-publishing.org

For more information visited: www.ibai-publishing.org/journal/massdata/about.php

ibai-publishing
Arno-Nitzsche-Str. 45
04277 Leipzig, Germany

ISBN 978-1-5108-9517-1

CURRAN ASSOCIATES INC.
proceedings.com

25th Italian Symposium on Advanced Database Systems (SEBD 2017)

Squillace Lido, Italy
25-29 June 2017